# HISTORY

OF

# TENNESSEE

From the Earliest Time to the Present; Together with an Historical and
a Biographical Sketch of Giles, Lincoln, Franklin and Moore
Counties; Besides a Valuable Fund of Notes, Reminis-
cences, Observations, Etc., Etc.

ILLUSTRATED.

Nashville:
THE GOODSPEED PUBLISHING CO.,
1886.

SOUTHERN HISTORICAL PRESS
% The Rev. S. Emmett Lucas, Jr.
P. O. Box 738
Easley, South Carolina   29640

ISBN   0-89308-116-7

# PREFACE.

THIS volume has been prepared in response to the prevailing and popular demand for the preservation of local history and biography. The method of preparation followed is the most successful and the most satisfactory yet devised—the most successful in the enormous number of volumes circulated, and the most satisfactory in the general preservation of personal biography and family record conjointly with local history. The number of volumes now being distributed appears fabulous. Within the last four years not less than 20,000 volumes of this class of works have been distributed in Kentucky, and the demand is not half satisfied. Careful estimates place the number circulated in Ohio at 50,000; Pennsylvania, 60,000; New York, 75,000; Indiana, 35,-000; Illinois, 40,000; Iowa, 35,000, and every other Northern State at the same proportionate rate. The Southern States, with the exception of Kentucky, Virginia and Georgia, owing mainly to the disorganization succeeding the civil war, yet retain, ready for the publisher, their stores of history and biography. Within the next five years the vast and valuable fund of perishing event in all the Southern States will be rescued from decay, and be recorded and preserved—to be reviewed, studied and compared for the benefit of future generations. The design of the present extensive historical and biographical research is more to gather and preserve in attractive form, while fresh with the evidences of truth, the enormous fund of perishing occurrence, than to abstract from insufficient contemporaneous data remote, doubtful or incorrect conclusions. The true perspective of the landscape of life can only be seen from the distance that lends enchantment to the view. It is asserted that no person is competent to write a philosophical history of his own time—that, owing to conflicting circumstantial evidence that yet conceals the truth, he can not take that luminous, correct, comprehensive, logical and unprejudiced view of passing events, that will enable him to draw accurate and enduring conclusions. The duty, then, of a historian of his own time is to collect, classify and preserve the material for the final historian of the future. The present historian deals in fact, the future historian, in conclusion; the work of the former is statistical, of the latter, philosophical.

To him who has not attempted the collection of historical data, the obstacles to be surmounted are unknown. Doubtful traditions, conflicting statements, imperfect records, inaccurate private correspondence, the bias or untruthfulness of informers, and the general obscurity which envelopes all passing events, combine to bewilder and mislead. On the contrary, the preparation of statis-

tical history by experienced, unprejudiced and competent workers in special-
ties; the accomplishment by a union of labor of a vast result that would cost
one person the best years of his life and transfer the collection of perishing
event beyond the hope of research; the judicious selection of important matter
from the general rubbish; and the careful and intelligent revision of all final
manuscript by an editor-in-chief, yield a degree of celerity, system, accuracy,
comprehensiveness and value unattainable by any other method. The publishers of this volume, fully aware of their inability to furnish a perfect history, an accomplishment vouchsafed only to the imagination of the dreamer
or the theorist, make no pretension of having prepared a work devoid of
blemish. They feel assured that all thoughtful people, at present and in
future, will recognize and appreciate the importance of their undertaking and
the great public benefit that has been accomplished.

In the preparation of this volume the publishers have met with nothing but
courtesy and assistance. They acknowledge their indebtedness for valuable
favors to the Governor, the State Librarian, the Secretary of the State Historical
Society and to more than a hundred of other prominent citizens of Nashville,
Memphis, Knoxville, Chattanooga, Jackson, Clarksville, Columbia and the
smaller cities of the State. It is the design of the publishers to compile and
issue, in connection with the State history, a brief yet comprehensive historical
account of every county in the State, copies of which will be placed in the
State Library. In the prosecution of this work they hope to meet with the
same cordial assistance extended to them during the compilation of this
volume.

THE PUBLISHERS.

NASHVILLE, September, 1886.

# CONTENTS.

# GILES COUNTY.

THE surface of Giles County is much broken and very rough, being made up of winding valleys and high ridges, some of which rise to a height of from 300 to 500 feet above the common level. The county is divided almost equally north and south by Richland Creek, the most important but not the largest stream in the county. This creek has a large, wide valley, which contains some of the richest farm land to be found anywhere in the State. Richland Creek has also many tributaries, each of which has its valley of fertile land. Elk River, the largest stream of the county, flows across the southeastern corner, receiving numerous creeks and branches. Sugar Creek, in the southwest part of the county, supplies splendid water-power for machinery. The water falls through a succession of cascades more than thirty feet within a distance of 100 yards, and it is cheaply utilized. Though called a creek, Richland is really a river, and was declared navigable by act of Legislature passed in 1809, the said act prohibiting the building of dams or other obstruction that would impede the passage of boats. The act was repealed in 1811, so much as related to that above the shoals, at Pulaski. Other creeks are Big Creek, Lynn Creek, Robertson Fork, Weakley Creek, Haywood Creek, Buchanan Creek, Silver Creek, Indian Creek, Jenkins Creek, Bradshaw Creek, Shoal Creek, Little Shoal Creek and Leatherwood Creek, all of which are very good streams. The northern boundary of the county lies on Elk Ridge, an arm of the highlands. This ridge runs nearly east and west, dividing the waters of the Elk from those of Duck River, and cutting off the portion of the Central Basin of Middle Tennessee lying in Giles and Lincoln Counties.

The geology of the county is simple and easily understood. The strata are horizontal, and, excepting the summits of the ridges, are mainly limestone. The ridges are capped with the lowest and flinty layers of the Lower Carboniferous Period, below which formation, outcropping on the slopes and underlying the lowlands, are the limestones which belong to the Silurian Age. There is also a thin formation of black slate, called the black shale, in the county, which lies next below the sub-carboniferous strata and above the limestones, and is often mistaken as an indication of stone coal. All the soils in that part of the county which lie in the Central Basin are fertile. The hillsides and slopes of the ridges are very fertile and productive, and the amount of alluvial soil in the county, owing to the numerous streams, is great. The lands bordering on Elk River and Richland Creek are the best in the county for cotton. On Big Creek around Campbellsville the lands are very fertile, and continue so on to the south and east, but on the north and west they run into "barrens," on the highlands, where the land is very thin. The products of the county are cotton, corn, wheat, oats, rye, barley, hay, tobacco, Irish potatoes, sweet potatoes, hops, grass and grass seeds, sorghum, all the different fruits and wine.

The cereal products of the county in 1885 were as follows: Corn, 1,545,605 bushels; oats, 33,289 bushels; wheat, 190,205 bushels; rye, 5,020 bushels. During the same year the live-stock in the county was horses and mules, 11,123 head; cattle, 15,126 head; sheep, 12,651 head; hogs, 46,762 head. In 1870 the county ranked first in the production of corn in the State, producing in that year 2,054,163 bushels of that product. In the same year 8,367 bales of cotton were produced in the county, and in 1885 between 12,000 and 15,000.

A treaty was made with the Chickasaw Indians in July, 1805, by which they ceded their claim to all lands north of Duck River and east of the Natches road as far as the ridge that divides the waters of Elk from those of Buffalo. This line passed through Giles County, entering it near the northwest corner, crossing the Lawrenceburg road at the eight-mile post, passed four or five miles west of Pulaski, crossed Elk River about three miles above Prospect and the State line at Phillips' mill, leaving a considerable portion of the western and southwestern part of the county in the Chickasaw territory.

Probably the first white men to penetrate and explore the forests and canebrakes of Giles County were the commissioners and their guard of citizens, who were sent to lay off a district fifty-five miles wide in the northern part of Middle Tennessee in satisfaction of land warrants issued by North Carolina to officers and soldiers of the Continental line, and also to lay off a tract of 25,000 acres south of said district, donated by said State to Gen. Greene. Among those to whom grants for land lying in Giles County were issued were the following: Martin Armstrong, 5,000 acres; William P. Anderson, 540 acres; Stockley Donelson, 5,000 acres; Robert Fenner, 300 acres; John Haywood, 5,000 acres; Henry Montford, 200 acres; Phillips and Shepperd, 5,000 acres; George Simpson, 152 acres; Henry Shepperd, 2,000; Howell Tatum, 311 acres; Henry Toomer, 340 acres; George Breckenridge, 150 acres; George Shields, 252 acres; Sam Shields, 116 acres; John Dobbins, 165 acres; James Reynolds, 5 acres; Charles Girard, 232 acres; James P. Taylor, 640 acres; James Williams, 100 acres; John Childers, 300 acres; John Dougherty, 500 acres; John Reynolds, 300 acres; James Montgomery, 200 acres; John Strother, 95 acres; John Temple, 83 acres; Richard Hightower, 100 acres; John Hughes, 50 acres; James Temple, 300 acres, and John Armstrong, 5,000 acres.

The first permanent settlement in the county was made in about 1805, on Elk River, near the mouth of Richland Creek, and in the neighborhoods of the present towns of Elkton and Prospect, one of which lies above and the other below the mouth of said creek, by William Crowson, his four sons and son-in-law, Vincent, Thomas Whitson, Jordan Word, James Ford, James Wilkerson, Parish Sims, Thomas Dodd, John Reynolds, William Jenkins, Thomas Kyle, Thomas Easley, Simon Ford, John Hunnicutt and John and William Price. When these pioneers came they found the county a vast canebrake and forest, the cane being from twenty to twenty-five feet high. The settlers united their forces and cleared away the cane and built log houses for each other, and the same kindness and courtesy was extended to each new-comer for years thereafter.

Other settlements were made in the county as follows: Thomas Reed, William Riggs, Joseph Moore, Daniel Cox, James Kimborough, Joseph and Elijah Anderson, Thomas Westmoreland, Rev. Aaron Brown and sons (Thomas and William). John Butler and John Barnett settled in the now Aspin Hill neighborhood from 1807 to 1809; Dr. Gabriel Bumpass, William Buchanan and sons (Maximillian, Robert, John and Jesse), Timothy Ezell, Mike Ezell and William Ezell settled in the neighborhood of Cross Waters in 1807 and 1808; John and Lewis Nelson settled a few miles northeast of Prospect in 1809; Lewis Kirk, Alex Black and Nathan and Robert Black settled on the site of Pulaski in 1806–07; Ralph Graves settled about 200 yards east of the present corporate limits of Pulaski, and in the neighborhood of the town Charles and James Buford, Somersett Moore, John Clark and son (Spencer), William Gideon, Nelson Patteson and sons (James and Bernard), Solomon E. Rose, Tyree Rhodes, William Kirley, Charles Neeley and John White settled between 1807 and 1809; Reese Porter and sons, Reese, John, David, James B. and Thomas C., settled in the Mount Moriah Church neighborhood in about 1807; John Dickey, James Ross, Hamilton Campbell, Joseph Bozler, James Ashmore and Daniel Allen settled in the Campbellsville neighborhood between 1808 and 1809; John Fry, William Dearing, George Malone, Gabriel and John Foulks, Daniel Harrison, John and William Rutledge, Jacob and Andrew Blythe, Joel Rutledge, Nicholas Absalom, Hugh Bowen, Thomas Moody, Andrew Pickens, John McCabe, James Angus, James Wilsford and James Brownlow settled on the waters of Lynn Creek between 1808 and 1810; John and Samuel Montgomery, Leander M. Shields, Samuel Shields, James Shields, Joseph Braden, Archibald Crockett, Alexander Shields and Robert Crockett settled in the neighborhood of Elk Ridge Church in 1808–10; Robert Gordon and sons (Thomas and John), the Widow Clark and sons, John and Sam Jones, Robert Alsop, Jacob Jarmin and John Henderson settled in the Brick Church neighborhood between 1808 and 1810; Adam Hightower, Hardy Hightower, John

Kennedy, John Eliff, James McKnight, Samuel McKnight, Joel Jarmin, John Young and Nicholas Holly settled in the Bradshaw Creek neighborhood between 1807 and 1810; Rev. Alex McDonald and brothers (Joseph, Robert and John) and their relatives, William McDonald and James McDonald, settled in the Mount Pisgah Church neighborhood in 1808; William Phillips, William Menifee, and sons (John and William, and son-in-law, Benjamin Long), and John Phillips, settled in the Elkton neighborhood in 1808 and 1809. Other early settlers were P. Moore, Peter Lyons, James Hurst, James Knox, Walter York, John Jones, William Woods, Allen Abernathy, William McDonald, N. Boss, Abner Cleveland, John Wilson, William McGuire, David Flinn, James Flinn, Nathan Farmer, John Reasonover, William Centhall, John White, Thomas Taylor, John M. Cabe, James Grimes, John Yancy, James Hart, Robert Curren, Warrick H. Doyle, Edmund J. Bailey, Benjamin Tutt, James Morgan, William Eubanks, Joseph Johns, Richard Little, Absalom Bosin, John Cunningham, Owen Shannon, James Shannon, Isham Carter, William Hanby, Benjamin Phillips, Gabriel Higenbotham, Robert Miller, Lawson Hobson, Jonas Kindred, Samuel Parmly, Charles McCallister, James Reed, Andrew Erwin, Drury Storall, John Bridwell, William Ball, Eaton Walker, Guilford Dudley, Jonas Kindred, John Scott, James Hunt, Douglas Blue, Joseph Boyd, Samuel Black, John Bryant, William Riddle, William B. Brook, James Lindsey, Henry Scales, William Pillows, Robert McAshley, Richard Briggs, Jelly Pemberton and Orpha Black.

A number of the early settlers located on the Indian lands, cleared away the cane and undergrowth, built log cabins and began cultivating the soil. Complaints being made to the Government, the United States soldiers stationed at Fort Hampton, on Elk River, about four miles above its mouth, were sent to drive out the settlers. The soldiers burned the settlers' houses, threw down their fences and destroyed their crops, and succeeded in driving the people across the reservation line. After the soldiers returned to the fort, the settlers returned to their ruined homes, rebuilt their houses and fences, and planted their crops, only to be again driven out as soon as word was received at the fort of their presence on the forbidden territory. This destruction of property and crops by the Government soldiers occurred during the years 1809–11, and was a great hardship to the settlers, many of whom held grants for the disputed lands they occupied.

Previous to 1809 the settlers of Giles County were compelled to go to mill in Williamson County, or crush the corn into meal by means of the mortar, as there were no mills at that period in the county. In that year, however, Nathaniel Moody erected a small water-power corn-mill on Robertson Fork, one-half mile south of Old Lynnville. Soon afterward Robert Buchanan built a water-power grist-mill on Buchanan Creek, and at about the same time George Cunningham built one on Richland Creek; Hardy Hightower built one on Bradshaw Creek; John White built one on Robertson Fork, near what was afterward Buford's Station; Jacob Bozler built one on Big Creek and John Williams built one on the south side of Elk River, near where Norvell's mill was afterward erected, all of which were common corn-mills of water-power. Lewis Brown built the first horse-power mill in 1810. After Pulaski had been selected as the county seat, Nathaniel Moody moved his mill to a point near town on Richland Creek. This was in 1811, and during the same year, Clacks or Mayfield's mill was built on the same stream, about one mile below Mount Moriah Church, and John Laird built a mill on Lynn Creek. James Cox. built a water-power mill on Sugar Creek in 1818, which was afterward known as Malone's mill, and during the same year James Paisley built a horse-power mill in the Shoal Creek neighborhood, and Elijah Ruthony built a water-power mill on Sugar Creek.

The powder used in the early days by the settlers was all manufactured within the county. One of the first powder-mills built in the county was owned by Daniel Allen, and stood near Allen's Spring, since known as Wright's Spring, a few miles northwest of the present site of Campbellsville. John Williams also operated a powder-mill near the State line, one mile southwest from Elk Mount Springs, and James Ross owned one in the western part of the county. The saltpeter used by these manufacturers was obtained from different sources, principally from a cave near Campbell's Station in Maury County.

Many of the early settlers brought with them cotton seed, and though at first only small patches of that useful article were grown from a production for home consumption only, it soon grew into one of the largest crops produced in the county, forming one of the chief exports, and as such continues at the present. Cotton-gins were soon established, and to-day the county is dotted over with them. One of the first cotton-gins built in the county was that of Lester Morris, and was erected in 1810 near Rehobeth Church. The power at first was furnished by hand, but later on the gin was enlarged and converted into horse-power. The first water-power gin was built in 1811 or 1812 on Lynn Creek, by John Laird. Soon afterward John Henderson built a water-power gin on a branch about a mile south of Cornersville, now in Marshall County, and Maj. Hurlston built a water-power gin on Dry Creek.

The mills and cotton-gins in the county at present are as follows, by districts: First District—Jacob Morrell has a steam saw-mill and cotton-gin; John Brown has a water-power grist-mill on Ragsdale Creek; S. H. Morrell has a water-power grist-mill on same creek; R. L. Donnevan has a water-power grist-mill on Sinking Creek; and J. N. Ruder, Edward Copeland, W. F. Smith, James Arnett, Thomas E. Dailey, Thomas Whitfield, A. R. Garrison, L. J. Bledsoe and Dr. Patterson each have one-horse-power cotton-gin. Second District—James Rivers has a water-power grist-mill on Richland Creek; M. B. McCal lister has a water-power grist-mill on Elk River; Smith & Bell have a steam saw-mill near Prospect, and cotton-gins are too numerous in the district to mention, there being not less than twenty-five or thirty, each farm of any consequence owning its own gin. Third District—Thomas E. Smith has a steam saw and grist-mill and cotton-gin combined; Joseph Edmunson has a similar mill, and Owen, English & Fowler have a steam saw and grist-mill; and Sterling Brownlow and Isaac Casey have each a horse-power cotton-gin. Fourth District—Graves & Dougherty have a steam saw and grist-mill, and James Marbett has a horse-power cotton-gin. Fifth District—James Patrick has a water-power corn and wheat-mill and cotton-gin on Shoats Creek, and J. E. Pryor, S. C. Johnson, James Tidwell, A. W. Parker and Felix Petty each have horse-power cotton-gins. Sixth District—The Vale Mills, corn and cotton-gin, water-power, on Richland Creek; Babe Nance has a steam saw-mill, and Elihu Coffman and William Edwards each have steam cotton-gins; David Shore, Samuel Williamson, Samuel Hower, James Short, Wiley Rogers and William Morris each have horse-power cotton-gins. Seventh District—W. I. Rainey and Mrs. Elder have water-power grist-mills on Richland Creek, and T. B. Wade has a horse-power cotton-gin. Eighth District—F. D. Aymett has a water-power grist-mill on Leatherwood Creek, and John M. Aymett, F. D. Aymett, Giles Reynolds, George Suttle and Thomas Harwell have horse-power cotton-gins. Ninth District—Andrew Chambers has a water-power flour, grist and saw-mill combined; Bud Morrell has a water-power corn-mill on Richland Creek; Jacob Morrell has a flour and grist water-mill on Elk River, and C. O. Bull, R. I. Baugh, E. N. Grigsby, John R. Beasley, Gray Hopkins, Wilburn M. Stephenson, James Scruggs, Marion Ellison and James Rivers have cotton-gins, all of which are of horse-power, except those of Baugh and Rivers. Tenth District—J. K. Craig has a horse-power cotton-gin. Eleventh District—Joseph Parsons has a steam flour and grist-mill; William Abernathy has a water-power grist-mill on Buchanan Creek, and Monroe Smith has a horse-power cotton-gin. Twelfth District—T. S. Williamson has a steam saw and grist-mill; J. M. Young has a water-power flour and grist-mill on Richland Creek; W. T. Copeland has a steam grist-mill and cotton-gin combined, and T. B. Wade, G. S. White, John Phillips, B. T. Reynolds, Frank Bramlett, William Rivers, Robert Rhodes and James Buford have cotton-gins, all with one exception, Wade's, being of horse-power. Thirteenth District—J. T. Steele has a water-power flour, corn and saw-mill combined on Big Creek; Joshua Morris has a water-power corn and saw-mill on the same creek, and Mrs. Buford and Mrs. Rhae have horse-power cotton-gins. Fourteenth District—L. Alexander has a flour, corn and saw-mill, water and steam-power, on Big Creek; Capt. Watson has a water-power flour and grist-mill on Brownlow Creek; A. Williams has a water-power wheat and corn-mill on Factory Creek, and Isaac Yokely and Mow Hays have horse-power cotton gins. Fifteenth District—Joseph Goldman and Griffis Bros. each have water-power grist-mills on Robertson Fork; Mrs. Fry has a water-power grist-mill on Lynn Creek; Wilkes & Calvert have a steam-power cotton-gin, and B. F. Walker has a horse-power cotton-gin. Sixteenth District—Horse-power cotton-gins are owned by Ephraim Gordon, Hugh Topp, Mack Dougherty, David Simmons, G. H. McMillan and Thomas Spofford. Seventeenth District—J. M. Gordon and R. F. Jackson have horse-power cotton-gins. Eighteenth District—Levi Reed has a water-power grist-mill on Egnew Creek; John Rector has a steam saw-mill, and Henry Purger has a horse-power cotton-gin. Nineteenth District—J. M. Parker and Sam Collins have horse-power cotton-gins. Twentieth District—J. M. Brownlow has a steam saw-mill, and J. H. McCormick has a horse-power cotton-gin.

Giles County was created in 1810 in pursuance of an act of the General Assembly passed November 14, 1809, and at the suggestion of Gen. Jackson was named in honor of Gen. William B. Giles, one of the governors of Virginia. Giles County was formed out of Maury County and is bounded as follows: North by the counties of Maury and Marshall, east by the counties of Marshall and Lincoln, south by the State of Alabama, west by Lawrence County, and has an area of 600 square miles. The act erecting Giles County is as follows:

AN ACT TO ESTABLISH A COUNTY SOUTH OF MAURY COUNTY, AND NORTH OF THE SOUTHERN BOUNDARY OF THE STATE.

SECTION 1. *Be it enacted by the General Assembly of the State of Tennessee,* That there be a new county established within the following described bounds, to wit: Beginning at the southeast corner of Maury County; thence due south to the southern boundary of the State; thence west as far as to form a constitutional county; thence north to the line of Maury County, and with said line to the beginning, which county shall be known by the name of Giles County.

Section 2 provides that James Ross, Nathaniel Moody, Tyree Rhodes, Gabriel Bumpass and Thomas Whitson be appointed commissioners to select a place on Richland Creek, near the center of the county, for a county seat, at which site the commissioners shall procure at least 100 acres of land, upon which they shall cause a town to be laid off, with necessary streets at least eighty feet wide, reserving at least two acres for a public square, on which shall be erected a court house and stocks, also reserving a public lot sufficient to contain a jail, in a convenient part of town, which town shall be known by the name of Pulaski. Section 3 provides for the sale of town lots by the commissioners at public auction to the highest bidders. Section 4 provides that the commissioners shall contract with suitable workmen to build a court house, prison and stocks, the same to be paid for out of moneys arising from the sale of town lots. Section 8 provides for the due administration of justice and for the time and place of holding courts. Section 9 provides that nothing in this act shall prevent the collection of taxes due Maury County at the time of its passage, by the sheriff of that county. Section 12 provides that this act shall be in force from and after the 1st of January, 1810.

On November 22, 1809, the General Assembly passed another act, electing the following magistrates for Giles County: John Dickey, Jacob Baylor, Somersett Moore, Charles Neiley, Robert Steele, Nathaniel Moody, William Phillips, Benjamin Long, Thomas Westmoreland, David Porter and Maximillian H. Buchanan; at the same time Thomas H. Stewart was appointed Judge and Amos Balch attorney-general of the Fourth Judicial Circuit, embracing Giles County.

The commissioners met early in 1810 and selected a place then known as the "Shoals," on Richland Creek, as a site for the county seat, which was named Pulaski, in honor of the gallant Polish count who fell at Savannah in 1779 while fighting for American independence. The land so selected was vacant land, lying south and west of the Indian reservation line. However, assurances of title were given, which authorized the commissioners to make the selection, and on November 11, 1812, a deed for the land was made to the commissioners by President James Madison.

There are 377,600 acres of land in the county, 194,479 acres being improved, and the total value of property assessed for taxation in 1885 was $4,587,977, an average of $8.82 per acre. The tax levy for 1886 was as follows: 30 cents for State, 30 cents for county, 20 cents for school, 11 cents for roads, and $1 each by State and county for school, making a total assessment of $2.91 on each $100 worth of property. In 1834 the first turnpike was built through Giles County, it being the Columbia, Pulaski, Elkton & Alabama Pike. The present pikes are the Pulaski & Elkton Pike, built about 1840, of which there are thirty miles; the Pulaski & Brick Church Pike, built in 1882, fourteen miles; the Pulaski & Bradshaw Pike, built in 1882, twelve miles. and the Pulaski & Vale Mills Pike, built in 1883, five miles. The Nashville & Decatur Railroad, the only one in the county, passes through from north to south. In 1856 the county subscribed $275,000 in aid of this railroad, payable in five annual installments. The road was completed in 1860, and has proven a great boon and benefit to the entire county. The Memphis & Knoxville Railroad has been surveyed through the county, and should the road be built the county would be quartered by railways, and Giles would have transportation facilities equaled by few counties in the State. The building of the latter road, however, is very indefinite.

The first court held in the county was a court of pleas and quarter sessions, and was held on the third Monday in February, 1810, at the house of Lewis Kirk, who lived in a log cabin on a bluff on the bank of Richland Creek at the foot of the "shoals," and about 200 yards above where the Nashville & Decatur Railroad depot now stands. The magistrates who had previously been appointed as such by the General Assembly, were sworn into office, and they at once elected John Dickey, chairman, German Lester, clerk, Jesse Westmoreland, register, and Charles Neeley, sheriff. By order of the court a log cabin was erected in Kirk's yard, in which the courts were held, and in a short while thereafter a rough log house was erected on the same yard for a jail. In this rude prison were kept those convicted of misdemeanors, contempt of court, etc., while the felons were sent to the Williamson County jail, and afterward to the Maury County jail for imprisonment. After the sale of town lots, August, 1811, the cave having been previously cut from a portion of the Public Square, a second court house was erected on the Public Square, and the records and courts moved thereto. This second building was constructed of round logs, which were covered with boards. The house stood for about two years, when it was destroyed by fire, presumably by the citizens, they having become impatient and indignant at the delay of the commissioners in giving them a more commodious and sightly building. A log jail was erected on the southeast corner of the Public Square at about the same time of the log court house, and it, too, was destroyed by fire soon after the court house burned.

The commissioners then contracted with Archibald Alexander, of Pulaski, to erect a new court house, and with Philip P. Many, of Williamson County, to build a new jail. This court house was a two-story brick, and answered well the purpose for which it was built. In about 1850 the building was torn down, and on the same site a handsome brick was erected, which stood until 1856, when it was destroyed by fire. The present court house was completed in 1859, and cost the county about $27,000. It is a large two-story brick, 60x150 feet, with four entrances and halls. Two large court rooms are on the second floor, while on the first are located six large well ventilated and lighted offices, including a chancery court room, an artistic cupola surmounts the building in which is a town clock, which was presented to the county court by Judge Henry M. Spafford, deceased in 1880. During the time between the destruction of the court house in 1856, and the completion of the present building in 1859, the courts were held on the first floor of the Odd Fellows Hall. The jail contracted by Philip P. Maney was of brick, and was erected on the northwest corner of the Square. When within a few hours work of completion it was destroyed by fire, having caught fire by sparks falling from someone's pipe or cigar into the shavings. Another jail was soon erected by the same contractor, which stood until about the close of the late war, when it was destroyed by fire by the retreating Confederates. The present jail is a handsome brick building, situated on First Main Street, about 150 yards from the Public Square, and was completed in 1867 at a cost of $25,000. It is provided with suitable apartments for a jailer's family, and has ten well-constructed cells, with necessary corridors.

In 1865, the County Court purchased 130 acres of land in the Eleventh District, four miles east of Pulaski, for a county poor farm, and erected log buildings thereon for the accommodation of paupers. In 1867, frame buildings took the place of the log house, and these were replaced with a good brick building in 1884, which cost about $4,000.

The Giles Circuit Court convened its first session in the log court house at Lewis Kirk's, on the second Monday in June, 1810, present and presiding the Hon. Thomas H. Stewart, judge; Amos Balch, attorney-general. James Berry was appointed clerk, and the session was opened by Sheriff Charles Neeley. The court continued to hold its sessions at the above place until the December term, 1811, when the court was opened at that place, and an adjournment was taken, to meet at once in the new court house on the Public Square. After the destruction of the court house in 1814, the court was held during the April term at the house of David Martin, in Pulaski. During the year 1815 the house of Isaac Smith, of Pulaski, was used as a temporary court house. From 1810 to 1822 there are no records of this court, they having been destroyed. The records are also missing between 1831 and 1836, between 1848 and 1852, between 1855 and 1858, and there were no courts between 1860 and 1865, but since the last date they are complete.

In 1827, for malicious stabbing, James Z. Maclin was sent to jail for twelve months; for an assault and battery, with murderous intent, Sterling Harwell was fined $25 and sent to jail for twenty days. In 1830 Arthur Jarnigar, for committing forgery, was given thirty-nine lashes on the bare back, sent to jail for one week and made to sit in the pillory two hours each morning for three consecutive days; and Dury Smith, for manslaughter, was branded on the brawn of the left thumb with the letter M; and sent to jail for one month. In 1836 James McNune was sent to the penitentiary for two years for an assault and attempt to commit murder.

In 1837 William Inzer, for larceny, was sent to the penitentiary for three years. James Tooey, five years for malicious stabbing, and Isaac Dale was convicted of murder and sentenced to be hung. In 1838 John W. Craft was sent to the penitentiary for three years for perjury. In 1853 William Hall was sent up for two years on a charge and conviction of malicious stabbing; in 1855 Martin, a slave, was convicted of murder and sentenced to be hung.

In 1860 N. C. Wisend, for grand larceny, was sent to prison for seven years; in 1865, Samuel Marks, for the same offense, was given ten years; and in 1866 Benjamin Abernathy, Stephen Brown, Jacob Kennedy and Meredith Dabney, for grand larceny, were given terms of imprisonment of three years, one year and seven years, respectively. In 1867 Henry Ars, for stealing a horse, was imprisoned for a term of ten years; Pleasant Beckwith, for murder, in 1868, was sent to prison for one year; and John Lightfoot and George Springer were tried jointly on a charge of larceny and each sent up for three years; in 1869, Cæsar Allen, for larceny, was given one year; James Kelley, for rape, was sent up for fifteen years; and Pleasant Madison, for horse stealing, ten years. In 1870, Sterling Eddins and Harup Mason, for larceny, were each sent to the penitentiary for one year; in 1871, James Montgomery, horse stealing, fifteen years; Lewis Swinnea, murder, twenty years; William Allen, larceny, five years; Green Turner, horse stealing, sentenced to be hung; Philip Maples, for administering poison, three years; and Lewis Taylor, larceny, three years. In 1872 Jesse Donaldson, Amanda Abernathy, Virginia Abernathy, Felix White and Richard Collier, for larceny, were given terms of imprisonment ranging from fifteen months to four years, while for murder, Jordan Petty was sent up for fourteen years; Jack McGuire, for stealing a horse, twenty-one years; and George Chapman, for forgery, went up for three years. In 1873, John Adams, Isaac Ballentine, Benjamin McDonald and Sterling Eddins, for larceny, were sent to penitentiary for three, one, four and six years, respectively; Andrew G. Downing and Richard Benson were given fifteen and ten years, respectively, for horse stealing. In 1874, William Jones, George Washington and Calvin Rhoades were sent to penitentiary for five, four and seven years, respectively, and for murder Walker Ingram was sent for twenty years, and John O'Connor ten years for horse stealing.

In 1875 Andrew Faran, Claibourn Johnson, James Vance and Fountain Walker were given terms of three, two, three and fifteen years, respectively, for larceny; and for stealing a horse John Caldwell was sent up for twenty years. In 1876, Neil S. Icter, for housebreaking; Andrew Beaty, for forgery; James Powell, house-breaking; and James Bell, C. T. Tramier and Sterling Butler, for larceny, received imprisonment of six months, three years, ten years, two years, fifteen months and four years, respectively. In 1877, James Johnson and Henry Matthews were each sent to the penitentiary for one year for larceny; Mirabeau Clark, ten years for horse stealing; Ralph Garrett, five years for arson; and George Riggan, ten years for house-breaking. In 1878, Arch Brown and Henry Smith were sent to penitentiary for three years each; William Jordan, murder, thirteen years; and George Washington and William Caldwell, eight and six years, respectively, for horse stealing. In 1879 Dick Collier was sent up for eight years on a charge of housebreaking; William Coats, ten years for attempt to poison; and Del Duncan, John Jackson, John Sweeney and Tom Ballentine, for larceny, were given terms of one year each in the penitentiary.

In 1880 W. T. Williams, for larceny, was sentenced to the penitentiary for 8 years; David Cheairs, for arson, 6 years, and Green Terry and Allan Shaw, 6 months and 5 months in the county jail for larceny. In 1881 Mat Pendegrass and Ben Eddins received 6 months and 3 years, respectively, for horse stealing: Felix Smith, 5 years for burglary, and Bill Smith, William Franklin and Alonzo Rhodes, 3 years, and 11 months, and 29 days, respectively, for larceny.

The Chancery Court of Giles County was held for the first time in April, 1832, with M. A. Cook as chancellor and Charles C. Abernathy, clerk and master. The members of the Pulaski bar have been as follows, the time in which they practiced being in the order given: John Minns, W. H. Field, William C. Flourna, John H. Rivers, Colin S. Tarpley, Aaron V. Brown, James W. Coombs, V. E. J. Shields, Adam Huntsman, Neil S. Brown, Thomas Jones, Robert Rose, Alfred Harris, Lunsford M. Bramlett, Archibald Wright, A. F. Gough, James Davenport, Davidson Netherland, Thomas M. Jones, Calvin Jones, John C. Brown, John C. Walker and Nathan Adams. The present bar is composed of. Thomas M. Jones, John S. Wilkes, Solan E. Rose, John A. Tinnon, E. T. Taliaferro, John T. Allen, Noble Smithson, Z. W. Ewing, Charles P. Jones, Andrew J. Abernathy, J. Polk Abernathy, Amos R. Abernathy, Hume Steele, Flourna Rivers and John C. Brown.

The following is a list of the court and county officers in the order in which they served: Judges—Thomas H. Stewart, Alford S. Harris, Robert M. Mack, William E. Kennedy, Lunsford M. Bramlett, Edmund Dillahunty, W. P. Martin, Henry Ward, A. M. Hughes, W. P. Martin, William L. McLemore and Edward D. Patterson. Attorney-generals—Alford Balch, Robert L. Cobb, Gideon J. Pillow, Edmund Dillahunty, James H. Thomas, Nathaniel Baxter, Archilaus M. Hughes, Nathan Adams, Archilaus M. Hughes, Austin C. Hickey, James Smithson, Joseph H. Fussell and John L. Jones. Chancellors—M. A. Cook, Lumsford M. Bramlett, Terre H. Cahal, A. O. P. Nicholson, Samuel D. Frierson, John A. Brien, Samuel D. Frierson, John C. Walker, David Campbell, Horace H. Harrison, William S. Flemming and Andrew J. Abernathy. Clerk and masters—Charles C. Abernathy, Daniel L. Morrison, James McCallum, W. H. McCallum, A. Cox, J. B. Stacy. Chairmen of county court since 1865—Daniel G. Anderson, J. F. Smith, W. H. Abernathy J. L. Jones. County trustees since 1868—Thomas S. Riddle, Sterling H. Brown, Daniel B. Garrett, W. G. Lewis, R. M. Bugg, H. C. McLaurine, H. L. Booth and W. R. Craig. County court clerks since 1810—German Lester, Edward D. Jones, J. L. Jones, A. R. Richardson, E. W. Rose, D. A. Wilburn, H. H. Aymett, P. H. Ezell, Will S. Ezell. Circuit court clerks since 1810—James Berry, Henry Hagan, Sterling Lester, Charles C. Abernathy, C. H. Abernathy, W. Williford, F. T. McLaurine, H. M. Stanley, J. H. Morris, J. W. Braden. Sheriffs since 1810—Charles Neeley, James

Buford, Max H. Buchanan, James Perry, Lewis H. Brown, Thomas C. Porter, Thomas S. Webb, John A. Jackson, Asa Ezell, James D. Goodman, Joshua Morris, John Kouns, Berry H. Piden, John W. West, D. H. Parsons, R. H. Mitchell, R. A. Blow, H. Arrowsmith, John D. Butler and J. Polk English. Registers since 1810—Jesse Westmoreland, Fountain Lester, David McCormack, P. T. T. McCanless, Andrew Fay, Daniel G. Anderson, John Dyer, J. J. Phillips and J. F. Fogg.

Quite a number of the Giles County pioneers served in the Revolutionary war, and for their services as soldiers of the line received grants from the State of North Carolina for the lands in this county, upon which they afterward settled. But of them there is no record accessible, and their names have long since passed from the memory of the citizens of the present, if memory of them they ever had. While no companies went from Giles County into the war of 1812 a large number of her citizens joined companies that went out from neighboring counties, among whom were Lester Morris, George Everly, Charles Buford, James Patteson, Sol. E. R. Rose, Wm. Kirley, Maj. Hurlston, Wm. McDonald, Wm. Kyle, Col. Cleveland, John Clark, Nelson Patteson, John Phillips, Thomas Smith, Dr. Gilbert, D. Taylor, Charles C. Abernathy, Wm. K. Gordon, and many others whose names could not be secured. Dr. Taylor served on Gen. Jackson's medical staff.

Within a short time after the organization of the county the county militia was established as an adjunct to the State militia, and for twenty years or more was in active organization. The first regiment organized was the Thirty-seventh, which embraced the entire county. Of this regiment Robert Steele was the first colonel elected, and Claibourn McVey and John Buford the first majors. After the war of 1812 the regiment was reorganized or divided, and a new regiment, the Fifty-second, was formed of the northern half of the county, leaving Pulaski with the old regiment. Thomas K. Gordon was the first colonel, and Richard H. Allen and James Simmons the first majors, elected for the new regiment. Of the old regiment James Terrill was elected colonel and Thomas Wilkerson and Wm. Rose majors. Col. Terrill removed from the county in 1821, when Maj. Rose was elected colonel, and Gillan Hamell and Abel Wilson majors. The militia was again re-organized in 1825, and an additional regiment, embracing the northwestern portion of the county, including Pulaski, was organized. Of this regiment Richard H. Allen was elected colonel; Simpson H. White, lieutenant-colonel, and John H. Rivers and Edward Tipton, majors. From 1830 the militia began to decline, and upon the adoption of the new constitution in 1834 ceased to exist. Previous to the new constitution's adoption the county was divided into Captains District, and the election or appointment of justices of the peace was regulated by companies or beats, or, as now, by civil districts. During its day the militia was a great institution indeed, and militia offices were much sought after. Giles County's contribution to the Florida war in 1836 consisted of two full companies, which were raised in June, 1836, and on July 4 following, were mustered into the First Tennessee Regiment of Mounted Volunteers, at Fayettville, Lincoln County. The companies were designated in the regiment as First and Sixth Company First was commanded by Capt. Thomas M. Jones, now Judge Jones, of the Pulaski bar, and Quincy Black and Robert L. Dixon were the lieutenants. Company Sixth was under command of Capt. James Gibson, with Joshua and John Morris, brothers, as lieutenants. Among the members of the above companies, whose names are obtainable, were Archibald Wright, Neil S. Brown, Sol. E. Rose, Jesse Mays, J. N. Patteson, Joseph E. Anthony, George B. Allen, Robert H. Rose, J. Carroll Smith, Samuel D. Wright, Homer Jones, Charles G. Keenan, Milton Payne, Wm. Baugh, Daniel Brinkle, Henry E. Pitts, Henry C. Lester, Jesse D. Page and Warren P. Anderson.

As in the Florida war Giles County furnished two full companies to the war with Mexico in 1846. The first company organized left Pulaski in June, 1846, under command of Capt. Milton A. Haynes and Lieuts. W. P. Chambliss, William Richardson and — Brownlow. They volunteered for twelve months, and were mustered into the First Tennessee Regiment of Cavalry, under command of Gen. Jonas E. Thomas, of Maury County. Among the members of this company were William Evans, Ira Martin, E. G. B. Lee,

Samuel Farmer, Sterling Farmer, David Hammond, James T. Wheeler, Samuel C. Johnson, Alexander Black, Samuel S. Williamson, David H. Hannah and Nathan Adams. At the expiration of the twelve months' service for which the company enlisted the survivors returned home, and when the second call for volunteers was made Lieut. W. P. Chambliss raised a second company, of which he was elected captain, and A. M. Flemming, first lieutenant; Thomas Gordon, second lieutenant; J. L. Jones (at present Chairman of the Giles County Court), brevet second lieutenant; Patrick Chambliss, orderly sergeant; William D. Everly, second orderly sergeant; William Fallis, third orderly sergeant, and Milton Rason, fourth orderly sergeant. The company left Giles County for Nashville in October, 1847, where it was mustered into the Third Tennessee Regiment of Foot Volunteers, Gen. Cheatham commanding, as Company C. Among the members of Company C were James Adams, Abe Cable, — Davis, W. R. Edwards, Samuel Elliff, Joseph Elliff, J. A. Foster, Hardaway Tucker, Calaway Tucker, George Chesser, Samuel Farmer, — Wilson, — Walker, A. A. Walker, J. N. M. Farmer, Edward Rasen, Michael Fry, Samuel Edmonson, — Spirey and John Carr.

Giles County took a decided stand in favor of secession at the breaking out of the late war, and cast an overwhelming majority vote in favor of separation from the Union and representation in the Confederate Congress. In response to the call of Gov. Harris for State volunteers early in 1861 the " Martin Guards," the first company raised in the county, was organized, placed in command of Capt. Hume R. Field, and dispatched at once to Nashville, where, upon the organization in April, 1861, of the First Tennessee Regiment of Infantry, the company was mustered into service as Company K. The regiment went into camp at Alisonia, Franklin County, which was given the name of Camp Harris, thence to Camp Cheatham, in Robertson County, where the soldiers were given full instructions. On July 10, 1861, it was ordered to Virginia.

Under special orders from Gov. Harris the Third Tennessee Regiment of Infantry was organized at Lynnville, this county, on May 16, 1861. The regiment consisted of ten full companies of picked men, five of which were supplied by Giles County. The roll of field and staff officers of the regiment was as follows: Colonel, John C. Brown; lieutenant-colonel, Thomas M. Gordon; major, Nathaniel F. Cheairs; adjutant, Thomas M. Tucker; quartermasters, Benj. P. Roy and J. L. Herron; commissary, B. L. Wilkes; surgeons, Samuel H. Stout and James A. Bowers; assistant surgeon, Wiley S. Perry; chaplains, Marcus Williams and Thomas J. Davenport; sergeant-major, William Polk; quartermaster-sergeants, J. F. Alexander and J. W. Littleton; commissary-sergeant, John S. Wilkes; ordnance sergeants, Wallace W. Rutledge and James J. Walker, hospital steward, Eber Fry. The Giles County companies in this regiment were as follows: Company A, first captain, John C. Brown, succeeded by Calvin J. Clack, numbered 120 men; Company B, first captain, Thomas M. Gordon, succeeded by E. H. F. Gordon, 130 men; Company D, captain, William Peaton, 108 men; Company G. captain, Calvin H. Walker, 110 men; Company K, captain, F. C. Barber, 110 men.

The regiment was mustered into the State service as soon as organized, and from Lynnville went into camp near Springfield, Robertson County, where it remained until July 26, 1861, when it moved to Camp Trousdale, Sumner County, from whence they were ordered to Fort Donelson, reaching the fort on February 8, 1862. On September 26, 1862, the regiment was reorganized as follows: Colonel, Calvin H. Walker; lieutenant-colonel; Calvin J. Clack: majors, Thomas M. Tucker and F. C. Barber; adjutant, David S. Martin, Giles County companies: Company B, captain Robert A. Mitchell 105; Company G, formerly Company A, captain David Rhea, 99 men; Company I, formerly Company D, captain, D. G. Alexander, 90 men; Company H, formerly Company G, captain, James J. Walker, 101 men; Company A, formerly Company K, captain F. C. Barber, 100 men. The reorganization took place at Jackson, Miss., after the exchange of prisoners at Vicksburg, and the regiment went at once into active service, their first engagement occurring a few days afterward at Springdale, Miss.

In the summer of 1861 the Thirty-second Tennessee Regiment of Infantry was organized at Camp Trousdale, Sumner County, in which regiment Giles County was represented as follows: Winstead's company, captain, John M. Winstead; Worley's company, captain, Willis Worley; Hannah's company, captain, John W. Hannah; Hunnicutt's company, captain, W. H. Hunnicutt. The regiment upon leaving camp went into East Tennessee, and thence into Kentucky, In October, 1862, the regiment was reorganized, the reorganization affecting the Giles County companies as follows: Winstead's company, captain, Field Arrowsmith; Worley's company, captain, James Young; Hannah's company, captain, John L. Brownlow; Hunnicutt's company, captain, J. M. Bass. The reorganization of this regiment also occurred at Jackson, Miss.

Holman's battalion of partisan rangers was raised under commission from Judah P. Benjamin, Secretary of War of the Confederacy; bearing date, June 27, 1862, directed to Maj. D. W. Holman. The battalion consisted of four companies, two of which were furnished by Giles County, they being those of Capt. Andrew R. Gordon, of 160 men, and of Capt. James Rivers, of 100 men.

The above is a list as near as could be obtained of the soldiers furnished to the Confederacy by Giles County. The county was continually overrun with both Federal and Confederate soldiers throughout the war, being on the line of march from Nashville to Huntsville, Ala. Pulaski, Lynnville, Elkton and Prospect were each visited by Federal troops in large numbers, and Pulaski and Lynnville were fortified, a formidable fort or earth-work was erected on Fort Hill, a high steep hill overlooking the town and surrounding country at the former place. The first Federals to visit Pulaski in any number was a detachment of Gen. Negley's brigade which was sent out from Columbia, under Col. Mark Monday, in April, 1862, to drive off Gen. John Morgan, who with his cavalry was harassing and plundering the Federal wagon trains on their way to Gen. Mitchell at Huntsville, Ala. After doing considerable damage, Gen. Morgan withdrew from Giles County in May, upon the approach of Col. Monday, going into Bedford and Wilson Counties. Col. Monday went into camp with his men at Pulaski, and remained until September, 1862, when his command joined Gen. Negley's brigade and went into Kentucky after Gen. Bragg. In August, 1863, Col. Hayes made a raid on Giles County with a regiment of cavalry, who made a camp of one day and night in Pulaski, and returned to Columbia. During the same year Lynnville and Elkton were both raided by the Federals, the whole county, in fact, being relieved of horses, cattle and grain. In October, 1863, Gen. Wheeler retreated south through Giles County, pursued by Gen. Wilder, who made a short stop at Pulaski on his way south, and in the course of a few days returned and again camped for a number of days, going thence to Shelbyville.

In November, 1863, Gen. W. T. Sherman and his entire army passed through Giles County, en route to Chattanooga, making a short stop at Elkton, and Gen. William Dodge, with the Sixteenth Army Corps, went into camp at Pulaski, remaining until April, 1864. A portion of the above corps was stationed at Lynnville, where earth-works were thrown up. Gen. Starkweather, with four regiments of infantry and as many regiments of cavalry, camped in Pulaski and Giles County, during the summer of 1864, engaged in guarding the Tennessee River. Gen. Starkweather was succeeded in command by Gen. R. W. Johnson, who remained at Pulaski until November of the above year. In that month Gen. Stanley was sent to Pulaski with the Fourth Army Corps, and camped for three or four days.

Gen. Schofield, in command of the Army of the Ohio, brought the Twenty-fourth Army Corps to Pulaski in the latter part 1864, and remained until Gen. Hood crossed the Tennessee River at Florence, Ala., and was approaching Columbia, when he evacuated the town and fell back to Franklin, and then to Nashville. Gen. Hood came on into Middle Tennessee. At Lawrenceburg, his advance composed of Gen. Forrest's cavalry, repulsed the Federals, who then fell back to Pulaski, and the following day quite an engagement occurred at Campbellsville, this county, when the Federals were again repulsed. Gen. Forrest's cavalry made sad havoc with the railroad, tearing up the rails and destroying all bridges in the county. At Pulaski he stationed a battery on East Hill and made a feint movement by throwing a few shells into the Federal fort on Fort Hill, to cover his move toward Shelbyville.

After the battle of Nashville, Gen. Hood retreated south through Giles County, followed by Gen. George H. Thomas, with the Twenty-third, Fourth and Sixteenth Army Corps. The retreat through Giles County was almost a continuous battle all along the Columbia & Pulaski Turnpike. At Anthony Hill, this county, Gen. Hood made a stand and repulsed the Federals, only to resume his retreat. Another stand was made at a point on Sugar Creek, where the Federals were repulsed a second time, after which they fell back to Pulaski, while Gen. Hood's army proceeded leisurely into Alabama. The command of the Twenty-third, Fourth and Sixteenth Army Corps was turned over to Gen. Johnson, who remained with them in camp at Pulaski, until the close of the war in 1865. During the stay of the Federals in Pulaski, at different times, the court house and Giles College building were used as quarters for the soldiers, and the different church buildings were converted into hospitals.

On November 20, 1863, Samuel Davis, a Confederate spy, was captured inside the Federal lines at Pulaski, with complete plans of the Federal fortifications at Pulaski, Franklin, Nashville and, in fact, all over Middle Tennessee. Davis was tried by a court-martial, on the charge of being a Rebel spy, and was hung on East Hill, in front of Squire James McCollum's residence, at 10 o'clock on Friday morning, November 27, 1863. Davis claimed that his plans had been furnished him by a Federal officer, high in command, whom he stated was standing in the crowd in front of the scaffold awaiting his hanging, but whose name he refused to divulge, even when offered his life and liberty as an inducement to do so. Opinion is divieed as to whether the doomed man was really a brave man, and sought death rather than divulge a friend's name, or whether he was playing for glory, even in his last moments.

The county seat and principal town of Giles County is Pulaski. which stands on the east bank of Richland Creek, and on the Nashville & Decatur Railroad, seventy-five miles south of Nashville and eighteen miles north of the Alabama State line. The town is one of the prettiest in the State and has a population of 2,500. The site for Pulaski was selected by the commissioners early in 1810, and during that year a portion of the cane and under-growth was removed from the Public Square. In August, 1811 the first town lots were sold at auction and a court house and stocks were erected on the Public Square. Lewis Kirk and Alexander, Nathan and Robert Black were the first white citizens of Pulaski; they settling on the town site at least three years before it was selected as such. Kirk built a log cabin on a bluff on Richland Creek, at the foot of the "shoals," while the three Blacks erected their cabins on what is now First Main Street. Other settlers or citizens of the town before the sale of town lots in 1811, were William R. Davis, William Ball, James Berry, German and Fountain Lester, David Martin, Richard Scott, James Drew, James H. Williams, William Hanby, Thomas Smith, John McCrackin, John G. Talbott, Henry Hogan, Dr. Shadrack Nye, Joseph Trotter, Joseph H. Hodge, Dr. Gilbert D. Taylor, David Woods, Lewis, James and William Connor, Sam G. Anderson, Nathaniel Moody, Alfred M. Harris and Lunsford M. Bramlett.

The first attempt at tavern-keeping was made by Lewis Kirk, who entertained the justices and officers of the court at his house during the sessions of court in 1810 and 1811. Richard Scott was the first merchant in Pulaski. He opened a small store near Kirk's house, on Richland Creek, in about 1809. In 1810 Scott sold his store to John G. Talbott and William Ball opened a grocery store in the same vicinity. At that time the above were the only houses in Pulaski. The first merchants to do business after the town was laid out were Richard Scott, David Martin, John G. Talbott, James Doren, John McCrackin and Henry Hogan. The taverns of that day were kept by Capt. Thomas Smith, on the northeast corner of the Public Square and by James Alexander, on the southeast corner of the the Public Square; the latter being afterward kept by —— Kennon and was known by that name. The physicians of Pulaski who practiced between 1809 and 1815, and probably later, were Dr. Gilbert D. Taylor, Dr. Shadrack Nye, Dr. David Woods, Dr. Alfred

Flournoy, Dr. Elisha Eldridge and Dr. Charles Perkins. The first tan-yards established in the town were those of James Hanby and Lewis and James Connor. The first comfortable residence erected in Pulaski was built by German Lester.

The Legislature declared Richland Creek navigable as far as Pulaski in 1809, and for thirty years thereafter the produce of the county was shipped from Pulaski in large flat-bottomed boats, which were made in the town, and frequently small keel boats and pirogues were made, which were loaded and taken to New Orleans, where merchandise was purchased and brought back in the boats. From three to four months were required to make the trip. Goods for the first merchants were hauled in wagons from Baltimore, Md., whither the merchants themselves would journey once each year with cattle, cotton, etc., which they would exchange for dry goods, groceries and other commodities.

In November, 1815, the Legislature appointed Tyree Rhodes, Ralph Graves and John Hicks commissioners to build a bridge across Richland Creek, at Pulaski, the bridge to be paid for out of moneys derived from the sale of town lots. The bridge was built near the depot, and was the first one in the county. A substantial covered frame bridge was subsequently erected in its place, which is in use at the present.

The manufacturers of Pulaski, between 1818 and 1825, were as follows: John E. Holden, cabinet-maker; James Lynch, turning-lathe; William Holden, woolen-factory, afterward converted into a steam saw-mill; Robert Hamby, tannery; George Everly, hattery; Thomas Wilkerson, gunsmith; Adam R. Farres, silversmith; Henry Cowper, saddlery; Henry Piden, blacksmith; Samuel Anderson, cabinet-maker. During the same period Capt. James Patteson kept a hotel, and William Willis a livery stable. A census of the heads of families in Pulaski, taken in 1820, returned the following: Samuel Pearson, Jeremiah Parker, Alfred M. Harris, Shadrack Nye, Nathaniel Moody, James Patteson, James Perney, Samuel J. Anderson, Thomas Wilkerson, James Connor, John E. Holden, William English, William Connor, Francis Guthrie, Nathaniel Allman, William Royle, Bernard M. Patteson, Lunsford M. Bramlett, German Lester, W. R. Davis, Robert Gibson, Tyran M. Yancy, Amos Davis, John Brown, Jesse Day, Francis Hicks, William Hamby, Mathias Sharon, John B. Connor, Robt. Crockett, Marterson, B. McCormack, A. V. Brown, Elizabeth Berry, Judith Birch, Elizabeth Hooks, Mary Scott, William Ball, Thomas White, Joseph H. Hodge, John McCrackin, William Rose, Francis Alexander, Joseph Trotter, Henry Hogan, Fountain Lester and Archibald Story.

The merchants of Pulaski in business between 1820 and 1830, were Thomas Martin, James Perry, Nathaniel G. Nye, Andrew M. Balentine, Andrew Fay, Samuel Kercheval and Toggert & Christy. Between 1830 and 1840 the merchants were Edward Rose, Keenan, Walker & Guy, James McConnell, H. E. Lester, Lester & Hoag, P. H. Brady, Andrew Fay, Joseph C. Ray & Co., Brown & Ezell, Block Bros., Bell & Mason, Litherman & McNairy, Simonton & Oliver, Jones & Armstrong, J. W. Carpenter, Riddle, Smith & Robinson and Butler & Story. Between 1840 and 1850: Balentine & Gough, J. H. Taylor, M. Nassau, H. C. Lester & Bro., Martin & Tapp, Booker & Shepperd, W. H. Lime, Samuel Kercheval, Bell & Mason, Yerger & Shawl, Balentine, Ezell & Co., Mason & Ezell, Martin & Ray, Benjamin Carter, J. C. Carter, B. F. Carter & Sons, A. M. Carter & Co., and May and Neil. Between 1850 and 1860: Ezell & Bro., May & Neil, Martin, Ray & Co., A. M. Carter & Co., May & Bros., Mason & Ezell, P. H. Ezell, Balentine & Son, Batte & Patteson, Martin & Amos, Armstrong & Nassau, Fuller & Abernathy, J. P. Skillerm, Davidson & Allen, Brannon & Carson, Martin & Stacey, John Kounts and Ray, Harris & Co. There were no merchants in business during the war, all stores, save an occasional sutler's stand, being closed. Between 1865 and 1870 the merchants were R. A. Gordon, Shepperd & Son., Ezell & Edmonson, Balentine & Ezell, Taylor & Son, May Bros., Cox & Reynolds, John B. Ezell, Flautt, Martin & Co., Rosenau & Bros., and A. Lazeress. The merchants of 1870 and 1880 were Arrowsmith & Brannon. H. Abrams, Dickenson & Co., J. R. C. Brown & Co., J. H. Cannon & Co., P. H. Ezell & Son, Flautt, Martin & Co., Heins & Hannaburgh, R. B. Gibson, Erwin & Lindsey, George W. McGrew, J. P. & A. E. May, James T. McKissack & Co., L. Nassau, Pullen & Childress, Pope & Toller, L. Rosenau & Bros., J. P. Rankin, Rosenau & Loreman, Sumpter & Lacy, S. P. Sternau, Robert Shepperd & Co., and H. O'Lenskey.

Business of Pulaski at present: W. H. Abernathy, clothier; Brannon & Smith, Abernathy & Lightfoot, L. Rosenau & Bros., A. E. May & Son, Solinsky & Feinburgh, F. Arrowsmith & Co., W. S. Rose & Son and H. G. Brown, dry goods; Nelson, May & Martin and Carter & Buford, hardware; H. M. Grigsby, Anderson & Arrowsmith, Craig & Co. and Pope & Gordon, drugs; F. M. Burch, W. J. Nance & Son, J. S. Reynolds, T. J. Wells, J. S. Childress & Co., R. W. Woodward, Spear & McGrew, D. E. Spear & Son, James Davis, J. P. Rankin, Barrington & Lewis and R. S. Williams, family groceries; W. R. Craig, grain dealer; John West and James T. Oaks & Co., undertakers and furniture dealers; Walter Moffitt, merchant tailor; J. H. Cannon & Co., boots and shoes; T. H. May and W. B. Smithson, books and stationery; B. S. Cheek and G. N. McGrew, confections; Miss M. A. Smith & Co. and Mrs. F. M. Rudd, milliners; John Matthews and H. Rosecrans, saddles and harness; P. M. Ezell and J. C. Young & Co., tinware; W. H. Rose and I. H. Rainey, livery stables; Maclin & Robinson, meat market; hotels—Linden House, J. A. P. Skillern, proprietor, and the St. Giles Hotel, Bledsoe & Brown, proprietors; Jones & White, real estate agents; W. B. Smithson, E. Edmonson, Will S. Ezell, James R. Crow and George T. Riddle, insurance agents; Edward F. McKissack, J. T. Grant, G. A. McPeters, dentists; Drs. C. C. & C. A. Abernathy, Dr. J. C. Roberts, Dr. William Batt, Dr. W. E. Wilson, Dr. Gordon and Dr. Millhouse, practicing physicians. The Giles National Bank, S. E. Rose, president, John D. Flautt, cashier, was established in 1872, and the People's National Bank, J. P. May, president, George T. Riddle, cashier, was established in 1883. Both banks do a general banking business. The town has one of the best opera houses to be found outside of the cities. The building is 42x84 feet, with an arched ceiling, beautifully frescoed, and has a seating capacity for 800 persons.

The manufactories of Pulaski are as follows: W. N. Webb & Son, general machine shops; Webb & McGrew, woolen factory; McCord & Co., flouring-mill; T. W. Pittman & Co., planing-mill; Williams & Watson, planing and saw-mill; Graham & Son, carriage factory; McGrew & Son, J. B. Childress, tan-yards; Leon Godfroy and J. A. Casey, silversmiths; Morris & Bro. and Woodring & Sullivan, marble works; Bradley Bros. and D. E. Spear, blacksmith; Owen Callihan and W. A. Manning, boot and shoe-makers. There are two newspapers in Pulaski, the only ones in Giles County, both of which are excellent papers with fair patronage, and both belong to the Democratic party in politics. The Pulaski *Citizen*, of which McCord & Smith are proprietors and L. D. McCord is editor, was established in 1858, and the Pulaski *Democrat*, J. G. Ford, editor and proprietor, was established in August, 1886. In addition to these two papers, there is a job printing office in Pulaski, of which Charles F. Carter is proprietor.

The secret societies of Pulaski are as follows: Lawrence Lodge, No. 16, F. & A. M., was the first lodge in Giles County, being instituted in August, 1816. In 1821 the lodge forfeited its charter by a failure to elect officers, and in 1824 a new charter was obtained and the lodge revived as Lafayette Lodge, No. 57. During the suspension of Masonry, between 1834 and 1841, the lodge ceased to work, and in 1842 was again revived under a new charter as Pulaski Lodge, No. 101, and continues as such at the present. Pulaski Lodge, No. 12, I. O. O. F., was established in 1845. The charter was destroyed during the war but the lodge did not suspend active work, and at the close of the war a duplicate charter was obtained and is in force at the present. Pulaski Chapter, No. 20, R. A. M., was organized in 1859; Stonewall Lodge, No. 112, K. P., was organized in 1874; Friendship Lodge, No. 104, K. of H., was organized in 1875; Richland Council, No. 407, A. L. of H., established in 1881; Mystic Lodge, No. 25, A. O. U. W., established in 1877; Giles Council, No. 409, R. A., organized in 1880; Pulaski Lodge, No. 170, G. T., organized in 1884; Pulaski Y. M. C. A., organized in 1880; Pulaski Commandery, No. 12, K. T., organized in 1871. There is one church each of Methodist Episcopal South, Cumberland Presbyterian, Presbyterian, Episcopal and Christian denominations in Pulaski.

Pulaski was incorporated in 1820, and Elisha Eldridge was the first mayor, and Shadrack Nye the first recorder and treasurer. The present town officers are as follows: Mayor, P. Smith; recorder and treasurer, John Dyer; marshal, J. M. McDonald; policeman, Joseph Flippin; aldermen—J. H. Lightfoot, M. C. Camody, T. J. Walls, R. B. Crow and H. A. Rosecrans.

The streets are as follows: Those running east and west—Washington, Madison, Jefferson, College, Flower, Hemp, Cotton and Depot; those running north and south—First, Second, Third, Mill Lane and Cemetery. The streets are lighted with gas, the gas being manufactured and furnished by the Pulaski Gas Company, the works of which were established in 1882. The company is composed of Messrs. Chess, Carley & Co., of Louisville, Ky. The local manager is Mr. F. Winship. The streets are also macadamized and furnish some delightful drives. The Giles County Agricultural Society was organized in 1876 and hold annual exhibitions at their grounds near Pulaski.

Elkton, one of the oldest towns of the county, is situated in the Ninth District, fifteen miles southeast from Pulaski, three miles above the mouth of Richland Creek, on Elk River, and has a population of between 150 and 200. Soon after the organization of the county two towns were laid off on Elk River, one immediately at the mouth of Richland Creek and the other a short distance below. They were named Upper and Lower Elkton. Later on another town was laid off about three miles above the upper town, on Elk River, and lots sold by Dr. Purcell and others, which town was named Elkton; thus at one time there were three separate and distinct towns on Elk River within a few miles of each other, and all bearing the same name with the prefix of Lower and Upper only to distinguish them. In the course of fifteen or twenty years Lower and Upper Elkton lost their identity as towns, the citizens moving from time to time to Elkton and other points, and of the three villages only Elkton remains at present. The business of Elkton at present is as follows: A. W. Moore and T. E. Dailey, general merchandise; A. G. Ezell & Milton Carter, J. J. Upshot, John R. Beasley and P. W. Nave, dry goods and groceries; N. M. Hollis & Co., and Stephen Dunn, blacksmiths. There are two white and one colored churches in Elkton, as follows: Methodist Episcopal and Cumberland Presbyterian, and Colored Missionary Baptist. The schools of the town consist of a chartered high school, or academy, and the common school for the colored people.

Lynnville, the second town in size and importance, is situated forty-three and a half miles north of Pulaski, in the Fifteenth District, and on the Nashville & Decatur Railroad, and has a population of about 400. Originally the town stood about a mile from the railroad, and was known as Old Lynnville, but in 1860, upon the completion of the railroad, was moved over to the road, being at present in the old town about seventy-five inhabitants and one store, which is kept by Smith & Reed, an undertaking establishment by J. C. Gibbs, and a blacksmith shop by Clifford Fry, while John Wagstaff runs a water power grist-mill on Lynn Creek, near town. The old town was laid off on Lynn Creek in about 1810–11. A Cumberland Presbyterian, Christian and Colored Methodist and Baptist Churches are situated in the old town, though no school is taught there. The business of Lynnville proper is conducted as follows: Smith & Bros., Geo. S. Tate, Wagstaff & Bro., C. H. Witt, and F. M. Walker, dry goods; J. B. McCall, Shields Bros., H. Thomas and Heindman & McIntosh, family groceries; W. B. Pepper and Royster & Co., drugs; Griffis Bros., grain dealers; John Boulie, tin shop; J. W. Dickerson, undertaker; J. B. Bray, planing-mill; James Ridenberry, wood-worker; Thomas Fry and J. H. Lancaster, blacksmiths. The churches are the Presbyterian, Methodist and Primitive Baptist, all white. Half way between Lynnville and Old Lynnville is a splendid high school, which is operated under a four-mile law charter, and which supplies the educational facilities for both towns.

Prospect, a flourishing village on the Nashville & Decatur Railroad, has a population of 200. The town lies thirteen miles south of Pulaski, in the Second District. The merchants of Prospect are R. F. Mays, Gilbert & Reed and J. H. Hazlewood, general stores, and Dr. Cardwell, drugs. N. V. Davis and Dr. Cardwell operate cotton-gins, and T. H. Browning has a blacksmith shop. The secret societies are the Masons, Knights of Honor and Good Templars, the first named order having a large and commodious hall. There are but two churches in the town, the Methodist South and Colored Baptist. The Prospect High School is the one institution of learning in the town.

Aspin Hill, with a population of 150, is another town in the Second District, situated eight miles south from Pulaski, on the railroad. The one store of the village is kept by W. G. Inman, who does a general merchandise business. There is also a Methodist Church and a good public school at Aspin Hill, and the people are a thrifty, moral class.

Campbellsville lies in the Fourteenth District, eight miles west from Lynnville, and has a population of about seventy-five. There are two stores in the village, those of Mirh & Hubbard and Cowan & Co., general merchants. Dew & Wright are the blacksmiths. The only church in the town is the Cumberland Presbyterian. A good high school is also located in the town. Other villages are Buford, Wales and Veto on the railroad, and Bunker Hill, Bradshaw, Bodenham and Pisgah away from the railroad.

The first school in Giles County of which there is now any record or recollection was the Pulaski Academy which was chartered by act of the General Assembly, passed November 23, 1809, just nine days after the passage of the act establishing the county. The act appointed as trustees of the academy John Sappington, Nelson Patteson, Tyree Rhodes, Samuel Jones, Somersett Moore, Charles Buford, and Charles Neeley. There being a surplus of money from the sale of town lots, the commissioners were authorized by the General Assembly to invest a portion of the same in a tract of land upon which to locate and erect a college building and the present commanding and beautiful site on East Hill was purchased. In September 1812, the name of the academy was changed from Pulaski Academy to that of Wurtemburg Academy, and William Purcell, David Woods and Alfred M. Harris were appointed additional trustees. In 1849 a college charter was obtained for the academy by the name of Giles College, when the present large, commodious brick building was erected at a cost of about $15,000.

In 1810 a school was taught by John Morgan in the Weakley Creek neighborhood, and in 1811 a school was taught in the same neighborhood by Rev. James B. Porter.

The first classic school taught outside of Pulaski was established by Rev. David Weir in 1812, near the junction of Lynn Creek and Robertson Fork. The school was one of the leading ones of its day, and was taught for many years.

At a very early date an excellent female academy was established in Pulaski, and suitable buildings were erected on the lot now owned by J. B. Childress. In 1830 the property was exchanged for the lot upon which the Episcopal rectory now stands, which building was erected for the academy. This building became damaged by a crack in the walls in 1853, to such an extent as to be considered dangerous, and a short time before the late war the property was sold and the school discontinued.

The teachers of Wurtemburg Academy from 1824 were as follows: William W. Patter, William Loring, William Price, Mr. Mendum, John C. Brown, Daniel G. Anderson, Benjamin F. Mitchell, John A. McRoberts, Woodberry Mitchell, James L. Jones, Prof. Sharp, John H. Stewart, Charles G Rogers and Alfred H. Abernathy. Of the Female Academy, the teachers were Rev. James Hall Brooks, Mrs. Thomasson, Mr. Davis, Dr. Rowles, and Rev. Robert Caldwell, the latter being one of the most celebrated educators of his day.

In 1870 Thomas Martin, one of the leading citizens and business men of Pulaski, and a pillar of the Methodist Church, died and left $30,000 to be expended in the establishment and endowment of a college for young ladies, to be located at Pulaski. In 1872, in accordance with Mr. Martin's bequest, Martin College was chartered, and handsome and commodious brick buildings were erected in 1873. The buildings will accommodate from 80 to 100 pupils. The study hall, recitation and music rooms, as well as parlors and sleeping apartments, are well lighted and ventilated, and are unusually large and pleasant. The many conveniences embrace a fire escape, elevator, covered galleries, etc. The grounds cover an area of about eight acres, and are beautifully laid out in walks and flower gardens. The buildings and grounds cost about $30,000. John S. Wilkes is the president and Ida E. Hood and Susan L. Heron, principals. The board of trust is composed as follows: J. S. Wilkes, president; William S. Ezell, vice-president; L. W. McCord, secretary; J. B. Childers, treasurer; J. P. May, John T. Steele, John D. Flautt, Wm. F. Ballentine, H. M. Brannan and J. S. Childers. There are chartered schools at Lynnville, Prospect, Elkton, Aspin Hill and other points in the county, all of which have a good attendance. The public schools are in a healthy condition, and are conducted for six months in the year.

In 1885 the scholastic population of Giles County was as follows: White, male 4,143, female 3,789—total, 7,932; colored, male, 2,695, female, 2,499—total, 5,194; total, white and colored, 13,126. The semi-annual apportionments of school money in 1885 was for Giles County as follows: April apportionment, $1,730.27; October apportionment, $1,730.27. During 1885 the numbers of teachers employed in Giles County was as follows: White, male, 74, female, 29; colored, male, 25, female, 18; total, 146. The number of schools and school districts in the county are as follows: White schools, 103; colored, 43; total, 146. Number of school districts in county, 20. In 1885 there were two institutes held in the county, which were attended by 103 teachers. The number of teachers licensed in the county in 1885 were as follows: White, male, 74, female, 29; colored, male, 25, female, 18; total, white and colored male and female, 146. There were in 1885 pupils enrolled as follows: White, male, 3,314, female, 3,031; colored, male, 2,156, female, 2,009; total, white and colored, 10,510. In the same year there were 51 frame and 26 log schoolhouses in the county, making a total of 77 schoolhouses in the county.

Probably the first church organization in Giles County was the Baptist Church at Cross Water, which was organized in 1808 by the Buchanans, Ezells and other settlers of that neighborhood. A log meeting-house was erected in 1809, which stood for a number of years, until torn down and a new and more commodious one was built, which was given the name of Old Zion. Other early churches of this denomination were erected as follows: Lynn Creek Church in 1810, Indian Creek Church, Robertson Fork Church, and a church near the Martin Wood's place in 1811. In 1815 the Baptists organized a church in Pulaski, and in about 1820 erected a substantial brick church building. The organization dying out in after years, the building was sold and converted into a private residence, since when there has been no Baptist Church in the town.

In about 1809 the Methodists organized their first church and erected a log meeting-house on Lynn Creek, one and a half miles north of old Lynnville, of which Rev. Pruit was the first preacher. In 1810 that denomination organized and erected a church at Mount Pisgah, and soon afterward the "Brick" Church was erected in what is now the Seventeenth Civil District. In 1811 Rehobeth Church, one of the most celebrated of the early Methodist churches, was erected on the Pulaski & Elkton Pike, four miles southeast of the former place. During the same year a Methodist Church was erected on Indian Creek, about three miles southwest of Bee Spring. Bethel Church, on Elk River, was erected in 1817, almost entirely alone by Wm. R. Brown. Mount Gilead Church was erected in 1830, and Hopewell Church in 1829. Sometime in 1820 a log church was erected on Third Street in Pulaski. Later on a large brick church was erected, which was afterward sold to the Odd Fellows, and in 1851 the present substantial brick church was erected at a cost of about $8,000. The twenty-second session of the Tennessee Conference was held in Pulaski, commencing November 6, 1833, being held in the court house. In 1830 a large camp ground was established at Prospect and a church subsequently erected, known by that name.

The Presbyterians organized and erected their first church in the county at Elk Ridge, two and one-half miles east of Lynnville, in about 1810, of which Rev. David Weir was the first preacher. Marr's Hill Church was erected the following year. In 1812 the Pulaski Church was erected, of which Rev. Gideon Blackburn was the first preacher. In 1820 the Presbyterians and Masonic lodge joined finances, and erected a large brick church and Masonic hall combined, and in 1852 the present brick church was erected at a cost of about $7,000. In 1822 the Tennessee Presbytery met at the court house in Pulaski.

The first church organized and erected in Giles County by the Cumberland Presbyterians was Mount Moriah, in the Thirteenth District, in the fall of 1811. The organization took place at the residence of Reese Porter, whose son, James B., was the first preacher in charge of the church. The Shoal Creek Church was erected in 1818 in the Paisley neighborhood, of which Rev. A. Smith was the first preacher. The Pulaski Church was organized in July, 1828. In 1840 a large brick church was erected, which was subsequently torn down, and the present handsome edifice erected, in 1882, at a cost of about $10,000. All of these early churches had their camp-grounds, and conducted camp-meetings until about 1840, and in some instances until within a few years of the breaking out of the late war.

The Pulaski Episcopal Church was organized in about 1849 or 1850, and held services in the Odd Fellow's Hall until 1854, when the congregation purchased the old Female College building, and converted the same into a rectory, which is in use at the present time. The congregation has a beautiful lot, and it is the intention to erect a handsome church edifice thereon at no distant day. The Pulaski Christian Church was established in 1859, and for a while held their meetings in the court house, but at present meet in the Odd Fellow's Hall.

The churches of the present, outside of the towns, in the county are as follows, by civil districts: First District—Smyrna; Mount Pleasant. Methodist Episcopal South, and Union Hill, Missionary Baptist. Second District—Fetusia, Cumberland Presbyterian; Liberty, Methodist Episcopal South; Ridge, Baptist, and Poplar Hill, used by all denominations. Third District—Pleasant Hill, Beach Grove, Cumberland Presbyterian; Mount Zion, Beach Spring, Baptists; Bethel, Carmel and Hebron, Methodist Episcopal South. Fourth District—Bluff Spring, Missionary Baptist; Puncheon Camp, Hard Shell Baptist; Booth's Chapel, Pleasant Ridge, Methodist Episcopal South; Shoal Bluff and Noblett's Chapel, Christian. Fifth District—Rural Hill, Christian; Loan Oak, Methodist Episcopal South; Weakley Creek and Old Side, Baptist; and Mount Joy, Colored Cumberland Presbyterian, and Chestnut Grove, Colored Missionary Baptist. Sixth District—Mount Moriah, Cumberland Presbyterian; Trinity, Chestnut Grove, Cedar Grove, Methodist Episcopal South; Cool Spring, Christian; and Cedar Grove, Martin Box, Anthony Hill, African Methodist Episcopal, and Rocky Point. Colored Baptist. Eighth District—Sharon, Presbyterian, and Rockey Mount, Colored Presbyterian. Tenth District—Mount Pleasant and Mount Zion, Methodist Episcopal South. Eleventh District—Blooming Grove, Friendship, Parson's School House, Methodist Episcopal South, and Old Zion, Baptist. Twelfth District—Union, Baptist; Mount Olivet, Methodist Episcopal South, and Lilburn Chapel, American Methodist Episcopal. Thirteenth District—Pleasant Valley, Pleasant Hill, Methodist Episcopal South; Minnow Branch, Methodist, Baptist and Cumberland Presbyterian combined, and Pleasant Hill, African Methodist Episcopal. Fourteenth District—Taylor's Chapel, Williams' Chapel, Methodist Episcopal South; Gibsonville, Primitive Baptist; Center Point, Christian, and Powell's Chapel, Christian. Fifteenth District—Antioch, Methodist Episcopal South. Sixteenth District—Ash Gap and Simpson's Chapel, Methodist Episcopal South. Seventeenth District—Mount Zion, Baptist and "Brick" Church, Methodist Episcopal South. Eighteenth District—Hurricane Creek, Shoal Creek, Egnew Creek, Methodist Episcopal South, and Scott's Hill, Baptist. Nineteenth District—Pleasant Valley, Hebron, Salem, Methodist Episcopal South; Pleasant Hill, Baptist, and St. Matthew, African Methodist Episcopal, and Philippi, Colored Cumberland Presbyterian. Twentieth District—Mount Pisgah, Bee Spring, Mount Zion, Methodist Episcopal South; Unity, Primitive Baptist, and Indian Creek, Hard Shell Baptist.

# LINCOLN COUNTY.

L INCOLN COUNTY is bounded on the north by the counties of Marshall, Bedford, and Moore; on the east by Moore and Franklin; on the south by the State of Alabama; and on the west by Giles County. It lies almost wholly within the central basin of Middle Tennessee, The geological situation of the county is about equally divided between the siliceous group of the lower Carboniferous formation, and the Nashville group of the Silurian formation. On the line of railroad may be seen large quantities of black shale, which is so impregnated with petroleum or bitumen that it will sustain for a month a fire when kindled on it. This black shale is also rich in sulphuret of iron, by the decomposition of which copperas and alum are formed. It easily disintegrates upon exposure and is valueless except for the manufacture of the salts mentioned. Many of the limestone rocks are but aggregations of fossil remains. A few miles east of Fayetteville is a quarry where a very fair article of reddish variegated marble is found. This marble is sometimes injured by particles of iron pyrites. The county is divided into two almost equal parts by the Elk River, which with its numerous tributaries affords it excellent water facilities. The streams which enter this river from the north are Bradshaw Creek, Swan Creek, Cane Creek, Norris Creek, Mulberry Creek, Roundtree Creek, Tucker Creek and Farris Creek. Those from the south are Shelton Creek, Duke Creek, Stewart Creek, Wells Creek, Coldwater Creek, and Kelley Creek. Between Elk River and the Alabama line is a belt of high land which is the watershed between Elk River and the Tennessee. This watershed embraces a strip about eight miles wide and includes nearly one-third of the county. It is an exceedingly level high plateau and is not well drained. The sub-soil is a pale yellowish clay porous and leachy except in swamps where the clay is bluish. However, a few spots are found with a good red clay subsoil, and when this is found, lands are rated higher. No limestone is seen on this plateau and the main vegetation is wild growth.

The remainder of the county comprises spacious valleys, alternating with productive hills and ridges. Upon some of the hills however, the loose limestone lies in such abundance as to preclude cultivation. The valleys of Elk River and Cane Creek will average a mile in width, and the latter is probably fifteen miles long. The land in these two valleys is as productive as any in the State. Many knolls near Elk River are upraised alluvium. An abundance and a general variety of timber grows in the county. It is mainly of the following varieties: Linn, buckeye, hickory, poplar, box elder, black walnut, wild cherry, black locust, chestnut, beech, gum, dogwood, ironwood, horn beam, sugar tree, hackberry, cedar and elm.

As early as 1784 land explorers passed through this section, and some surveys were made and grants issued prior to 1790. North Carolina grants for land in this county were issued to John Hodge, Robert Walker and Jesse Comb in 1793. There are also land grants recorded in the office of Lincoln County Register, bearing date of 1794, to the following persons: William Smith, Elizabeth W. Lewis, Ezekiel Norris, William Edmonson, Alexander Greer, Thomas Perry, Thomas Edmonson, Matthew Buchanan, Matthew McClure, Andrew Greer and John Steele. In the spring of 1806 James Bright, at the head of a surveying party, passed where Fayetteville now stands, striking Elk River near the mouth of Nelson Creek. He found a very rank growth of cane and occasionally discovered Indian trails. Near Fayetteville he found a deposit of periwinkle and muscle shells, giving evidence of an Indian village site, and by some it is supposed that this was the village in which De Soto camped through the winter of 1540–41. This supposition has recently been strengthened by the finding of a coin bearing the inscription of the Cæsars.

It is impossible to tell who first settled within the present bounds of Lincoln County. The first settlers are now all in their graves and many have no descendants in the county. In the fall of 1806 Ezekiel Norris settled on his grant of 1,280 acres of land at the mouth of Norris Creek, and this creek is all that now bears his name in the county. He was a shrewd man. Being led to donate 100 acres of land for the county seat under the false representation that other parties had made the same offer, he afterward sued the county and recovered $700 for the land. He was probably the first permanent white settler in the county.

James Bright also became a citizen of the county, and many deeds are recorded transferring land from him to other parties. For twenty-five years he was clerk of the circuit court and was clerk and master of the chancery court for a term of years. John Greer, a very wealthy man, settled near the mouth of Cane Creek on his large tract of land. He took interest in organizing the county and in conducting the public affairs afterward. He was once general of the militia. He erected a valuable mill for those days on Elk River, two miles from Fayetteville.

Joseph Greer settled on his vast domain on Cane Creek near Petersburg. He was a giant in stature, standing six feet seven inches and "well built proportionately." He was one of the forty gallant defenders of Watauga Station in 1769. He was also a hero of King's Mountain, and it was he who bore the news of that splendid victory to Congress, then sitting in Philadelphia. He dressed in the style of the old aristocratic Virginia gentleman. Thomas Leonard, Hugh M. Blake, Jesse Riggs, Peter Luna, James Blakemore, Capt. William Crunk and John and Ezekial March were also settlers on Cane Creek in the first and second decades of this century. Crunk and Blakemore were noted for their social qualities, and dances were frequent at their homes. On Swan Creek, N. G. Pinson, Joel Pinson and Wright Williams were prominent "first cane cutters," and men who bore their share of the load in administering public affairs. In what is now embraced in the Twelfth and Thirteenth Civil Districts the first settlements were made by James McCormick, John Anderson, Henry Taylor and Richard Wyatt. On Norris Creek early homes were made by Fielden McDaniel, Moses Hardin, William Edmonson, John Ray, George Cunningham, Samuel Todd, Isaac Congo, —— Jenkins and —— Parks. On Mulberry Creek were John J. Whittaker, a good and prominent man; John Morgan, grandfather of Hon. John M. Bright, Brice M. Garner, who soon removed to Fayetteville, and Gen. William Moore. Others were the several Whitakers, Hardy Holman, William Brown, Enoch Douthat, the Waggoners and Isaac Sebastian.

Other settlements on Norris Creek were made prior to 1810 by Ebenezer McEwen, Robert Higgins, Amos Small and Philip Fox. It is said that Davy Crockett also lived in the vicinity of the waters of Mulberry, in the eastern part of the county, in 1809–10.

In Fayetteville James Bright, who is mentioned above, was one of the most prominent first settlers. James Buchanan, Francis Porterfield, Brice M. Garner, John P. McConnell, Robert C. Kennedy, Benjamin Clements, and many others, made up the first citizens of the town. Alexander Beard settled near Fayetteville, south of the river. He had a large body of land, but lost a great portion of it in confirming his title, which, among many other North Carolina grants, was contested. Philip Koonce settled between Shelton Creek and Duke Creek in 1807 or 1808, and near by him, on Shelton Creek, settled Henry Kelso, about the same time. Tunstall Gregory settled on the waters of Shelton Creek, and John Duke on Duke Creek. Michael Rolinson was one of the first settlers on Coldwater Creek; but an old man, named Abbot, lived in that part of the county "five years, before he knew any one else lived within one hundred miles of him," so says one who vouches for the truth of it. A great many settlements were made prior to 1810, on the waters of Coldwater, but names can not be obtained. A man named Peyton Wells was the first to make a home in the vicinity of Wells' Hill. He kept a noted "ordinary" or tavern. A man named Harper was the first to settle on the branch that now bears his name. Joseph Dean and William Todd soon became his neighbors.

The southeastern part of the county was sparsely settled along in the "twenties," but the barrenness of the soil has deterred many from locating there.

Many other settlers suffered privations and hardships, as well as those above given, but their names and places of settlement are lost to reliable tradition. In 1808 land entries were made by the following: Anthony Foster, Daniel Cherry, John Morgan, Benjamin Fitzrandolph and George Maxwell. Other land entries were made as follows: 1809—Adam Meek, William Richey, Robert Davis, Nicholas Perkins, John Richardson, Joseph Greer, Michael Robertson, W. P. Anderson, Oliver Williams, Nicholas Coonrod, Newton Cannon, Wright Morgan, Abram Maury, Stephen Holbert, Malcom Gilchrist, William Martin, Edward Bryans, Jacob Castleman, Nimrod Williams, Jesse Franklin, John Tesley, Daniel Kinley, Philip Phillips, Michael Campbell, Samuel Garland, William Townzen, Robert Bigham and Robert Tucker. 1810—Armstead Stubblefield, Abner Wells, William Rountree, Lemuel Koonce, Thomas R. Butler, Francis Nichson, John Cunningham, William Edmiston, James Buchanan, Morris Shaw, Thomas Edmiston, John Alcorn, Robert Elliott, Robert Nelson, James Winchester and Thomas Hickman. 1811–12—Reuben Stuart, John Cone, Timothy Hunter, James Coats, Roger B. Sapington, Henry Rutherford. 1813–14—Robert C. Kennedy, Robert Henry, Alexander Newberry, Brice M. Garner, John Coffman, Francis McCown, Mary Gray, David Cowen, Hugh Heartgrave, James McBride, Joseph Garner, Jeremiah Burks, Elyan Clements, Alden Tucker, Thomas Clark, Joel Butler, Daniel Read, William McGehee, Jesse George, Edward Harding, Samuel Ragsdale, Samuel Yager and Aaron Dutton. 1815–20—William Dickson, Jr., Jesse Pugh, William Smith, Warren Calhoun, Lavis Pugh, John Russell, Andrew Greer, William Dickson, David McGlathery, Henry Rutherford, David Dodd, James Boyle, John Clark, George Price, Joseph Byers and Joseph Street.

Doubtless many other grants were issued, the records of which are lost. Many of the above persons settled here before obtaining their grants, and some who obtained grants did not permanently settle, and even some were speculators who never lived in the county. On account of the climate and the fertile soil settlers were attracted to Lincoln County, and in 1833 it had a population of 10,788 free white persons. Since then parts of the county have been formed into other counties. In 1880 the population was 26,960.

Among the oldest persons now living in the county and who have been in the county since its pioneer days, are Hon. John M. Bright, Rev. J. W. Holman and C. A. French, of Fayetteville, and Hugh M. Blake and Joseph Gill, of Petersburg. Early pioneers found it no trival matter to develop their farms and raise their families. Not only was farming to be developed, but milling, merchandising, schools and churches, all required attention. However, these people were happy in their condition, and various were their amusements. Fayetteville, Petersburg and Arnold's Grocery (now Smithland) were noted places for settlement of all grudges, in "pummelling" fights. The lookers-on enjoyed this very much, and it was their duty to see fair play. No weapons or missiles were to be used, and "it was not fair to bite." In Fayetteville was a "grocery," in which fighting was such a common occurrence that it was known as the "war office." Militia musters were "big days" for the people.

Grist-mills were erected on the creeks and on Elk River, and there were several horse-mills in the county. To these horse-mills each man took his own horse or horses, and hitched them to the sweep to turn the mill while his grist was grinding. The water-mills were more economical, that is, they needed no horse power.

Joel Yowell, an early citizen of Petersburg, had a large horse-mill two miles from Petersburg, with a hand-bolting machine attached. Jesse Riggs and Thomas Leonard also had mills of this kind. Leonard and Yowell had wheat threshers attached to their mills, and Leonard also had a cotton-gin attached. However, threshing was mostly done by "tramping it out."

In 1811 the county court granted Elias Lunsford permission to build a saw mill on Mulberry Creek. This mill was built the following year. In 1814 David P. Monroe built a grist-mill on the west fork of Cane Creek. Francis Finchee built a grist-mill in 1815. In 1820 Nathaniel B. Binkingham built a mill on Cane Creek on a tract of school land.

Taverns were numerous, and were situated in all parts of the county without regard to towns. Ephraim Parham, Vance Greer, William Cross, Brice M. Garner and John Kelley obtained tavern license in 1811. Collins Leonard, Jesse Riggs, Cornelius Slater, John D. Spain, John P. McConnell, Elisha Boyles, Willie Garrett, George Stobah, C. R. Milborn, David Cobb, Joseph Dean, John Parks, William Smith, Walter Kinnard, Enoch Douthat, John H. Zevilly, John Houston, John Parks, Thomas Rountree and William Mitchell were other tavern keepers in the teens. These taverns were also known as "ordinaries," "houses of entertainment," etc.

Elk River was crossed by means of ferries. Ezekiel Norris had one of the first ferries on the river. William P. Anderson established a ferry at the mouth of Farris Creek in 1820, and Andrew Hannah, in 1822, established one at Hannah Ford.

Produce was marketed by means of flat-boats carrying it out of Elk River and down to New Orleans, and by wagons to Nashville. The very earliest merchants obtained their goods mainly from Baltimore, and brought them here by wagons from that city. Estill & Garner were experienced flat-boatmen. They took out boats each year, and returned on foot from New Orleans. At first cotton was not raised here to any extent, and that article was obtained in Alabama and freighted by wagons. Scouting Indians frequented these first settlements, but very few depredations were committed by them. It is handed down by reliable tradition that three men, whose names were Taylor, Anderson and Reed were scalped by the Indians while out searching for a horse. Another incident occurred wherein the Indians forced their way into a house where a woman was making soap. The woman had secreted herself behind the door with a gourd full of boiling soap, and upon their entrance she "anointed" the dirty red-skins with telling effect, causing them to flee for cooler parts.

Lincoln County was created by an act of the Legislature in 1809. The following is the act so far as it relates to establishment of the county:

AN ACT TO ESTABLISH A COUNTY SOUTH OF BEDFORD, TO BE KNOWN BY THE NAME OF LINCOLN.

SECTION 1. *Be it enacted by the General Assembly of Tennessee,* That Lincoln County shall be laid off and established within the following bounds, to wit: Beginning on the northeast corner of Giles County and extending south with the eastern boundary line of Giles County to the southern boundary line of the State; thence with that line east to a point due south of the mouth of Cove Spring Creek; thence north to the southern boundary line of Bedford County; and thence, with the said line, westwardly, to the beginning.

SEC. 2. *Be it enacted,* That John Whitaker, Sr., Wright Williams, Eli Garret, Littleton Duty and Jesse Woodruff be, and they are hereby, appointed commissioners with full power to procure by purchase, or otherwise, 100 acres of land on or near the north bank of Elk River, as near the center of the county, east and west, as a proper situation will admit of, and at all events not more than two miles from said center.

SEC. 3. *Be it enacted,* That the said commissioners, immediately after procuring the aforesaid 100 acres of land, shall cause a town to be laid off thereon, reserving near the center thereof a public square of two acres, on which the court house and stocks shall be built, likewise reserving a lot in any other portion of said town for the purpose of erecting a jail; and the said town, when so laid off, shall be named Fayetteville.

SEC. 6. *Be it enacted,* That the court of pleas and quarter sessions for the county of Lincoln shall be held on the fourth Monday in the months of February, May, August and November annually, at the house of Brice M. Garner until a place is provided for holding the said court in the town of Fayetteville.

SEC. 11. *Be it enacted,* That the militia of the county shall compose the Thirty-ninth Regiment and be attached to the Fifth Brigade.

SEC. 14. *Be it enacted,* That this act shall be in force from the first day of January, in the year one thousand eight hundred and ten.

The county thus established assumed the form of a rectangle in outline, but in 1835 a part of the territory now constituted in Marshall County was taken from the original Lincoln County, and in 1872 Moore County was created, embracing a part of Lincoln.

The first county court met Monday, February 26, 1810, at the house of Brice M. Garner, and the following men were qualified justices of the peace by Oliver Williams, Esq., of Williamson County: Thomas L. Trotter, Wright Williams, William Smith, John Whitaker, Sr., William Dickson, William Roundtree, Eli Garrett, Philip Koonce, Henry

Kelso, Robert Higgins, Samuel Barns, Littleton Duty, James Fuller, James Stallard, Jesse Woodruff and Nathan G. Pinson. Philip Koonce was appointed chairman and Thomas H. Benton was made clerk *pro tem.*, and entered the first minutes upon record. County officers were elected, an allowance of $1 each for wolf scalps was made, stock marks were recorded, constables were sworn in, justices were appointed to "take the tax," etc. At this term 2,662 acres of taxable land were reported. Harvey Holman, Wright Williams, Littleton Duty, Eli Garrett and John Whitaker were appointed to locate the county seat. They bought 100 acres of land of Ezekiel Norris and platted the town of Fayetteville.

At the May term William Allen was fined $3 for "profane swearing," and at the August term taxes were laid as follows: 6¼ cents on each 100 acres of land; 6¼ cents on each poll (white and black), and 12¼ cents on each stallion. Ferriage rates across Elk River were established at the following: Wagon, team and driver, 50 cents; cart or other two-wheel carriage, 25 cents; man and horse, 6¼ cents; footman, 6¼ cents, and live stock 2 cents per head. Tavern rates were made: Good whisky per half pint, 12¼ cents; good peach brandy, 12¼ cents; good West India rum, 25 cents; good "diet," 25 cents; good lodging, 6¼ cents; good "stableage with hay or fodder for 12 hours," 25 cents; good corn per gallon, 6¼ cents. Brice M. Garner was allowed $15 for the use of his house for the holding of court, and $30 for furnishing county seal and record books. Jurors were allowed 50 cents each per day for service. At this term a man entered court with an ear bleeding from being bitten off in a fight. He had the incident recorded at length to avoid the imputation of having been "cropped under the penal laws." The clerk charged the usual fee for recording a hog mark. At a term in 1811 two men were each fined $125 for not attending as witnesses in an important civil suit.

The county officers, so far as names and dates can be obtained, have been as follows: Sheriffs—Cornelius Slater, 1810; John Greer, 1812; Francis Porterfield, 1822; William Husband, 1826; Andrew Kincannon, 1828; Alfred Smith, 1833; William C. Blake, 1836; Constant Smith, 1840; William B. McLaughlin, 1844; E. G. Buchanan, 1847; Eli L. Hodge, 1848; James Hanks, 1852; W. M. Alexander, 1854; Moses Cruse, 1856; W. M. Alexander, 1858; Moses Cruse, 1860; William Moffett, 1862; John H. Steelman, 1864; William F. Taylor, 1866; C. S. Wilson, 1868; F. W. Keith, 1868; H. B. Morgan, 1870; W. A. Millard, 1872; R. F. Holland, 1878; W. A. Cunningham, 1882; George W. Poindexter, 1884. Trustees—John Rhea, 1810; Ebenezer McEwen, 1816; William Neeld, 1826; Samuel E. Gilleland, 1828; E. M. Ringo, 1836; John J. Ramsay, 1838; Richard White, 1842; E. M. Ringo, 1844; S. J. Isaacs, 1850; William B. Rhea, 1853; William Neeld, 1854; A. S. Randolph, 1858; William R. Smith, 1862; William P. Neeld, 1864; J. D. Scott, 1866; J. H. Carey, 1868; J. D. Scott, 1870; J. J. Cummins, 1872; H. C. Street, 1874; Henry Henderson, 1876–86. Registers—Samuel Barns, 1810; Cornelius Slater, 1816; Peter M. Ross, 1832; John Goodrich, 1836; Daniel J. Whittington, 1852; Peter Cunningham, 1860; Miles Ramsay, 1862; A. T. Nicks, 1864; A. J. Childress, 1869; P. D. Boyce, 1870; B. B. Thompson, 1874–86. Rangers—Philip Koonce, 1810–41; William Neeld, 1841; William T. Berry, 1843; A. H. Berry, 1848; N. O. Wallace, 1853–86. County Court Clerks—Brice M. Garner, 1810–32; Robert S. Inge, 1832. F. L. Kincannon, 1832; Charles Boyles, 1836; George W. Jones, 1840; Harmon Husband, 1843; Henry Kelso, 1844; George Cunningham, 1852; E. L. Hodge, 1854; Norris Leatherwood, 1857; Daniel J. Whittington, 1858; John T. Gordon, 1864; E. P. Reynolds, 1868; John Y. Gill, 1870; P. D. Boyce, 1874; E. S. Wilson, 1882

In 1856 J. R. Chilcoat was elected county judge, and served until the war. Afterward were elected T. J. McGarvey, 1869; H. C. Cowen, 1870; M. W. Woodard, 1873; N. P. Carter, 1874. Circuit court clerks: James Bright, 1810–36; Alfred Smith, 1836; J. R. Chilcoat, 1848; R. S. Woodard, 1856; M. W. Woodard, 1868; Rane McKinney, 1870; A. B. Woodard, 1873; Theodore Harris, 1874; W. C. Morgan, 1878.

Chancery clerks and masters previous to the war were Davis Eastland, James Bright, Robert Farquharson and John Fulton served successively. Afterward were Robert Farquharson, until 1869; Davis Clark, 1869; A. S. Fulton, 1876; W. B. Martin, 1879. Chancellors: B. L. Bramlitt, Terry H. Cahall, B. L. Ridley, John Steele, A. S. Knox, J. W. Burton and E. D. Hancock.

The first court house built was only for temporary use, until another could be erected. It was 18x20 feet in the clear, built with round logs, and "covered with a good cabin roof." It had a "seat for the jury, court and bar, and a resting place for the feet of the court, all of good plank." It was built in 1811 on one corner of the Public Square, by James Fuller, for $35. The first jail was built in 1810, with logs not less than twelve inches in diameter and ten feet long." The walls, floor and loft were "all of logs of the same description." In November, 1811, a contract to built a new two-story brick court house on the Square, was taken by Micajah and William McElroy, for $3,995. The court afterward allowed $750 extra for the work, thus making the total cost of the building $4,745. This court house was torn down in 1873, and the present one was erected by William T. Moyers, James N. Allbright and William E. Turley, for $29,579.30. J. H. Holman, H. C. Cowan and John Y. Gill composed the committee to report the plans, specifications and estimates for the building; Theodore Harris superintended the work. The second jail that was built, was a two-story brick building, lined on the inside with logs, the logs being protected by sheet iron. It was built about the same time as the court house. The present jail was built in 1868, and by contract was to cost not more than $23,000. It is of stone.

The stone bridge across Elk River is one of the best structures of the kind in the State. It was built in 1861 at a cost of about $40,000. It is of limestone, contains six elliptical arches, and is 450 feet in its entire length. The roadway is flanked on either side by a stone wall three feet high and two feet wide.

The civil divisions of the county were first designated by the companies of militia in the respective parts of the county, i. e., the civil officers of the county were elected from the various militia companies, as they now are from the civil districts. In 1835 the county was laid off into twenty-five civil districts. The lines have been changed from time to time, but still the same number is retained. The school districts have not always coincided with the civil districts, but are now one and the same.

Among the first acts of the county court was one to provide for the poor, and in 1815 a special tax was assessed for the county poor. About 1826 a poor farm was purchased and a poor house erected, the supervision of which was put under three commissioners, regularly appointed by the court. The poor are still cared for in this manner.

At different times agricultural societies have been organized, but have as often proved to be institutions of short life. The first one was organized in 1824.

In the year 1858 Fayetteville was connected with the main line of the Nashville & Chattanooga Railroad by the branch built from Decherd to Fayetteville, and in 1882 the narrow gauge road was built from Columbia to Fayetteville. The main support of these roads is the agricultural product, which in turn brings in articles of general merchandise. Pikes connect Fayetteville with Lynchburg and Shelbyville, and extend from Fayetteville for several miles in all directions.

The political cast of the county is strongly Democratic. In 1884 the vote for president and governor stood as follows: Cleveland, 2,382; Blaine, 890; Bate, 2,220; Reid, 941.

Financially old Lincoln is on a strong foundation. She has first class public buildings, good general improvements, with a firm backing of a good agricultural soil. The tax for 1884 shows a total valuation of taxable property of $3,564,340; number of acres of land, 345,722, valued at $2,628,780. The State tax for 1886 is $10,192; county tax, $12,692; school tax, $16,257; road tax, $2,393; making a total tax of $41,535. These figures include the estimate on railroad and telegraph property valued at $166,890. In 1885 there was reported in the county 9,325 horses and mules, 14,090 cattle, 11,969 sheep, 42,415 hogs, 1,070 bushels barley, 213 bushels buckwheat, 1,252,919 bushels corn, 37,908 bushels oats, 1,641 bushels rye and 275,463 bushels wheat.

Upon the bench of the circuit court sat Judge Thomas Stewart to hold the first court in this county. Then came Judge Kennedy for a time, who was succeeded by Judge Edmund Dillahunty, who held for a number of years. A. J. Marchbanks was the next judge, and continued on the bench until the war. Gov. Brownlow then appointed N. A. Patterson, who became the laughing stock for the lawyers who attended court. He was "deficient in the organs of hearing," and very "eccentric in nature." Then came W. P. Hickerson, who did not serve a full term. He resigned and was succeeded by Judge J. J. Williams, who was afterward elected to fill the term now closing. For many years Erwin J. Frierson was the attorney-general, and he was superseded in turn by A. F. Goff, James H. Thomas, Joseph Carter, George J. Stubblefield, J. H. Holman, J. D. Tillman and A. B. Woodard, the present incumbent of the office. The court in early days was engaged mainly in trying petty offenses, and not until 1825 was there a sentence of death pronounced. Duncan Bonds had murdered Felix Grundy, and was found guilty. He took an appeal to the Supreme Court of the State. A jury in 1828 rendered a verdict of guilty upon a charge of murder committed by a man named McClure, upon D. C. Hall. He received the sentence of death, and was hung in the spring of 1829. About 1847 a negro named Bill Moore was sentenced and hung for an attempted rape. In 1862 John George was sentenced to be hung for murdering Hosea Towry. He escaped from jail. Two years previous to this, in 1860, a negro, Alf, was hung for murdering his master, William Stevens. The whipping post and pillory often received the victims of the judge's sentence for the various offenses, and men were imprisoned for debt.

The bar of Lincoln County is one that ranks high in Tennessee. Not only are the members at present eminent and able lawyers, but from the first Lincoln County has given a home to many able men. At the first meeting of the county court was present Thomas H. Benton. He drew up the minutes of the first session of that court, and was the county's legal advocate on organization. He resided in Fayetteville for a number of years. He then arose to adorn the nation's highest legislative council, of which he was a member for thirty-two years, and was truly "an eminent man of America." Contemporary with him was L. P. Montgomery, widely known as the brave Capt. Montgomery, who began the practice of law in 1810, and who fell at the battle of Horse-Shoe. In 1810 George B. Baulch, George Coalter, William White, Joseph Phillips, Marmaduke Williams, Matthew D. Wilson and Alfred Harris were permitted to practice in the county. In 1811 Eli Tolbert, Samuel Acres and Charles Manton were allowed to practice. George C. Witt and W. S. Fontine also practiced here in that year. Hon. C. C. Clay, of Huntsville, Ala., attended this court as early as 1811, as also did John McKinney and John Tolbert. Other lawyers from adjoining counties visited this court professionally, among whom were Judge Haywood, and, later, Nathan Green, James Campbell, William Gilchrist, Oliver B. Hays, Lunsford M. Bramlett and Thomas M. Fletcher. Other prominent early lawyers were James Fulton, Samuel W. Carmack, Charles Boyles, William C. Kennedy, William P. Martin, William M. Inge and John H. Morgan. John H. Morgan, after a number of years in Fayetteville, moved to Memphis, thence to Mississippi, and was elevated to the bench in that State. He was the father of Hon. J. B. Morgan, of Mississippi. William P. Martin moved from Fayetteville to Columbia, Tenn., and there was a judge for many years.

Kennedy also removed to Columbia, where he too was elevated to the bench. He became the owner of quite a number of slaves, which he emancipated and transported to the African colony of Liberia. W. M. Inge was for many years associated in law with L. W. Carmack at Fayetteville. He served one term in Congress from the district which then included Lincoln County, and afterward made his home in Alabama.

Carmack was born in 1802; was an able and learned lawyer. In 1832 he moved to Florida, although retaining a summer home in Fayetteville. He arose to prominence in Florida, and died in 1849.

James Fulton has been styled the "father of the Fayetteville bar." He located in Fayetteville in 1820, when twenty-two years of age. He filled one term as attorney-general in early life, but devoted his time to the prosecution of his profession rather than pursue official honors. He was an able lawyer and a highly respected citizen. His death occurred in 1856.

Previous to 1825 the following were permitted to practice law in the county: E. B. Robertson, William Kelly, Tryon Yancey, besides those above mentioned. Others were W. D. Thompson and Henry B. Ely, 1827; Davis Eastland, 1829; John R. Greer and Robert Inge, 1832; Andrew A. Kincannon and Elliott H. Fletcher, 1834; George W. Jones, 1839. Mr. Jones was born in 1806, and came to this county when young. He was three times elected to the Legislature. For sixteen years he was a member of Congress, and was in the Senate once. In his congressional career he received the nickname of "the watch dog of the treasury." He was also a member of the Confederate Congress and of the constitutional convention of 1870. He was a very able and popular man, filling many of the county offices and taking especial pride in his county's welfare. His death occurred in 1884. He devoted no time to the practice of law, but lived almost wholly in political circles. Other prominent early attorneys of the county were Felix G. McConnell, who went to Alabama and afterward served in the United States Congress, committing suicide while a member of that body; W. T. Ross, a very able advocate; John C. Rodgers, who died young, but was an able lawyer; and Archibald Yell, who was a man of "ability and temper." He and Hon. G. W. Jones once engaged in a physical combat before the county court, of which Jones was chairman. Yell threw a book at Jones, and Jones immediately returned the salute by a personal presentation with knife in hand. By the interference of other parties, no injury was done. Yell commanded a regiment in the Mexican war and was killed at the battle of Buena Vista.

The influence of W. H. Stephens, R. G. Payne, W. F. Kercheval, F. B. Fulton and J. W. Newman, has been felt at the bar. Since 1840 Robert Farquharson, who was prominent in the county, but did not give much time to law; David P. Hurley, who was a member of the bar but a short time, and Jas. M. Davidson, an able young lawyer, have held licenses to practice in these courts. Others were D. B. Cooper, who died when yet young; Davis W. Clark, who pursued the profession but a short time, but was an influential man; J. R. Chilcoat, who was the first county judge; Thomas Kercheval, now the mayor of Nashville; Ed R. Bearden, O. P. Bruce and Thomas B. Kercheval.

Hon. John M. Bright is the oldest member of the bar now living, and has probably acquired the most prominence in political circles. He was born in Fayetteville about 1818, and has ever since made this his home. He is able as an attorney, and was a prominent member of the Legislature of Tennessee before the war. In 1880 he retired from Congress, where he had served for several years. J. B. Lamb is one of the oldest and most successful attorneys of the county, and has been a member of the Legislature. He is the senior member of the law firm of Lamb & Tillman, of which Col. J. D. Tillman is the other member. He is a son of the Hon. Lewis Tillman, late of Bedford County. He was lieutenant-colonel (afterward colonel) of the Forty-first Regiment of Tennessee Infantry in the late war. J. H. Holman has been a member of the bar since 1866, and is widely known for his ability. J. H. Burnham is a good speaker, and was on the Hancock electoral ticket. He is now making the race for chancellor of this district. N. P. Carter is the county judge and a practicing lawyer. A. B. Woodard, the attorney-general, was reared in Fayetteville, the son of R. S. Woodard, who was a prominent man of the county. M. W. Woodard, also a son of R. S. Woodard, is a practicing attorney, and has been identified with public offices of the county. Joe G. Carrigan and G. W. Higgins are also able attorneys, and have both been in the Legislature. G. B. Boyles is an attorney at law, and now fills the office of recorder at Fayetteville. Others are Col. N. J. George, who was a lieutenant-colonel in Turney's First Tennessee; A. M. Solomon, an ex-member of the Legislature; R. L. Bright, S. W. Carmack, C. C. McKinney, F. P. Taylor, W. B. Lamb, John Routt and George H. Newman.

The sobriquet of "The Banner County," so often applied to Lincoln, appropriately represents its attitude in military matters. Hardly had the first few settlers begun to call this their home before Jackson's troops for the war of 1812 asked and received recruits from the county, among whom were Gen. William Moore, who commanded a company; Charles McKinney, S. S. Buchanan, William B. McLaughlin, Frank Smith and others—

as many as fifteen altogether. These troops made Fayetteville their rendezvous, and upon starting upon the campaign they marched out 2,500 strong and crossed Elk River, near where the stone bridge now is. These men served throughout the war, participating in the battle of New Orleans. A patriotic response was again made to the call for troops in 1836. A full company, commanded by Capt. —— Tipps, entered from Lynchburg, and another company was raised by Capt. George A. Wilson, but was not mustered into service. However, Capt. Wilson raised a spy company of about fifty men and entered the service. The following are remembered as members of this company: Augustus Steed, lieutenant; W. H. Bright, bugleman; William Robertson, David F. Robertson, Henderson Robertson, C. B. Rodgers and Oliver Garland. These were from Fayetteville and the immediate vicinity, while many from the various parts of the county also enlisted in this company, as well as in that of Capt. Tipps. By the act organizing the county the militia of Lincoln was made the Thirty-ninth Regiment and was attached to the Fifth Brigade. For many years the militia musters were largely attended, and amusements invariably attended them.

In the spring of 1846 a company of eighty-three men, known as the Lincoln Guards, was raised at Fayetteville for the Mexican war. It was officered as follows: Captain, Pryor Buchanan; first lieutenant, A. S. Fulton; second lieutenant, John V. Moyers; third lieutenant, C. A. McDaniel; orderly sergeant, William T. Slater. The company left Fayetteville March 31, 1846, and participated in the battle of Monterey, where several members were killed.

Early in the spring of 1861, and after the fall of Fort Sumter, and the call of President Lincoln for troops from Tennessee, war was the only thing discussed in Lincoln County. Old gray haired men, devoted wives, sisters and mothers talked of war until the whole atmosphere was full of it. Children after listening to the discussions and imagining that they could almost see the blood flow were "afraid to go to bed," and were often afflicted with nightmare. Little tow-headed boys were shouting the battle whoop from every cabin. Old saws, hoes, etc., were soon upon the forge or held to the grindstone, to make the large, ugly, ill-shaped bowie knives. Almost every man carried two of these knives which were to repel the invasion in the hand-to-hand conflict which was imagined to be approaching. Public meetings were almost daily occurrences and fiery speeches were "long and loud." Men, women, and children, of all ages, sizes and colors, went out to these meetings and joined in the general enthusiasm. Even ladies fell into the ranks of the drilling companies—even the most refined and intelligent; willing to part with—sacrifice, if necessary—those most near and dear to them, were enthusiastic and materially aided in sending forth the grand array of volunteers.

When the question of separation was submitted to the people, Lincoln polled 2,892 votes for separation and not one for no separation. However, even before the State seceded companies were organized and war preparations were rapidly going on. The first companies raised were four, which composed a part of Turney's First Tennessee, and one of which was raised principally in what is now Moore County. The others were officered as follows: Company G— B. F. Ramsey, captain; John Shackelford, first lieutenant; F. G. Buchanan, second lieutenant; Thomas Wilson, third lieutenant; and John Thoer, orderly sergeant. Company K— N. C. Davis, captain; T. J. Sugg, first lieutenant; Joe Davidson, second lieutenant; J. B. Turney, third lieutenant; John W. Nelson, first sergeant. Company H—Jacob Cruse, captain; M. V. McLaughlin, first lieutenant; N. J. George, second lieutenant. These companies left Fayetteville April 29, 1861, for Winchester, where the regiment was organized. These companies were with Turney's First Tennessee Confederates from the first of the war to its close, being in the hottest parts of many of the great battles of the war.

The field officers of this regiment who were from this county were, upon organization J. H. Holman, lieutenant-colonel; D. W. Holman, major. Upon re-organization John Shackelford, lieutenant-colonel; M. V. McLaughlin, major. These officers were killed at Gaines Mill and their places filled by N. J. George, lieutenant-colonel, and F. G.

Buchanan, major.    Dr. C. B. McGuire was surgeon of the regiment and was afterward brigade surgeon.

While these companies were organizing and going forth to duty, others were also forthcoming. On May 14, 1861, four other companies left Fayetteville, and on the same day arrived at Camp Harris, in Franklin County, where they were mustered into the service of the State on the 17th of the same month by Colonel D. R. Smythe of Lincoln County. These companies were assigned to the Eighth Tennessee, under the command of Col. A. S. Fulton, of Lincoln County. Lincoln County was also represented in this regiment by W. Lawson Moore, lieutenant-colonel; Chris C. McKinney, adjutant; Dr. G. B. Lester, assistant surgeon; and David Tucker, chaplain. Company B, known as the Petersburg Sharp Shooters, was raised at Petersburg, with A. M. Hall as captain; Chris C. McKinney, first lieutenant; T. W. Bledsoe, second lieutenant; C. N. Allen, third lieutenant; and N. P. Koonce, orderly sergeant. Company C was officered as follows: Rane McKinney, captain; N. M. Bearden, first lieutenant; T. W. Raney, second lieutenant; A. M. Downing, third lieutenant; and R. D. Hardin, orderly sergeant. It was known as the Comargo Guards. Company G, Norris Creek Guards, was raised at Norris Creek with George W. Higgins, captain; W. C. Griswell, first lieutenant; David Sullivan, second lieutenant; E. S. N. Bobo, third lieutenant; Joseph G. Carrigan, orderly sergeant. Company H was commanded by W. L. Moore until he was elected lieutenant-colonel, and was then officered as follows: W. J. Theash, captain; William Bonner, first lieutenant; W. L. Shofner, second lieutenant; T. H. Freeman, third lieutenant; G. W. Waggoner, first sergeant.

The Eighth Tennessee was one of the two regiments that made the almost unparalleled Cheat Mountain campaign, enduring those severe privations, marching through rain day and night, leaving the roads stained with blood from their feet, and almost starving for want of food. Without blankets or tents and with very little food, for eight days these troops were undaunted in their onward march and in their flight for life, but many took sick and died from exposure and fatigue. Two companies were raised in the western part of the county and constituted in the Thirty-second Regiment. One of them was known as the Millville Men: J. J. Finney, captain; W. P. A. George, first lieutenant; Jno. W. Wright, second lieutenant; Jno. P. McGuire, third lieutenant; David F. Hobbs, first sergeant. The other was the Swan Creek Guards: C. G. Tucker, captain; John Roach, first lieutenant; J. T. Pigg, second lieutenant; H. H. Tucker, third lieutenant; J. S. Finley, first sergeant. The quartermaster of this regiment was E. S. Wilson, of this county.

Then came the organization of the Forty-first Tennessee, whose colonel was Robert Farquharson, of this county, and whose lieutenant-colonel (afterward colonel) was J. D. Tillman, now of Lincoln, then of Bedford. Lincoln furnished four companies to this regiment, viz.: One (company C) commanded by Capt. J. D. Scott, whose lieutenants were B. J. Chafin, J. R. Feeney, and Jacob Anthony, and afterward commanded by Chafin and Feeney successively; one from Mulberry (Company A) commanded by W. W. James, whose lieutenants were L. Leftwich, Christopher Carrigher and A. D. Johnson; one (known as Liberty Guards) commanded by J. H. George, with the following lieutenants: William Smith, T. D. Griffis and S. A. Hopkins; and one commanded by W. B. Fonville, whose lieutenants were W. S. Bearden, A. A. Woods and E. R. Bearden. These companies left Fayetteville about the last days of September, 1861, and the regiment was organized at Camp Trousdale.

The Forty-fourth Regiment of Tennessee Volunteer Infantry was organized at Camp Trousdale in November, 1861, with C. A. McDaniel, colonel, and D. J. Noblett, assistant surgeon, from this county. It also included four companies from Lincoln; one commanded by C. A. McDaniel, who, upon being elected colonel, was superseded by T. M. Bell, and he by J. E. Spencer, with the following lieutenants, Joseph Cunningham, A. B. Rhea, and J. J. Martin; one by W. A. Rhodes, with J. H. Patterson, Jacob Van Hoozer and C. K. Moody as lieutenants; one from Shelton Creek, commanded by Capt. Smith; and one from Swan Creek, commanded by Capt. Stiles.

The Forty-fourth was actively engaged in some of the fierce conflicts of the war. At Shiloh forty-two per cent of those of the regiment actually in combat were killed and wounded. Afterward this regiment and the Fifty-fifth Tennessee were consolidated, still retaining the name of the former, and embracing another company from this county, which was organized in the latter part of 1861, by W. H. Moore, and embraced in the Fifty-fifth upon the organization of that regiment. Early in 1862 another company was raised by Capt. James R. Bright, with R. B. Parks, J. L. Moore and Stephen Loyd, as lieutenants, and entered an infantry regiment of Kentucky. After the battle of Shiloh the company was reorganized with W. P. Simpson, captain, and J. B. Price, T. D. Hill and G. W. Jones, lieutenants. J. L. Moore who was second lieutenant at its first organization, afterward raised another company and entered the service.

December 21, 1861, there were twenty-one companies of infantry from Lincoln County in the service. However, this number included those raised in Moore County, which was then a part of Lincoln. The company of J. L. Moore, was probably the last full company of infantry to leave the county as a company. Recruits were added to the old commands throughout 1862–64. About September, 1862, Freeman's Battery, which was a part of Hardin's Artillery, received about fifty members from Lincoln County, only one of whom was killed in the service. A great many of Forrest's escort were from this county, probably the majority of the members. Capt. Nathan Boone was captain of the escort. Other cavalry regiments received members from the county. Wheeler's First Tennessee Cavalry was composed of some Lincoln County boys, as was the Eleventh Tennessee Cavalry and also the Fourth Tennessee Cavalry.

Including all men in the service from first to last, Lincoln County furnished nearly 5,000 soldiers. Besides the regular companies of infantry there were several who entered war in companies from adjoining counties. This was also the case with artillery men and cavalry men. At all times recruits were entering the old commands.

At the organization of Capt. Higgins' company of the Eighth Tennessee, the ladies of Norris Creek and vicinity presented the boys with a beautiful large flag, the presentation being made by Miss Sallie Landess in an eloquent and stirring address. On the 25th of August, 1861, a magnificent flag was presented to the Eighth Regiment by the ladies of Lincoln County, accompanied by an inspiring address from the Hon. John M. Bright. On the flag were written in large gold letters the words, "Patience, Courage, Victory." Many times did the ladies send stores of provisions, containing delicacies for the sick, clothing and all kinds of hospital and camp supplies. Much of the inspiration that enabled the troops to remain in the field with sickness, danger and deprivations, came from the encouragement received from the ladies at home.

The Federals first entered Fayetteville April 9, 1862, causing a sudden suspension of business. They withdrew after about two months' stay, and again occupied the town in the spring of 1863, remaining until 1865. The court house was used as a stable for the horses a part of the time, and for the protection of troops at other times. It was surrounded by a bomb proof wall about six feet high, built of brick. The whole county was almost impoverished by the foraging armies passing to and fro. Sherman's whole army, on its march from Memphis to Chattanooga, passed through Fayetteville and crossed Elk River on the stone bridge, which, affording an excellent passage over the river, caused many of the passing armies, both Federals and Confederates, to pass through here. While Fayetteville was occupied by the Federals, business was at a standstill and many depredations were committed. When requested to do anything the citizens did not wait for time to argue points. The depredations, however, were mostly committed by Brixie's band of robbers, who in the main, claimed to be Yankees. Among the most dastardly acts, which the people suffered, was the murder of Judge J. R. Chilcoat. Afterward John Massey, a Confederate soldier, who had returned home (together with two other men named Pickett and Burrow), was brutally murdered—riddled with bullets. Some buildings were burned, county records were destroyed and, of course, property was confiscated. Guerrillas did not injure the people to any great extent.

The war over, the soldiers laid down their arms to return to their avocations of life. They found their farms in a deplorable condition. Their stock was gone, fences burned, buildings going to rack or entirely destroyed. The cost of the war to Lincoln County can hardly be estimated. However, she has now almost recovered from the effects; the hard times and desperate conflicts are remembered as in the past, and all unite in one grand army for the upbuilding of the general welfare of the country.

There was a difference of opinion as to the expediency of the location of the county seat where it was located. One-hundred acres of land was obtained of Ezekiel Norris, and a town of 128 lots was platted. On September 5 and 6, a sale of lots was made, the following, among others, being purchasers: Potter & Wilson, 11; Eleanor Buchanan, 1; John Buchanan, 2; Charles Porter, 2; Francis Ross, 1; Robert Ramsey, 1; Joseph Sumner, 2; John Kelly, 2; William Whitaker, 2; Hugh Blake, 2; Joseph Commons, 2; Walter Kinnard, 2; Rice M. Garner, 2; Peter Looney, 1; Joseph Jenkens, 2; Joseph McMillan, 1; James Bright, 2; John Angel, 1; James Cochran, 1; Stephen Chinnault, 1; Jacob Van Zand, 1. The records in the register's office are not all preserved, hence, the names of all the first purchasers can not be obtained.

Among the earliest merchants were Francis Porterfield, Robert Buchanan, Robert H. McEwen, and Robert H. Dickson, all of whom were successful. Mr. Dickson also ran a tan-yard and saddlery. Ephraim Parham was the first man to obtain tavern license; John P. McConnell and Vance Greer also kept taverns in Fayetteville very early. Between 1820 and 1830 existed the following firms: General merchants—Buchanan & Porterfield, R. & W. Dickson, Mason & McEwen, Alex R. Kerr & Co., A. A. Kincannon, Akin, Bagley & Co., McEwen & Gilleland, Daniel Dwyer, H. S. Morgan, William F. Mason & Co., Thompson & Wardaw, John Thompson, Dickson & Wallace, J. H. Wallace, William Akin & Co. Grocers—Parks & Moyers, and J. G. Selph & Co. Physicians—J. B. Sanders, G. & R. Martin, William Bonner, A. C. Gillespie, Charles & J. V. McKinney, J. J. Todd, C. J. Smith and R. Stone. Besides these, James Crawford had a saw-mill, grist-mill and distillery; S. A. Pugh ran a saddlery and Barclay & Ross a furniture store; E. M. Ringo was a watch-maker, Jacob Moyers a coppersmith, I. H. Wallace a shoe-maker, Weigart & Bryant and H. Worsham, tailors. C. Wilson had a bookbindery. An inn was kept by W. H. Talbot. Wool cards were run by Frost & Co., and by Johnson & Garner.

In December, 1823, Robert Dickson, Esq., was elected mayor. Vance Greer, R. H. McEwen, Chas. McKinney, Elliott Hickman, Joseph Commons and J. P. McConnell were elected aldermen; Wm. F. Mason, recorder; Vance Greer, treasurer, and Wm. Timmins, constable. In the "thirties," the most prominent general merchants were Wm. Dye & Son, Napoleon Garner, Gilliland & Roseborough, Gilliland, Smith & Co., Martin & Murphy, and A. C. McEwen & Co. The physicians were J. B. & Chas. McKinney, Wm. & M. C. Bonner, and Elliott Hickman. In the "forties" general merchandising was carried on by H. & B. Douglas, A. T. Nicks, John Goodrich, Jno. A. McPhail, S. Hart & Co., R. H. C. Bagley, Fulghum & Short, J. S. & J. T. Webb, Morgan & Neil, A. B. Shull, H. C. Holman & Bro., W. W. Petty, Southworth & Co., D. M. Tucker, T. C. Goodrich, W. H. Webb, Webb & Thompson, George F. Smith, B. L. Russell, Southworth, Morgan & Neil, and Scott & Gray. Rane McKinney and Deimer & Hampton were druggists. Webb & Smith had a book store.

In the "fifties," Wright & Trantham, T. C. Goodrich, Wright & Ransom, Thomson & Buchanan, Goodrich, Buchanan & Beavers, W. D. & S. M. Ewing and Russell & Tucker were general merchants. Fletcher & Stogner were produce dealers. Groceries were kept by all the general merchants. Scott & Gray were merchant tailors and furnishers. The first carriage manufactory ever established was by Raboteau, Hobbs, & Walker. C. S. Wilson kept a livery stable and Chilcoat & Edmonson a tavern. Diemer & Hampton were druggists.

In the "sixties" after the halt caused by the war had given place to business, general merchandising was carried on by Wright & Trantham, Newman & McLaughlin, J. C. & J. F. Goodrich, Murray & Morgan, P. T. Murray, Morgan Bros., and F. W. Brown &

Co. Druggists were Diemer & Miles and Smith & Blake. Grocers were Foster & Co., and Woods & Woodard. Moyers & Wilson were dealers in furniture. In the "seventies" business assumed wider proportions. Morgan Bros., P. T. Murray, Wright & Wright, J. C. Goodrich, T. J. Gray & Co., Smith & Miles, J. E. Caldwell, Nassauer & Hipsh, Hart & Fisher and F. W. Brown did a general mercantile trade. B. J. Chafin & Co., Bagley Bros., Bryson & Lauderdale, J. W. Barnett & Co., J. C. Goodrich, R. L. Gains & Co., W. H. Webb and W. R. Smith dealt in groceries. J. B. Hill, who had been in business for many years, and S. Heymann were jewelers. E. C. McLaughlin, J. S. Alexander and C. S. Wilson ran liveries. S. W. Brown & Co., Blake & McPhail and R. H. Ogilvie were hardware merchants. Douthet Bros. and Gray, Hatcher & Waddle were dealers in boots and shoes. J. T. Medearis ran a tan-yard.

The present business is as follows: General merchants—Wright & Wright, Nassauer & Hipsh, Kilpatrick & Co., Morgan Bros., J. A. Murray & Co., J. A. Lumpkin, J. W. Naylor & Sons, Whitaker & DeFord and T. C. Goodrich & Co. Groceries—J. C. Goodrich, Lauderdale & Rowell B. J. Chafin, Bagley Bros., E. E. Feeney, Stonebraker & Co., Bryson & Francis, J. L. McWhirter, W. K. Woodard, Blake & Rawls, Z. P. Gotcher, J. A. Bunn & Son, H. Nevill and J. W. Bennett. Hardware—Lamb & Robertson and Benedict & Warren. Drugs—W. A. Gill & Co., Smith & Miles, W. W. Christian and C. A. Diemer & Son. Jewelers—J. B. Hill, S. Heymann and A. D. Ruth. Bookstore—R. S. Bradshaw. Saloons—W. W. Alexander & Co., Eaton & Evans, Alexander & Copeland, B. J. Chafin and J. L. McWhirter. Livery stables—C. S. & R. M. Wilson and J. S. Alexander. Physicians—W. C. Bright, C. A. Diemer, C. B. McGuire, R. E. Christian and W. W. Christian. Grain merchants—Holman & Woods and Bruce & Cowen. General produce—C. Bonds and Caldwell & Scott. Furniture and undertaking—J. B. Wilson and J. A. Formwalt. The leading hotel is the Petty House. Others are kept by Sanford Prosser, S. G. McElroy, Mrs. A. Johnson, and T. S. King has a restaurant. Bearden & Thomas have a flouring-mill, J. L. Waggoner a planing-mill, and L. Peach runs a stone, saw and marble works. J. L. Vaughn manufactures carriages and buggies.

The first newspaper in Fayettville was the Fayetteville *Correspondent*, edited and published by David Augustine Hays; only a few numbers were issued. The *Village Messenger* was then published from March 11, 1823 to July 18, 1828, by Ebenezer Hill. In 1829 the *Western Cabinet* was commenced by Ebenezer Hill and John H. Laird. Mr. Hill published one volume of Haywood's reports in his office. He published Hill's Almanac for a great many years, making it a part of the standard literature of southern Tennessee and northern Alabama. As early as 1833 the *Independent Yeoman* was published by Joe B. Hill, afterward by Joe B. & E. Hill. Then it was purchased by W. L. & A. H. Berry, and published as the *Lincoln Journal*, from 1840 to 1848, at which time C. A. French, became the editor and publisher, continuing it until the war. In 1840 a Whig paper, the *Signal*, was started and issued but a few numbers. After the war the *Lincoln County News* was started by Ebenezer Hill, Jr., and continued by W. P. Tolley for some years. The Fayetteville *Express* was established in 1873 by S. H. McCord, was afterward published by McCord & Lloyd, and is now by Lloyd & Blake. The Fayetteville *Observer* was established in 1850, stood the "war stroke," and continues to be a thriving paper, edited and published by N. O. Wallace.

The Lincoln Savings Bank was established in 1870 with a capital of $100,000, did a seemingly good business, but suspended in 1884, "jarring" the financial status of the whole county considerably. The First National Bank was organized in June, 1873, with a capital stock of $60,000. Its first president was Hon. George W. Jones. Its present president is Dr. C. B. McGuire; its cashier, J. R. Feeney.

As early as the year 1824 a Masonic Lodge was established but existed only a few years. Jackson Lodge, No. 68, F. & A. M., was chartered October 9, 1828, and now has a membership of over 40. Calhoun Lodge, No. 26, I. O. O. F., was chartered April 6, 1846, and now has nearly 30 members. Fayetteville Lodge, No. 181, K. of H., was established April 1, 1875, and has a membership at present of nearly 65. Protection Lodge, No. 8. A.

O. U. W., began its existence from charter dated May 2, 1877. Jewel Lodge, No. 59, K. & L. of H. was established April 1, 1879, and has about 60 members. There are five church edifices in the town, owned respectively by the Cumberland Presbyterians, Presbyterians, Methodist Episcopal Church South, Christians and the Protestant Episcopalians. The Missionary Baptists have an organization but no building. There are four churches for the colored people of the following denominations: African Methodist Episcopal, Primitive Baptist, Missionary Baptist and the Cumberland Presbyterian.

About 1815 George L. Leonard settled where Petersburg now is and cleared up the land there. He put up a cotton-gin, and afterward began the first mercantile trade of the place by selling small articles of merchandise, such as thread, etc. Porterfield & Akin established a small store in 1828, and Wm. DeWoody conducted their business. In 1833 they were superseded by Rowlett & Hill, and soon others followed. Holman & Loyd, Jones & Yowell, Rives & Hayes and Stone & Reese were merchants before 1840, and all did a large business. Then came a lull in the business tide of Petersburg until the war; however, Metcalfe & Son did a good business during this time, as also did Wynus, Blake & Co., Smith, Blake & Co. and Fonville & Bledsoe. Since the war the principal merchants have been W. J. Hamilton, P. B. Marsh & Son, Fogleman & Cummings and Hall & Hamilton, together with the present business firms. General merchants—G. A. Jarvis, Cummings & Bledsoe and B. S. Popflanus grocers—E.₮M. Crawford and L. L. Rebman; W. R. Hanaway, undertaker and furniture dealer; Rives & Christopher, saddlers and harness-makers; saloons—J. W. King & Co., F. D. Cummings & Co. and Pack & Byrd; blacksmiths—Alex Lancaster and George Morrison. J. C. Montgomery has a large frame flouring-mill, and Dwiggins & Co. are erecting a fine brick mill. Gillespie Bros. do a livery business.

The secret societies are Unity Lodge, No. 84 I. O. O. F., which has a membership of twenty; Petersburg Lodge, No. 123, was organized in 1846, and for many years was very strong, but now has only a weak organization; Petersburg Lodge, No. 607, K. of H., has a membership of thirteen, and was organized in 1877. Petersburg has a good school, and five churches of the following denominations: Methodist Episcopal South, Presbyterian, Cumberland Presbyterian, Missionary Baptist and Christian. It is a chartered town, but by some the charter is considered a burden. It is situated on the Duck River Valley Railroad, twelve miles from Fayetteville.

Mulberry began to exist as a village about 1840. Among the merchants that have transacted business there were Booker Shapard, Drury Conley, Abner Brady, R. N. Whitaker, W. W. James & Co., Hoots & Logan and J. & W. H. Reese, previous to the war. Since the resumption of business after the war have been W. W. James & Co., W. L. Shofner, R. A. & J. H. Reese, Whitaker & Yates, E. S. Terry and J. G. Reese, the last two of whom are now in business. Several family groceries, etc., have existed from time to time. The Mulberry Academy began about 1830, and has become a noted school. There was once a male and female academy, but it is now known as the Mulberry Male and Female Academy. There is one Missionary Baptist Church, one Cumberland Presbyterian Church, one Methodist Episcopal Church South and one Christian Church. Physicians are G. W. Jones, A. R. Shadden and S. Dance. Mulberry Lodge, No. 404, F. & A. M., was organized in 1870, and is in a prosperous condition. It had twelve charter members. Mulberry Lodge, No. 148, was chartered in 1871 and has only a very weak organization. The Good Templars have a lodge of about ninety members. There are two good mills near by. In the village are two blacksmith shops, two wood-work shops and a cabinet-maker and undertaker.

Boonshill was one of the first postoffices established in the county. Previous to the war Wood & McDaniel, Hudson & Horton and Sumner & Ewing were merchants there. Since the war have been Buchanan & White, E. S. Wilson & Co., Swinebroad & Co., Templeton & Son and H. D. Smith, the present merchants. Physicians have been Dr. John Wood, Dr. Dunlap, Dr. Porter, Dr. Parks and Dr. Sumner. Stephen Hightown first settled where Millville now is. Stone & Baird were the first merchants; others were

Frank McLaurine, G. L. McLane, Sam Isaacs, Thomas McLaurine, McGuin & Son, Mc-Guire & Franklin, Ezell & Hudspeth.   Since the war have been Ezell & McGuire, F. L. Ezell, Ally Smith and Finney & Son.   Dr. C. B. McGuire practiced medicine there from 1847 to 1859; others have been Dr. M. P. Forehand and Dr. G. W. McGuire.

Dellrose was first known as "Roosterville."   "Hog" Bruce was the founder and first merchant.  It has only been a village since 1867.  D. C. Sherrill & Co. are now doing business there.  There is a good school.  Dr. B. S. Stone is the physician of the place.  Molino postoffice was established in 1849, by D. C. Hall, the first postmaster and merchant.  Since the war, merchants have been Robert Stewart, James W. Rawls, Joe Montgomery and J. H. Dale & Co.   J. W. Rawls was a blacksmith, and John Hays the present one.  It has a Missionary Baptist Church there, and is located in a good locality.  Howell is a small station on the narrow-gauge railroad, seven miles from Fayetteville.  It was first known as Renfroe Station.  Harris Bros. and George Bros. are merchants.  It has a good railroad depot and a Cumberland Presbyterian Church.  Oak Hill is a village nine miles north of Fayetteville.  The postoffice is Norris Creek.  H. L. Cole and James Bell are merchants. It has a good school, a Cumberland Presbyterian Church and a Missionary Baptist Church. There is also a Masonic lodge of thirty-eight members—Mount Hebron, No. 344, and a weak lodge of I. O. O. F.—Oak Hill, No. 39.  A pike connects Oak Hill with Fayetteville. Stonesborough is a chartered town and consists of a distillery owned by Stone & Thomas, and a store and saloon owned by Stone & Patterson.  W. J. Landers has a tan-yard between this place and Oak Hill.  Chestnut Ridge is also in the north part of the county.  J. N. Stallings is a merchant.  James Freeman a blacksmith, and Wash. Gilbert a wagon-maker.  Chestnut Ridge Lodge, No, 499, F. & A. M., has about fifteen members, and Chestnut Ridge Lodge, No. 157, I. O. O. F., has nearly fifty members.  There is a church near by.

Booneville, received its name from Capt. Nathan Boone.  Musgraves and Shofner, and J. E. Reese are merchants.  It is about three miles from Mulberry Village.  Blanche was first known by postoffice as Pleasant Plains.  Samuel Parker was the first postmaster, and W. W. Petty the first  merchant in 1849.  It began to assume the proportions of a village after the war, and is now a pleasant and thriving little town.  Dr. J. C. Coats is the merchant and physician.  There is located here Pleasant Plains Lodge, No. 305, F. & A. M., and a church.  There are several county stores near by.

Smithland was known as George's Store until 1884.  At first the postoffice was on the north side of Elk River, having been established about 1840.  It was moved to "Arnold's grocery" about 1850, and there Smithland has been built.  This was a notorious fighting place.  Taylor & McLaughlin and R. Smith are the present merchants.  An I. O. O. F. Lodge, Sereno No. 195, is located at Smithland.

Camargo was established in 1849 and was a flourishing village prior to the war.  John Caughran was the first merchant.  Others have been Nicks & Webb, J. N. & W. A. Stallings, Wm. Ashworth, Samuel Dehaven and J. A. Corn.

Lincoln is settled mainly by northern people who went to that place after the war. J. F. Montgomery, J. R. McCown, J. E. Ramsey and J. C. McClellan have been merchants there.  In 1837 —— Crosby started a small spinning factory at Oregon.  In 1839 it was bought by Henry Warren, was afterward operated by H. & T. K. Warren, and is now operated by Henry Warren & Son.  This factory has about 1,000 spindles, a cotton-gin and a flouring and grist-mill attached, being an investment of about $20,000 capital. Oregon is three and one-half miles from Flintville, its shipping point.  It has a Cumberland Presbyterian Church.

Elora was formerly known as Baxter Station, and only dates its beginning since the building of the Fayetteville & Decherd Branch Railroad.  It is in the southeast corner of the county, and is the proposed junction of the Winchester & Alabama Railroad with the one now existing from Fayetteville to Decherd.  J. B. Hamilton and W. M. Parker & Co. are the merchants.

Flintville, twelve miles from Fayetteville, on the Nashville & Chattanooga Railroad, has sprung into existence since the building of that road. The first merchants were Cunningham & Myrick; J. A. Grills was the first blacksmith; Peter Cunningham put up a grist-mill, and then he and L. P. Myrick engaged in distilling. The town was all destroyed by the Federals the time of the war. Since the war merchandising has been carried on by D. M. & J. C. Mimms, Mimms & Knowles, D. M. Mimms, Kilpatrick & Co., Merrit & Golden (saloon), Chas. Kelley, D. M. & W. G. Mimms, Richard Routt, A. Smith, Peter Cunningham, Brady & Hall, Henry Warren & Son, and Chick & Eslick. J. W. Cooper & J. J. Coston have been blacksmiths and wagon-makers, and Joseph Richardson, a saddler; E. J. Cambron is a carriage and cabinet-maker; Tolley, Eaton and Sims have run distilleries, and Copeland & Co. now have a large distillery. They also have a good mill. John Young also has a mill. Surprise Lodge, No. 153, I. O. O. F., is located there with sixteen members. There are four church organizations at Flintville.

Kelso's first merchant was A. S. Fulton. Subsequent merchants have been Hill Southworth, D. M. Eslick and Jenkens McKinney. Present merchants are J. A. Taylor, G. D. Wicks and M. S. Eslick. Kelso Lodge, No. 490, F. & A. M., and Kelso Lodge, No. 172, I. O. O. F., are located there, and also a Cumberland Presbyterian Church is at Kelso.

The attention of the early pioneers was required by almost everything else before it was given to means of educating the children. This most important subject was not long entirely neglected, for those who had sufficient education taught short terms of school at the different private residences early in the "teens.'" After a time, by agreement, the settlers would meet to build a schoolhouse in the different localities. These buildings were of logs, with a door in one end and a fire-place in the other. However, not all of them had fire-places, and those that had them generally allowed the escape of the smoke through a large hole in the roof, there being no chimneys to them. This was the condition of the schoolhouses even through the twenties. The seats were made of poles split open, supported on legs about three feet long, and with the flat side up. Light was admitted through an aperture made by "leaving out" one log along the sides of the building. A bench or plank for writing was supported on pins driven in the log just beneath the window. The roofs of these primitive institutions of learning were of boards held to their place by "weight poles." Each pupil took whatever book he could find. Some studied the "Life of Washington," others the "Life of Marion," and a few would take a *Clarion* (the paper then published at Nashville) to school, and learn from that. These were pay-schools, the tuition being from 75 cents to $1 per pupil for one month. Various were the "rules" and requirements of these schools. Each teacher had new rules. An invariable custom was to make the teacher "treat or take a duckin'" on Christmas and at the close of school. If a mischievous boy passing the schoolhouse desired to be chased at a lively rate it was only necessary for him to yell out "school butter," when the teacher would say to his pupils: "Take him in, boys." Reading and writing were the main branches taught, and arithmetic was sometimes taught. Pupils recited one at a time. They were by most teachers allowed to seek the the out-door, pure atmosphere in fair weather to prepare their lessons. Prior to 1820 (probably as early as 1815) the Fayette Academy was established. This was a county academy, and derived its support from a State fund. The building became untenable about 1854, and the new building just then erected by the Cumberland Presbyterian Church was to be used by Milton College, which did not materialize, was purchased, and Fayette Academy continued for some years, and then sold the building to the county school commissioners.

The Fayetteville Female Collegiate Institute began its existence almost as early as the Fayetteville Academy. The land was donated by James Bright. This institution is under the control of a company and board of trustees. The building first used was torn down in 1884 to give place to the present splendid brick building. The enrollment for the past year was about 220 pupils. Although it, by name, is known as a female school, both sexes are admitted.

The Mulberry Female Academy was established in 1830 and existed as such until 1869, when it was consolidated with the Mulberry Male Academy, and since the institution thus formed, has prospered under the name of the Mulberry Male and Female Academy. The Mulberry Male Academy was formed and put in working order in 1844.

Viney Grove Academy was founded by the Rev. Henry Bryson and conducted with great success by him for many years. This once ranked with the standard educational institutions of the South, but it has died away. It was five miles west of Fayette-ville. Boonshill Academy has existed since before the war. The building is a nice brick house, and good schools are taught there.

The Petersburg Masonic Academy was founded by that fraternity in 1858 and is taught in the lowest story of the brick Masonic Hall at Petersburg. Oak Hill Institute flour-ished from 1865 to 1880 with considerable success. The building is frame. Nixon Springs Academy, near Smithland, was a good institution from 1875 to 1880. Hopewell Academy at Lincoln was endowed by the United Presbyterian Church and is a well-conducted school. Greenwood Academy, between Mullberry and Booneville, was established in the fifties, and has a brick building. Cane Creek Academy, at Howell, also has a brick build-ing and is comparatively a new institution.

The public schools of Lincoln County are gaining in favor, but are yet in their infancy. There are eighty-two public schools in the county for white, and thirty-one for colored people. There are but eighty-four public school buildings, but school is taught in other buildings. The buildings are as follows: Stone and brick, 3; frame, 47; log, 34; total, 84. Value of school buildings is estimated at $23,460, and the value of apparatus, etc., at $1,570. The scholastic population of the county for this year is 9,912, and the amount of school fund, at $1.75, per capita, is $17,346.

As in all new countries, the first settlers of this section were more accustomed to the sound of the hunting horn and chasing hound than to pulpit oratory on the Sabbath. However, many good Christian people were among the first pioneers, and they established Scripture readings, and even preached sermons at the different private residences. Early services were held in the court house, and not unfrequently did people assemble at some designated place in the woods to hear a sermon.

In 1811 the earthquake shock which was so sensibly felt here was by many regarded as the approach of the Last Great Day, and consequently many accessions to the Chris tian flock were made. For a considerable time "big meetings" were held, and a great revival was experienced, but after a time the lull in the tide came, the "spirit of the meet-ings died down." Yet there was a good work being done by some of the good Christian people. As early as 1808 a church was organized at the Forks of Mulberry, and it pros-pered greatly, and even at the present time is in a flourishing condition. This is a Primi-tive Baptist organization. Hardy Holman was the first pastor. In about 1812 the Shiloh congregation was organized by the same denomination. Other churches of this (the Primitive or old-school Baptist) denomination, are Concord, which was organized prior to 1820; Mount Olivet, probably organized in the twenties; New Hope, a small congre-gation, but an old one; Kelly Creek, which began existence in the forties. Pleasant Grove; Rocky Point; Bethel; and Buckey, which was organized as late as 1866 with a mem-bership of nineteen and now has 165 members. Nearly all of these churches are in a good condition and prospering.

In the fall of 1812 the Presbyterian Church of Fayetteville was organized with the Rev. John Gillespie as pastor. The first elders were David Turner, Andrew Hannah, Francis Patton, John Armstrong and Ebenezer McEwen. Private members were Peggy Hannah, Mrs. Armstrong, Mrs. Patton, Mrs. Turner, Peggie Gillespie, Mary McEwen, Elizabeth Ferguson, John B. Alexander and Barbara Alexander. Subsequent pastors of this church have been John R. Bain, James McLinn, Amzi Bradshaw, E. McMillan, M. M. Marshall, W. C. Dunlap, D. D., James Watson, A. N. Cunningham, D. D., George Hall, A. D. McClure, J. H. Bryson, W. H. Groves and R. M. DuBose. The present member-ship is 105. First worship was in the court house; afterward an edifice was built, which was destroyed by a storm in 1851, and then the present one was erected. Other Presby-terian Churches of the county are: Unity, eight miles from Fayetteville, organized about 1820, and now having a membership of about forty; Petersburg, organized May 5, 1860, and now having about forty members; Swan Creek, organized as early as 1830, now having a membership of fifty; and Young's Chapel, with a membership of twenty-five, and having existed only since 1870. One other church, by the name of Old Unity, once existed, but is now extinct.

Bethel Church of the Associate Reformed Presbyterian denomination was organized in 1830, by the Rev. H. Bryson, who continued as its pastor until his death in 1874, and was superseded by Rev. A. S. Sloan, the present pastor. There are three other churches in the county of that denomination known as the New Hope, Prosperity and Pleasant Plains.

Early in 1829 a camp-meeting was held near Fayetteville by distant workers in the Cumberland Presbyterian Church. Great success blessed this meeting and an organization of the Cumberland Presbyterian Church of Fayetteville was accomplished the same year. Rev. S. M. Cowan was the first pastor, continuing many years, and under him the church multiplied in numbers and strengthened in good work. Subsequent ministers have been Herschel S. Porter, W. D. Chaddick, D. D., Stokely Chaddick, S. M. Cowen, again M. B. DeWitt, —— McElree, Nat Powers, C. P. Duvall, —— McDonald and J. S. Weaver. Among the first members were Benjamin Clements and wife, William Norris and wife, Benjamin Wear and wife, S. O. Griffis and wife, George Stonebraker and wife, Jacob Stonebraker and wife and Dr. Charles McKinney and wife.

Cane Creek Cumberland Presbyterian Church was organized in 1817 by Rev. R. Donnel, and now has 138 members. J. B. Tigert has been its pastor for twenty-five years, and in its seventy years of existence the church has never been without a pastor, although but five men have served as pastors. There are thirteen other Cumberland Presbyterian Churches in the county, viz.: Mulberry, with a membership of about 50; Mount Zion, organized by Rev. D. Tucker about eight years ago; Hebron, an old church with about 125 members; New Unity, with 100 members; Petersburg, with about 70 members; New Salem, an old church, with a membership of about 75; Pisgah, organized about 1856, and now having about 40 members; Liberty, organized about 1878, present membership about 50; Sulphur Spring, with 75 members, built and supported by Henry Warren for his factory hands; Moore's Chapel, a young congregation of about 100; Elkton, a small congregation; Flintville, a new congregation with a small membership; and New Lebanon, about twelve years old and having a large membership.

The Methodist Episcopal Church of Fayetteville was organized prior to 1829. Rev. Joshua Kilpatrick was its pastor that year. Present membership is 162. The present church building was erected about 1846. The other Methodist Episcopal Churches South and their approximate memberships are as follows: Shady Grove, 100; Lloyd's Chapel, 75; Providence, Beech Grove, Union and Boonville, 331; Petersburg, —; Macedonia, Hermon, Flintville and Liberty, 350; Medium and Moore Chapel, 263; Mulberry, 90; Shiloh, 100; Dellrose, —; Blanche, Smith's Chapel, Shiloh and Ebenezer, —; and New Bethel, a new organization. This denomination is in a prosperous condition.

The Christians have nine organizations. They are as follows: Fayetteville, which was organized in 1865 and now has a membership of about 75; Gum Spring, Philadelphia, Friendship, Chestnut Ridge, Mulberry, Antioch, one on Lane's Branch, and one at McAlister's chair factory.

The Hard Shell Baptists have two small congregations—Mount Carmel and Sulphur Springs.

The Protestant Episcopal Church of Fayetteville is the only one of that denomination in the county. It was organized in 1882, and in 1883 was built the elegant little stone edifice which is used for worship.

The first organization of the United Presbyterian Church in Tennessee was Lebanon Church in this county. It was organized September 15, 1865, by Rev. A. S. Montgomery. The church building cost about $2,000 and the present membership is 145. Other organizations of that name are Hopewell and Pisgah.

The Missionary Baptists also have a number of congregations in the county. They have an organization at Fayetteville, but no church house.

# FRANKLIN COUNTY.

FRANKLIN COUNTY is bounded on the north by Coffee County, northeast by Grundy, east by Marion, south by the State of Alabama, west by Lincoln, northwest by Moore, and contains about 500 square miles, one-fourth of which lies on the Cumberland Mountain and its western escarpment.

The topography of the county is greatly diversified, a portion of it lying on the Cumberland Plateau, a portion in the valley of Elk River, a portion on the Highland Rim and a very small portion in the Central Basin. The rim is in the Devonian formation, the basin in the silurian, the Cumberland Table-land in the carboniferous. The carboniferous strata are the surface rocks of the Highland Rim and the table-land. The soils of the rim are the siliceous or flinty, found in the basin on the inner half of the rim, and calcareous, found on the outer half, which is a red clay. The soil of the basin is almost entirely calcareous; that of the table-land is the sandstone soil. The limestone of the rim is the coral or St. Louis formation, while that of the basin is the Nashville group. The latter is a blue limestone; the former is gray, or grayish and blue. The rim is about 1,000 feet above the level of the sea; the table-land about 2,000; and the basin about 700.

The mean annual temperature of table land is 54°, of the rim 57°, of the basin 58°. The soil of the Cumberland Table-land is thin and sterile, but well adapted, on account of its climatic advantages, to the raising of all kinds of fruit. Along the western base of the mountain is a wide belt of land with a dark clay surface and red clay subsoil, furnishing a fine agricultural land. Then come the valley lands of the Elk River, which flows through the county from northeast to southwest. West of the river lie the barrens, so-called, which afford considerable pasture, but the soil is thin and not good for agriculture. In the western portion of the county, and running down the river, is found the black shale formation with its "rock houses," or alum and copperas caves, in which are often found native alum and copperas. There are several coves, among which Farmers' Cove, Lost Cove, Round Cove and Sinking Cove lie upon the table-lands, and are wholly shut in by the mountains, beneath which their waters find outlet. Buncombe Cove lies along the base of the mountain and is almost shut in by an outlier. It is watered by the head waters of Bean Creek. There are several other coves, among which is Roark's, one of the largest in the county. The most fertile lands are found in these coves and in the valleys of the Elk and its tributaries. The best timber is found on the mountain slopes, and consists principally of oak, ash, chestnut, beech, poplar, cherry and walnut. The barrens are covered mostly with a light growth of scrubby oak. The Elk River and its tributaries furnish the principal drainage of the county. Mineral springs are abundant, the most noted of which are Hurricane Springs, Estill Springs and Winchester Springs. The former of these springs is a noted summer resort, where thousands of pleasure-seekers make their annual visits. There are also many noted cave springs which furnish pure free-stone water.

There is an extensive marble bed upon Elk River, commencing about five miles below Winchester, and extending down the river ten miles and five miles on either side. The marble is of excellent quality and consists of gray and red, clouded with green porphyry and various shades. This vast mine of wealth has only been slightly developed. Coal has found to exist in great quantities near University Place, and at Anderson, Keith's Spring, Maxwell and other points, but, as yet, it has not been mined to any considerable extent.

Many beautiful cascades and waterfalls and caves are found upon the mountains. Natural scenery in the county is extensive. Viewing the mountains from Winchester, their grandeur arises to sublimity. And standing upon the mountains and overlooking the grand valleys of the Elk and its tributaries, with Winchester and its church spires in the foreground, one is led to exclaim with the poet:

> "God hath a being true,
> And that ye may see
> In the fold of the flower,
> The leaf of the tree;
> In the wave of the ocean,
> The furrow of land;
> In the mountain of granite,
> The atom of sand!
> Ye may turn your face
> From the sky to the sod,
> And where can ye gaze
> That ye see not a God?"

The settlement of the territory now composing Franklin County began with the beginning of the present century, when all was a vast wilderness, inhabited only by Indians and wild animals. It was a hazardous undertaking to come here in that day and open up a new country west of the mountains where the light of civilization had never shone, and where neither schools, churches, mills, factories, nor any conveniences existed, such as the pioneers had been accustomed to. None but brave and courageous men and women could ever have accomplished such a dangerous and hazardous undertaking. The early settlers came mostly from Virginia and the Carolinas, and some from Kentucky and Georgia. It may be truthfully said that with the exception of those who have settled since the war the inhabitants of the county are nearly all descendants from the best families of "Old Virginia" and the Carolinas. It is claimed that Maj. William Russell, who settled on the Boiling Fork, near Cowan, and Jesse Bean, who settled on Bean Creek, both about the year 1800, were the first two settlers in the county. This is quite probable, as these two families are prominently mentioned elsewhere in the organization of the county, the first court being held at Maj. Russell's house, and Mr. Bean being one of the commissioners to locate the county seat. Bean Creek took its name from the Beans who settled thereon.

Samuel Miller and his wife, *nee* Elizabeth Montgomery, were both born in this county, the former in 1801 or 1802, and the latter, who is still living, in 1803. The parents of these persons were, of course, among the very early settlers. The families of Larkin and Hunt, settled on Bean Creek, about 1806. The Beans who had previously settled there, established, in 1812, a gunsmith shop and powder mills in two caves on Little Bean Creek, the remains of which can still be seen. David Larkin, hearing of the massacre of two children by the Indians, one night in 1812, mounted his horse and rode to the place: Finding no one about the house, he endeavored to arouse some one by calling, but the lady of the house, thinking him one of the Indians, would not come from her place of concealment. The next morning the bodies of the children were found and buried. James Russey, grandfather of James Russey, proprietor of the Ballard House, in Winchester, and William M. Cowan, Christopher Bullard, James Cunningham, George Taylor, Samuel Norwood, James Dougan, John Bell, John Cowan, George Davidson, John A. S. Anderson, William P. Anderson and James B. Drake, were all prominent early settlers, who came to the county about 1800 or soon thereafter.

The following were early settlers with date of settlement accompanying their names: Edward Finch, 1808, from South Carolina, settled on what is known as the Anna Finch farm, near Winchester. He brought with him Lewis Finch (colored), who was then four years old, and is now living. William Lucas, 1808; George Grey, on Crow Creek, 1809; Alexander Faris, Robert and Isaac T. Hines, 1812; Joseph Miller, from Georgia, 1815; John B. Hawkins and Isaac VanZant, 1817. The latter settled on the farm where his son Isaac now resides. Matthew R. Mann, 1819, afterward engaged in cotton spinning; Thomas Gore, Sr., 1822; William L. Sargent, 1829; Col. Davie Crockett was also one of the early settlers of the county, who came soon after the war of 1812, and settled in a "face camp," on Rattlesnake Spring Creek, near Salem. Here he married the Widow Patton.

It is said that he attracted much attention at the early camp-meetings, as all were anxious to see him.  He remained in the county only a few years.  George Grey settled on Crow Creek in 1809, and built a cabin and planted some corn.

An old lady by the name of Londey, and member of Grey's family, was ill and in bed on an occasion when a party of Indians approached with evil designs.  The family seeing the "red skins" approaching fled into the mountains, leaving Mrs. Londey in the house.  The Indians carried all the goods out of the house, placed the invalid lady on a bed a safe distance from the house, then burned the latter, cut down the corn, and fled without doing further damage.  Mr. Grey then moved upon and improved the farm now owned by Isaac Grey, about three miles from Winchester.  John A. S. Anderson and William P. Anderson, assisted by George Grey, made most of the early surveys of land, especially the Government survey, whereby the lands were surveyed into sections of 640 acres each.  In May, 1809, while J. A. S. Anderson, assisted by George Grey and James B. Drake, was surveying a Government line, he discovered "a remarkable cave and a remarkable spring."  They had with them a dried beef tongue, which Mr. Anderson threw into the water, and it sank beyond all recovery.  Thereupon they named the spring "Tongue Spring," hence the name of Tongue Spring Creek.  On May 25, 1809, they planted some corn and deadened some timber, and camped on Rattlesnake Point, and "bark was their food."  On May 30 they came upon an Indian camp, "and shouted around them and advanced, and the Indians absconded and left their meat and one horse," which, as Mr. Anderson said, the party got, "the horse to ride and the meat to eat."  There were nine Indians in the camp.  Rattlesnakes were then abundant and "monstrous," as related by Mr. Anderson.  On one occasion, when he was obliged to undress his feet to enable him to walk over the slippery rocks, he stepped his heel on the head of a rattlesnake, discovering which he made his escape unharmed.  The foregoing facts about the surveying party are taken from Mr. Anderson's field notes made at the time, and now in possession of Mr. Isaac Grey.

The greater portion of the best lands in Franklin County were entered by location of land warrants and other claims granted by North Carolina to individuals for military services while the territory belonged to that State.  Henry M. Rutledge was executor of the last will and testament of Gov. Edward Rutledge, of South Carolina, who in his lifetime owned a large tract of land, mostly in this county.  As executor, Mr. Rutledge sold this tract, consisting of 73,000 acres, to Col. Thomas Shubrick for £535 of English money.  As an individual he then purchased the whole tract back from Col. Shubrick, and the deeds of these conveyances are the first that appear on the records of Franklin County.  The Rutledge lands lie mostly in Districts 8 and 9.  In May, 1808, Gen. Andrew Jackson and John Hutchins, assignees of John G. and Thomas Blount, received a patent from the State of Tennessee for 1,000 acres located on the Boiling Fork, just below Winchester.

The following is a condensed list of a few early grants, entries and purchases; July, 1796, State of North Carolina to Thomas Dillon, an assignee of the Blounts, 5,000 acres on Elk River, including Fendleton's Spring, and a large camp made by Major Ore & Co., on their way to Nickajack; March 5, 1805, Thomas Dillon to E. Thursby, for $4,500, 18,000 acres on Elk River; April, 1807, Henry M. Rutledge to Wm. P. Anderson and John Strother a large tract on Elk River and on both sides of Logan Creek; in 1808, State of Tennessee to John Maclin and John Overton 4,935 acres, and to Nicholas Tramel 640 acres, both on Elk River; and to Solomon Wagoner, Wm. Russell, Absalom Russell and John Cowan each 200 acres on the Boiling Fork, and to James Cunningham and Robert Bean each 200 acres on Bean Creek; to James Metcalf 200 acres on Metcalf Creek, and to Wm. Metcalf 200 acres on Elk River; in 1809, State to James Patton and Andrew Erwin 1,000 acres, to Andrew Jackson 640 acres, and to John Winford 640 acres, all on Elk River.

We have cited the foregoing grants, which are only a few among the many, to show how a few individuals originally came into possession of so much of the best land of the county.  In 1824 the State of Tennessee began to sell the remaining lands at 12½ cents per acre, and purchasers were allowed to select and enter these lands in quantities to suit themselves.  The first of these entries was made by Thomas Newland, April 5, 1824, for thirty acres, the whole tract costing only $3.75.  During the years 1824 and 1825 there were 508 entries made in the county for tracts mostly under 100 acres each.  Entry 508 was the last one made at that price.  The entries have never been permanently closed for the mountain lands, but are still being made.  It is believed that all of the lands have been entered once.  In many instances the original purchasers have abandoned or neglected their lands, and in this way some tracts have been entered the second and perhaps the third time.  The last entry, No. 3,868, was made May 22, 1886, by Peter H. Plumer for 150 acres.

The first grist-mill in the southern part of Franklin County, was built by George Stovall about the year 1810, and as early as 1815 Districts Nos. 2 and 3 had over a dozen cotton-gins.  This county at that early day was one of the leading cotton-producing counties of the State.  The cotton was shipped out of the Elk River on flat-boats, and thence by way of the Tennessee and Mississippi Rivers to New Orleans, where it was sold for from $1\frac{1}{4}$ to $2\frac{1}{4}$ cents per pound.  Peter Simmons, John R. Patrick and Dick Holder, early merchants of Salem, used to ship large quantities of cotton on "flats" from the mouth of Bean Creek to New Orleans, and then walk back through the Chickasaw and Choctaw Indian nations.  In 1828 a Mr. Heiston, from Ohio, established a tan-yard on Bean Creek.  He sold it to Mr. Smith, and he to Mr. Lipscomb.  This was the first tan-yard in that part of the county.

Among the early cotton-gins were those erected in the upper end of the county by Sims Kelly, John Oliver, Wm. Faris, Wm. O'Rear, Geo. McCutcheon and James Sharp, and one in the Cowan neighborhood by John Holder, and one at Wm. Bledsoe's place, by Wm. Street, and one were Isaac Grey now lives, by George Grey.  Isaac Gillespie had a cotton-gin, tan-yard and grist-mill in Owl Hollow.  At the same time gins were owned and operated in the lower part of the county by James F. Green, James Woods, Mr. Trigg and others.  The owners of the cotton-gins would receive all cotton brought to them and give the farmers receipts for the amounts.  The latter would then sell the receipts to the merchants for goods.  About the year 1836 Franklin County raised 4,500 bales of cotton all of which was shipped on "flats" to New Orleans.  During the early settlement of the county the merchants went on horseback to Baltimore to buy their goods, which were then brought in wagons from that city to their destination, being about 700 miles.  Enough goods were purchased at one time to last a year; and goods were hauled on the same route through this county from Baltimore to Nashville.  It is claimed that as high as 300 wagons loaded with goods en route to Nashville and other points encamped at one time on the side of the road near Caldwell's Bridge.  This method of obtaining goods continued until near the year 1840, when transportation was opened up by way of the Ohio and Cumberland Rivers to Nashville, after which time and until railroads were constructed, the merchants of Franklin County bought their goods in Nashville, and had them brought from thence in wagons to their places of business.  The shipment of cotton on flats to New Orleans was discontinued about the same time.  The Winchester Sulphur Springs were then a fashionable summer resort, and were visited annually by the wealthy planters of the South.  For some years before the war a Mr. Butterworth had a cotton-mill in Owl Hollow, which was burned during the war and afterward rebuilt and again burned.  Another cotton-mill was erected near Estill Springs, about the year 1851, and was destroyed by fire a few years thereafter.

The Nashville & Chattanooga Railroad was completed through the county in 1851.  It has stations within the county, at Estill Springs, Decherd, Cowan, Sherwood and Anderson.  It passes through the Cumberland Mountains in this country by deep cuts, and a tunnel 2,200 feet long.  The Sewanee Mining Company has a railroad from Tracy City passing by University Place, and connecting with the Nashville & Chatanooga Railroad at the base of the mountain near Cowan.  This road was completed in 1858.  The Decherd, Fayetteville & Columbia Railroad was completed to Fayetteville about the same time.  It has stations in this county at Decherd, Winchester, Belvidere, Maxwell and Huntland.

The Falls Mill Manufacturing Company are operating a cotton-mill on Bean Creek near Salem. Whit Ransom now owns the Town Creek Mills, which were established by Anson Butterworth. These mills consist of a woolen-mill, with about twelve looms, a carding-mill and a large grist and flouring-mill, all run with water-power. They are located about five miles west of Winchester. R. C. Handley, Ben. A. Oehmig, A. J. Kinningham and Estill Bros. each own and operate grist and flouring-mills on Boiling Fork. Corn & Miller have a grist and flouring-mill on Elk River. There is also a grist and flouring-mill in Sinking Cove. Grist-mills and saw-mills are found on almost every stream. There are also a number of steam saw-mills and other manufacturing establishments throughout the county outside of the village. An agricultural and mechanical society existed for a few years before the war. And along in the "seventies" the Grange movements struck the county. A number of Granges were organized, and some stores were attempted to be run on the Grange plan, but all this has passed away.

When the county was new malarial fevers prevailed to some extent. In 1843 and 1844 typhoid fever made its first appearance in the county. At first it nonplussed the physicians, but they soon learned to treat it successfully. The first cases of cerebro-spinal meningitis made their appearance in the winters of 1848 and 1849. The temperature of the climate is mild and pleasant, and never goes to the extremes of heat and cold. The people of the county are remarkably healthy. No cases of cholera or yellow fever have ever been known in the county, except one or two, which were brought here from abroad.* The raising of cotton has been dispensed with, and the farmers are now turning their attention to the cultivation of cereals, grasses and live-stock. In 1855 there were raised in Franklin County 135,816 bushels of wheat, 475,293 bushels of Indian corn, 71,980 bushels of oats, 1,283 bushels of rye, and 1,110 bushels of barley. And the live-stock was enumerated as follows: 4,580 horses and mules, 7,906 cattle, 6,296 sheep, 25,379 hogs.

The county of Franklin was created by an act of the General Assembly of the State of Tennessee, passed December 3, 1807. The act provided "that there be a new county established within the following bounds, to wit: Beginning on the southeast corner of Warren County; thence with the south boundary line of Warren County to the eastern line of Bedford County; thence with said line to the southern boundary line of the State; thence east with the State line to the southwest corner of Bledsoe County; thence northwardly to the beginning; which said bounds shall constitute a new and distinct county, to be known by the name of Franklin."

The act also provided that the courts should be held at the home of Maj. William Russell, near Cowan, until otherwise provided by law; and that the general musters and courts-martial should be held at the same place, or place of holding courts. By a subsequent act, passed November 14, 1809, creating the county of Lincoln, all the territory east of Lincoln, south of Bedford and north of the State line, was attached to and made a part of Franklin County. And by later acts of the General Assembly creating Moore, Coffee, Grundy and Marion Counties, Franklin has been reduced to its present limits. Before the organization of Franklin County a portion of its territory lay in what was then called White County, and in many of the original conveyances the lands were described as being in White County. The early records of the county court, or court of quarter sessions, were lost or destroyed during the late civil war, and consequently no account of the first election of magistrates and county officers can now be given. It is certain, however, that such election was held in the year 1808, and the first county court organized at the home of Maj. William Russell, as provided by the act of creation.

An act of the General Assembly, passed November 22, 1809, provided for the holding of an election "at the place of holding courts on the first Thursday and Friday of February, 1810, for the purpose of electing seven fit and proper persons as commissioners to fix on and establish a permanent seat of justice in and for the said county of Franklin," with power to fix on a place for the seat of justice, and to purchase a tract of land "not less

---

*Information pertaining to health from Dr. J. C. Shapard.

than forty acres;" to lay off the same into lots, streets and alleys, and to reserve in the most convenient place two acres for a public square, on which to erect the public buildings; to sell the lots at public sale, and make deeds of conveyance to purchasers; "to let out the building of the court house, prison and stocks, and to appropriate the money arising from the sale of lots in payment for the same."

And the act further provided that the town so laid off should be called and known by the name of Winchester, and should be the place of holding courts for the county of Franklin, as soon as the improvements would authorize an adjournment thereto. This election was accordingly held, and George Taylor, Jesse Bean, Samuel Norwood, James Dougan, John Cowan, John Bell and George Davidson were duly elected as such commissioners. In compliance with the foregoing, it is evident that the commissioners selected the site for the seat of justice, and caused the town to be surveyed and platted, but owing to reasons already given, neither the original plat nor the record thereof, nor the record of the sales of lots can now be found.

The register's office shows that on the 10th day of February, 1812, the said commissioners purchased of Christopher Bullard, for a consideration of $1, twenty-six acres of land, upon which the town was located; and that they afterward sold the town lots and made deeds of conveyance to the purchasers. And it is to be presumed that they performed all the duties incumbent upon them pertaining to the erection of the public buildings, etc., the details of which can not be given in full on account of the loss of early records. The first court house and jail were erected soon after the foregoing purchase. The former was a small brick structure on the site of the present court house. The latter was erected on a lot at the west end of College Street, and in 1813, very soon after its completion, it was consumed by fire. On the 8th of November, the General Assembly passed an act authorizing the drawing of a lottery for the purpose of rebuilding the public prison in county of Franklin, and for other purposes; and Wallis Estill, William Russell, Sr., Col. James Lewis, Christopher Bullard, James S. M. Wherter and Thomas Eastland were by said act appointed commissioners to superintend the lottery, and upon the receipt of the proceeds thereof, to proceed to rebuild the public prison in said town, erect stocks, and finish the work of the court house therein, by the appropriation of said moneys thereto. From the foregoing it is evident that the first court house was finished in about 1814. It was small and inconvenient, having no room sufficient for holding the sessions of the courts. However it was used until the year 1839, when it was torn down and the present court house erected in its stead. The contract for the brick work was let to Elisha Meridith, and that of the wood work to Reeves & Oehmig. The building cost about $10,000. It is a substantial brick structure of medium size, with county offices on the first floor, and the court room on the second.

The prison was rebuilt as provided by said act, on the west end of College Street, and was used until 1855, when it was condemned on account of its being insecure.

A committee, consisting of W. W. Brazelton, L. W. Gonee, John T. Slatter and Thomas Finch was then appointed by the county court to erect a new jail. Accordingly at the July term, 1855, of the county court, this committee reported that they had sold the old jail for $300, and that the new one had been constructed on Main Street and was then completed and occupied by the jailor and his prisoners. The new jail was built under contract by John Steele, of Lincoln County.

In January, 1881, the county purchased of Luke Kelly and wife, for a consideration of $2,200, a farm consisting of 150 acres, with buildings thereon, as a home for the paupers of the county. This farm lies about seven miles northwest of Winchester. The authorities have employed a man to superintend the farm and oversee the paupers at a salary of $350 a year.

The average number of inmates in the poor-house thus far has been about fourteen. Prior to the purchase of this farm the paupers of the county were provided for by annual appropriations made by the county court, and a few outside of the poor-house are still furnished relief in that way.

The county is divided into civil districts numbering from one to eighteen, respectively. The First District has four magistrates, and all the others have two each, making a total of thirty-eight.

We give herewith the vote of Franklin County at the presidential elections commencing with 1848:

1848—Lewis Cass, Democrat, 1,207; Zach. Taylor, Whig, 390.

1852—Franklin Pierce, Democrat, 1,135; Winfield Scott, Whig, 330.

1856—James Buchanan, Democrat, 1,427; Millard Fillmore, American, 331.

1860—John C. Breckinridge, Democrat, 1,526; Stephen A. Douglas, Democrat, 26; John Bell, Union, 388; Millard Fillmore, American, 331.

1864—No election.

1868—Horatio Seymour had a majority of about 1,200 over Gen. Grant. The vote of some precincts were thrown out, and the exact figures are not now accessible.

1872—Horace Greeley, Democrat. 1,740; U. S. Grant, Republican, 267.

1876—Samuel J. Tilden. Democrat, 2,275; R. B. Hayes, Republican, 276.

1880—Gen. Hancock, Democrat, 2,187; Gen. Garfield, Republican, 357; Gen. Weaver, Independent, 16.

1884—Grover Cleveland, Democrat, 2,091; James G. Blaine, Republican, 645; St. John, 30.

It will be observed that Mr. Tilden received the largest Democratic vote ever cast in the county, and Mr. Blaine the largest Republican. Up to and including the year 1880 the voters of that part of Moore County which was cut off from Franklin County, voted in the latter. The vote of 1884 is the true vote of the county as it now stands geographically.

In 1860 there were 10,249 white and 3,599 colored people in the county, making a total of 13,848; in 1870 there were 11,988 white and 2,972 colored, making a total of 14,970; and in 1880 there were 13,646 white and 3,530 colored, making a total of 17,176. The colored population in 1860 were nearly all slaves, who became free by virtue of the emancipation proclamation, after which it seems that a large number migrated from the county, as shown by the fact that in 1870 there were 627 less negroes than in 1860; during the same time the white population increased 1,748 in number. During the last decade the whites have increased 1,648 and the blacks 538.

The county court clerks were Absalom Russell, 1808-13; Edmund Russell, 1813-34; W. B. Wagoner, 1834-36; W. W. Brazelton, 1836-40; Isaac Estill, 1840-44; Sherwood Williams, 1844-48; Wm. E. Taylor, 1848-58; R. F. Sims, 1858-60; John G. Enochs, 1860-64; Thos. Short, 1864-66; John G. Enochs, 1866-71; Clem Arledge, 1871-82; Wm. E. Taylor, 1882-86. The registers were: John Keeton, 1808-26; Solomon Wagoner, 1826-36; Jesse T. Wallace, 1836-44; James L. Williams, 1844-48; Jesse T. Wallace, 1848-52; W. D. McNeil, 1852-56; Adam Hancock, 1856-60; M. G. Osborn, 1860-64 (war interval.) Wm. Stewart, 1865-66; D. R. Slatter, 1866-69; J. J. Martin, 1869-74; N. R. Martin, 1874-78; J. B. Ashley, 1878-86. The chancery court clerks and masters were: John Goodwin, 1834-38; Hu Francis, 1838-58; H. R. Estill, 1858-71; T. H. Finch, 1871-85; Clem Arledge, present incumbent, 1883 to—

Since the late civil war the office of county trustee has been held respectively by the following named gentlemen, to wit: Wm. Buchanan, Wm. R. Francis, Sanders Faris, R. J. Turner, R. G. Smith and the present incumbent, A. J. Skidmore. Circuit court clerks, since the war: George W. Hunt, 1865-66; Thos. J. Jackson, 1866-74; W. W. Estill, 1874-78; H. P. Stewart. 1878-82; Nathan Francis, 1882-86. Sheriffs since the war, omitting dates: John W. Custer, J. W. Williams, H. D. Willits, D. J. Martin, H. P. Stewart, R. F. Oakley, J. J. Turner, and the present incumbent, C. A. Majors. J. W. Syler is the present county surveyor, J. P. Waddington coroner, and W.B. Watterson superintendent of schools. Owing to the loss of some records, and the manner in which others have been kept, it is impossible to compile as full and complete a list of county officers as might be desired. The average annual expense of the county for the last ten years has been $9,000, and according to the financial report of J. W. Williams, judge of the county court, filed July 5, 1886, county warrants had been issued between October 1, 1885, and the date of his report amounting to $10,057.81; and the total amount received into the treasury for the same time was $9,291.61, leaving the county in debt in the sum of $766.20 at the date of said report.

The tax duplicate of the county for 1886 shows 337,930 acres of land assessed, and the total taxable property assessed at $1,687,170. And the amounts of taxes levied are as follows, to-wit: State, $5,061.51; county, $5,670.26; school, $8,948.84; highway, $2,530.75; total, $22,211.16. Number of taxable polls, 2,435.

The first term of the county court* was held in the spring of 1808 at the house of Maj. William Russell, near Cowan, where the county business was transacted until the seat of justice was established at Winchester, and a place provided for holding the courts. The courts were first held at Winchester about the year 1814, when the first court house was completed. An act of the General Assembly passed October 16, 1812, provided "that the county courts should be held in the county of Franklin on the third Mondays in February, May, August and November;" and the sessions were accordingly held on those dates until a subsequent act provided that the county courts in each and every county in the State should be held "on the first Monday in every month."

The "minute books" of the county court prior to year 1832 have been lost or destroyed. The officers of this court are a county judge and the magistrates of the several civil districts of the county. Prior to 1868 the county court was presided over by one of their number elected as chairman, and since that date by a judge elected by the people. This court continued to hold its sessions up to and including the June term, 1863, when, on account of the war, it suspended action until April, 1865, since which time it has held its regular sessions. J. N. McCutcheon served as judge of the county court from 1868 to 1870, and Judge J. W. Williams, the present incumbent, has held the office ever since. There are no records of the circuit court in the county prior to the fourth Monday of January, 1824, when the court was held by Judge Nathaniel W. Williams. Nathaniel Hunt, Esq., was then the high sheriff and James Fulton attorney-general, and Jonathan Spyker clerk. Judge Williams served one year, and was succeeded by Judge Charles F. Keith, who served until 1830, when he was succeeded by Judge J. C. Mitchell, who served a series of years. On the 26th day of January, 1825, Robert L. Mitchell, then seventy years of age, appeared and filed an affidavit, attesting his services in the war of the Revolution. In January, 1829, Samuel Suddarth was tried for manslaughter, found guilty, and sentenced "to be forthwith branded on the brawn of the thumb of the left hand with the letter M in the presence of the court, and that he be imprisoned in the jail of the county six months, and to pay the costs of this prosecution, and to remain in jail until the same be fully paid."

The most dramatic and most lasting of all the historic episodes in the history of Franklin County, was the killing of Tom Taul and the trial of Rufus K. Anderson as the murderer. In this case the sheriff summoned, in all, 168 men to appear in court, all of whom were examined touching their qualifications to act as jurors in the cause, and out of this number "twelve good and lawful men" were found competent to try the prisoner. The killing took place in 1829 and the trial in 1830, but the social and political estrangements which they brought still linger here. Rufus K. Anderson was the son of Col. Wm. P. Anderson, of whom mention has been made in connection with the settlement of the county. The Andersons were wealthy and aristocratic. Thomas P. Taul was the son of Col. Micah Taul, who had been a colonel in the war of 1812 and a member of Congress from Kentucky. Coming to Tennessee, he located at Winchester, and soon took rank among the first lawyers of the State, and he and Hopkins L. Turney were then the leading members of the Winchester bar. Tom Taul is said to have been the most brilliant young lawyer in Tennessee at that time. He married Miss Caroline, the accomplished daughter of Col. Wm. P. Anderson, and sister of Rufus K. In a few years Mrs. Taul died of consump-

*This was originally called the "Court of Quarter Sessions."

tion, childless. On her death bed she gave her property to her husband by a deed. After her death the Andersons claimed that Taul had never been kind to her and that he had coerced the deed. Rufus K. Anderson, a young man of the highest notions of civil life, had gone to Alabama before his sister's marriage and before Col. Taul moved to Tennessee, and had never seen his brother-in-law, Tom Taul. After the death of his sister, he returned to Winchester, and asked to have Tom Taul pointed out to him, which being done, he walked across the street to where Taul was standing, and shot and killed him. The trial came off in less than a year and Col. Taul employed Col. Sam Laughlin, a most powerful prosecuting lawyer, and other lawyers of distinction to prosecute Anderson, who was defended by Hon. Felix Grundy, Hopkins L. Turney and other distinguished lawyers. By the time the trial came on the whole county was divided under the respective banners of the contending parties. The jury returned a verdict of "not guilty." Whether the verdict was just, or whether the jury was led to commit an error, will never be known with certainty.

The State of Tennessee vs. John Farris, was an action brought against the defendent at the June term of 1830, for killing his slave named James. The trial took place at the July term following. One hundred and thirty-four men were brought into court and examined before twelve "good and lawful men " could be found competent to act as jurors. Able counsel was employed by the defendant, and the jury returned a verdict into court of "not guilty." The foregoing causes have been mentioned because of their historic importance. There have been other murder trials, and many important civil cases, which might be mentioned if space permitted.

In May, 1862, the circuit court convened for the last time until the close of the war. In July, 1865, it again convened with Judge Wm. P. Hickerson on the bench, since which time it has held its regular sessions. Judge J. J. Williams is now the presiding officer, whose term is about to expire.

The first records found of the chancery court are its proceedings in 1834, when L. M. Bramlett was chancellor. For a number of years following, this court was held at Winchester, for Franklin and Coffee Counties. Bloomfield L. Ridley was chancellor from 1842 up to the late late civil war, as shown by the records. Only one session of this court was held between 1861 and 1865. At the August term, 1865, John P. Steele presided as chancellor, and served as such until 1870, since which time Hons. A. S. Marks, John W. Burton and E. D. Hancock, have filled the office of chancellor, in the order named.

A few persons have been hanged in the county by due process of law, but a greater number have probably been hanged without it. It is believed that the first hanging which took place in the county, was that of Adkinson or Adkins, who killed his wife with a shoe last. This occurred about the year 1821. Just after the close of the late civil war, Rolly Dotson, a noted bushwhacker, murderer and desperado, was taken from the jail by an organized body of men and hanged to a tree in the court yard until he was dead. Henry Huddleston, colored, was hanged to the same tree in 1882, for committing a rape on a white woman. In 1871, three negroes were hanged under the bridge of the Boiling Fork, at Winchester, for burning a church at Hawkerville. All these, excepting the first, were without process of law. Other hangings, both legal and otherwise, have taken place within the county.

Perhaps no county in the State has ever had, according to its population, such an able bar as Winchester has produced.

The eminent jurist, Judge Nathan Green, came from Virginia when he had reached middle life, and settled on land owned by his uncle, John Faris. He was plain in dress, and not known for two years as anything but a farmer. No little merriment took place one day when Mr. Farris brought Green into court to take charge of and conduct a law suit in which the former was involved. The trial made the lawyer-farmer famous, and he at once stepped to the head of the bar and in a short time became chancellor, and soon thereafter a member of the supreme court, where he so long distinguished himself. This was the home, for many years, of Tom Fletcher, one of the greatest criminal lawyers the State has ever produced. He, like Green, came to the bar in middle life, after failing as a merchant.  He was the author of a paper anonymously written in 1824, styled "The Polit ical Horse Race," which attracted much attention in the race between Jackson, Clay, Adams and Crawford.

Maj. Edward Venable, who in 1857 was appointed embassador to Gautemala, and died immediately after reaching that country, was also a prominent member of the Winchester bar.  Frank Jones the gifted stumper and brilliant congressman, lived here and was the most popular man of his day.  Thomas and Isaacs, brothers-in-law, both marrying the daughters of Col. Bullard, and both at times, in turn, representing the distr ct in Congress, lived here and were men of rank.  Judge Isaacs was among the ablest lawyers the State ever had.  Forrester, a man who made his mark, and was several years a member of Con gress, lived here.  James Campbell was a man of great legal reputation with an un blemished life.  He also married a daughter of Col. Anderson, and practiced a number of years at the Winchester bar, then went to Nashville, and about 1847 made a visit to the Winchester Springs, where he committed suicide.  Hopkins L. Turney, father of Judge Peter Turney, was a self-educated man, and for many years one of the leading members of the Winchester bar.  He was a man of fine personal appearance, kind and affable, in fluential and popular.  As a jury lawyer he was rarely equaled.  He served in the Legis lature, in Congress, and in the United States Senate.  Micah Taul, of whom mention has been made, was a man of great learning and eminent as a jurist.  While he and Hop kins L. Turney were the leading members of the bar, they were generally employed on opposite sides of the principal trials in litigation.  Frank Estill was a very prominent member of the Winchester bar for many years prior to his death, which occurred only a few years ago.  A. S. Colyar, now of Nashville, began the practice here about the year 1844.  He was a close student, and a man of great firmness, and devoted to his client's cause, and it is too well known to need further mention.  To him acknowledgement is made for much valuable information compiled in the foregoing concerning the Win chester bar and the trial of Rufus K. Anderson.

Judge Peter Turney, who was colonel of the First Tennessee Confederate Infantry, and who since the war has served sixteen years on the bench of the Supreme Court of Tennessee, lives here, and was for many years a member of the Winchester bar.  Many other prominent lawyers have been members of this bar, and Felix Grundy, in his day, practiced here.  The present members of the bar are ex-Gov. A. S. Marks, Capt. Tom Gregory, T. A. Embry, John Simmons and Estill and Whitaker, whose biographies appear elsewhere in this work.  Other members are Scott Davis, Burt Russey, J. B. Ashley, Nathan Francis, Mr. Curtis, Brannon and Thompson, John H. Martin and James Taylor. Senator Isham G. Harris was born, reared and educated in this county.  The old log cabin in which he was born is still standing a few miles from the town of Winchester.

Many of the early settlers of this county were survivors of the war of the Revolution; and when the war of 1812 broke out between this country and Great Britain, the young men of Franklin County, sons of the veterans of 1776, formed themselves into "ranks of war," under the heroic Jackson, and others, to maintain the flag of the young republic.  In evidence of the foregoing the following from the *Home Journal* of September 30, 1880, is inserted: "In the *Home Journal* office we have the manuscript of what we print.  It is yellow with dust, age and decay.  The paper is just such as could be had in those days. This document was found among the papers of our grandfather, Wallis Estill, who has left quite a family of descendants in this county.  It appears that the county had been drained of young men, and the old men—those over forty-five—formed themselves into a company to protect the honor of the United States against any disaffected persons, and against those who might do injury to the property of the younger men who had to go to battle.  In the list of names will be found many familiar here in Franklin County.  Read it, and see how nobly ministers of the gospel entered in behalf of liberty:

"WHEREAS, The honor of the United States has made it necessary that war should be declared against Great Britain by the United States; and whereas, in this contest it may evidently happen that the active part of our force may be called off to distant service, by which an opportunity will be afforded to the disaffected (if any such there should be amongst us), to do much mischief: Therefore, for the purpose of defending the frontiers, and property of our younger brethren when fighting our battles abroad, and to suppress and put down any combination which may manifest itself inimicable to our beloved country, we, the undersigned, all over forty-five years of age, and most of whom fought in the late Revolutionary war, have embodied ourselves into a company, to be denominated the Revolutionary Volunteers of Franklin County; and when the company is formed, officers to command the same shall be elected by the suffrages of the members of the company. Captain, Wallis Estill; first lieutenant, Richard Farris; second lieutenant, John Woods; ensign, James Russey; sergeants, A. Berryhill, Alex Beard, James Holland, Jacob Casterline; adjutant, James Lewis. Rev. John Davis, Rev. Wm. Ginnings, Jesse Embry, Jesse Bedu, John Champion, Samuel Henderson, Jos. Champion, John Chilcoat, Ralph Crabb, Jesse Toulan, Francis Adams, John Poe, Wm. Thompson, George Waggoner, Benj. Johnson, Samuel Rosebary, Archibald Woods, Rev. Andrew Woods, Rev. Peter Woods, Rev. Robert Bell, David Milligan, Elijah Williams, Ebenezer Picket, Moses Ayers, John Denson, Joseph McClusky, James Weeks, Alex. Borehill, Nicholas Robinson, James Busby, Thomas Green, Samuel Reynolds, Jesse Perkins, James Holland, John Robinson, William King, Samuel Runnells, William Crawford, James King, Richard Miller, John Barnett, David Larkins, William McCloud, Samuel Handley, Jacob Van Zant, Sr., James Harris, Robert Hudspeth, Jesse Ginn, Thomas Herlep, John Cowan, William Russell, Sr., Daniel Champion, William Faris, John Herrod, John Nellum, John Dellehide, William Greenwood, John Stokes, David McCord, Charles Weeks, Randolph Riddle, Matthew Taylor."

These noble men were among those who first secured, and afterward maintained, our liberties, and Time, the great leveler, has long since closed the green earth over all that was mortal of every one of them. Many of the citizens of this county served under Jackson in the Florida war, and, according to tradition, Jackson encamped with his troops just below Winchester, on one occasion, while the Indians were encamped on the opposite side of the Boiling Fork. In the brief but brilliant war with Mexico it is learned that Franklin County furnished Capt. George T. Colyar's Company E, of the Third Regiment Tennessee Volunteer Infantry, commanded by Col. B. F. Cheatham. This company, consisting of 115 men, rank and file, left Winchester in September, 1847, and was mustered into the United States service near Nashville about October 10, 1847, and left for Mexico in the same month. Capt. Colyar died January 8, 1848, in the city of Mexico. His remains were sent to his home in Winchester. First Lieut. Sherrod Williams then became captain, and continued as such to the close of the war. The company was discharged about July 22, 1848. The following is a list of the survivors of the company now living in this county: A. J. Caldwell, John Thurman, F. M. Williams, Ed Jackson, William Adcock, David Smith, Nathan Boone and Gordon McCutcheon. The following are living elsewhere: T. H. Finch, Texas; W. H. Jones, Lincoln County; M. N. Matthews. Bedford County; Wilson Clark. Alabama; Berry Logan and William Taylor, Moore County; Ed Anderson and Alpheus Green, Texas. Oliver Posey is a survivor of some other command in the Mexican war, and lives in Franklin County.

Early in September, 1860, while court was in session at Winchester, two or three public meetings of a political nature were held, and speeches were made by M. Turney, A. S. Colyar, T. W. Newman, H. T. Carr, Jesse Arledge, Dr. B. W. Childs and others. Much excitement prevailed, and the following was offered by H. T. Carr:

" Resolved, That it is the sense of this meeting, that in the event of any one of the Southern States, or more, should, under the grievous wrongs now pressed upon by the sectional States of the North, secede from the Union, we hold it to be our duty to sympathize with, aid and assist our Southern brethren if an attempt is made to coerce them into submission."

Pending the discussion of the resolution the meeting adjourned without action thereon. The citizens of Franklin County were mostly extremely Southern in sentiment, and as soon as South Carolina and other States seceded from the Union, were anxious that Tennessee should do likewise.

The most intense excitement prevailed, and early in the spring of 1861 companies began to form and drill for the contest; and soon Capt. Miller Turney's Company C, Capt. Clem Arledge's Company F, Capt. Jos Holder's Company I and Capt. N. L. Simpson's

Company D, of Col. Peter Turney's First Regiment Tennessee Infantry, were completely organized and ready for the service. These companies were led with their regiment into the Confederate service, long before Tennessee seceded from the Union. Then followed Capt. A. S. Marks' Company E, Capt. James Engle's Company I and Capt. Thomas H. Finch's Company D, all of the Seventeenth Regiment Tennessee Infantry. Many joined the Forty-first Regiment Tennessee Infantry, some joined Forrest's cavalry, and many others joined other commands. Including all of the foregoing, together with the recruits that subsequently joined these and other commands, it is safe to say that the county furnished over 3,000 soldiers for the Confederate Army.

The first command of Federal troops that made its appearance in this county was that of Gen. Lytle, who came here in the spring of 1862, with a small command from General Mitchell's division, then encamped at Huntsville. He was in search of Terry's Texas Rangers, who were encamped at Goshen. The day after the arrival of the Federal troops Col. Cox came in on the Decherd road with a squad of rangers. A sharp skirmish ensued, in which one ranger was killed. Col. Cox then retired, and two days later Gen. Lytle returned with his command to Huntsville. Soon thereafter Gen. Negley, with his command, passed through Winchester, on his way to Chattanooga. Gen. Buell's army advanced to Decherd, but retired therefrom when he fell back toward the Ohio River in August, 1862. On July 2, 1863, the army of Gen. Rosecrans took possession of Winchester and in force occupied all the surrounding country. Gens. Rosecrans, Garfield, McCook and others had their headquarters at private houses in the town. The provost-marshal occupied the old office of Dr. Wallis Estill, and Rosecrans' staff occupied the building of the Mary Sharp College. The Normal School building (then Carrack Academy) was used as a hospital; and when Winchester was in the rear of Bragg's army almost every available house was used as a hospital. Briggs & Herrick kept a store in Winchester while it was under Federal rule, and were allowed to sell goods to the citizens. Rosecrans was here about six weeks, during which time all the forage in the surrounding country was gathered in for the support of his army. Soon after the Federal Army left, a company of citizens galloped into town and gutted the store of Briggs & Herrick, carrying away nearly all its contents. Gen. Slocum and his command occupied the town a short time thereafter, and Gen. Sherman's army passed through Winchester, on its way to Chattanooga, in the winter of 1863–64.

Franklin County was directly on the line of the contending armies, and consequently her citizens suffered greatly from the ravages of war. No great battles were fought, nor were any extensive fortifications made within the county, and strangers passing through it now could not observe that there had ever been a war here.

The town of Winchester was laid out in 1810, when the site thereof was covered with timber. A Mr. Norwood cut the first tree on the Public Square, and the same year James Russey, grandfather of James Russey, now of the Ballard House, built the first house, locating it on the corner where the Ballard House now stands. It is said that the United States troops were quartered therein during the war with the Creek Indians. The latter James Russey is the oldest native-born citizen of the town.

Thomas D. Wiggins was the first merchant in Winchester, and sold his goods in a log cabin. The next merchants were Col. Crabb, Hayter, Spyker and Daugherty, and following them were the Decherds, Tom Pryor, Alfred Henderson, Tom Wilson, Joe Klepper, Mark Hutchins and Mr. Blackwood. The first saloon or grocery where liquors were sold was kept by Daniel Eanes & Son, between 1810 and 1820. The town grew rapidly at its commencement, and by an act of the General Assembly of the State, passed October 28, 1813, Ralph Crabb, Jonathan Spyker, James S. M. Wherter, James Estill and James Russell were appointed commissioners for the purpose of regulating the town, with authority to levy and collect taxes and compel the inhabitants to work on the streets and alleys. The first doctors were Higgins and Kincaid. In 1816 the learned Dr. Wallis Estill came from Virginia and located here. He soon rose to eminence, particularly as a surgeon, and did nearly all the surgical practice in the county for nearly fifty years.

Telfair Hodgson

FRANKLIN COUNTY.

Soon thereafter his brother, William Estill and  Dr. John Fitzpatrick, of Virginia settled in Winchester, and both became prominent physicians.  The latter died in 1854, and the former in 1874.

Soon after the town was laid out a hotel was erected opposite the Ballard House, and was for many years headquarters for the stage route.  The site is now vacant.  The Ballard House was built about 1830, and the block on the opposite corner about 1833.  By an act of  the General Assembly passed August 20, 1822, Winchester was incorporated, and the town council given full power to enact all ordinances necessary to restrain vice and immorality and to otherwise govern the town.  As early as 1826 or 1827 a branch of the State Bank was established in the brick building still standing opposite the southeast corner of the Public Square, and Dr. M. L. Dixon was the first cashier thereof. This bank suspended early in the "thirties," and the town has never had a bank since.  In 1832 the population of Winchester was about 600, and the business of the town nearly equal to what it is now.  The merchants of the town during the "thirties" were Thomas Wilson, Joseph Klepper, Oehmig & Wells, Tolls & Russell, M. W. Howell, W. Williams, James Robertson, A. L. & J. W. Campbell, William & J. H. Knox, A. M. Cowan, Benj. Decherd, H. A. Rains, Hutchins & Pryor and J. & R. Snowden.  Madison Porter was a blacksmith, and Wm. Buchanan had a tan-yard.  There were two saddle and harness shops, one by Joe Bradford and the other by James Russey.  M. Robertson had a cabinet shop, and Edmond Dyer was the silversmith.  Winchester was then the only town of importance on a long stage route and in a vast country surrounding it, hence its business activity. There were then three hotels in the town: The Ballard House, which was built and kept by Henry Runnells; the old frame hotel on the opposite corner, kept lastly by P. I. Curl; and the third hotel was kept by Col. Crabb, in the third brick building in the town.  It is now occupied by Mark Henderson and others.  Dr. Matthew L. Dixon and Dr. Turner were the prominent physicians of the town and Dr. Wallis Estill was at the head of the profession.

Business of the forties:  Merchants—Mark Hutchins, Thomas Pryor, Thomas Wilson, Ben Powell, F. A. Loughmiller, the Decherds, Brazeltons, J. T. Slatter, and others.  Carriage and coach manufacturers—Thomas Logan and Hutchins, Porter & Co.  The carriages were mostly sold to the wealthy planters of the South, and the business was very extensive.

Business of the fifties:  Merchants—D. & A. R. Brazelton, Harris & Williams, Horton & Kennington, C. C. Brewer, Sanders & Henderson, H. Leonard & Co., N. R. Martin, Templeton & Stewart, Crutcher & Tennison, J. W. Templeton, W. B. Wagner, G. A. Shook, Houghton & Decherd, S. A. & T. J. Lockhart.  Tailors—L. Stone & Co. and J. S. Kelly.  Livery stable—John W. Curtis.  Blacksmith—Owin Hill.  The carriage making was continued by Thomas S. Logan.

The business continued about the same until the commencement of the civil war. For the history of the town during the war period the reader is referred to "Military." On the return of peace a noticeable event was the occupation of one house at the Russey corner, now burnt, by two merchants, one a Federal soldier and the other a Confederate— one having his goods on one side, and the other occupying the other side.  Soon after the war the merchants of the town were M. D. Embry, Avery Handley, D. S. Logan, John Vaughan, W. L. Bickley, Moffett & Clark, W. B. Miller, Matterson & McDowell, J. W. Degresse and P. H. Achey & Co.  Nearly all business was suspended during the war, and twenty years have passed away since it began to recruit.  A reference to the business of the present will show how it has been re-established and increased.  The merchants now are: Dry goods—Wiley S. Embry, J. L. Baugh, Mark Henderson, Sim Venable and A. C. Plumlee.  Dry goods and groceries—J. A. Gaines, T. J. Gaines, J. C. Garner, T. J. Jackson & Son and Whit Ransom.  Hardware—Carter & Brother.  Tinner and stove dealer— John F. Vaughan.  Drugs—G. G. Phillips and John M. Hutchins.  Family grocery—H. H. Embry.  Confectioner and baker—Johnnie Schrom.  Manufacturer of leather, boots, shoes, saddles and harness—Matt P. Petty.  Provisions—B. Templeton and Mrs. Rosa

Ayers. Milliners—Mrs. Emma Brazelton and Mrs. N. E. Days. Furniture dealers and undertakers—Fred Wenger and Jacob Weidman. Repair shop—John Lawing. Jewelers— C. S. Crane and George R. Martin. Wagon-makers—John Kissling and Jack Miller, the latter colored. Manufacturers of carriages, wagons, etc., and dealers in all kinds of farm implements—Ruch & Little. The proprietors of the Winchester Spoke and Handle Factory are Wenger, Girton & Woodward, who employ ten hands, and do an extensive business. The blacksmiths are George Lefeber, James Lee, A. Knapper and Charlie Coleman. The boot and shoe-makers are R. Kleinwaechter and Bill Street. Looney and Estill are dealers in coal; James N. Logan, painter; R. B. Williams, picture gallery; W. E. and M. A. Lockridge, livery stable. Hotels—Estill House, by Isaac Estill; Ballard House, by James Russey; Cole House, by Mr. Cole. Physicians—Shapard, Murrell, Grisard and Blalock. Dentists—Baird, Gattis and Slaughter. Societies—Cumberland Lodge of F. & A. M., A. L. of H., K. of H., K. & L. of H. and Temperance Alliance. For schools and churches see under their appropriate heads.

In 1855, the General Assembly passed an act authorizing the mayor and aldermen of Winchester to lay off the town into a suitable number of wards, and providing for the election of a constable and two aldermen in each ward. The town was accordingly divided into four wards, and the officers were elected, as provided in the act, which conferred upon them full power of the then existing laws for the government of incorporated towns. The last meeting of the council, during the war, was held June 16, 1862, and the action of the corporation was then suspended until January 7, 1867, after which a new council had been elected and convened. On the 13th of March, 1883, the General Assembly, upon petition of the citizens of Winchester, passed an act repealing their charter, to take effect at the close of the year. Accordingly the council held a meeting December 31, 1883, and made full and final settlement of finances, and adjourned *sine die*. According to the census of 1880, Winchester had a population of 1,039, which has not greatly increased since. The town has no saloons, but it has two colleges, and two free schools, and seven churches. "The young ladies wear the blush of modesty and the crown of culture and refinement. The young men are thrifty, energetic and sober."

The first newspaper published in the county, of which there is any account, was *The Highlander*, established and published in Winchester, in 1839, by H. Mabry. How long its publication continued is not known. The next seems to have been *The Winchester Independent*, which was established in 1850, by Alexander R. Wiggs, with George B. White as editor. Its publication continued about three years. Hon. F. A. Loughmiller, it is said, once published a paper in Winchester, the name of which and date of publication is clouded with uncertainty. *The Winchester Appeal* was established in February, 1856, by George E. Pulvis & William J. Slatter. It was American in politics and advocated the election of Fillmore and Donelson. Its publication suspended with the close of the year. *The Home Journal* was established in January, 1857, by Metcalfe & Pulvis, who published ten copies and then sold it to William J. Slatter, who was connected with it until October, 1884, when he leased it to H. H. Dulin, who had for many years been connected with it in the capacity of printer. It is now published by Taylor & Dulin. W. D. Watterson, Lewis Metcalfe and others have been connected with it for short periods. It has always been Democratic in politics.

The *Franklin County News* was established in June, 1883, by Phillips, Embrey & Co., who continued to publish it until 1884, when they leased it to Morrell & Snodgrass, who published until June, 1886. The company then sold it to Nathan Francis, the present publisher. It is also Democratic in politics.

Decherd is situated on the Nashville & Chattanooga Railroad, at the junction of the Decherd & Fayetteville Railroad, and two miles from Winchester. It had its origin with the completion of the former railroad in 1851. The only house then was the log cabin in which Richard Holder was living. The place was named in honor of Peter S. Decherd. A good depot was built and Joseph Carter made agent, and Mrs. Davidson was put in charge of an eating house for the railroad company, which she kept up to the war. Among its first merchants were Carroll Walker, John March, Aaron Lynch and Cyrus Barnes.

Before the war a good academy was built at a cost of about $1,000.   It was destroyed during the war.   A union church was built by the Methodists, Baptists, Cumberland Presbyterians and Christians.   This was destroyed by Federal troops in the early part of the war.   After the army of Rosecrans occupied Decherd, it became and continued to be an important military station until the close of the war.   It was incorporated by an act of the General Assembly passed January 30, 1868, and the charter was repealed by another act passed April 3, 1885.   The town contains three general stores, one family grocery, queensware and hardware store, one drug store, one steam grist and flouring-mill, some mechanical shops, two churches and a public school.

Cowan lies on the Nashville & Chattanooga Railroad, at the base of the Cumberland Mountains on the north side, and is noted for its extensive iron manufactory.   The Sewanee Furnace was established here in 1880, with a capital stock of $200,000.   It has since passed into the hands of the Tennessee Coal, Iron & Railroad Company, with the capital increased to $300,000.   The company employs 100 hands, and manufactures seventy tons of pig iron per day.   The buildings are large and extensive.   Cowan is an old town located in one of the earliest settlements made in the county.   It is at the junction of the Sewanee & Tracy City Railroad.   Its present business, aside from that of the iron furnace, consists of four general stores, one drug store, one family grocery, one grist-mill, some mechanical shops, five churches (three white and two colored), two good hotels and one academy.   The place has about 800 inhabitants, a large proportion being colored.   It is pleasantly located and the surrounding scenery is delightful.

Sherwood is located on the Nashville & Chattanooga Railroad, in the romantic valley of Crow Creek, and is 1,100 feet above sea level.

Ex.-Lieut.-Gov. C. D. Sherwood, of Wisconsin, after whom the place is named, located there in 1875, and purchased a large tract of land, and organized the Sherwood Colony, of which he is the president, his object being to build up a health resort, and manufacturing town.   The town has been platted into lots of the most convenient size to suit purchasers, including a large number of tracts suitable for fruit farms on the top of the mountain, to which a wagon road of easy grade has been made.   This road leads from Sherwood to the University of the South, at Sewanee, only a few miles distant.

The colony consists at present of thirty Northern and ten Southern families.   And the town, which is only nine years old, has two general stores, a steam saw, planing and shingle-mill combined, two churches, the Sherwood Academy, and one free school, the railroad depot and offices, a large number of dwellings, and some mechanical shops.   There are fine mineral springs at the top of the mountain, and A. J. Smith, of Wisconsin, has purchased a tract of land, and made arrangements to build a hotel costing $20,000.   To this hotel he intends to conduct the mineral waters through pipes.   There are also fine springs of pure water at the site of the hotel.   A son of Mr. Smith will commence the publication of a newspaper there in September next.   The contract is let, and the office for the press is now being constructed.

Mr. Hersheimer, of Wisconsin, has made arrangements to move his machinery to Sherwood and establish a large foundry which will employ sixty hands.   It is a most romantic place, and as soon as the improvements now under way are completed it will no doubt become a popular health resort.   The leading industry at present is the getting out of chestnut-oak tan-bark and shipping it to St. Louis and Louisville.   About ninety car loads of this bark are shipped annually.

Anderson, a station on the Nashville & Chattanooga Railroad, near the State line, is a small village containing three general stores, a station house, one church and a public school.

Sewanee, at University Place, has a fine railroad depot and a three-story business block, built of stone.   Also a large frame hotel, kept by Col. S. G. Jones, six general stores, one drug store and an extensive coal mine.   The latter is operated by Col. Jones.

Salem was an old town in the lower part of the county, which had much importance in its day. Some of the early merchants were John R. Patrick, Hedspeth & Simmons and Thomas B. Moseley. Prior to 1840 Salem was a noted cotton market. It had good merchants and for many years Mrs. Cowan's hotel was considered one of the best in the country. On the 7th of March, 1873, the town was nearly all destroyed by fire. Mrs. Cowan's hotel, some dwellings and every business house in the village were consumed. The loss was estimated at $34,000. The town has never been rebuilt. In its "palmy days" it had a flourishing academy, the building of which is now used for the public school.

Belvidere, on the Decherd & Fayetteville Railroad, five miles below Winchester, has a station house, general store, blacksmith's shop, etc.

Maxwell, further down on the same railroad, has a station house, two general stores, one church, a shoe shop, two doctors and a few residences.

Hunt's Station on the same railroad, near the western line of the county, has a station house and express office, four general stores, one church, a public school, etc. Estill Springs on the Nashville & Chattanooga Railroad, was formerly a summer resort, and frequently contained a summer population of several hundred. It was almost entirely destroyed during the war, and has not been rebuilt. There are two general stores there at present. Hurricane Springs lie near the Moore County line and about four miles from the railroad. It is now the great fashionable resort for invalids and pleasure-seekers. It has a large hotel and cottages for visitors. Winchester Springs, formerly a great summer resort for the wealthy planters of the South, are located in a romantic dell near Elk River, and about five miles from Winchester. The Springs furnish red, yellow and white sulphur, chalybeate, freestone and limestone water. It is a fine summer resort. J. R. Warner is the proprietor.

In the settlement and growth of Franklin County, very little attention was paid to education, until villages with their academies became established. No adequate system of free schools existed prior to the late civil war. The first effort to establish an academy within the county, was made in the General Assembly of the State, by an act passed November 22, 1809, establishing Carrick Academy. Wm. Metcalfe, James Hunt, James Cunningham, Richard Callaway, Christopher Bullard and Geo. Taylor, were constituted a body politic and corporate, by the name of the Trustees of the Carrick Academy of the county of Franklin. The academy was established on the present site of the Winchester Normal, but when it was first organized and by whom first taught can not be stated. Prof. Witter conducted the school for some years prior to 1827 or 1828, when the school building was consumed by fire. In 1829, the trustees contracted with Wallis Estill to erect a new building, which cost $629. They then employed Prof. Robert Witter, a son of the former professor, to teach the school. In 1855, a brick building (which forms a part of the present building) was erected at a cost of about $5,000. And in 1865 it was leased to the Bishop and Diocese of the Protestant Episcopal Church of Tennessee for ninety-nine years. A school was opened under the auspices of said church, and continued about two years, when the lease was surrendered back to the trustees who gave it. The war coming on the academy was neglected for a series of years, and in 1871 Prof. R. A. Clark took charge of it, and in 1873, he was joined by Prof. J. M. Bledsoe and together they conducted the school until 1878. Carrick Academy was for males only.

Referring to early times it is found that among the very early teachers were Jonathan Burford whom, it is thought, taught the first school in Winchester, in a log cabin, near the Davidson Spring; and Rev. Andrew S. Morrison, who taught in a cabin, on the south side of Little Mountain. Abram Shook and M. K. Jackson were also among the early teachers. The Locust Hill Female Seminary, two miles southeast of Salem, was a flourishing school for many years before the late war. There was also an academy at Salem, which is now used by the free school. The Acme Academy, at Cowan, was chartered in 1882. It has an average of seventy pupils. The Sherwood Academy was chartered in 1881, and is doing a good work in that new and romantic village.

The Winchester Female Academy was founded by Rev. W. A. Scott, of the Cumberland Presbyterian Church. The building was erected in 1835, and the school opened in December of the same year. Rev. Scott and his wife were the first teachers. They continued about three years, and were succeeded by Rev. T. C. Anderson, two years. He was followed by Rev. Biddle, who taught until his death, which occurred about 1856. About this time the name of the academy was changed to that of The Robert Donnell Institute, and the faculty changed frequently thereafter. Profs. Syler and Crisman taught at different periods, and after the war Rev. McKinzie taught, and was followed by Prof. A. M. Burney. In the early sessions of this academy there were from 80 to 120 pupils in attendance, and the number afterward increased to about 160, and finally decreased so that the school had to be closed for want of patronage. The building is now used by the free school.

The Winchester Normal, for both sexes, was chartered in May, 1878. Capt. B. Dufield. J. L. Baugh, W. W. Garner, G. G. Phillips, T. J. Gaines, John Simmons, James H. Davis, John Kaserman and H. G. Hampton were constituted a body politic and corporate under the name of "The Winchester Normal." At the organization Capt. Dufield was elected president of the board of trustees, and Prof. J. W. Terrill was chosen president of the faculty and teacher of logic, mental and moral philosophy, etc.; Prof. R. A. Clark as teacher of mathematics, astronomy, etc.; and Prof. J. M. Bledsoe as teacher of Greek, Latin, etc· In May, 1878, the trustees of Carrick Academy, by authority of the county court, leased to the trustees of the Winchester Normal, the buildings and premises of the former academy for a period of fifteen years; and in December, 1881, a lease was made for fifty years more, to commence at the expiration of the first lease. This school was opened in September, 1878, with 220 students, including 160 free-school pupils, leaving only 60 who paid tuition. The free-school pupils were taken out at the end of the first year. The Normal has met with excellent success, and it is deservedly popular. From 60 paying students of the first year, the number has increased to 417 which were in attendance during the last year. Prof. Bledsoe retired from the faculty in 1881, and at present the faculty consists of President James W. Terrill, Prof. R. A. Clark, Miss Matt Estill, Miss Maud Terrill, Mrs. Colie Terrill, Miss Lillis Bledsoe, and Miss Fannie Stewart.

The history of the Mary Sharp College has been ably written and published in *The Illustrated Baptist*, from which is quoted a few extracts. This college, located at Winchester, "was founded in 1850, for the purpose of giving to the daughters of the South a more thorough and practical education than could be obtained in any school for girls, North or South." Two of the men most active and efficient in securing a departure from the custom of superficially educating girls, were Rev. J. R. Graves, the well known Baptist divine, now of Memphis, but then of Nashville, and Col. A. S. Colyar, now a distinguished member of the bar at Nashville, but at that time a citizen of Winchester.

" In the latter part of 1849, the services of Z. C. Graves, of Kingsville, Ohio, were secured. He was widely known as a most successful educator, and brought with him the entire faculty of the institution he left; Prof. W. P. Marks, for the chair of mathematics, his wife Mrs. Graves, for Latin and *belles-lettres*, and his sister Mrs. Marks, for the preparatory department. The professor of music was Johann Svensen, of the Conservatory of Music, at Stockholm, in Sweden. Two years after, Prof. Marks was succeeded by a brother of Mrs. Graves, Prof. G. D. Spencer. Save the music department, the teachers were all of one family, and a most harmonious and efficient band they were. Prof. Spencer taught until his death in 1864."

" In January, 1850, school was commenced in a commodious private dwelling, which was purchased for a boarding house for the embryo college, the families of the faculty living in the same house. The pupils were at first less than twenty, and the teachers five. At the close of the year the students were more than a hundred, and the school was removed to the service and basement rooms of the Baptist Church, where it continued to be taught for two years, whence, at the beginning of 1854, it removed to its permanent quarters, in the main building of the present college edifice." A thorough course of study was prepared, in which mathematics had a prominent place, English branches also, the Latin and Greek languages, with an extended and thorough drill in logic and metaphysics. The study of the Greek language was unknown at that time in any institution for girls.

The name of the college was at first the "Tennessee and Alabama Female Institute," but when the charter was procured it was changed to Mary Sharp College, to perpetuate the memory of the estimable lady who had made the largest donation for this first real "woman's college" in this or any other land—Mrs. Mary Sharp—the childless widow of an extensive planter in the vicinity of Winchester. The college edifice consists of a main building, three stories high, 80x40 feet, with two wings, each 24x40 feet, two stories high, and a laboratory, 24x18 feet, at the rear, the whole making twenty-five rooms for teaching purposes.

The prosperity of the Mary Sharp College has been unexampled. Commencing with less than twenty pupils, in ten years it had a patronage of 320 from eleven different States. The war left nothing but the bare walls of the college edifice standing. The expense of repairs fell heavily on President Graves, who paid it out of his own pocket. In 1865 pupils began to return, and although other prominent institutions of learning have sprung up in the immediate vicinity, this college has made rapid progress, and stands at the head of female colleges, and is able to prove that it is the pioneer college established for the higher education of woman. That is, it is the first college founded in America for women where Latin and Greek are a *sine qua non* for graduation. At the last commencement, 1886, the Mary Sharp College graduated a class of nineteen students. Over 5,000 young ladies (students) have attended this college since its commencement. The college is now in a flourishing condition and has the following able faculty: Z. C. Graves, LL. D., president; A. T. Barrett, LL. D., Prof. J. M. Bledsoe, Prof. C. F. Utermoehlen, Prof. E. M. Gardner, Miss Florence Griffin, A. M., Miss Mary Taylor, Miss Nannie Henderson, A. B., Mrs. K. C. Barrett, Mrs. J. M. Bledsoe, A. B., Miss Nannie Huff, Mrs. A. C. Graves, A. M.; A. T. Barrett, secretary. During the thirty-six years existence of this college, Dr. Graves, the founder thereof, has been its constant president.

Gen. Leonidas Polk (founder of the University of the South), a native of Tennessee, but late bishop of Louisiana, first conceived the idea of concentrating the interests of the Southern dioceses of the Protestant Episcopal Church upon one great school of learning. In 1856 he issued an address to the bishops of the Southern States, proposing to establish a university upon a scale that would reach the demands of the highest Christian education. Receiving the proposal with favor, the bishops of the South and Southwest, with delegates, assembled, for the first time, on Lookout Mountain on July 4, 1857, and decided to establish the proposed university. After many places were scientifically examined, Sewanee, Tenn., was chosen, on account of its healthfulness and delightful and picturesque scenery, as the site of the university. A charter was soon afterward procured from the State of Tennessee, granting the fullest power, and a domain of 10,000 acres of land was secured for the university.

An endowment of nearly $500,000 was obtained, and the corner-stone laid with great ceremony. Offices and buildings were erected, when the late civil war broke out and put a stop to all further operations. At the close of the war little remained, except the university domain. A movement was inaugurated in 1866 to revive the work. Funds were generously contributed in England, and in September, 1868, the trustees were enabled to put the university in operation upon a moderate scale. The prosperity of the institution from its opening until 1874 was on the rapid increase. At the latter date its numbers fell rapidly in consequence of the financial depression throughout the country, from which it did not recover until about 1880. Since then it has grown rapidly. The following is a list of the public buildings of the university, with cost of construction annexed: St. Luke's Hall, $45,000; Hodgson Library, $12,000; Thompson Hall, $12,000; St. Augustine Chapel and Quadrangle, $70,000; Temporary building, 1866, $15,000. The school opened in September, 1866, with fifteen pupils, and closed its recent term, June 30, 1886, with 281 pupils. The faculty consists of Rev. Telfair Hodgson, D. D., Dean, and Revs. George T. Wilmer, D. D., W. P. DuBose, S. T. D., Thomas F. Gailor,

M. A., S. T. B., Sylvester Clark, F. A. Shoup, D. D., and gentlemen—Gen. E. Kirby Smith, F. M. Page, M. A., Greenough White, M. A., B. L. Wiggins, M. A., W. A. Guerry M. A., J. W. S. Arnold, M. D., and Dr. Albert Schafter as professors ; Rt. Rev. John N. Galleher, D. D., Bishop of Louisiana, and Rt. Rev. J. F. Young, D. D., Bishop of Florida, as lecturers; J. W. Weber, instructor in book-keeping, and Robert W. Dowdy, second lieutenant Seventeenth Infantry, United States Army, commandant of cadets and instructor in military science. Sewanee, the site of the university, is on the elevated plateau of that name—a spur of the Cumberland Mountains. Its elevation above the level of the sea is about 2,000 feet and about 1,000 feet above the surrounding country, and its climate is unsurpassed. There are many elegant residences, and Sewanee and University Place combined contains about 1,000 inhabitants.

Under the present free-school system the educational interests of the county have reached the following statistics, to wit: Scholastic population—white males, 2,626; white females, 2,346; colored males, 690; colored females, 530. Grand total, 6,192, of which 4,100 attended school in 1885. The number of free schools are as follows: White, 62; colored, 9. During the last school year there were 38 white male and 28 white female, and 9 colored male and 3 colored female teachers employed, at an average compensation of $30 per month. The length of the school year was four months. About $17,000 are annually expended in the county for the support of the free schools.

The pioneer settlers of Franklin County were a Christian people, who worshiped God while undergoing the hardships of frontier life. A large number of the first settlers were ministers of the gospel. Public worship was held in every neighborhood in the cabins of some pious settlers. And as the people became more numerous they established camp-meetings at various places throughout the county. The early Methodist camp-meetings were located at Farris' Chapel, Walnut Grove, Caney Hollow, Marble Plains and Dabb's Ford. The Presbyterians established a camp ground at Goshen, and the Baptists established one near Salem. At these places the good people met annually "in God's first temples," the groves, to worship Him. These camp-meetings were mostly continued until the late civil war, since which time all have been discontinued, except the one at Goshen, where services are annually held for a season on the camp grounds. But no tents are now used, as the people go to the grove in the morning, and worship during the day, and return home in the evening. The pioneer religious denominations were the Methodists, Baptists, Presbyterians and Lutherans, and Revs. James Faris, James Rowe, Elijah Brazier, Henry Larkin, Robert Bell and Wm. Woods were some of the pioneer preachers. Early churches were established by the respective denominations in the neighborhood of the location of the camp grounds before mentioned.

The Goshen Presbyterian Church was organized soon after the first settlement, and Rev. Robert Bell was the first pastor. Immediately after the organization of the Cumberland Presbyterian Church, the Goshen Church joined it in a body, It still exists and has a very large membership. There is now only one Presbyterian Church in the county, and that one was established at Decherd about 1874, and has now a membership of about sixty. Decherd also has two colored churches—one Missionary Baptist and one Southern African Methodist. At Winchester divine services were first held in private houses, and next in the court house, until 1827, when the Cumberland Presbyterian Church edifice was erected on the lot where the Christian Church now stands. This was the first church building erected in the town. The first Sunday-school in Winchester was organized about 1828, and was conducted by Benjamin Decherd and others in a room of the second story of the court house, where white and colored children were taught together. About 1830 the Methodists built a log church in the Moseley neighborhood. The Cumberland Presbyterian Church in Winchester was organized about 1820, by Benjamin Decherd and Judge Green, their wives, and others. Rev. Joseph Copp was pastor of this church early in the thirties. He was succeeded by Rev. W. A. Scott, who founded the Winchester Female Academy. The present church edifice was built in 1858. At present it has a membership of about 125.

The Missionary Baptist Church in Winchester was founded about 1849 by Rev. A. D. Trimble, pastor, with a membership of about twenty-five. The church edifice was completed in 1852. The present resident membership is about fifty, and about twenty-five of the Mary Sharp College students, who reside abroad. Rev. Enoch Windes is the pastor.

The Catholic Church, at Winchester, was built soon after the close of the late civil war. Its members reside principally in the country. The edifice of the Christian Church at Winchester, was completed in 1885, Elder Floyd is the present minister.

The original trustees of the Methodist Episcopal Church South, at Winchester, were Robert Dougan, Robert Haukins, Wiley Densen, Charles Farris, William Stewart and John Fennell. A lot was donated to this church by J. Gordon, and the church built thereon in 1834. The church was organized with a small membership—twenty-five, perhaps. In 1854 the church edifice and lot were sold to Prof. Charles Guita for the sum of $400. The new church building was dedicated in 1852 by Dr. McFerrin. The present membership is 140. Rev. W. T. Haggard is the present pastor. The Episcopal Church at Winchester was founded principally by Ashton Butterworth, the most liberal donor, and Rev. J. L. Park. The edifice was erected in 1874 and the church has a membership of about forty. The Christian Church at Cowan was built in 1880. At Sherwood there is a Union and also a Methodist Church, the edifice of the latter being built in 1881, and the former in 1883. There are two colored churches in Winchester—one Methodist and the other Baptist. There are many other churches throughout the county, of which, for want of space, we can not speak in detail.

Franklin County has had her full share of suffering on account of intemperance. It can now be recorded that intemperance is on the decrease, while temperance is on the increase. Only a few years ago nearly every village in the county had its tippling saloons; but in 1876 the "Star of Hope Lodge," of the I. O. G. T., was organized in Winchester by J. J. Hickman, Grand Worthy Chief Templar, with a membership of sixty-five, which afterward increased to about 300. This lodge began the battle with intemperance and so prevailed upon the people as to induce them to petition the General Assembly to abolish the charter of Winchester, The charter being abolished the tippling houses had to immediately close up under the "four-mile law." This induced other towns to have their charters abolished, and now there is not an incorporated town in the county and not a tippling saloon. But the colleges and schools are incorporated. It seems that under the laws of Tennessee incorporated towns mean saloons, intemperance and degradation, while incorporated colleges and schools mean temperance, education and good morals. It is to be regretted, however, that such a town as Winchester has to sacrifice its municipal government in order to suppress the "traffic."

# MOORE COUNTY.

MOORE COUNTY lies in the south central portion of Tennessee, and is bounded on the north by Bedford, east by Coffee, south by Franklin, and west by Lincoln. It contains about 170 square miles, and its surface is greatly diversified. About one-half of the county lies on the Highland Rim, and the remainder in the Central Basin. The eastern portion has a high, flat, slightly-rolling surface, known as the "barrens," which breaks off to the south and west into ridges and ravines, some of the latter having a depth of 300 to 400 feet. These ridges are spurs which shoot out into the valley of the Elk and Mulberry and their tributaries, the valleys constituting a part of the broken southern division of the Central Basin which is partially cut off by Elk Ridge. These ridges are very fertile. They are composed mainly of the Nashville limestone, upon which rests the black shale or Devonian, and upon this shale rests as a protecting rock, the siliceous layers of the barren group, which is characteristic of the barren portion of the Highland Rim. Marble of a fair quality is found in the county.

The eastern portion, known as the "barrens," is covered mostly with a light growth of scrubby oak timber, and the soil has a whitish clay surface, with a porous, leachy subsoil, and is very sterile, except for the cultivation of fruits and tobacco. Elk Ridge is very fertile, and almost as productive as the best valley lands. It is heavily timbered with poplar, oak, chestnut, walnut, sugar, linden and locust. The valleys of the Elk, Hurricane, Mulberry and their tributaries, have a rich alluvial soil, which is very productive. The staple crops of the county, are wheat, corn, rye and oats. Blue grass is indigenous to the soil. Clover, timothy and most other grasses yield bountifully with proper cultivation. Stock raising is carried on to some extent, and the county, with its numerous springs, is well adapted to dairy farming, which however is not carried on to any considerable extent. The farms are not in as high a state of cultivation as they are capable of being brought. A good turnpike road leading from Shelbyville to Fayetteville passes directly through the county, via County Line and Lynchburg. The county is high, healthy, and well drained. It has no swamps to contaminate its atmosphere with malarial poison.

The first settlements in the territory now composing Moore County were made near the beginning of the present century, when bears, wolves, deers, and all kinds of game were abundant. Just when and by whom the first actual settlement was made cannot be stated, but the names of a considerable number of the earliest settlers can be given. William B. Prosser came from North Carolina and settled in this county in 1806, and William Spencer came in 1808. Isaac Forrester, born in South Carolina in 1790, settled here prior to the war of 1812, in which he participated. In 1816 he married Miss Matilda Hodges, and both are yet living. They are the parents of fourteen children, eleven of whom are still living. They have had eighty-nine grandchildren, sixty-nine of whom are living, and they have had nearly seventy great†grandchildren, sixty of whom are living, and two great-great-grandchildren, both living. A remarkable family—certainly they have obeyed the Scriptural injunction "Be ye fruitful, multiply, etc."

A Mrs. Wiseman, who was also born in 1790, is still living in this county. Frederick Waggoner and family settled in the county before the war of 1812, in which he participated in the battle of the Horse Shoe Bend. Woodey B. Taylor and his wife, Nancy (Seay) Taylor, parents of John H. Taylor (Uncle Jack as he was familiarly called), came from Georgia with their family in 1809, and settled on East Mulberry, about two miles below the site of Lynchburg. There was only one house then between their settlement and Lynchburg, and that one was at the place now owned by Mrs. B. H. Berry. At that time there were only two log-cabins in Lynchburg, one where Dr. Salmon now lives, and the other at Mrs. Alfred Eaton's place; Mr. Joel Crane then lived in the former. The same year, 1809, Andrew Walker came from South Carolina, and settled upon and mostly cleared the farm, and soon thereafter erected the house where Smith Alexander now lives. Samuel Isaacs then lived on the Jack Daniel's farm, and Daniel Holman lived in the next house down the valley. Anthony and Thomas Crawford, James Clark and Champion Bly were then living near Lynchburg. Mrs. Agnes Motlow, widow of a soldier of the war of the Revolution, settled in this county in 1809 or 1810, with her five sons, Zadoch, William, James, John and Felix, and two daughters, Elizabeth, who married Andrew Walker, of whom mention has been made, and Lauriet, who married Mr. — Massey. The Motlow family in this part of the State originated from the above ancestors. Reuben Logan settled here soon after 1800, and had many successful encounters with the wild animals. He killed many bears and deers, and was a soldier in the war of 1812.

James Cox and Mary, his wife, were among the first children born within the limits of Moore County. Dempsey Sullivan and Naomi, his wife, were born in this county in 1811 and 1812, respectively.

Michael Tipps settled in the county in 1813. His wife, nee Leah Scivally, was born here in 1810, and she is still living. Thomas H. Shaw, father of Elder Shaw, born at Perryville, Ky., in 1798, settled in this county before the war of 1812, in which he was a soldier under Gen. Jackson. He married a daughter of Thomas Roundtree, and was a magistrate for many years, and died in 1872. In 1815, James P. Baxter and family settled on the farm where John F. Taylor now resides. He was a county surveyor thirty-three years, and was a member of the commission to locate the Creek Indians. John F. Baxter was born in 1827, on the farm where he has always resided and still resides, without ever having been away from home seven days at a time. James S. Ervin settled in the county in 1816, and Martin L. Parks in 1818. The latter was an officer in the war of 1812. About the year 1812, a Mr. Brown and others erected the first grist mill in the county near where Jack Daniels' distillery now stands. Soon thereafter a distillery was established there, which was probably the first one in the county.

The first cotton-gin was erected near the same place in about 1818. Thomas Roundtree built the cotton-mill on the creek at Lynchburg, about the year 1820. At this time there was a cotton-gin and cotton-mill on East Mulberry Creek near the county line, owned by Levi Roberts. The grist-mill and cotton-gin at Lynchburg, was then operated by Wm. P. Long. A large tannery was also in operation at Lynchburg about this time. A Mr. McJimsey is said to have opened the first store in Lynchburg some time prior to 1820, at which time Wm. P. Long kept a general store in the same place. Barnes Clark, Wm. Howard, Wm. Bedford Mr. ——— Bird and Wm. Burdge were all among the earliest settlers in the county, and the three latter were among the pioneer school-teachers. For a number of years after the first settlements were made, and before local mills were erected, the people had to go all the way to Murfreesboro and to Mill Creek, near Nashville, to get their grinding done. John Guthrie with his family settled near the site of Dance & Waggoner's mill in 1820, and lived there until his death. Wm. Tolley, whose death occurred in 1884, settled in this county in 1825. Samuel Edens and his family were living at Lynchburg at that time. Stephen M. Dance and family settled in 1826, on the farm where J. T. S. Dance now resides. Joseph Call and Rebecca, his wife, settled in 1834, on a farm in the present District No. 6, where he died in 1842. Mrs. Call subsequently had three husbands and outlived all of them, and died in 1880, in this county.

Col. Davie Crockett, the great pioneer hunter and adventurer, resided for a time on a branch of the East Mulberry in this county. Moses Crawford came to this county in 1809, and lived at or near Lynchburg, and attended the "sale of lots when the town was laid off in lots and sold." The valleys were then covered with cane-brakes. The *Falcon* of March 20, 1885, published a letter from Mr. Crawford dated at Grand Island, Neb., where he then resided. This letter refers to the early settlement of this county, and especially the great earthquake shock so sensibly felt here in 1811. He says "the prevalent idea was, judgment is knocking at the door. The earth reeled as a drunken man. Mercy was sought and pardon found in many cases. * * * Preaching every four weeks at my father's house. Rev. Adams, of Flat Creek, was minister or pastor in charge. My father and mother were old members of said church for years before. People came from far to hear the Scripture propounded. The ministers were Adams, Hardy, Holman and Whittaker. The addition to the church was large every Sabbath. There were none but Baptists in this neck of woods. They used to take the applicant for baptism down to the ford, singing as they went. The place for immersion was near where Roundtree built his dam across Mulberry. Revivals stopped and drinking liquor began. I think I knew some of your ancestors. Two brothers by the name of Parks came there some time between 1815 and 1820, I think with Smiths. Time rolled on and rolled them off, and I soon shall follow."

Mr. Crawford then says "that after the war of 1812 closed, a clan of thieves was found in and about the present town of Lynchburg. And that in the neighborhood of Barnes Clark, a blacksmith three or four miles southeast of Lynchburg, stealing was as common as going to church. A member of this clan by the name of Woods, or something else, was lynched till he told of or showed the cave or warehouse of stolen goods. Old Hickory Jackson permitted the shooting of John Woods and a brother for stealing."

About this time it seems there were no laws in force here for the suppression of crime, and consequently the good people organized themselves into vigilance committees, and took the administration of justice into their own hands, and "Judge Lynch" presided at their meetings. They selected the large beech tree which stood over the spring, afterward known as the town spring of Lynchburg, for a whipping post, and after arresting offenders and becoming satisfied of their guilt, tied them to this tree and authorized some one to administer the whipping, which was generally very severe. Uncle Jack Taylor says he saw about twenty persons whipped at that famous tree, and three others at another tree, near which he now resides. In this way public offenders were punished for all kinds of crime until the courts were established, and the civil authorities sufficiently empowered to enforce the laws for the protection of society. The noted lynching tree stood until about the year 1880.

Like most rural counties Moore's industries have been limited principally to agriculture. Manufacturing, except in the article of whisky, has never been developed to any considerable extent. A few grist-mills and saw-mills, sufficient for the accommodation of the people, have been erected and operated. The manufacture of whisky has been extensive. In addition to what has already been mentioned, Samuel Isaacs and John Silvertooth erected a distillery on the German branch of East Mulberry, one and a half miles below Lynchburg, in about 1825; and near the same time another was erected by Mr. Isaacs, three miles below town.

Alfred Eaton erected a distillery in an early day, about two miles below Lynchburg. Calvin Stone erected one on West Mulberry in 1852. As the country improved numerous distilleries were constructed and operated, from time to time, in the territory composing the county. There are now fifteen registered distilleries in Moore County. Tolley & Eaton's, established in 1877, at County Line, is said to be the largest sour mash distillery in the State. It has a capacity of 98 bushels of corn and 300 gallons of spirits per day. It is all run by machinery. Jack Daniels', the next in size, was built in 1876, at the Cave Spring, at Lynchburg, where, it is claimed, the first one in the county was erected. The capacity of this distillery is 50 bushels of corn and 150 gallons of spirits per day. The other thirteen distilleries have an average capacity of 23 bushels of corn and 70 gallons of spirits per day. Then, when all are running, they will grind 447 bushels of corn per day and produce about 1,360 gallons of whisky. This is an immense industry. Suppose these fifteen distilleries to run their full capacity for six months, or 156 days, in the year, they would manufacture the immense amount of 202,160 gallons, or 5,054 barrels, of 40 gallons each, which, at $2 per gallon, would amount to the sum of $404,320. When these distilleries are running they consume, at an advanced price, all the surplus corn that the farmers can raise. They also consume thousands of cords of wood annually. They thus make for their farmers a home market for their grain and wood; and the revenue to the people of the county for the corn, wood and whisky is immense. The whisky manufactured here is known in commerce as Lincoln County Whisky, and is among the best manufactured in the United States. The capital employed in this branch of industry is said to pay 20 per cent. The manufacture of domestic goods is carried on, in the families, to a great extent.

The lands of the country are rich and productive, teeming with thousands of horses, mules, cattle, sheep and hogs. All kinds of grain, fruit and vegetables can be raised in great profusion. All kinds of grass, clover and millet grow to perfection. The highlands of the eastern part are especially adapted to the production of grape. The people are cordial and hospitable—primitive in their habits, and manufacture and wear a great deal of home-made clothing.

The county of Moore was organized in accordance with an act of the General Assembly of the State of Tennessee, entitled " An act to establish a new county out of portions of the territory of Lincoln, Franklin, Coffee and Bedford Counties, to be called the county of Moore, in honor of the late Gen. William Moore, of Tullahoma, Tenn., one of the early settlers of Lincoln County, Tenn., a soldier of the war of 1812, and for many years a member of the General Assembly of the State of Tennessee," passed December 14, 1871.

The act provided that the county should be bounded by a line described therein. And for the purpose of organizing the county, the following commissioners were appointed by said act, to wit: Berry Prosser, Lewis Morgan, J. B. Thompson, John D. Tolley, H. H. Smith, William Copeland, J. E. Spencer and S. J. Green, of the county of Lincoln; C. T. Shiver, A. J. Simpson, Goodwin Miller and Harvey Farris, of the county of Franklin; James G. Aydelotte, Mike Campbell, Thomas Colley and S. J. McLemore, of the county of Coffee; William Smith, W. P. Bobo and John Sullivan, of the county of Bedford; who, before entering upon their duties, should take an oath to faithfully and impartially discharge the same as such commissioners, And to ascertain the will of the people of the fractions of the old counties out of which the new county was to be composed, said commissioners were to cause elections to be held at as early a day as practicable in each of the fractions of the old counties to be included in the new one. And if the requisite constitutional majority was found to be in favor of the new county, the said commissioners were to complete the organization in accordance with the provisions of the act.

The act provided that said commissioners should have power to make any change in the lines of said county, if found necessary, so as to conform with the requirements of the constitution of the State—i. e., that none of the old counties out of which the new one was to be formed should be reduced below 500 square miles; and that they should cause an actual survey of the county to be made, and an actual enumeration of the qualified voters in the limits of said county to be taken, to ascertain if said new county contained 275 square miles, and 700 qualified voters. Accordingly, on January 6, 1872, said commissioners met at Lynchburg and organized by electing A. J. Simpson chairman and John D. Tolley secretary, and at once employed J. B. Thomison and R. F. Darnoby to survey the boundary line of the new county, to begin at 12 o'clock M., on Monday January 8, 1872, at or near Rev. J. W. Holman's place, on the Mulberry & Lynchburg Turnpike. The commissioners then adjourned until the 23d day of January, when a plat of the survey of said county was presented to them by said surveyors. The plat was accepted, and the surveyors ordered to make a full and complete written report of the survey, which they afterward did.

Three hundred and forty-one square miles were found to be included in this survey. Subsequently the commissioners learned that Coffee County contained less than 500 square miles, and consequently no portion of it could be attached to the new county. By this survey the county line was run eleven miles from the county seats of Bedford, Lincoln and Franklin Counties by surface measurement. This was not satisfactory to Lincoln and Franklin Counties, consequently each brought suit against Moore County to reclaim their lost territory. The matter was fully litigated in the Lincoln County Chancery Court, and finally decided that the line of Moore County should be established eleven miles, on a straight air line, from the county seats of the old counties from which it was composed. This made a new survey necessary between this county and both Lincoln and Franklin Counties. Bedford County brought no suit to enforce this "straight line rule," but allowed the line to stand as originally surveyed. This very materially reduced the county in size, so that it now contains only about 270 square miles, or about seventy-one square miles less than the original survey included.

On Saturday, April 13, 1872, elections were held in each of the fractions of the old counties to be included in the new, to ascertain the will of the people on the formation of a new county, and the votes cast were as follows: In fraction of Lincoln County for new county, 799; for old county, 51. In fraction of Bedford County, for new county, 59; for old county, none. In fraction of Franklin County, for new county, 284; for old county, 6. The requisite number of two-thirds having voted in favor of the new county, the county of Moore became established, and it only remained to perfect its organization. The commissioners then appointed Wm. Tolley, J. M. Spencer, Berry Leftwick, G. W. Byrom and F. T. Davis to divide the county into civil districts. The subdivision was made and the districts formed and named as follows: Lynchburg, Ridgeville, Marble Hill, Reed's Store, Tucker Creek, Wagoner's, Prosser's Store, Charity, County Line,

Hurricane Church and Wm. B. Smith's mill. The districts were numbered in the order named, from one to eleven. The commissioners then ordered an election to be held on on Saturday, May 11, 1872, for the purpose of electing county officers. Accordingly elections were held in each of the several districts, and the following officers duly elected: John A. Norman, sheriff; James W. Byrom, county court clerk; W. R. Waggoner, circuit court clerk; John A. Silvertooth, trustee; E. F. Brown, register; W. J. Taylor, tax collector. Magistrates, J. D. Tolley, J. W. Martin, B. F. Womach, A. J. Simpson, G. W. Byrom, C. H. Bean, A. C. Cobble, J. E. Spencer, R. L. Gillespie, Wm. Copeland, John Swinney, John L. Ashby, T. G. Miller, D. J. Noblet, A. M. Prosser, J. A. Prosser, L. Leftwich, Samuel Bobo, T. J. Baxter, J. L. Holt, J. M. Byrom, J. W. Eggleston and J. J. Burt. These magistrates elect assembled on the third day of June, 1872, at the house of Tolley & Eaton in Lynchburg, and organized and held the first county court ever held in the county, They organized the court by electing A. J. Simpson, chaiman, and John D. Tolley & D. J. Nobblett, associates. At this term the court ordered an election to be held in the several districts of the county on the first Saturday of July, 1872, to determine where the people desired to have the county seat located. The elections were accordingly held, and out of 499 votes cast, 465 were in favor of Lynchburg as the county seat.

The court then appointed a committee of one from each district to select suitable grounds for a jail and jailer's house, and a public square for a court house site. This committee selected a plat of ground 300 feet square on Mechanic Street for a public square, and a tract of one acre belonging to E. Y. Salmon, and lying across the creek, between the town and Parks' tan-yard. The Public Square was located by the court, as reported, and title acquired thereto by donation from the owners. The tract for the jail was purchased of Dr. Salmon, for $100. Before building the jail, the court decided that this lot was not suitable and convenient, and thereupon sold it at public outcry for $10, and at the August term, 1875, the court bought the present jail lot of Col. J. M. Hughes for $200. A committee, consisting of M. L. McDowell, A. C. Cobble, J. E. Spencer, B. F. Womack and J. L. Holt, was then appointed to let the contract for the building of a jail and jailer's house. The contract was awarded June 7, 1875, to Bobo & Stegall for $2,550, the building to be completed by the first Monday in October of the same year. At the January term, 1876, of the county court, the committee reported that the jail and jailer's house had been completed according to the contract. It was accepted and the committee discharged. The jail has two cells, 8x8 feet, made of heavy oak timber, and large nails driven in almost every square inch. It is a very safe jail. The house is in the shape of an L, the front consisting of two nice rooms for jailer's residence. It is situated on the lot bought of Col. Hughes, nearly opposite the Methodist Episcopal Church, and is a very neat and comfortable building.

On the 8th of January, 1884, the county court appointed a committee to select and secure a new location for a public square. And in July of the same year the committee reported that they had deeded the square on Mechanic Street back to its former owners, and secured title to the Public Square where the court house now stands. Their action was approved, and a building committee, consisting of R. B. Parks, John E. Bobo and W. D. L. Record, was then appointed, with instructions for the construction of a court house. This committee awarded the contract to S. L. P. Garrett. And at the April term, 1885, they reported that the house was completed according to contract, and that they had paid the contractor $200 for extra work over and above the original contract, thus making the total cost of the court house $6,875. The building was accepted by the court and the committee discharged. The court house is a very substantial two-story brick structure, 40x60 feet, with the county offices on the first floor, and the court rooms on the second. The people of the county are very fortunate in having good and sufficient county buildings. The county has no asylum for the poor. The latter are provided for by appropriations from the public treasury, by authority of the county court.

The sessions of the courts were first held in Tolley & Eaton's Hall; then the county bought the Christian Church, which stood on Main Street, on the east side of the Public Square. The courts were held in this church building until it burned down in December, 1883, after which the sessions were held in the schoolhouse on Mechanic Street until the court house was completed. The following is a list of the county officers and the time served by each:

County court clerks—James W. Byrom, the present incumbent, was elected at the first election, which was in 1872, and has been re-elected and held the office continuously ever since. This shows the high estimation in which he is held by the people. Circuit court clerks —W. R. Waggoner, 1872–74; Dr. W. D. Frost, 1874–78; J. A. Norman, 1878 to June, 1880, when he died; then B. H. Berry was appointed to fill vacancy. H. H. Neece, 1880 to present time. Sheriffs—J. A. Norman, 1872–78; H. S. Hudson, 1878–80; A. J. Travis, 1880–82; J. S. Hobbs, present incumbent, 1882. Registers—E. F. Brown, 1872–74; M. G. Osborn, 1874–82; J. R. Brown, present incumbent, 1882. Tax collectors—W. J. Taylor, 1872–74; E. F. Brown, 1874–76; J. A. Silvertooth (the trustee), 1876–82; B. E. Spencer (trustee), 1882. Trustees—J. A. Silvertooth, 1872–82; B. E. Spencer, the present incumbent, 1882. Clerk and master—Dr. E. Y. Salmon, 1872–80; W. A. Frost, 1880–84; R. B. Parks, present incumbent, 1884 to ——. Coroner—R. C. Hall, 1872–73; H. B. Morgan, present incumbent, 1873 to ——.

The following table shows the amount of taxes charged on the tax duplicates for the several years since the organization of the county, for county purposes, and the total amount charged for all purposes:

|        | County. | Total. |
|--------|---------|--------|
| 1872   | $3,863 29 | $ 7,726 59 |
| 1873   | 5,022 17 | 13,307 68 |
| 1874   | 2,953 20 | 11,265 81 |
| 1875   | 3,091 55 | 10,852 87 |
| 1876   | 1,984 36 | 8,962 91 |
| 1877   | 2,158 48 | 6,410 10 |
| 1878   | 2,358 97 | 6,057 07 |
| 1879   | 2,215 88 | 5,940 79 |
| 1880   | 2,461 13 | 6,131 12 |
| 1881   | 2,864 03 | 8,088 53 |
| 1882   | 2,418 30 | 6,684 89 |
| 1883   | 2,938 35 | 8,654 74 |
| 1884   | 3,458 63 | 9,393 21 |
| 1885   | 3,946 82 | 8,685 02 |

The indebtedness of the county for current expenses is about $1,000, and for balance due for the court house $1,431. The levy on the duplicate of 1886 will be about sufficient to liquidate the latter, thus leaving the county in a very good financial condition.

Prior to the year 1882 the general elections in the territory composing the county, for State and National purposes, were controlled by the old counties, the same as though Moore County had never been organized. In 1882, after the census of 1880 had been published, and Moore County was recognized in redistricting the State, it held its first election for officers of the Legislature. At the presidential election in 1884, the vote in the county stood as follows: For Cleveland, 906; Blaine, 53; St. John, 5; Butler, 5.

According to the census of 1880 Moore County contained the following number of inhabitants: White males, 2,766; white females, 2,691; colored males, 376; colored females, 355. Total white, 5,457; total colored, 731. Grand total, 6,188.

The county court is composed of the several civil magistrates of the several civil districts of the county, and is presided over by one of their number, whom they elect as a chairman. The county court clerk and the sheriff are officers of this court. The court meets in quarterly sessions the first Mondays of January, April, July and October. Quorum courts convene on the first Mondays of each month. For the organization of this court and a sketch of its proceedings, the reader is referred to the organization of the county, in which its history is interwoven.

The first term of the circuit court was held in the room used for court purposes in Lynchburg, beginning on the third Monday of June, 1872, the time fixed by act of the General Assembly of the State. W. P. Hickerson, judge in the Sixth Judicial District, of which Moore County forms a part, presided. The court was opened by proclamation made by J. A. Norman, sheriff. Whereupon W. R. Waggoner, clerk-elect, produced to the court his certificate of election and filed his bonds as required by law, and was duly sworn into office. J. W. Byrom, clerk of the county court, then officially certified the names of twenty-four "householders and freeholders" of the county, appointed by said county court at its June term, 1872, out of which the circuit court should select a grand jury. And out of the number so certified the following named persons were selected as the first grand jury of Moore County, viz.: J. T. Metlow, J. H. Taylor, B. F. Womach, Jacob Tipps, J. E. Spencer, J. W. Franklin, Wm. Tolley, J. L. Ashby, A. M. Prosser, P. G. Prosser, J. M. Byrom, J. J. Burt and J. F. Leach. Wm. Tolley was made foreman. H. S. Hudson and Wm. Cooper were appointed constables to wait upon the court. W. H. Allen and E. S. N. Bobo each presented his license as an attorney at law, and was admitted to the bar. The first cause of action in this court was Pique, Manier and Hall *vs.* John Read, to recover a judgment of $249.15 rendered by F. P. Fulton, a justice of the peace. The case was tried, and the court decreed that the land of the defendant be sold to satisfy the said judgment and costs. The grand jury, after having retired to inquire into "indictable offenses," etc., returned into court an indictment against Jeff Berry (colored) for assault, and four presentments against other offenders, to wit, Calvin Shofner, James Simpson, Daniel Downing and Hiles Blythe, for "carrying pistols." And thus ended the business of the first term of the circuit court.

At the next term, the court ordered that the first Monday of each term be fixed "as State's day for the county." Jeff Berry, colored, was then tried for assault by the first petit jury of "good and lawful men of the county," viz.: J. D. Smith, Wm. Richardson, W. A. Hobbs, A. C. Cobble, N. Boone, K. J. Bobo, E. J. Chambers, John N. Morehead, Wm. Copeland, Wm. Waller, Henderson Gilbert, and Walter Holt. The defendant was found guilty, and fined $5 and costs.

At this term, T. P. Flack, who professed to be an attorney at law, was arraigned for larceny. The attorney-general, being related to him, declined to prosecute, whereupon the court appointed Hon. W. D. L. Record attorney-general *pro tem.* to prosecute the defendant. Wm. Wricketts was then arraigned and tried for "horse stealing and larceny." He was found guilty, and was sentenced to jail and penitentiary for five years. At the February term, 1873, of this court, the grand jury found a true bill against Wesley Speck for the murder of John Jean. The defendant was tried, found guilty, and sentenced to twenty years in the penitentiary. An appeal was taken to the supreme court, where the sentence was affirmed. After serving for a few years the defendant was released by executive clemency. At the February term, 1885, Jordan Whitaker, colored, was tried for the murder of John Kiser, colored. The jury found the prisoner "guilty of murder in the first degree, with mitigating circumstances," and fixed his penalty at imprisonment in the penitentiary for life. Whereupon the attorney-general, A. B. Woodard, and Judge Williams joined in suggesting to the governor that sentence ought to be commuted to twenty years instead of for life. Also at this term James Silvertooth, marshal of the town of Lynchburg, was indicted for the murder of Bird Millsap. He asked for and obtained a change of venue to the Lincoln County Circuit Court, where he was tried and acquitted, on the ground that he committed the act in self defense. These are the principal criminal cases that have been brought in this court.

In the year 1875 there were 37 prosecutions for carrying pistols, 8 for assault and battery, and 7 for disturbing public meetings. In 1885, ten years later, there were 21 prosecutions for carrying pistols, 5 for assault and battery, and 3 for disturbing public meetings; thus showing that crime is on the decrease. Judge W. P. Hickerson presided over this court, either in person or by proxy, from its organization up to and including its October term, 1877, and Judge J. J. Williams, the present incumbent, has presided over it since.

The first term of the chancery court was held in the court room at Lynchburg, beginning on the fourth Monday of July, 1872, with Hon. A. S. Marks, chancellor, presiding. The court was opened in due form by Sheriff John A. Norman. Dr. E. Y. Salmon was appointed clerk and master, and filed his bond, to "safely keep the records of said office and faithfully discharge the duties thereof," and took the oath of office. He also filed a bond to faithfully collect and account for fines, taxes, etc., and another as special commissioner and receiver. There being no other business the court adjourned to "term in course."

At the next term of this court William Thomison and others filed a petition for a turnpike road from Lynchurg to Prosser and Sullivan's store, in Moore County, a distance of about six miles. A number of the petitioners were then named and appointed a body politic and corporate, by name of The Lynchburg & West Mulberry Turnpike Company. The capital stock was divided into shares of $95 each. At this term, December, 1872, the charter of the town of Lynchburg was amended so as to enlarge its powers and immunities. The first case brought in this court was "Lewis Newson vs. Mollie Neece and others." At the October term, 1873, E. S. N. Bobo, the county superintendent filed his report of the formation of school districts for Moore County, numbering them from one to eleven; and the court declared each one an incorporated town, with all the privilege conferred thereupon by law. At the June term, 1877, the members of the bar and visiting attorneys held a meeting, and passed resolutions of condolence upon the death of Hon. Abe Frizzell, a member of the Moore County bar, who died June 17, 1877. The first resolution reads as follows: "That in the death of Abe Frizzell this bar and community have lost a member, who in generosity of nature, kindness of heart, and charitable conduct was without an equal, and one who loved his neighbor better than himself. That while he had faults, they were so far outweighed by his many distinguished virtues, that the first are lost in the splendor of the last." Judge Marks served as chancellor of this court from its organization to the close of the June term, 1878. And from time to the close of the October term, 1883, Judge J. W. Burton served as chancellor. And since then Hon. E. D. Hancock, the present chancellor has officiated. R. B. Parks, the present obliging clerk and master was appointed in 1884.

Hon. Abe Frizzell was a member of the bar from the organization of the county until his death, in 1877. He was an able lawyer and fine business man. The following attorneys were all members of the bar at the organization of the county: W. A. Cole, a young and studious lawyer, who moved to Alabama some years ago; E. S. N. Bobo, who practiced until 1880, and then went into other business; W. H. Allen, who practiced only a short time; James M. Travis, who practiced a few years, and J. T. Galbreth, likewise; R. A. Parks, who now edits and publishes the Lynchburg *Falcon*, joined the bar soon after its organization, and has practiced ever since; W. D. L. Record joined the bar at its inception, and has been a constant practitioner ever since; R. E. L. Montcastle, a young and energetic attorney, joined the bar in 1885. The latter three are now the only resident attorneys.

The citizens of the territory composing Moore County have contributed their full share of soldiers to fight the battles of their country. A few of the early settlers were survivors of the war of the Revolution, and some of them served in the struggle of 1812, but it is impossible now to obtain an account of their names and services. A few survivors of the Mexican and Florida wars still reside within the county. Public excitement ran very high here at the outbreak of the late civil war. Public meetings were held at Lynchburg, and at other points throughout the county, and were addressed by Hon. Peter Turney and others, and the people were almost unanimously in favor of a Southern Confederacy.

The first company to enter the service was Company E, of the First Tennessee Confederate Infantry. This company was raised at Lynchburg in March, 1861, and joined its regiment at Winchester in the next month. The following is a list of the officers and privates who were mustered into the service, together with the recruits: Officers—Dr. E.

Y. Salmon, captain; T. H. Mann, first lieutenant; C. W. Lucas, second lieutenant; W. F. Taylor, third lieutenant; W. P. Tolley, first sergeant; J. P. Edde, second sergeant; T. H. Parks, third sergeant; J. N. Taylor, fourth sergeant; M. C. Parks, first corporal; J. H. Silvertooth, second corporal; A. W. Womack, third corporal; F. W. Motlow, fourth corporal; W. B. Taylor, ensign. Killed—Lieut. T. H. Mann, Sergt. J. P. Edde, Corp. J. H. Silvertooth, and Privates William T. K. Green, B. W. Shaw, B. R. Bobo, T. E. Brown, J. J. Lucas, J. W. Stockstill, John McCulley, W. M. Jones, W. A. Dillingham, J. F. Metcalf, J. T Hunter, C. M. Wade, William F. Morris, F. G. Motlow, Clay Hoskins and J. S. Green. Wounded—Lieut. W. F. Taylor, Sergt. W. P. Tolley, Sergt. J. N. Taylor and Privates M. L. Parks, A. F. Eaton, B. H. Berry, R. H. Crawford, O. J. Bailey, S. W. Edens, W. H. Hutchenson, George Jones, T. C. Spencer, T. D. Gregory, B. A. W. L. Norton, J. H. Brandon, M. A. L. Enochs, John Gray, and Alex. Bailey. Ensign W. B. Taylor and Private M. V. Hawkins each lost an arm, and Private Joseph S. Hobbs lost a leg. Died— Corp. A. W. Womack, Privates John W. Brown, W. C. Kirtland, W. H. Waggoner, David Roberson, W. A. Strawn, J. C. C. Felps, John R. Cates, F. D. Bedford, J. C. Jenkins, William F. Scivally, John D. Hinkle, F. A. Thurman, and Olla Overby.

The following are those who passed through the war without being wounded: Capt. E. Y. Salmon, Lieuts. C. W. Lucas, and A. F. Eaton, Sergt. T. H. Parks, Corp. M. C. Parks, Corp. F. W. Motlow, T. J. Allison, M. L. Parks, Jr., T. J. Eaton, C. D. Williams, Z. Motlow, J. K. Bobo, Anderson Edens, A. H. Parks, S. E. H. Dance, C. W. Felps, T. A. Chapman, J. M. Rhoton, F. F. Brown, W. C. Jones. J. R. Strawn, J. S. Hubbard, W. M. Miles, W. A. Parks, J. W. Robinson, J. P. Rives, J. S. Kirtland, Joseph Miles, J. R. Mullins, Jacob Mullins, Williiam M. Cowan, M. R. Cobbs, J. M. Shaw, W. M. Pearce, S. C. Tucker, James H. Holman, W. B. Daniel, F. Motlow, William M. Banks, Frank Edens, Sanford Stewart.

Officers after reorganization were W. P. Tolley, captain; T. H. Mann, first lieutenant; O. J. Bailey, second lieutenant; A. F. Eaton, third lieutenant. Capt. Tolley was wounded and retired, and Lieut. Mann was promoted to the captaincy, and at his death Lieut. Bailey was promoted to the captaincy and held it to the close of the war. Lieut. Lucas resigned during the first year of the war, and his place was filled by the election of Private A. H. Parks.

Company D, First Tennessee, Confederate States Army, was organized at Ridgeville in March, 1861, and joined its regiment at Winchester the next month. Its captain, N. L. Simpson, died during the war, and John Bevel then became captain. First lieutenant, ——— Awalt; lieutenants, William Davis, Thomas Baggett, Nat Norvell; Tuck Hill, Thomas Davis, Allen Pogue, Jacob Mitchell, Ben George, Henry Driver, Giles Powers and Thomas Taylor were among the killed in the service. Capt. John Bevel, Lieut. H. J. Byrom, Alex Reedy, John Clark, were among the wounded. J. W. Byrom lost left hand. R. H. Anthony, William Lewis and Isaac Mitchell each lost a leg. Thomas Reedy, John Clark, wounded; ——— Tribble, Olla Overby and Ezekiel Shasteen died in the service. Lieuts. John Tribble and Monroe Farris, and Privates Thomas Rogers, James Allen, Thomas Anderson, Tobe Anderson, Milt. Byrom, James Bailey, R. S. Anthony, Rev. William Anthony, chaplain of the regiment, L. A. Rogers, Larkin Rogers, Benjamin Shasteen, H. W. Farris, Joseph Pogue, George Sanders, William Fanning, Wes. Fanning, Watch Cook, William Jones, Dick Jones, James A. Sanders, A. A. Davis, E. J. Chambers, Henry McGivens, G. Raney, W. Weaver, George Weaver, Ben Hutton, James Hutton, E. Brown, Toliver Hendricks, John Hendricks, Turner Childs, Dr. ——— Childs, R. A. Overby, H. C. Bolen, Joseph Bolin, ——— Smith, John McKinzie, John Strong, John Cobble, William and Robert Majors, H. Pilot and Gabriel Lewis—all are supposed to have served to the close of the war. The information concerning this company were given by county court clerk, J. W. Byrom, who gave it to the best of his recollection.

Company H, Eighth Tennessee Confederate States Army, was raised by Capt. William L. Moore from this and adjoining counties, and consisted of 104 men. When the regiment was organized Capt. Moore was elected lieutenant-colonel, and

William J. Thrash, was made captain of the company. The company was organized with its regiment at Camp Trousdale, in Sumner County, May 29, 1861. The following named persons enlisted from what is now Moore County: Benjamin Morgan, Frank Johnson, Lieut. J. G. Call, W. L. Davidson, W. H. Martin, Joseph Stacy, P. Y. Mitchell, Alexander Brady and John Reese, all of whom were killed in the service. And L. A. Farrer, W. J. Taylor, Nat. S. Forrester, Lieut. John Sullivan, Berry Leftwich, Brittain Carragan, P. A. Raby, Lieut. John D. Tolley, H. L. W. Boon, Alex. Crane, Stephen Johnson, M. M. Dean, Wilson Call and John Raby, all of whom were wounded. And James and Rufus Morehead, both of whom died in the service. The following are supposed to have served to the close of the war: Albert H. Boon, Joseph Broughton, Wiley H. and John S. Carrigan, Jas. H. C. Duff, John Eslick, Isaac V. Forrester, Enoch Glidewell, Geo. C. Logan, H. D. Lipscomb, W. M. Montgomery, Geo. F. Miller, E. M. Ousley, B. H. Rives, John C. Raney, John B. and Robt. F. Steagall, John B. Thomasson, Daniel J., George A., Geo. W., Sr., Geo. W., Jr., Felix M. Daniel N., George H., Felix, Henry A., and Riky Waggoner, Edward D. and James W. Whitman, Wm. A. Woodard, Elijah W. Yates, Benj. Broughton, Green B. Ashby, W. N. Bonner, Isaac Evans,'W. R. Evans, Geo. W. Gattis, Sr., J. H. Leftwich, Jacob C. Morgan, Jas.ꝑF. Massey, J. F. M. Mills, Ellis Mills, F. M. Moyers, Jas. W. Mitchell, Jas. Marr, Jas. M. Major, Wm. Norvall, John Owens, E. B. Raby, Jos. M. Sebastian, Stephen P. Wiler, John C. Waid, W. H. Webb.

Company C, Fourth Confederate Infantry, was raised by Capt. J. W. Smith, with headquarters at Ridgeville, and consisted of over 100 men. It joined its regiment at Knoxville in July, 1861. It was raised wholly within the territory now belonging to Moore County. Capt. Smith has kindly furnished us the following list of names of members composing his company: James Osborn, James Cobble, Henry Farrar, James Jackson, John Graves, John Steagall, T. W. Steagall, George Shasteen, Alfred Travis, Joseph Rose, Thomas Pearson, T. Roberson, M. J. Brown, Robert Brown and Tom Shasteen—all of whom were killed in the service. And Marion Bedford, M. A. and W. B. Couser, S. Dillingham, John Eaton, Robert Farmer, James Gore, H. Gore, John Byrom, George Damron, H. Nelson, Samuel Rolan, Thomas Raney, H. Rosenberger, J. F. Mitchell, J. Hammontree and Polk Nix—all of whom were wounded. And William Brannon, J. A. Cobb, Enoch Garner, Davis Marshall, Javan Nelson, John Buchanan, P. Osborn, William Runnells, Allen Revis, A. Shasteen, Ed. Rose, C. L. Parks and N. M. Ivey—all of whom died in the service. A. Cummins, James Osborn and James Burt were discharged on account of disability. And Capt. J. W. Smith, Lieuts. G. W. Byron, D. P. Muse and R. Simpson, and Sergt. S. J. Shasteen and the following non-commissioned officers and privates: G. W. Anderson, D. G. Branch, George and Samuel Brown, W. M. Browning, D. R. Bedford, J. R. Bolin. A. W. and E. A. Cobble, E. Bolin, J. P. Damron, D. Ellis, William Evans, Henry Fullmore, J. C. Gobble, Stephen Hanes, Doll Byrom, Henry Miles, Isaac Dannel, Henry Ivey, Tom Graves, Tom Muse, William Curle, Sam Ray, M. Runnells, Doe Runnells, William Shasteen, Elijah and Jacob Shasteen, H. and R. Smith, Ralph Gray, R. Riddle, J. Pardon, Dan Baker, Levi Lawson, Stephen and John Pilant, Sam Parks, Henry Bevell, J. Y. Price, J. Hendricks, James and William Travis, A. J. Parks, J. J., William and M. and C. Tankesley, W. W. and Alfred Burt, E. Brown, Jack Ivey, James Hudgens, James Rodgers, William Smith, George Tipps, Joe Ford, H. M. Bean, M. Holt, N. Thompson, W. M. Tucker, J. Timms and J. R. Parks—all served to the close of the war.

Company G, Forty-first Tennessee Confederate Infantry, was raised in the vicinity of Marble Hill by C. H. Bean, who was its original captain. Sergt. J. M. Waggoner has kindly furnished us the following roll of officers and men: Captain, W. E. Murrel; lieutenants, W. N. Taylor, G. S. Tipps (killed) and H. H. Johnson; sergeants, J. J. Matlock, A. Smith, G. Hall and J. M. Waggoner; corporals, G. W. Davis, R. C. Hinds, J. Hill, W. H. Noah and G. W. Reneger. Privates, Conner Awalt, E. M. Bean, J. W. Bowling, J. B. Benson, Wm. and Abe Brazzelton, Nick Copeland, Fletch Church, James

Cooper, H. Church, Jesse and James Ethridge, W. C. Grant, T. H. Hall, Zib Frily, Rich Groves, Richard Hill, Jack Hall, J. F. Hall, I. H. Hall, T. J. Hise, J. K. Higgenbotham, J. H. Higgenbotham, S. M. Lewis, Samuel Morris, J. M. Mayes, George McClure (killed), Z. R. Murrel, F. M. McCoy, John Morris, J. M. McKinzie, P. J. Noah, M. Powers, H. G. Renegar, W. C. Roach, G. R. Scivalley, J. V. Scivalley, G. W. Syler, J. N. Scivalley. S. W. Smith, Kit Smith, Pen Sandredg. John Tipps, J. F. Tipps, J. C. Tipps, W. J. Tipps, C. M. Taylor, J. H. Vanzant, Izaac Vanzant, W. M. Wiseman, R. C. Wiseman. J. T. Wiseman (killed), M. G. Waggoner, G. W. Wicker, J. M. Woods, W. D. Young, M. V. Wiseman.

Company A, Forty-first Tennessee Confederate Infantry, Capt. James, was partially raised in the vicinity of Charity, and the following is a list of names of those who joined it from the territory now belonging to Moore County. Lieut. H. B. Morgan, who lost his left arm at the battle of Franklin, H. H. Neece lost right arm at Atlanta. Lieutenant L. Leftwich, Henry Davidson, J. C. Davidson killed at Franklin, Mart Collier, J. R., T. M. and Robt. Rees, J. B. Rainey, M. A. Prosser, Wash Cox, Joseph Brock, Nat and M. B. Rees, and Thos. Albright.

The following named persons joined Forrest's escort, which organized at Shelbyville in the fall of 1862, and joined the army at Murfreesboro after its return from Kentucky: F. G. Motley, S. J. Green and W. T. K. Green, killed in the service; W. F. Taylor, received seven wounds; Lieut. John Eaton and Privates J. N. Taylor, T. J. Eaton, D. R. Bedford, D. H. Call, E. Clark, T. M. Dance, M. A. L. Enochs, C. W. Lucas, and Orderly-Sergt. M. L. Parks were among those who served to the end of the war without being wounded. This command served under Gen. Forrest during the war, and surrendered May 10, 1865, at Gainesville, Ala.

In 1862 Samuel Dillingham, of Confederate fame, while at Cumberland Gap visited a distillery, and filled a canteen with "Mountain Dew." He corked it tight, and sent it home, and afterward declared that when the next Democratic President was elected he intended to uncork it. Accordingly, in May, 1886, he turned it over to a select committee, consisting of H. B. Morgan, J. Y. Price and W. W. Holt; and on Saturday, June 13, following, due notice having been given, the committee. after appropriate remarks had been made by H. B. Morgan, uncorked the canteen in presence of a large audience in the court house. Drs. Dancer and Taylor inspected the contents. and pronounced it old bourbon, of the genuine article.

The people of the territory composing this county suffered great loss during the late civil war, and lived in constant fear of death from marauding parties and bushwhackers. Being a rich agricultural district it was constantly preyed upon by foraging parties sent out from the armies stationed at these points. It is hardly probable that any county in the State of Tennessee furnished more, if as many, soldiers in the late civil war as did Moore County, or rather the territory now composing it, in proportion to its population.

Thomas Roundtree, who lived in the log house on the lot where Dr. E. Y. Salmon now resides, was the original proprietor of the lands on which Lynchburg is located. He laid out the town about the year 1818, and, as the famous beech tree, used as a lynching post, where early offenders were punished, stood over the spring near his house, he very appropriately named the town Lynchburg. Lots were laid out and numbered on the street south of the court house, and sold at public sale; but, no records having been preserved, it is impossible to give date of sale and names of purchasers. For the early settlement of the town and its first business interest, the reader is referred to "early settlements." It being a rural town, without an outlet for its commerce, its growth has been generally slow. Lynchburg was incorporated by an act of the General Assembly of the State, at its session in 1841-42. The charter was amended in 1872, by the Chancery Court of Moore County, in conformity with an act of 1870-71, Chapter 54, Section 1, and following. It was so amended as to confer all the rights and privileges, powers and immunities conferred upon municipal corporations, from Sections 1358 to 1399 inclusive, of Thomson and Steger's Code. The early ordinances and record of proceedings of the municipal authorities were destroyed in the fire of 1883. The revised ordinances, now in force, were adopted January 12, 1885, and published in the *Falcon* of January 16, 1885. Within a few years, about the time of the organization of Moore County, the population of Lynchburg more than doubled. The fact of its becoming a county seat gave it an impetus to improve. In 1874 it contained five dry goods houses, whose signs read Parks, Eaton & Co., Hiles & Alexander, J. L. Bryant & Co., D. B. Holt, M. N. Moore & Co.; one drug store, Salmon & Frost; three drinking saloons; two good flouring-mills, under the firm names of Hiles & Berry, Womack, Dance & Co.; two planing-mills, Spencer & Co. and Bobo & Steagall; one tannery, by M. L. Parks; the boot and shoe shop of M. T. Allen; the saddle and harness factory of Stafford & Cummins; one cooper-shop, by Colsher Bros.; a tin-shop; two wagon-shops, and three blacksmith-shops.

In December, 1883, a fire broke out, which consumed a large portion of the town, including the old Christian Church, then owned and used by the county as a court house. The town has been rebuilt and the business re-established. In 1867 Womack, Dance & Co. erected a cotton-mill with a capacity of over 300 spindles. It required about a dozen hands to run it, and did a flourishing business until 1870, when it burned down. Then in 1871 the flouring mills now owned by Dance & Waggoner were erected on the same site.

Dr. S. E. H. Dance commenced the practice of medicine here in 1856, and still continues. And Dr. E. Y. Salmon, whose biography appears elsewhere in this work, began practicing here in 1857. Dr. J. N. Taylor began the practice in April, 1872, and is still in practice.

The societies at present are Lincoln Lodge, No. 50, I. O. O. F., which has a charter dated May 14, 1849. Jas. McBride, W. C. Byron, Thos. J. Lindley, J. A. Silvertooth and W. F. Smith, were the members named in the charter. The lodge has a membership of thirty-five, and is in a flourishing condition.

Lynchburg Lodge, No. 318, F. & A. M., has a charter dated December 5, 1866. The officers named in the charter are J. T. Motlow, W. M.; E. Y. Salmon, S. W.; and D. L. Enochs, J. W. There are about twenty-five members belonging to the lodge at the present writing, "who dwell together in peace and harmony."

The first newspaper published in the county was the *Moore County Pioneer*. It was established at Lynchburg in 1872 by James R. Russ, who continued its publication until near the close of 1874, when it suspended. The Lynchburg *Sentinel*, W. W. Gordon, editor, was established in April, 1874, the first number being issued on the third day of that month. Mr. Gordon continued to edit and publish the paper until December, 1878, when he sold it to Mr. W. A. Frost, who continued its publication until it was burned out in the great fire of 1883.

The first number of the Lynchburg *Falcon*, R. A. Parks, editor and proprietor, was published February 15, 1884. It is a good county paper, well patronized, and satisfied the demands of the people. The press of Moore County has been ably edited, and has always been, as it now is, Democratic in politics.

Dr. J. N. Taylor, the present able and obliging postmaster in Lynchburg, has the honor of being the first postmaster appointed under the new administration by Postmaster-General Vilas. His commission dates early in April, 1885. At present writing (June, 1886) Lynchburg contains the following business houses: J. L. Bryant & Co., general store and millinery store—the latter superintended by Mrs. M. J. Morgan; Dr. S. E. H. Dance & Son, drug-store; Parks & Evans, saloon; Billingsley & Bailey, general store; Parks, Taylor & Co., general store; Waggoner & Roughton, general store; Tolley & Eaton, wholesale liquor dealers, warehouse; Tolley & Bedford, pork packers; McDowell & Son, undertakers; M. F. McGregor, carriage manufacturer; Warren & Co., blacksmith-shop; J. H. Warren, wagon-maker; J. W. Stafford, saddles and harness; W. J. Walker, and George Daniel, colored boot and shoe shops; Wash. Chrisman, colored, barber-shop; Dance & Waggoner, merchant mills; Jack Daniels, distillery; G. G. Mitchell, tannery; Colsher Bros., cooper-shop; Allison & Moore, first-class livery, sale and feed stable. The town has two good hotels, one conducted by Mrs. McClellan and the other by Mrs. Salmon. There are two good schools and five churches—one Primitive Baptist, one Methodist Episcopal South, one Christian, and two colored churches, one Methodist and the other Christian. The population is about 350. The municipal officers are R. A. Parks, mayor; J. T. Bickley, recorder; M. L. Parks, treasurer; A. R. Hinkle, T. F. Roughton, S. M. Alexander, W. H. Colsher, aldermen; H. R. Blythe, town marshal.

The first house in Marble Hill was built by Allen Johnson, about 1835. It stood alone about ten years, and has been occupied, in order of time, by Allen Johnson, John J. Angel, Dr. Thomison, Mrs. Cole and Jacob Tipps, the present occupant. The first business house was built by Allen Johnson about 1844. About 1855 three other business houses, general stores, were erected by Robert Wiseman and John Whitfield, Wm. Whitfield and Isaac Parks. Also, there were erected two saddlery-shops, two shoe-shops, two blacksmith-shops —one of the latter was run by Thomas & John Graves, the other by "Pink" Cole. Over a dozen dwelling houses were built about the same time (1855). R. Richardson & Co. have erected the only business house since the war. There are two churches, one large schoolhouse, two doctors, Drs. Ferass and Tripp. The town was nearly destroyed during the war. County Line contains one distillery (Tolley & Eaton's), one school, two churches, two general stores, a blacksmith-shop and postoffice. Ridgeville contains one general store, one school, one church and a blacksmith-shop. Charity contains one general store, two churches and a blacksmith-shop.

The early settlers of the territory composing Moore County had, in common with the early settlers of all new counties, very meager opportunities for educating their children. No free public schools were then established. The country was a vast wilderness, which had to be cleared and subdued in order to furnish homes and provisions for the pioneer, his wife and children. They had to labor hard, and had but little time which they could devote to the education of their children. There were a few school-teachers among the early settlers who taught private subscription schools. They would contract with the parents to teach their children a specified time for a stipulated price, usually agreeing to teach spelling, reading, writing and arithmetic—rarely anything more. Those who could afford it sent their children to these schools, and those who could not had to raise their children with scarcely any educational advantages.

As time rolled on, and the country developed, small academies were established at a few villages, and later a meager school system was inaugurated by the State, and finally the present system of free schools, which promises efficiency in the future, was formulated and established. Among the early teachers we may mention Andrew Walker. William Bedford, Mr. Bird and William Burdge. The two latter taught school on the old Taylor place, near the present residence of Uncle Jack Taylor. William Pegram was a later teacher. The old school-masters kept order and enforced obedience with the rod. Uncle Jack Taylor was a pupil of Andrew Walker, and the latter whipped twenty-four boys in his school in one day—all the boys except two, Uncle Jack being one of the latter.

The Lynchburg Male and Female Institute was chartered by an act of the General Assembly of the State, passed January 24, 1870. J. T. S. Dance, D. B. Holt, Dr. S. E. H. Dance, M. N. Moore and J. A. Silvertooth were named therein as charter members of the association. This school opened soon after receiving its charter, and has always been well sustained by the people. It has had an average attendance of from 80 to 100 pupils, and has had as high as 150 at one time. It is deservedly popular, and is doing excellent educational work. The school year consists of two sessions of five months each. It has generally had two teachers; Prof. W. W. Daffron is the present able principal. He is assisted by Miss Rosa Tolley, who is also a successful teacher. This institute is controlled by a board of trustees, the members of which are elected annually. The school building, which is large and commodious, is very pleasantly located on the east bank of the Mulberry, just above the town. This school is an outgrowth of the academy which was established there several years before the late civil war. The building was erected in 1856, and enlarged in about 1866. Prior to the war, and up to the date of its charter, as the "Lynchburg Male and Female Institute," the school was conducted as an academy, and it is one of the few schools in this paat of the State that did not suspend its sessions during the war.

The Lynchburg Normal School was chartered by an act of the General Assembly of the State. The charter is dated June 25, 1885, and the charter members are John D. Tolley, J. T. Motlow, T. J. Eaton, Dr. J. N. Taylor, C. M. Wilson, Dr. S. E. H. Dance, Dr. E. Y. Salmon and M. N. Parks.

This school opened on the first Monday of August, 1885, with about forty-five pupils. Prof. T. W. Estill is the principal, and Miss Lura L. Motlow, teacher of music. The school year consists of two sessions of five months each. The Lynchburg Normal School is centrally located, and is the young rival of the Lynchburg Male and Female Institute, and is making laudable efforts to excel the latter, if possible, in educational work. It has been well sustained and patronized during its first year's work. Persons desiring to locate in a healthy, rural town, with first-class educational facilities, can not do better than to locate at Lynchburg. To show the present condition of the schools of Moore County, is appended the following items from the county superintendent's report for the year ending June 30, 1885: Scholastic population, between the ages of six and and twenty-one years—white males, 976; white females, 962; colored males, 140; colored females, 104. Total, 2,182. Number of pupils enrolled during the year—white males, 710; white females, 627; colored males, 74; colored females, 65. Total, 1,476. Average daily attendance—white, 924; colored, 82. Total, 1,006. Number of schools in the county—white, 25; colored, 4. Total, 29. School districts, 16; consolidated schools, 2. (These latter are the Lynchburg Male and Female Institute and the Lynchburg Normal School.) Receipts of school funds for the year, $3,348.18; expenditures for the same time, $3,193.13. Number of teachers employed—white males, 17; white females 14; colored males 5. Total, 36.

Average compensation of teachers per month, $25.35. By reference to the foregoing it will be observed that only two-thirds of the scholastic population attend school, and less than one-half are in daily attendance. There are seven frame and twelve log schoolhouses in the county.

The religious history of the territory composing this county began with its first settlers. Among them were pioneer ministers who began to labor in the "Lord's vineyard" when they struck the first blow to erect their log cabins in which to shelter their families. A Mr. Adams, Hardy Holman, John Whittaker, Levi Roberts and Aldrich Brown were ministers and Christian workers among the first settlers, who began their labors, both physical and spiritual, with full faith that God would reward their efforts.

The Christian workers among the first settlers seem to have been Primitive Baptists and Episcopal Methodists. The former erected the first church within the territory composing this county in the year 1812 or 1813. It was a log structure located at the place known as Bethel, a short distance above Lynchburg. Anthony and Thomas Crawford, James Clark, Champion Bly, William Smith and his son, William, were members of this church.

About 1814 a Methodist Episcopal Church, "Wesley Chapel," was built at "Enoch's Camp Ground." And soon thereafter the Allen Church was erected about one and a half miles below Lynchburg. The Baptists established a church at County Line about the year 1820, and Brannon's Methodist Episcopal Chapel was erected about the same time, and later the Olive Branch Methodist Episcopal Church was erected. Revs. Joseph Smith, Lem Brannon and Stephen M. Dance were among the pioneer Methodist ministers.

The Ebenezer Church near Marble Hill and the Union Church about five miles southeast of Lynchburg, both belonging to the Evangelical Lutherans, were organized about 1826, and the church of the same denomination at Pleasant Hill was organized about 1845. Rev. William Jenkins was the principal worker in the organization of these churches. He was assisted in pastoral work by Revs. John and Benjamin Scivally and Richard Stephens, who were prominent among the pioneer preachers. The Waggoners, Scivallys, Awalts and Beans were early members of these churches. Services are continued at these three churches, Rev. L. R. Massey, a resident minister, and others officiating.

Before many church edifices were erected the people of all denominations met at the old camp grounds, near the sparkling waters of some noted spring, and there in the cool shade of the forest mingled their devotions to Him through whose care they had been enabled to endure and overcome the hardships of pioneer life. As the country developed and more churches were erected the camp-meetings were finally discontinued.

The first Christian Church in the county was built in Lynchburg in 1849 and dedicated in June of that year by Elder S. E. Jones. This building stood on the present Public Square and was purchased by the county soon after its organization, and used as a court-house until it burned down in 1883. The first regular ministers of this church were Elders T. W. Brents and Calvin R. Darnall. Since the late civil war Elder Thomas J. Shaw has been and still continues the regular minister. The first members of this church were Thomas J. Shaw and wife, E. H. Womack and wife, Nancy C. and Eliza Womack, W. P. Bobo and wife, B. H. Berry, R. B. Parks, James McBride, T. E. Simpson and wife, and Sarah J. Simpson.

The Christian Church at County Line was erected in 1877, and dedicated the same year by Elders Wm. H. Dixon and C. M. Crawford. The new Christian Church in Lynchburg was dedicated September 26, 1875, by Elder Thomas J. Shaw. The Methodist Episcopal Church at Lynchburg was established in 1872. The first trustees were J. T. S., J., W. M. and S. E. H. Dance, J. B. Price and B. M. Edens. The ministers have been G. W. Anderson, J. P. Funk, W. C. Collier, T. H. Hinson, G. W. Winn, J. W. Bell and the present pastor T. L. Darnall. When this church was established, it had a membership of about forty, which has increased to about ninety. The Methodist Episcopal Churches now in the county are—the one just described, one at Marble Hill, Brannon's Chapel on Coffee Creek, one at Pleasant Hill, Smith's Chapel, Friendship and Wiseman's Chapel. The Missionary Baptists have a church at Charity. The Baptists, one at County Line, one at Chestnut Ridge and the Hurricane Church. The Cumberland Presbyterians have one church, Moore's Chapel, recently established near Charity. The Christians have a church at County Line and one at Liberty Hill. The Primitive Baptist Churches are Bethel, Harbor and Mulberry. There are three colored churches in the county, one Methodist Episcopal and two Christian.

# FRANKLIN COUNTY.

OLIVER N. ALDEN was born August 16, 1817, in Yarmouth, Barnstable Co., Mass., being a son of Oliver and Lucy T. (Alden) Alden. The parents were direct lineal descendants of the sixth generation of John Alden, who was one of the pilgrim flock that immigrated to America in 1620. The grandfather of our subject, Timothy Alden, was for sixty years pastor of one church in Yarmouth, Mass. The subject of this sketch moved with his parents from Massachusetts to Meadville, Penn., at the age of twelve; thence the family removed to Cleveland, Ohio. The father died in Ohio and the mother died in Wisconsin. Oliver N., in early life, learned the carpenter's trade, at which he worked till 1849, when he went to Wisconsin and entered land near Oshkosh, where he successfully remained in the pursuit of farming till 1873, when he removed to Neenah, Wis., and lived there until 1884, when he removed to Sherwood, Tenn., on account of his health. Here he engaged in merchandising in the spring of 1885, continuing but a short time. He now owns his Wisconsin farm of 120 acres. He was married, in 1841, to Miss Theodosia H. Morton, of Ohio, the fruits of this union being six children, three of whom are now living: Clinton H., in Papillion, Neb.; Violet M., in Oshkosh, Wis.; and Oliver N., in Orcas, Washington Territory. The mother of these children died in 1868, and December 21, 1870, Mr. A. wedded Miss Caroline Alden, also a direct lineal descendant of John Alden. Mrs. Alden was born in Springfield, Mass., and her last residence in that State was in Boston. Her maternal ancestry were direct descendants of the Sears family that first appeared in England in 1016, in the person of Knight, who was engaged with Edward Ironsides against Canute. Through the intermarriages of this noted family, Mrs. Alden is a descendant of the house of Norfolk and of the royal houses of both England and France.

JOHN F. ANDERSON, one of Franklin County's oldest citizens, was born February 27, 1808 in Sullivan County, Tenn., being a son of Thomas and Mary (Davis) Anderson. The father was born in Abington, Va., and when a child immigrated to Sullivan County, Tenn., whence in 1812 he removed with his family to Bedford County, Tenn., and in 1819 near where Sherwood now is. Here he entered twenty-two acres of land and engaged in the pursuit of farming and hunting. He removed to West Tennessee in 1834, and afterward to Mississippi, where he died. The mother was born in Philadelphia. Her father was killed in the Revolution, and she then moved to Sullivan County, Tenn., with a stepfather. She died in West Tennessee about 1835. The subject of this sketch was eleven years old, when coming to Franklin County. In 1828 he bought ten acres of land on credit, and began the pursuit of farming. He surmounted the primitive and numerous obstacles in his road and continued to farm until he amassed an immense estate; at one time owning 26,000 acres of land. He was active in securing the building of the Nashville, Chattanooga & St. Louis Railroad, and for many years was a director of that road. He now owns about 16,000 acres of land. He was married August 23, 1827, to Miss Mary Hendricks, a cousin of the late Thomas A. Hendricks. The fruits of this union were twelve children, two of whom are now living—Cyrena (the wife of Larkin Willis) and Thomas B. The mother of these children died about 1854, and on August 23, 1855, Mr. Anderson was again married to Mrs. Mary Stephens, *nee* King, the results of this union being nine children, seven of whom are now living—George C., Luke W., Lou H. (wife of Dr. Jones Keith), Fay (wife of Henry M. Bunn), Virginia L., Charles W. and May B. Mrs. Anderson was the mother of three children by her former marriage. Two of them are living—William Stephens and Elizabeth (Stephens), wife of James Brown. Mr. Anderson, wife, and several of the family are members of the Christian Church. Mr. Anderson has built a church of worship himself, to which he invites all Christian denominations. He also employs a minister, and he often says: "If the minister don't preach to suit me, I'll turn him off and hire another." He is a Democrat in politics and is a member of the F. & A. M. He has the name of being "the most liberal man in Tennessee."

CAPTAIN CLEM. ARLEDGE, clerk and master of the chancery court, was born June 1, 1826, being one of nine children, the fruits of the union of Clem. Arledge, Sr., and Martha Ginn, natives of South Carolina, from whence they came to Franklin County, Tenn., in 1818. The father was a farmer; he departed this life in 1851, and the mother followed him in the year 1857. Clem. Arledge was reared on a farm. At the age of twenty-six he married, and settled to farming. In 1856 he removed to Texas, and in two years returned to his native county. He was in the Confederate service as captain of Company F, Turney's First Tennessee, from 1861 to 1862—one year—when he resigned on account of temporary loss of sight in both eyes, and perpetual blindness in one eye. In 1871 Capt. Arledge was elected clerk of the county court of Franklin County, efficiently holding that office for twelve years, until 1882. In January, 1883, he was appointed to the office of which he is now the incumbent. He was married, in 1853, to Eliza Roseborough, a native of Franklin County. She has borne ten children to this union, one of whom is dead—viz.: Josiah J., James C., John, Jesse B. (deceased), Robert L., Samuel L., Thomas M., Mattie S., Dora and Willie. Mrs. Arledge is a member of the Methodist Episcopal Church South. Capt. Arledge is a firm Democrat in politics, and is an enterprising and respected citizen of the county.

GEORGE E. BANKS, of the law firm of Simmons & Banks, was born in Bridlington, England. When eighteen years of age he crossed the ocean to America, landing in New York in April, 1867. He then taught school in Delaware one year, and in April, 1868, came to Franklin County, Tenn., where he taught two years. He then went to Kansas, and remained two years; thence returning to Franklin County, where he engaged in the manufacture of boots and shoes until the spring of 1885. He then went on a visit to Europe, and remained there three months. He then returned to Winchester, and engaged in the practice of law, at which he has since been occupied. He was married, January 10, 1869, to Miss Mattie Johnson, of this county, the fruits of this union being four children, one of whom—George E.—is now living. Both Mr. Banks and his wife are members of the Episcopal Church. Mr. Banks has no relatives in America, he being the only one of the family that came to this country.

JAMES P. BARTON, M. D., of Maxwell, this county, was born in Wilson County, Tenn., February 12, 1851, and is one of a family of seven children born to William and Margaret (Lane) Barton. The father is still living, and has been a minister of the Missionary Baptist Church in Wilson County, Tenn., since nineteen years old. He was born in that county in 1814. The mother is a daughter of William Lane, an old soldier in the Revolutionary war, and is also still living. Our subject was educated at Gibson University, and also taught school prior to his majority. May 7, 1872, he married Miss Anna Pate, native of Putnam County, Tenn. To this union three children have been born: James O., William O., Ada A., all still living. Our subject attended the Louisville Medical College in 1876, and then the medical department of the University of Tennessee at Nashville, in 1877, and soon after moved to this county and has since been practicing medicine. Dr. Barton and his family are members of the Missionary Baptist Church. Politically he has always been connected with the Democratic party.

EZEKIEL M. BEAN was born August 31, 1833, in Franklin County, Tenn., and is a son of William Bean, who was born in Lincoln County, and married Sallie Lindsey, who was born in East Tennessee. They became the parents of five children, only two of whom are living—our subject and a brother. After the mother's death the father married Anna Weaver, and both are still living in the county. After attaining his majority Ezekiel M., in the month of August, 1854, wedded Louisa Marshall, who was born in Franklin County, Tenn., and to their union were born fifteen children, all of whom are living and five are married. During the late war he was with Ferguson's command two months, but returned home on account of ill health. In 1874 he purchased and located on his present farm. Mr. Bean and part of the family belong to the Methodist Episcopal Church, and the rest are identified with the Lutheran Church. Our subject votes the Democratic ticket.

JOHN K. BENNETT, a prominent merchant of Decherd, Tenn., was born April 23, 1840. His father, H. K. Bennett, was a son of John Bennett, one of the very early settlers of Franklin County, and a well-to-do man, having dealt extensively in lead-mining interests. H. K. Bennett was a farmer; he died in 1847. The mother of John K., was Clarissa Keeton, a daughter of John Keeton, one of the very first pioneers of the county and a very prominent citizen, having held the different public offices in the county. When fourteen years of age our subject found himself on his own support. He went to Atlanta and engaged at manual employment for a time, and in 1857 engaged as a mercantile clerk there, which he continued till the fall of Atlanta before Sherman. He then returned to Franklin County, and soon established his mercantile trade, which he has continued very successfully ever since. Besides merchandising he carries on farming and stock-dealing. His stock of merchandise is about $3,500, and he transacts a yearly business of from $10,000 to $15,000. He was first married in 1858 to Miss M. T. Allen, of Atlanta, who bore him three children, viz.: John E., Lycurgus L. and Bettie, now the wife of C. D. Jackman, of Kentucky. Mrs. Bennett died in 1872, and Mr. Bennett married Mrs. Lavina Parks, who became the mother of two children—Charles and Lavina—and died in 1877. In 1878 Mr. Bennett chose and wedded Miss Florence Hines, the result of this union being four children—Daisy, Robert, Edgar and Minnie. Mr. Bennett and family are members of the Christian Church. Politically he has always been a Democrat. He is an enterprising and respected citizen of the county.

HENSON G. BLANTON (deceased) was born in Bedford County, Tenn., February 12, 1821, and died in Franklin County, Tenn., December 10, 1877. His father, William Blanton, was a North Carolinian, and came with his mother to Bedford County, Tenn., in the early settlement of that State and county. Our subject remained with his parents until his majority, then read medicine, and attended the Louisville Medical College, after which he began practicing in Franklin County. In 1844 he was united in marriage to Miss Eunice Van Zant, who was born in Franklin County, and eight children were born to this union, six of whom are living—James (a physician practicing in Alabama), Mary, Joseph, Charles (also a physician of Alabama), Edward (a physician at Maxwell, Tenn.) and Hugh.

WILLIAM M. BOUCHER, proprietor of the Franklin Hotel, at Cowan, Tenn., was born in Randolph County, Mo., February 2, 1825. His father, Robert Boucher, was born about 1795, in Madison County, Ky., where he was reared. He then went to Howard County, Mo., in 1818. He married Elizabeth Willcockson, in 1821, and then removed to Randolph County, Mo., where he died in 1871. The mother was born in Clark County, Ky., in 1805 and died in Randolph County, Mo., in 1867. These were parents of twelve children. William M., our subject, at the age of twenty-one, entered Masonic College, Missouri, and attended one term. In 1850 he went to California and engaged in gold mining three years. Returning home, he married Sophia Darby, in 1853, and followed farming until 1870, with the exception of a few months, near the close of the war, when he was drafted and assigned to Company I, Sixth Missouri Infantry, joining his company at Washington, he was sent to Louisville and thence to Little Rock, where he was mustered out of service. In 1871 he moved to Huntsville, Mo., where he remained six years and thence immigrated to Franklin County, Mo., where he has since lived. Mr. Boucher has a family of three children now living, there having been eight born to his marriage. In 1884, Mr. Boucher opened up the Franklin Hotel, in the building which was built by Drs. Sloan and Williams, at a cost of $6,000, for that purpose. By the hospitality of both Mr. and Mrs. Boucher, the Franklin Hotel has gained no little fame along the Nashville, Chattanooga & St. Louis Railroad as a first class hotel. Mr. and Mrs. Boucher are members of the Missionary Baptist Church.

PETER C. BREEDEN was born in Memphis, Tenn., November 29, 1846, and is one of a family of three born to Archibald and Mary A. (Heistand) Breeden. The father was a native of Virginia, and when a young man came to Franklin County, Tenn., where he followed the carpenter's trade all his life, and died in the same county May 8, 1859; the mother having preceded him in the year 1851, August 23. From the time of his mother's death our subject lived with an aunt until he attained his majority, after which he followed manual labor and clerking until 1874, when he engaged in the mercantile business at Huntland, Franklin Co., Tenn., and followed that with success for ten years, when in March, 1885, he disposed of his stock of goods and retired from the business, at least for a short time. But since then Mr. Breeden has not been idle, as he has built a good commodious dwelling house on his property in Huntland, in addition to the one occupied by himself and family. December 11, 1878, he married Lila M. Deford, a native of Lincoln County, Tenn. To this union three children, all girls, have been born—Susan, Mary and Sallie, all living. Mr. and Mrs. Breeden are members of the Christian Church, and Mr. Breeden is a strong advocate of the principles of prohibition.

W. W. BRITTAIN, fruit grower and nurseryman, was born June 13, 1827, in Rutherford County, Tenn. His father, John Brittain, was born in North Carolina, in 1791, and in 1812, came to Rutherford County, Tenn., where he lived and died. In his early day, he, the father, was a cabinet-maker and also an extensive fruit grower and nurseryman, and at his death, in 1859, left an orchard of sixty acres. He was the first man to peddle fruit in Nashville, and was at one time awarded a ten-dollar silver cup as first premium on grape wine at the State Fair. The mother, nee Martha M. Smith, was born in Rutherford County, Tenn., in 1802. and lived all her life in her native county, her death occurring in May, 1882. The subject of this sketch was the third of a family of eight children. He came to Franklin County, Tenn., in 1856, and began farming and fruit-growing, which he has continued very successfully, now owning 140 acres in Franklin County, and 80 acres in Florida on which is an orange grove. He has the most extensive nursery in the county, and an orchard of about 20 acres. He was married in about 1855, to Sarah H. W. Blair, of Rutherford County, the result of this union being three children, two of whom are now living—Martha Ann, John (deceased) and William. The mother of these children died in August, 1864, and in December, 1871, Mr. B. was married to Elizabeth T. Lyons, who is the mother of these children—Ethel, Columbus L., James D., Elmer and Floyd. Mr. B. is a Master Mason and an active Democrat in politics. He enlisted in May, 1862, in Company F, Fourth Tennessee Cavalry, and served three years, receiving a gunshot wound in the knee. He is an enterprising and highly respected citizen of the county.

STEPHEN W. BROWN, a noted mill-wright of this county, was born in McMinn' County, Tenn., in 1825. Of the family of nine children born to his parents, James and Anna (Kelley) Brown, eight are still living, The father was born in Virginia in 1780, but came to East Tennessee when a child, where he met and married the mother. They followed the tanning trade and farming all their lives. The father died July 4, 1876, the mother in 1877–78. Our subject remained with his parents until his majority, then spent seven years in the Cherokee Nation, after which he moved to Franklin County, Tenn., where he has since resided, following farming in connection with his trade. August 24, 1848, he married Mary A. L. Patton, a native of Coffee County, Tenn. To this union six children have been born, all still living. Mr. Brown, with his family, are members of the Cumberland Presbyterian Church, he being an ordained minister in the Jackson Presbyterian. Mr. Brown has recently constructed and fitted up one of the very best flour-mills in the county. It is located on Bean Creek, two and a half miles north of Huntland, near his residence, and was begun on President Cleveland's inaugration day. The water wheel for this mill is constructed upon an entirely new principle, and was designed and built by Mr. Brown, its chief superiority over the old wheel being the simplicity of the gear, thereby considerably economizing power.

DAVID L. BUCKNER is a native Tennesseean, born in 1846. He is one of five children born to James and Susan (Stephenson) Buckner, both of whom were born in Tennessee, the former in 1820.    James Buckner was a dentist of considerable note.    He was sheriff of his county and frequently conducted his prisoners to Nashville on horseback. The father died in 1863 and the mother in 1857.    Our subject made his home with his parent until the breaking out of the war, when he enlisted in Company H, Forty-third Tennessee Infantry, which, after the siege of Vicksburg, was changed to cavalry.    Three of his brothers were in the service, and all except our subject were officers.    After return-ing home David began the study and practice of dentistry, and in two years' time moved to Bedford County, where he remained five years.    One season was spent in Texas, after which he returned to Tenneseee and located in Maxwell, Franklin County, where he has a lucrative practice.    The Doctor has a very desirable country home, and in connection with his profession takes pleasure in following horticultural pursuits.    In 1866 he married Elvie Jenkins, a native of Sullivan County, Tenn., and to them were born two children— one now living, Edward.    Mrs. Buckner died in 1868, and October 29, 1873, Mr. Buckner wedded Mary Justin, a native of New York.    They have two children—James and Freddie.

JOHN M. DONALDSON is one of six surviving members of a family of seven chil-dren, and was born in Franklin County, Tenn., in 1837.    His parents, William and Ellen (Morris) Donaldson, were born in North Carolina and Tennessee, respectively.    The for-mer was born in 1811, and came to Tennessee with his parents in 1819.    He married the mother in 1836, and followed farming until his death, which occurred June 7, 1864.    The mother died August 31, 1883.    John M. assisted his parents until the breaking out of the war, when he, in 1862, enlisted in Company K, Fourth Tennessee Cavalry.    He participated in the battles of Chickamauga, Mission Ridge, Lookout Mountain, Kenesaw Mountain, At-lanta, Goldsboro, N. C., and was fortunate in not being wounded during service, although his horse was killed under him in the battle of Dover.    May 4,1875, he married Ara Phillips, of this county, and this union was blessed with one child, Ellen L.    In 1876 they moved to their farm of 250 acres.    They also own a tract of 105 acres elsewhere in the county. Mr. and Mrs. Donaldson are members of the Christian Church, and he has always been identified with the Democratic party, and believes in prohibition.

REV. WILLIAM PORCHER DU BOSE, S. T. D., professor of ethics in the academic department and of exegesis in the theological department of the University of the South, was born April 11, 1836, in Winnsboro, S. C., being of Huguenot descent on both sides. He was graduated from the Military Academy of South Carolina in 1855, and received the degree of M. A. from the University of Virginia in 1859.    He then entered upon the study for the ministry.    In 1864 he entered the Confederate Army and served as adjutant until 1864, when he was ordained and appointed chaplain of Kershaw's Brigade, serving in that capacity until the close of the war.    He was then successively rector of the churches of Winnsboro and Abbeville, S. C., and, in 1871 was elected chaplain and professor in the University of the South at Sewanee.    He resigned the chaplaincy in 1883, but has filled the chair of professor ever since coming to Sewanee, being one of the ablest and most de-voted members of the faculty.    He was married, in 1863, to Miss Anne B. Peronneau, who bore him four children, of whom three are living—Susan P., Mary P. and William H.    The mother of these children died in 1873, and Dr. Du Bose was then married to Mrs. Maria L. Yerger, nee Rucks, daughter of Judge Rucks, of Nashville.    Dr. Du Bose received the degree of S. T. D. from the Columbia College of New York.

THOMAS A. EMBREY was born in Winchester, Tenn., February 27, 1861.    His father, Alexander S. Embrey, was also a native of Franklin County, Tenn., his birth oc-curring in 1833.    He was a merchant all his life, and was in business in Winchester with a brother for over thirty years, doing a leading business of the place.    He departed this life July 7, 1884, having been preceded by his wife on January 21, 1883.    The parents reared but one child, and his name heads this sketch.    Thomas A. was reared in Winches-ter, having good educational advantages.    He began the reading of law in Winchester, and then took a course in the law department of the Vanderbilt University, of Nashville. He was admitted to the Franklin County bar in February, 1883.    He was married Octo-ber 19, 1883, to Miss Fannie Lindsey, of Gainesville, Tex.    Mr. Embrey and wife are mem bers of the Methodist Episcopal Church South. He is a Democrat in politics, and is one of the highly respected attorneys and business men of the county.

FLOYD ESTILL, an attorney of Winchester, is a son of Frank T. and Catharine (Garner) Estill. The father was also an attorney; he was a native of this county, and a son of Dr. Wallis W. Estill, one of the most eminent physicians who ever lived in the county. Dr. Wallis W. Estill came from Virginia to Franklin County in the early settlement of the county, where he lived nearly all his life. He died in Georgia in 1862, while acting as a surgeon in the Confederate Army. Frank T. Estill was born in 1822, and died in 1878, being a leading member of the bar and a popular citizen of Franklin County. He was elected to the Legislature of Tennessee when but about twenty-one years of age. He was county surveyor for a time after the war. He reared a family of eleven children; of fourteen born to his marriage, ten are now living. Floyd Estill was born November 11, 1859, and was reared in Winchester. He read law in Winchester and at Fayetteville, and engaged in the practice of law before twenty years of age in Nashville, and in January, 1883, formed his present partnership under the firm name of Estill & Whittaker. He married Miss Nora Landis, of Bedford County, Tenn., November 10, 1885. Himself and wife are members of the Cumberland Presbyterian Church. Politically Mr. Estill is a firm Democrat.

NATHAN FRANCIS, the editor and publisher of the *Franklin County News*, was born August 23, 1858, in Franklin County, Tenn., being one of the family born to the matrimonial union of W. R. Francis and Margaret McIlheran. The father is a farmer of Franklin County; he was born in Virginia. The mother was born in Franklin County, Tenn. The subject of this sketch was reared on a farm to the age of fifteen, at which time he entered the State University at Knoxville, Tenn., which he attended one year. He then attended the Winchester Normal School and graduated from that institution. He was elected to the office of clerk of the Circuit Court of Franklin County, efficiently serving in that trust till 1886—one term. For four years he taught school in his county, previous to his term of office. In 1886 he took charge of the *News*, his first issue being June 4 of this year. Mr. Francis was united in marriage December 25, 1883, to Miss Lulu Wood, of Scottsboro, Ala., the fruits of this union being one daughter, Grace. Both himself and wife are members of the Cumberland Presbyterian Church. Politically he is a firm Democrat. He is an advocate of prohibition, and is a promising young man of the county.

REV. THOMAS FRANK GAILOR, M. A., S. T. B., professor of ecclesiastical history and polity, and chaplain of the University of the South, was born in Jackson, Miss., September 17, 1856. His mother, who is still living, was Miss Charlotte Moffett, the youngest daughter of an Irish family which came to the United States in 1849, and which boasts that for nearly 200 years it has given one or more of its sons in each generation to the ministry of the Episcopal Church. His father was Frank M. Gailor, a New Yorker by birth, who went to Mississippi in 1853, but moved to Memphis, Tenn., and was associated with M. C. Gallaway on the editorial staff of the Memphis *Avalanche*. When the war broke out he entered the Confederate Army, and after gaining distinction on the fields of Shiloh, Munfordsville and other places, he was killed while leading the Thirty-third Mississippi Regiment to the charge at the battle of Perryville, Ky., October 8, 1862. Rev. Prof. Gailor received his early education in Memphis, Tenn., which he still claims as his home. He was graduated with the degree of B. A. at Racine (Wis.) College in 1876, and took the M. A. degree from the same institution in 1879. He received his theological training in the General Theological Seminary, New York, where he was graduated in 1879, and earned the degree of S. T. B. In 1879 he was ordained to the ministry of the Episcopal Church, and for three years had charge of the Church of the Messiah in Pulaski, Giles Co., Tenn. In 1882 he was elected to the professorship of ecclesiastical history and polity at the University of the South, and in 1883, was made chaplain of the university, both of which positions he now holds. In November, 1885, Prof. Gailor married Miss Ellen Douglas Cunningham, daughter of George W. Cunningham, Esq., of Nashville, Tenn.

J. A. GAINES, dealer in a general line of merchandise in Winchester, established business October 1, 1882, and has been successfully selling goods ever since. He was born in South Carolina, in 1835, and was reared in that State. He remained in his native State till 1881. When young he had the advantages of a common school education. When twenty-one he began the blacksmithing business, having learned the trade before. This he pursued and doing a general mechanical business, as long as he lived in South Carolina, also carrying on merchandising there for several years. In 1881, he moved to Sweetwater, Tenn., and in 1882 came to Winchester, as stated above. He was married in 1859 to Miss Margaret Pegg, of South Carolina. Eleven children were born to this union, nine of whom are living, viz.: Ora A., Nettie F., Pauline, Carrie, Julian, Raymond P., Charles, Ira and Frank. Mr. Gaines and wife and his three older children are members of the Methodist Episcopal Church South. He is a Royal Arch Mason. Politically he is a Democrat. His parents were from Virginia and were of Welsh descent.

IRVIN C. GARNER, a merchant of Winchester, was born March 23, 1837, near Winchester. His father, Charles C. Garner, was born in Rutherford County, N. C., January 18, 1800, and when two years old went to Kentucky where he lived a short time, and then, with his parents, came to near Winchester, where he died May 6, 1882. He was a farmer by occupation, was a well known man, and was also one of the prominent farmers of the county The mother, nee Beulah Wadlington, was born near Princeton, Ky., in 1806, and when a girl came to this county, where she is now living. Irvin C. began clerking in a store at the age of fifteen, and continued to do so till the war. In May, 1861, he enlisted in Company C, Turney's First Tennessee, and was in the service till September, 1861, when he was discharged on account of disability. He returned to his command in May, 1864, and remained till the close of the war. He then resumed mercantile pursuits till 1867, when he began general merchandising for himself, which he has continued ever since. He was married, March 20, 1866, to Mary C. Pryor, a native of Winchester, born September 29, 1844, the result of this union being two children—Nannie P. and Beulah T. Mrs. Garner and oldest daughter are members of the Cumberland Presbyterian Church. Mr. Garner is a member of the K. of H. and of the K. & L. of H. Politically he has always been a Democrat.

JOHN H. GILLESPIE is a native of Huntsville, Ala., born in 1813, and an only child of James T. and Clarkia (Gillespie) Gillespie. The father was born in Pennsylvania, and was in the war of 1812 and was killed at Horseshoe battle, on the Coosa river, September 14, 1814. The mother was born in Louisiana, and died in 1870. John H. remained with his mother until her death. He was married to Sarah Morris in 1832, and to them were born nine children, seven of whom are living—Mary E., William J., John D., Cynthia, Ruth, Monroe and Charles E. Mr. Gillespie and family are earnest members of the Christian Church. Originally he was an old-line Whig but at the present time has no particular preference. He is a strong advocate of prohibition.

ZUINGLIUS C. GRAVES, LL. D., president of the Mary Sharp College, of Winchester, Tenn., was born April 15, 1816, in Windsor County, Vt., being a son of Zuinglius C. and Lois M. (Snell) Graves, natives of Massachusetts and of German descent. When our subject was but five years old his father died, and he was then reared by his mother to the age of sixteen. At this age he entered the Chester Academy of Vermont, and afterward attended the Black River Institution at Ludlow, Vt., graduating from this school in 1837. He then went to the Western Reserve, Kingsville, Ohio, and founded the Kingsville Academy, of which he was president for twelve years. In December, 1850, he was called to Winchester, Tenn., to establish and conduct the Mary Sharp College, the presidency of which he has held ever since. From the very germ he has developed Mary Sharp to be one of the very best colleges for the education of women in the country. Dr. Graves was licensed to preach in the Missionary Baptist Church when nineteen years of age. The degree of A. M. was conferred upon him by the Madison University of New York, and the degree of LL. D. by the Union University of Murfreesboro, Tenn. He is a man wholly attached to his work, and has had under his charge as many as 10,000 different pupils during his career. He was married at the age of twenty-five, in Kingsville, Ohio, to Miss Adelia C. Spencer, the fruits of this union being four children—James R., who was killed in the late war; Florence M., who died after becoming the wife of Henry Green, a commission merchant of Columbus, Ga.; Zu. D., deceased; and Hubert A. Dr. Graves is an enterprising and valued citizen of Franklin County, and one of the eminent instructors of the State.

ISAAC GRAY is a son of George Gray, who was married to Lucy Benning and became the father of seven children, only three of whom survive. George Gray was born in 1777, in North Carolina (his father being in the Revolutionary war at the time), and came to Kentucky when a boy. In 1809 he came to Franklin County, Tenn., and soon located on the farm where our subject now lives. There the father died in 1859, and the mother in 1844. Isaac Gray was born in 1815, and spent three years, from 1847 to 1850, in Arkansas, in the tanning business; and with the exception of these three years has always lived in Franklin County. He is well preserved and is a hale, hearty and jovial old bachelor, and, although over seventy years old, can see to read without the aid of glasses better than most men of fifty. He owns a fine tract of 1,200 acres of land, and is considered one of Franklin County's successful financiers. He is a member of the Christian Church, and was formerly a Whig, but is now a Democrat and a firm believer in the principles of prohibition.

THOMAS D. GREGORY, one of Tennessee's eminent attorneys, was born December 31, 1842, in Lincoln County, Tenn. His father, Brown Gregory, was also a native of Lincoln County, and by occupation was a farmer. In 1852 he removed from his native county to Franklin County, Tenn., where he remained till his death in 1858. The mother, *nee* Mary McClellan, is yet living; she was born in Lincoln County, Tenn. The subject of this sketch was reared on a farm and received a common school education. At the age of eighteen he entered Turney's First Tennessee Regiment, Confederate States Army, and served throughout the war, being promoted to adjutant of the regiment and serving in that capacity the last eighteen months of the war. Returning from the war he began the reading of law with A. S. Marks, of Winchester, and in September, 1866, was admitted to the bar. He is a man of fine physical build and of marked firmness of character. He was married, in 1868, to Miss Mary Simmons, a native of this county. Two daughters have been born to this union. Their names are Lena and Lou. Politically Mr. Gregory is a firm and active Democrat. He is a member of the State Democratic Executive Committee. He has never aspired to official honor, but is a popular and leading member of his party in that part of the State in which he lives. He is a member of the I. O. O. F. and of the K. of H.

GEORGE O. HANNUM, principal of the Sherwood Academy, was born February 2, 1833, in Belchertown, Hampshire Co., Mass., being of English descent. He is the son of a farmer, his parents both dying in Massachusetts, of which State his father was a native. His mother was a native of Connecticut. He received a fair early education, and remained with his parents to the age of twenty-one, when he was married. He then engaged in farming and teaching until 1868, in his native State. He then removed to Winnebago City, Minn., where he taught school and farmed; also, a part of time, he was engaged in the flouring-mill business. In the spring of 1883 he removed to Sherwood, Tenn., and has since had charge of this academy. His marriage ceremony was solemnized in 1856, uniting him in wedlock to Amelia Nutting, a native of Amherst, Hampshire Co., Mass. Both Mr. and Mrs. Hannum are members of the Union Church at Sherwood, and are valued citizens of the place. In Massachusetts Mr. Hannum was on the board of superintendents of schools, and was for a series of years an assessor and supervisor under municipal government; and in Winnebago, Minn., he was justice of the peace.

JAMES L. HATCHETT was born in 1838 in this county, and is one of three children born to Archard and Sarah (Lucky) Hatchett. The father was born in 1782, in Virginia; came to Rutherford County, Tenn., in 1806, where he remained a few years, and then came to this county, locating on the farm where he lived and died, which is also the birthplace of our subject and his present home.  He followed farming, making stock raising a specialty, and was an associate of David Crockett, with whom he frequently hunted game in this vicinity; and even now their initials may be seen carved together on many trees in this county.  His first wife, Susan Sublet, bore him eleven children, and died about 1834; he then married our subject's mother, a native of North Carolina.  She was born in 1799, and died in May, 1879.  The father died May 24, 1852.  Our subject remained with his parents until their deaths; but on the day of his majority he married Jane Larkin, a native of this county, to whieh marriage eight children were born, all living.  The mother of these children died March 23, 1875.  In the fall of 1862 he enlisted in Company K, Fourth Tennessee Cavalry, with which command he remained until the close of the war, and then returned to his farm, which he has since cultivated, devoting considerable attention to stock raising.  Mr. Hatchett and family are members of the Cumberland Presbyterian Church.

JOHN HESSLER, an enterprising farmer of Franklin County, was born December 18, 1823, in Saxony, Germany.  His father was Conrad Hessler, and his mother was *nee* Margaret Kluge.  The father was born in Prussia.  He served eight years under Napoleon I, participating in the great battles of Leipsic, Moscow and Waterloo.  He died in Saxony in 1856.  The mother was also a native of Saxony, where she died a few weeks before the death of the father occurred.  In 1844 John Hessler came to America, where he found employment in carpet factories in New York and Baltimore for about twelve years.  In 1856 he moved to Fort Wayne, Ind., where he followed the same occupation for two years.  He then removed to Wabash, Ind., and there worked at his trade a short time, and then engaged for about ten years in tenant farming.  He then immigrated to Franklin County, Tenn., where he farmed as tenant for seven years, and then bought the farm whereon he now lives.  While in New York he married Margaret Klein, a native of Darmstadt, Germany, who became the mother of ten children, eight of whom are still living.  She died May 24, 1855, in Wabash County, Ind.  Mr. Hessler has a good farm of 250 acres, which he has paid for with the products of the place.  It is splendidly improved, considering that when he bought it it was an old and worn-out farm.

ISEBRAND H. HEIKENS is a native German, born in 1839, and is one of six surviving members of a family of seven children, born to Heije and Trientje, who were born in 1804 and 1806, and died in 1858 and 1884, respectively.  Our subject remained with his parents in Germany and worked on a farm until twenty-two years of age, and then, in company with a twin brother, came to America locating first in Stephenson County, Ill., and later purchased a farm in Iowa, where they remained eleven years.  Our subject then came to Tennessee, and purchased the farm of 460 acres where he is now living.  October 30, 1866, while in Iowa he married Aafke Jaspers, who was born in Germany and immigrated to America about the time our subject did.  After having borne seven children Mrs. Heikens died August 11, 1880; and June 4, 1883, Mr. Heikens married Laura Pack, of Franklin County, Tenn.  They became the parents of two children, one of whom is living, and the mother died February 13, 1886.  Mr. Heikens' children's names are—Heije, Berend, Trientje, Hinderina and Margarethe by his first wife, and Georgia by his last wife.  Mr. Heikens has never taken much interest in American politics, but is a civil and law-abiding citizen.

REV. TELFAIR HODGSON, D. D., of the Protestant Episcopal Church, was born in Columbia, Virginia, March 14, 1840.  He graduated at the College of New Jersey at Princeton, N. J., in 1859.  He studied theology in the General Seminary, New York, 1860; entered the Confederate Army in 1861.  In 1863 he was ordained to the lower order of the ministry (the Diaconate) at Savannah, Ga., and to the priesthood at Columbus, Ga., in 1864.  From 1866 to 1869 he had charge of St. Mary's Church, Keyport, N. J.; then, in 1869–70, he traveled in Europe, returning to Keyport, N. J., in 1871.  He was professor of philosophy at the University of Alabama 1872–73, and was assistant in Christ Church, Baltimore, Md., 1874.  From 1874 to 1878 he was rector of Trinity Church, Hoboken, N. J.  In 1878 he took the chair of vice-chancellor of the University of the South,

Sewanee, Tenn., and is still in that office, much of the grand success of that institution being due to him. While at Keyport, N. J., Mr. Hodgson was president of the New York & Freehold Railroad Company and of the Matawan & Keyport Gas Light Company. Dr. Hodgson has published several sermons, reports and fugitive pamphlets. He is a man of high intellectual powers and a vigilant worker.

SAMUEL C. HOGE, one of the leading merchants of Sewanee, was born in Alabama in 1839, and was reared in his native State, receiving a common school education. At the age of eighteen he began mercantile clerking, which he continued until the war, when he enlisted in Company C, Third Confederate Cavalry, remaining in the service until the close of the war. After the war he moved to Cowan, Tenn., and engaged at farming one year, and then in merchandising for a time. He then went to Jasper, Tenn., and for one year engaged in merchandising, and in 1869 came to Sewanee, and established his present business three years later, in 1872, since which time he has done a thriving business. He has a stock of about $4,000, and transacts a yearly business of about $20,000. He was married, in 1872, to Miss Tommie Holland, the fruit of this union being four children: Nellie W., Eunice H., Nannie and John E. Mrs. Hoge is a member of the Cumberland Presbyterian Church. Politically Mr. Hoge is a Democrat. He was postmaster for ten years under Republican administrations, and is now the postmaster at Sewanee. The parents of Mr. Hoge were James and Nancy (Kelly) Hoge, natives of Virginia. They died in Alabama, having been among the very early settlers of Wills Valley, Ala.

WILLIAM B. HOLT was born January 15, 1824, within eight miles of where he now lives, being one of ten children, the fruits of the union of Jacob Holt and Elizabeth Byrom. The father was one of the early pioneers of the county; he was born in 1799, and died in 1874. He was married four times and had a family of twenty-seven children. The mother was a daughter of Henry Byrom, one of the earliest citizens of Franklin County, who came from South Carolina and died in this county. He reared a family of ten children, and was a highly respected old citizen of the county. William B. Holt was reared on the old-time farm and has seen the county develop from a howling wilderness to its present state of civilization and cultivation. He delighted in the sports of hunting and fishing. When twenty-two years of age he was married, in the year 1846, to Miss Sallie Holt, who bore him nine children, eight now living: James H., Eva E., deceased; Turley C., the wife of Rufus Daniel; William J., John A., Thomas M., Joe L., Mary J., wife of Henry Furgerson; and Martha A., wife of James Chilton. He engaged in farming, and has continued it ever since. For fifteen years after his marriage he ran a blacksmith-shop, and then engaged in gunsmithing, which he has continued ever since. He now owns 450 acres of good land. Himself, wife and six children are members of the Baptist Church. Mr. Holt has taken notice of things that have passed by him, and enjoys his old days in thinking over pioneer times.

HENRY S. HUDGINS, dealer in a general line of merchandise at Estill Springs, was born June 7, 1847, in Williamson County, Tenn., being a son of John J. and Maria (Coleman) Hudgins. The father now resides in Franklin County. He was born in Mecklenburg County, Va., in 1803, and has been a farmer all his life. When young he came to Williamson County, where he lived till 1856, when he removed to Franklin County. When Henry S. was but six years old his mother died; he remained with his father to the age of twenty, when he engaged in farming in Franklin County, until November, 1884, when he began merchandising, which he has very successfully continued. He was united in the bonds of matrimony in 1866, to Rebecca B. Muse, a native of Franklin County. This union has been blessed in the birth of five children, all of whom are living: Mary A., James H., William D., Kindred W. and Burthal. Mr. Hudgins, his wife and his oldest daughter are members of the Baptist Church. He is a Democrat in politics, and is one of the enterprising and respected citizens of the county.

CHARLES L. JONES, an enterprising farmer of this county, was born in Franklin County, Tenn., in December, 1829, and is the youngest of two sons and one daughter born to Wm. L. and Mary (Arnett) Jones. The parents were both born near Richmond,

Va., and married there, but afterward moved to this county, where their family of three children were born and raised. The father was born May 31, 1792, and died January 16, 1857. The mother was born May 6, 1806; died July 28, 1861. In 1852 our subject married Rebecca J. Harris, native of this county, and to them was born one child, dying in infancy, the mother of which also died in 1853. October, 1858, he married Susan Horton, also native of this county, to whom five daughters have been born, one dying in infancy, and another, Mary E., in October, 1882. The names of the three remaining are Ella J., Belle and Willie. Mr. Jones has followed farming all his life on the place where he now resides—a splendid farm, well improved, and on which are several very fine and never-failing springs. He and his family are members of the Baptist Church; he also being a member of the F. & A. M., and identified with the Democratic party.

WILLIAM M. KEITH, a prominent and successful farmer of Franklin County, was born March 22, 1844, and is one of a family of eight children born to James N. and Nancy E. (Larkin) Keith. The father was born in North Carolina about 1814, and came with his grandparents to this county when quite young, and followed farming here until his death, which occurred in 1876. The mother was a native of this county, lived here all her life, and died March 9, 1872. Our subject remained with his parents until the commencement of the war; he then enlisted in Company E, Seventeenth Tennessee Infantry, with which he remained until the battle of Murfreesboro, at which place he lost an arm, and then came home staying with his father about ten years. In 1874 he, in partnership with a Mr. Lipscomb, embarked in the mercantile business at Huntland, this county, which he continued two years, and then returned to the farm, remaining with his father until his (the father's) death. January 22, 1878, he married Julia Ann Lipscomb, of this county, since which he has followed farming, where he now lives. To the above marriage three children have been born, all living: Buford, Floyd and Elizabeth. Mr. Keith has always been identified with the Democratic party, and is a supporter of the principles of prohibition.

JOHN M. KELLY, justice of the peace and postmaster at Sherwood, was born in Franklin County, Tenn., in 1846, being a son of William and Angeline (Prince) Kelly. The father was born in Franklin County, Tenn., was a farmer all his life, and died in 1851, his father being John M. Kelly, Sr., a very prominent early settler of the county. The mother is a daughter of Squire William Prince, who is now among the very oldest citizens of Franklin County, and yet resides near Sherwood, and has been justice of the peace for about twenty years. The mother of our subject is now living. The immediate subject of this sketch was reared on a farm. He enlisted in May, 1861, in Company I, Seventeenth Tennessee, remaining in that command throughout the war. After the war he engaged in farming, which he continued until about 1882, when he was elected justice of the peace, and has since lived in Sherwood. He was appointed postmaster in 1885, and now holds that office. He was married, in 1867, to Elizabeth Garner, the fruits of this union being five children, four of whom are still living: Jennie, Annie, Tina and Willie. The mother of these children died in 1880, having been a member of the Cumberland Presbyterian Church, as is Mr. Kelly. Mr. Kelly is a member of the Franklin Democratic Executive Committee.

HENRY M. LAIRD, car-inspector at Cowan for the Nashville, Chattanooga & St. Louis Railroad Company, and for the Tennessee Coal, Iron & Railroad Company, was born in June, 1857, being an only child born to James A. and Martha E. (Williams) Laird, both natives of Tennessee. The father published the first Know-nothing paper ever published in Tennessee. He died in Bedford County, Tenn., in 1861; the mother still lives in Nashville. The subject of this sketch was married, October 15, 1880, to Miss Ida Williams, daughter of William E. Williams, one of the pioneers of this part of the State. To this union two children have been born, whose names are Colie E. and Bessie A. Both Mr. and Mrs. Laird are members of the Cumberland Presbyterian Church.

WILLIAM T. LEAGUE was born March 10, 1830, in Alexandria, Va. When one year old his parents removed to Baltimore, and he was reared in that city. At the age of fifteen he began mercantile clerking, and also learned the trade of manufacturing silk hats, which trade he pursued very successfully till the war, when he engaged in the hotel business at Annapolis, Md., for about two years. After the war he came to Estill Springs for the purpose of again establishing a silk hat manufactory. He soon disposed of his stock of hats, and in 1866 engaged in general merchandising, which he has ever since continued. He was appointed postmaster in 1866, and has held the office continuously ever since. He was first married in Fredericksburg, Va., in 1850, to Miss Fannie Bradshaw, the result of this union being five children, viz.: Jared H., Metamora, Rosa B. (wife of R. T. Miller), William T. (a prominent lawyer in Poplar Bluff, Mo.) and Emma. He lived with the mother of these children until 1866, and in 1871 he was married to Miss Nannie Hill, of Franklin County, who bore him two children, one of whom—Achaen—is now living. This wife died in about 1875. Mr. League and his two daughters are members of the Christian Church. Mr. League is a Democrat in politics, and is a well respected citizen of the county. The League family originated in America through one James League, who, with seven sons, immigrated to Maryland in Revolutionary times. He was very wealthy. The father of our subject was also James League. He was a defender of Baltimore in 1812, and died in 1873.

DAN LENEHAN, one of the leading merchants of Decherd, Tenn., was born October 17, 1839, in Winchester, Tenn., being a son of Peter and Narcissa (Champion) Lenehan. The father was born in Dublin, Ireland, and when about nineteen he immigrated to America. In a short time he found his way to Franklin County, Tenn., in the very early settlement of the county. He taught school here for many years, but afterward engaged in farming, which he continued till his death, at the age of ninety, in 1878. The mother was a daughter of Daniel Champion, one among the first settlers of the county. She died a few months before the father's death occurred. The subject of this sketch remained with his parents to about the age of eighteen, when he lived with his grandfather, Daniel Champion for a time. He went to Illinois and taught school and worked on a farm for about two years. He afterward returned to Franklin County; in 1861 enlisted in Company I, Turney's First Tennessee Regiment, Confederate Army, and served throughout the war. He had three brothers in the same company with him, only one of whom returned from the service alive. He also had a brother in the Forty-fourth Tennessee, who safely returned. Coming from the war our subject taught school and clerked a while. In 1870 he established his mercantile trade, which he has continued successfully ever since, carrying a stock of about $6,000, and transacting annually about $12,000 worth of business. He was married, December 23, 1869, to Miss Susan Featherstone, the result of this union being three children, viz.: Richard, Pearl and Thomas. Mr. Lenehan was bereft of his wife May 13, 1882. He takes an active interest in politics, acting with the Democratic party. He is a moral and enterprising citizen of Franklin County.

JOHN LIPSCOMB, merchant at Bean's Creek, Franklin County, Tenn., was born in this county in 1838, and is one of seven children born to Granville and Jane (Breeden) Lipscomb. The father, a native of Virginia, was born about 1805, and married his first wife in Virginia, then moved to Franklin County, Tenn., where she died, having borne one child. Mr. Lipscomb then married his second wife, also a native of Virginia, and removed to Illinois, where he remained two years, and then returned to this county, where his second wife died, leaving two children, William and David, the latter being editor of the *Gospel Advocate* at Nashville, Tenn. Mr. Lipscomb's third wife was our subject's mother; she was also born in Virginia. At the age of sixteen John entered Franklin College, near Nashville, and attended two terms. In 1863 he enlisted in the Forty-first Tennessee Infantry, with which he remained about eight months, then returned home, and in 1865 began operating the tan-yard at Bean Creek, now owned by him, and recently remodeled with the view of running it on a large scale. It was the pioneer manufactory establishment of this part of Franklin County, being first operated in 1823. In 1876 Mr. Lipscomb began merchandising at Bean Creek, and in 1881 a cousin, J. C. Breeden, became his partner. In 1863 Mr. Lipscomb married Ann Smith, who has borne him nine children, all living. Mr. Lipscomb is a supporter of the principles of Prohibition, and he with his family are members of the Christian Church.

JOHN T. LIPSCOMB, farmer, was born October 22, 1840, in this county, and is one of seven children born to William C. and Elizabeth (Lipscomb) Lipscomb. The father was born in Spottsylvania County, Va., June 7, 1804, and came to this county in 1833; remaining one year, he returned to Virginia and married our subject's mother, a native of Louisa County, Va. In 1835 they removed to Franklin County, Tenn., where they remained farming until their deaths, which occurred March 16, 1847, and December 20, 1877, mother and father, respectively. Our subject remained with his parents until his majority, attending Franklin College, near Nashville, two years previous to the commencement of the war, when he enlisted in Company F, First Tennessee Confederate Infantry, joining his command in Virginia. He was captured at the battle of the Wilderness, and taken to Point Lookout, Md. At the close of the war he embarked in the mercantile business at Huntland, this county, which he continued successfully ten years. He then moved to his present farm, which he had purchased while in business. He has since followed farming, and is considered one of Franklin County's successful farmers. In August, 1869, he married Mrs. Mary M. Rutledge, nee Montgomery, who had two children by her former husband, both still living: George C. and Eva D. To this marriage one child was born—William Ira, still living; and the mother died April 8, 1871. On October 21, 1879, he married Mrs. Lina E. Porter, nee Montgomery (sister of his first wife), who had three children by her former husband—Flora M., Tinie L. and Willie G., all living. To this marriage one child has been born—Thomas Colville, living. Mr. and Mrs. Lipscomb are members of the Cumberland Presbyterian Church. He has always voted the Democratic ticket, and is a firm supporter of the principles of prohibition.

HUGH N. LUCAS was born in 1827, a native of this county and one of a family of seven born to William and Grissella Lucas. The parents were natives of North Carolina and South Carolina, father and mother, respectively. The father was born in 1798, and came to this county in 1818; he married the mother of our subject in 1820, she having moved to this county in 1816. They followed farming here in the county, the father dying in 1861 and the mother in 1882. Our subject remained with his parents until 1847, then spent eleven years in Texas, but returned to this county, where he purchased a farm and afterward located where he now resides. He has a controlling interest in the Falls Mills Manufacturing Company, of this county. In October, 1862, he was drafted into the Twenty-eighth Tennessee Infantry, with which he remained but a few months, owing to bad health. In 1865 he married Nancy Hannah, a native of Franklin County, which union has been blessed by the birth of six children, all still living. Mr. and Mrs. Lucas are members of the Methodist Church. He is also a member in good standing of F. & A. M.

JOHN D. LYNCH, one of the leading merchants of Sherwood, Tennessee, is the fourth of a family of seven children, born to the marriage of John D. Lynch and Hettie Wilkinson. The father was born in 1818, being a son of David Lynch a prominent early settler of Franklin County. John D. Lynch, Sr., was a farmer by occupation, and for many years was a magistrate of the county, his death occurring in 1883. The mother of our subject is still living. The immediate subject of this sketch was reared on a farm, having been born in 1844. In May, 1861, he enlisted in the Confederate service in Company I, Seventeenth Tennessee, in which he served until the surrender, and at Chickamauga lost a leg. Returning from the war he farmed a short time. Since then he has been dealing in lumber and tan bark, and has also been merchandising. He does an extensive business in the tan bark trade. He was married, in 1867, to Nancy Jane King, a native of this county, who has borne nine children to this union, six of whom are living, viz.: John B., Hettie, David, Lucinda, Rebecca, and Nancy Jane. Politically, Mr. Lynch is a Democrat. He is an enterprising and successful business man and a good citizen. His grandfather, David Lynch, was a soldier in the war of 1812. His uncle, Elijah Lynch, was a soldier in the war of 1812 and in the Florida war.

DAVID LYONS, a farmer, living in the Tenth District, was one of five children born to the marriage of William Lyons and Catharine Howp, *nee* Corner. He was born in 1815 in Augusta County, Va., and is the only one of the family now living. The father came to Franklin County, Tenn., with his family, about 1826, and died in the county in 1858, having been preceded by his wife about ten years. David Lyons remained with his parents till attaining his majority, when he began farming for himself. In 1859 he bought the farm whereon he now resides. In 1839 he married Nancy Ferrall, a native of this county, who bore him eight children, seven of whom are now living. This wife died in 1878, and in 1881 Mr. Lyons was united in marriage to his second wife, Mrs. Boyle, *nee* Black, a native of Blount County, Tenn. Mr. L. lives in a brick house, one among the first, if not the first one, ever built in Franklin County. In a little cemetery on his farm lie the remains of Col. James Lewis, an officer in the Revolutionary war, and one of "Washington's Forlorn Hope" at the battle of Brandywine. Col. Lewis was born in Albemarle County, Va., in 1755, came to Franklin County about 1811, locating on the farm now owned by Mr. Lyons, and died February 21, 1849.

EX-GOV. A. S. MARKS was born in Daviess County, Ky., October 16, 1836. He was reared in his native county to the age of twenty, on a tobacco plantation. His father was a well-to-do farmer, and died when A. S. was but about ten years old. At the age of twenty our subject came to Winchester and began reading law in the office of A. S. Colyar, and he was admitted to the bar just before the war. He then enlisted in 1861, as captain of Company E, Seventeenth Tennessee, in the Confederate service. In May, 1862, he was elected colonel of that regiment. At Murfreesboro he lost a leg, and after his recovery, he was in Forrest's military court till the close of the war. After returning home he resumed the practice of law in Winchester until 1870, when he was elected chancellor of the Fourth Division of Tennessee, and in 1878 was re-elected without opposition. He soon afterward, in 1878, received the nomination by the Democratic party for governor, and was elected, serving one term, 1879-81. He has since been engaged in the practice of law, being one of the very able lawyers of the State, and one of the popular and leading men of his party. He was married, April 28, 1863, to Miss Novalla Davis, of Wilson County, Tenn. Gov. Marks has two sons, one of whom, Arthur H., is now consular clerk in the United States Diplomatic Corps in London, being a lawyer by profession, and the other one, Albert D., is practicing law in the firm of Marks & Gregory, having been admitted to the bar when seventeen years of age.

WILLIAM W. MARTIN, one among the old citizens of Franklin County, was born within two miles of Decherd October 17, 1829. He is one of a family of eleven children born to the marriage of Nathan R. Martin and Jane Witt. The father was born in South Carolina December 1, 1804, where he lived till the age of twelve, when, in 1816, he immigrated to Franklin County, Tenn., where he married, lived and died, his death occurring in 1859. The mother was born December 20, 1804, in Virginia, whence she came to this county when seven years old. She lived in this county till 1874, when she removed to Houston County, Ga., where she now lives. Our subject was reared on a farm. He learned the blacksmith trade, and when twenty-one he began the pursuit of his trade for himself, which he continued until 1858, when he entered the mercantile business, which he continued till 1861. He then raised a company for the Confederate service, but the company was not received. He then remained at home till 1863, when he went to Houston County, Ga., there worked at his trade in the Confederate service till the close of the war. After the war he engaged at his trade in Decherd, and continued till October, 1865, when he established his present merchandising trade, which he has successfully continued ever since. He was married, March 19, 1853, to Miss Lizzie Hines, the result of this union being ten children, eight of whom are living: Edward H., Annie, Lou B. and Isaac H. (twins), Nathan E., Theodosius W., Meredith P. and Clyde. Mr. Martin and all of his family, except the two youngest children, are members of the Presbyterian Church, Mr. Martin being an elder in the church. Politically he is a Democrat, and is one of the leading and influential citizens of the community.

JOHN H. MARTIN, one of Winchester's attorneys, was born December 27, 1844, in Franklin County, Tenn., being one of a family of children, the fruits of the marriage of Daniel J. Martin and Sarah Martin, natives of this county, and of the same surname, although of no blood relation. The father was a farmer by occupation, and a prominent man of the county. He held the office of constable about ten years, that of justice of the peace six years, deputy sheriff four years, and sheriff four years. He raised four children, all now living in this county. He died in 1875, but the mother is still living. Our subject was reared on a farm, securing a good common school education. He began reading medicine in 1866 and continued until 1869; he then abandoned that profession and began the reading of law, and was soon admitted to the bar, since which time he has continued in that profession. He also owns 200 acres of land in the Fourth District. Politically he has always been a Democrat.

ISAAC N. MARTIN, farmer of this county, was born in 1828, in Franklin County, Tenn., and is one of a family of two children born to William and Elizabeth (Sandidge) Martin. The parents were both born in this county about 1801, and married about 1826. The father dying in 1831, the mother afterward married Jesse Garnett, a native of Mississippi, who died a couple years later. The mother died in August, 1855. Soon after his father's death, our subject made his home with his grandparents Sandidge, and remained with them until fifteen years old, when his mother returned to housekeeping. He lived with her until his marriage in 1853, to Sarah Horton. He then embarked in the mercantile business at Salem, this county, which he continued until 1876. He then followed farming near Maxwell, until the year 1881, at which date he began the mercantile business at Maxwell, in which he has been interested since. The marriage of Mr. and Mrs. Martin was blessed with the birth of five children, three of whom are now living. The mother of these children died December 16, 1885. Mr. Martin and family are members of the Missionary Baptist Church.

JOHN W. MASON, a leading merchant of Decherd, Tenn., was born in Franklin County, October 18, 1858. His parents were James and Melvina (Buckner) Mason, both natives of Franklin County. The father was at one time sheriff of this county, but now lives in Alabama. The mother is yet living near Decherd. John W. Mason was reared on a farm and received his education in the common schools of the county. When about thirteen years old he began clerking for Lenehan & Holland and continued with them for eight or nine years. He then succeeded his employers in business. He has been very successful, and now carries about $8,000 in stock, transacting a business of about $2,000 annually. He began with nothing but what he had earned himself, and is an example of a self-made successful man. His marriage ceremony was solemnized January 21, 1880, uniting him to Miss Laura Hines, a native of this county. Four children have blessed this union, whose names are as follows: Ward, Clara, Mary and Buford. Mr. Mason and wife are members of the Presbyterian Church. He is a Democrat in politics.

CAPT. STEPHEN D. MATHER was born in Penn. in 1842, and is one of a family of five born to Daniel and Roxana (Underwood) Mather. When five years of age he went to Illinois with his parents, who died in 1885 and 1859; father and mother, ninety and sixty years of age, repectively; both of old New England Puritan stock. Our subject remained with his parents until his majority, and graduated at Cornell College, Iowa, receiving the degree of A. B., in 1860, and since, A. M. At the commencement of the war he enlisted in the Nineteenth Iowa Infantry and was orderly sergeant, and afterward captain and quartermaster. He remained until the close, participating in the whole campaign of the Cumberland, once being taken prisoner at Nashville, but soon escaped, walking by night through to the Ohio River. In 1867, he came to Franklin County, Tenn., which place had attracted his attention and admiration during the war, buying at first 300 acres with the expectation of starting a colony for Northern settlers. Owing to the political difficulties which for a time disturbed the South, his first intentions were never carried out, although by his influence this section (around Belvidere) has been settled mainly by thrifty, enterprising Northern farmers, who, by systematic farming, with the use of fertillizers and systematic rotation of crops, have given the place no little fame as being the "garden spot of Tennessee." In 1866 he married Rebecca Stamper, a native of the county. To this marriage four children have been born, two of whom are still living— Bessie and Nellie. Mr. Mather met with the bereavement of the loss of his wife on June 29, 1880. Politically, Mr. Mather is a stanch Republican, and is a member of the State Republican Executive Committee, and he is a firm believer in the principles of prohibition.

HON. LEWIS METCALFE, the oldest living member of the Franklin County bar, was born in Lexington, Ky., February 22, 1818. His father, Barnett Metcalfe, was born in Fauquier County, Virginia, and when young went to Kentucky, where he married Letitia Martin, a native of Jessamine County, of that State. The father was a farmer and merchant. He removed to Huntsville, Ala., in 1822, and afterward to Fayetteville, Tenn. There Lewis began the study of medicine. He afterward attended Medical College at Lexington, Ky., graduating in that institution. He then engaged in the practice of medicine for ten years in Franklin County, Tenn., and in Mississippi. Returning to Franklin County from Mississippi he read law, and in 1852 was admitted to the bar, and since then has practiced law in Franklin County, having attained prominence in his profession. He is highly educated. He was elected to the Senate of Tennessee, in 1884, and has held that office one term. He was married, in 1843, to Miss Sarah A. Stamper, a native of North Carolina, who came to this county when young. This union was blessed in the birth of one daughter. She became grown, graduated in the Mary Sharp College, and died on April 9, 1865, at the very hour of Lee's surrender. Mrs. Metcalfe is a member of the Cumberland Presbyterian Church. Politically, Mr. Metcalfe was a Whig before the war; since then he has been a Democrat.

JACOB MIESCHER, an extensive and influential farmer of Franklin County, Tenn., is one of two children born to the marriage of Peter and Elizabeth Miescher. Our subject was born in Switzerland November 23, 1822, and with his parents came to America in 1853, and located in Wayne County, Ohio, where the parents passed the remainder of their lives. The father died in August, 1865, and the mother in June, 1855. July 6, 1847, our subject married Elizabeth Reinhard, who was also born in Switzerland. Two sons and one daughter were born to this union, two of whom were born and died in Switzerland. In 1870 Mr. Miescher came to Tennessee to choose a home. He made a second visit in 1871, and still another in 1872. On his last visit he purchased the home where he now lives, a splendid farm of 180 acres, which he has greatly improved. Since that time he has added 600 acres to the original tract. Mr. Miescher has been an exceptionally successful man, and is identified with the Democratic party, and he and family are members of the German Reformed Church.

SAMUEL M. MILLER, a farmer of Franklin County, living in the Tenth District, was an only child born to Montgomery C. and Melvinie (Buckner) Miller. He was born in Franklin County, Tenn., June 30, 1850. The father, Montgomery C. Miller, was also born in this county, where he lived all his life. He, the father, departed this life to join the innumerable dead in 1850, having been a farmer throughout his life. Samuel M. was reared to the years of maturity with an uncle. He then bought the farm whereon he now resides. He chose his helpmeet in the person of Joan Hines, daughter of I. F. Hines, one of Franklin County's prominent pioneer settlers. The marriage ceremony was solemnized in September, 1872. This union has been blessed in the birth of four sons, one of whom is deceased, and one daughter. Those now living are Walter, Montgomery, Burk and Leuvinie. In political affairs Mr. Miller cooperates with the Democratic party. Mrs. Miller is a member of the Baptist Church.

JEFFERSON D. MILLER was born July 14, 1861, in Franklin County, Tenn., and is one of a family of nine children born to the matrimonial union of John H. and Nancy (Brazelton) Miller. The father was born in Franklin County in 1834. At the commencement of the late war he enlisted in the First Tennessee Infantry, but owing to bad health he was discharged at the end of six months. The mother is also a native of this county.

Both parents are yet living. Jefferson D. remained with his parents to the age of twenty-one, when he accepted the position of telegraph operator at Cowan, which position he has ever since held. He has also been the regular correspondent of the *Franklin County News* for two years. In February, 1881, he married Miss Fannie Miller, a native of Bullock County, Ala. One daughter, Lilly Corene, has blessed this union. Both Mr. Miller and his wife are members of the Cumberland Presbyterian Church.

JNO. C. MONTGOMERY, a prominent citizen of Franklin County, was born September 24, 1820, in this county, being the only child born to the marriage of William H. Montgomery and Susan Cowan. The father was born about the year 1795, in Blount County, Tenn., and in 1806 came to Franklin County, where he followed farming until his death in October, 1829, his wife having preceded him to her long home in October, 1820. The subject of this sketch lived with his grandparents till attaining the years of majority. He was elected constable of the Tenth District in 1842 and taught school in 1844. Soon afterward he bought the farm on which he has ever since lived. He was elected justice of the peace in 1846, which office he held for eighteen years. On January 15, 1850, he married Nancy Cowan, daughter of James P. Cowan, an old pioneer of Franklin County, who was born December 1, 1792, and died April 7, 1862. To the above marriage were born nine children, five of whom are still living. The names of those now living are: William M., born in 1850; James C., born in 1853; Mary A., born in 1856; Ellen, born in 1863; and Kittie born in 1869. Squire Montgomery is a firm Democrat in politics. He is a thoroughly self-made man, having begun life with nothing, and by thrift and economy has become a well-to-do farmer, now owning 300 acres of fine land. Besides this his wife owns 100 acres. Both Mr. and Mrs. Montgomery are members of the Cumberland Presbyterian Church.

HORATIO R. MOORE, an enterprising and intelligent citizen of this county, was born near Florence, Lauderdale County, Ala., in 1833. He is of a family of five sons and two daughters that has been remarkably well preserved. The brothers—John J., Robert J., Hugh B. and James Knox Moore, and the sisters—Mrs. Sarah Millican and Mrs. Rebecca Patrick, are all living. Two of the brothers were wounded during the war, but all are now in good health, and the youngest is now over forty-one years old. The father, Stephen R. Moore, was born in Moore County, N. C., a county that was named for his grandfather, Robert Moore, who was a native of Ireland, and who came to America with his father, Patrick, and his brothers, Hugh and Patrick, and settled in South Carolina, and subsequently moved to North Carolina, where he lived at the breaking out of the war of 1776. He belonged to the Colonial Army and fell just before the close of the war at Guilford's Court House in Marion's command. Stephen, with his father, mother, brothers and sisters, left North Carolina and settled among the pioneers of north Alabama in the year 1820. The mother, Lucy (McDougal) Moore, was born in Cumberland County, N. C., and settled in north Alabama about the year 1820 with her parents. The parents of our subject were married in Alabama in 1829, and lived in that productive section till 1837, at which time they settled in north Mississippi, where they prospered farming. The mother died in 1845. The father never married a second time. His home fell within the Federal lines in 1863. He was taken North with many others of that section, and put in prison because he was true to his convictions, as a Southern citizen, where he died in 1864. Our subject was a regular laborer on the farm, occasionally attending the old style schools of that section till 1853, at which time he left home, without the approval of many friends, with the view of enjoying better educational advantages than that country afforded. He soon entered Franklin College, near Nashville, where he remained working and teaching during vacations till he completed the course of study and graduated in 1857. He then returned to Mississippi and taught till the fall of 1860. On the 5th of September of that year he and Miss Annie Hunt, with whom he became acquainted while students at Franklin College, were married in this county. After a short stay in Mississippi they returned to Huntland, where they have lived ever since. Our subject entered as a partner into the mercantile business with his wife's father, Clinton

A. Hunt, who is reputed to be the first white child born in Franklin County. The civil war soon put a stop to this undertaking. Insecure farming was then tried, next the Confederate service was entered, which ended with the surrender of Forrest's command in May, 1865. He át once went to farming, and has been busily engaged in this business on his 400 acre farm that lies adjacent to Huntland, on the Fayetteville branch of the Nashville, Chatanooga & St. Louis Railroad, ever since. He has at times been connected with the mercantile business, and is now secretary and treasurer of the the Fall Mills Manufacturing Company. He represented Franklin County in the General Assembly of the State in 1873–74, and has always taken an interest the public enterprises and issues of the country. He and his good wife are members of the Christian Church. They have had born to them seven sons and five daughters, the names of whom we give consecutively in this connection: Barclay D., Miss Elma, Miss Lou, William L., Miss Annie, Miss Mamie, Hugh B., Hunt C., Knox J., Horatio R., Miss Lexie and Tom P. Moore.

T. F. MOSELEY, a well known and popular old pioneer of Franklin County, Tenn., was born in the "Palmetto State" November 28, 1816, and is one of two children living out of a family of seven born to the marriage of George Moseley and Nancy Wakefield. The father was born in South Carolina and the mother in North Carolina. They came to Tennessee in 1818, and located on Bean Creek November 28 of that year. Our subject's paternal grandparents preceded them to Tennessee two years. Our subject made his home with his parents until nineteen years of age, and then accepted a clerkship in a general merchandise store at Salem, Tenn., receiving $50 for his first year's service, $100 for his second, and $150 for his third. He soon after took an interest in the business, continuing until 1841. December 12, 1839, he wedded Arie V. Simmons, and then located on the farm, where he still resides. The mother was born November 6, 1820, and died July 4, 1879, having borne eleven children. May 10, 1881, Mrs. Lucy (Dean) Noblett became his wife. She was born in South Carolina January 28, 1824, and died July 18. 1884·

HON. JOHN R. OLIVER, an active business man of Franklin County, at Estill Springs, was born January 17, 1837, in Tishamingo County, Miss. His parents were R. H. and Malinda Myra (Petty) Oliver. The father was born in Franklin County, Tenn., his father having emigrated from Virginia at a very early date. The father of our subject lived in his native county all his life, except about three years, which time he lived in Mississippi. He was a very prominent citizen, having been deputy sheriff of the county. His death occurred in 1837, and the mother's death about four years later. John R. was then reared with an only sister by an uncle, Lanson Rowe, a very prominent and public spirited citizen of Franklin County. He received his education at Irving College, Warren Co., Tenn., graduating in 1858. He then engaged in teaching as principal in the county academy at Woodbury, Cannon Co., Tenn., till the war. He then enlisted in Company E, Thirty-second Tennessee, and served in that company until the battle of Fort Donelson. Being absent from his command he was not captured with his company. He then joined Company K, Forty-fourth Tennessee. He was elected first lieutenant just before the battle of Shiloh, and acted as captain through that battle, afterward being promoted captain of the company, commanding it until after the battle of Chickamauga, when he was appointed captain of an engineer corps in A. P. Stuart's Division, and was on detached service on Gen. Stuart's staff until the close of the war, being paroled at Greensboro, N. C. He then resumed his profession at Woodbury, as principal of that school, until 1867, when he removed to Estill Springs and engaged in merchandising, and by thrift and energy has been very successful. He deals in railroad timber supplies and carries on farming very extensively, now owning about 1,000 acres of good land. He owns an interest in a store at Marble Hill, Moore County, and is the agent for the Nashville Chattanooga & St. Louis Railroad at Estill Springs. He was married, December 22, 1858, to Miss Callie McFerrin, oldest daughter of A. F. McFerrin, of Woodbury, Tenn. Mr. Oliver has a family of five children: Robert A., Joseph L., Eliza C., Myra S. and Ida M. Robert A. is married and has two children, and lives in Nashville. He is a traveling salesman. The subject of this sketch and his wife are members of the Methodist Episcopal Church

South. Mr. Oliver is a member of the F. & A. M. Besides being an active and popular business man Mr. Oliver has interested himself in the public affairs and represented Franklin County in the Legislature in 1876–77.

R. C. PATRICK was born in Madison County, Ky., in 1825, and is one of a family of ten children born to Jno. R. and Matilda (Callaway) Patrick. The father was born in Virginia in 1797, and moved to Kentucky while young, and was married in Franklin County, Tenn., after which they returned to Kentucky, but moved to this county about 1827, where he farmed and followed merchandising until his death, which occurred in 1847. The mother was born in this county in 1807, and died here in the county, where she lived all her life. Our subject remained with his parents until 1849, when he went to California, and engaged in mining about a year, after which he returned to Franklin County, Tenn., embarking in the mercantile line at Salem, where he remained nine years; then he moved to Maxwell, and took Franklin County census of 1860, after which he farmed for about seven years; but again embarked in merchandising, this time at Maxwell, about 1867, which he continued twelve years He has also been acting as agent for the Winchester & Alabama Railroad at this point, since its reconstruction after he war. August, 1854, he married Mary M. Clements, native of this State. This union has been blessed by the birth of five children, four of whom are still living—Anna, Emma, John and Jesse.

JOHN A. RUCH, a farmer of this county, was born September 28, 1842, in Holmes County, Ohio. The parents, Jacob and Magdelene Ruch, were both natives of Switzerland, and came to America about 1835, locating in Ohio, where they remained all their lives farming. The mother died in 1870, the father in 1876. Our subject remained with his parents until the commencement of the war, and then joined the Nineteenth Ohio Infantry, with which command he remained throughout the war, participating in the battles of Shiloh, Murfreesboro, Chickamauga, Mission Ridge, Nashville and Atlanta, escaping without a wound, there being but one other who had been with the command all the time so fortunate. After the war he returned home and engaged in the saw-milling business seven years. In 1868 he married Anna Graber, a native of Ohio, to which union four children have been born. In 1872 he, with his family, moved to Franklin County, Tenn., locating on the farm where he now lives. Since 1876 he, with others of his neighborhood, began the use of bone fertilizers, which, with thorough cultivation and systematic rotation of crops, has given the Belvidere settlement fame as an agricultural district. Politically Mr. Ruch is a Republican and a firm supporter of the principles of prohibition. He and his family are members of the German Reformed Church.

WM. M. RUTLEDGE was born in Roane County, Tenn. in 1848, and is one of a family of six children born to Geo. P. and Delia (Tedford) Rutledge. The father was born in Sullivan County, Tenn., June, 1813, and followed farming in that and Blount Counties until about 1861, when he moved to Spalding County, Ga., and from there in 1865, to Huntland, Franklin Co., Tenn., at which place he embarked in merchandising, and continued that until a short time before his death, which occurred in February, 1884. The mother, a native of Alabama, preceded him May 11, 1878. Wm. M., the subject of this sketch, remained with his parents until their death, and in 1878 he began merchandising for himself, and in partnership with Geo. C. Rutledge carries a splendid line of general merchandise at Huntland, this county. In November, 1879 he married Martitia Staples, daughter of Jno. W. Staples, of this county. This marriage has been blessed by the birth of two children, both girls: Roxie and Nettie, both still living. Mr. and Mrs. Rutledge are active members of the Cumberland Presbyterian Church. Mr. Rutledge has always been a Democrat, and is a strong advocate of the principles of prohibition.

LARKIN R. SARTAIN was born September 18, 1832, in Franklin County, Ga., being one of a family of three sons and two daughters, the fruits of the marriage of Elijah Sartain and Sarah Williams. The father was a native of Georgia, and died about 1850, at Barnesville, in his native State. The mother was born in North Carolina, and died March 11, 1862, in Franklin County, Tenn., whither she had removed in 1857. The subject of this sketch came to Franklin County, Tenn., before the war, and has ever since been employed as engineer on the Nashville, Chattanooga & St. Louis Railroad. During the war he was employed in hauling supplies for the Confederate Army, the above named railroad company having all their rolling stock then in the South. Mr. Sartain has met with two very narrow escapes with his life, having twice gone through bridges, each accident occasioning several deaths. He each time escaped injury, but afterward met with an accident on November 6, 1875, which cost him a leg. November 6, 1873, he was united in marriage to Jenney Hawkins, the result of this union being four daughters, viz.: Clara, Nettie, Eleanor and Daisy. Before the war Mr. Sartain was a Whig, but since the war he has been a Democrat. He is now an advocate of prohibition. Both himself and wife are members of the Christian Church at Cowan, where they reside.

DR. J. C. SHAPARD, one of the leading physicians of Winchester, was born August 30, 1823, in Rutherford County, Tenn. His father, James P. Shapard, was born in North Carolina, and immigrated to Rutherford County, Tenn., when very young. He was a merchant, and lived in Rutherford County till near his death, when he removed to Texas, where he died in 1850. The mother also died in Texas in 1875. Dr. Shapard was the oldest of ten children. When a young man he came to Winchester and conducted merchandising for his father two years. He began the study of medicine when twenty-two years of age, and soon entered the practice. He attended one course of lectures at Louisville, and then, in 1859, graduated in the medical department of the Vanderbilt University. He then entered upon the practice of medicine in Franklin County. In 1862 he removed to Winchester, where he has ever since continued, and has been justly successful. He was married, in 1846, to Miss Elivira Clark, of Bedford County, Tenn. This union has been blessed in the birth of seven children, six of whom are living, viz.: Melissa H., wife of J. W. Thornton, of Chattanooga; Mary E., the one who died; Henry C., Thomas N., Charles J., Leonora and Florence. Dr. Shapard and two of his sons and three daughters are members of the Episcopal Church, and his wife and youngest daughter are members of the Cumberland Presbyterian Church. Dr. Shapard is a firm Democrat in politics, and is a valuable citizen of Franklin County.

E. E. SHERWOOD, senior member of the firm of Sherwood & Whittemore, is a son of C. D. Sherwood, who, in 1875, organized a colony of settlers at Sherwood, Tenn. C. D. Sherwood was born in 1832, in Connecticut, where he was reared. In his native State he married Miss Charlotte Ferriss, and in a few years he moved to Minnesota, where he remained until 1875, attaining prominence in political circles in that State. He has been a member of both branches of the Legislature of Minnesota, and was lieutenant-governor of that State one term. The subject of this sketch was born in 1861, being the second of the family. He remained with his parents till coming to Tennessee, when he opened his mercantile business, in which he has been very successful. He was united in marriage, in 1884, to Miss Esther Foote, also a native of Connecticut. One son, Ambrose E., has blessed this union. Walter D. Whittemore, of the firm of Sherwood & Whittemore, was born in Minnesota in 1861, being the son of Reuben and Nancy (West) Whittemore, natives of Massachusetts. The father is a farmer and stock-raiser. He removed from Massachusetts to Rushford, Minn., where he lived until removing to Sherwood, where he now lives. In the spring of 1886 Walter D. entered the firm of Sherwood & Whittemore. This firm carries a stock of about $2,000 and transacts a yearly business of about $15,000. Both are young men of business ability and are highly respected.

JOSEPH A. SHORT, the present superintendent of the Tennessee Iron, Coal & Railroad Company's works at Cowan, was born April 12, 1850, in Rowan County, Tenn. His parents were George W. and Eliza (Parks) Short; they being parents of fourteen children. The father is a native of Virginia, the mother of Tennessee. They now reside in Roane County, Tenn., where the father follows farming, having formerly been engaged in iron interests in Roane County. The subject of this sketch remained with his parents to the age of nineteen, when he engaged in the iron business in his native county for four years. He was then engaged in the same business in Dade County, Ga., about three and a half years. He then went to Dickson County, Tenn., still in the iron business, remaining there a few months. Thence he went to the Chattanooga Furnace for a few months; thence to Baxter County, Ga., in the employ of a New York Iron Company for one year. In 1881, he took charge of his present business at Cowan, where he now resides. He was united in marriage, in 1871, to Miss Caroline Underwood, a native of Roane County, Tenn., the fruits of this union being two children, viz.: Michael and Cora. This wife died at her parents' home in Roane County, Tenn., in 1875. In 1879, Mr. Short married Lizzie Allison, a native of Alabama.

GEN. FRANCIS A. SHOUP, D. D., professor of physics and engineering in the University of the South, was born in Laurel, Franklin Co., Ind., March 22, 1834. His father, George Grove Shoup, was a member of the State Constitutional Convention of Indiana, and for many years was a member of the Legislature of that State. He was an extensive merchant, and was a man of large property. The maternal grandfather of Gen. Shoup, James Conwell, was also a man of large property. He founded the town of Laurel, Ind., and was for a number of years a member of the Legislature. When Gen. Shoup was nineteen years old his father died, and about three years later his mother died. He was educated in the Asbury University, Greencastle, Ind., and in the Military Academy, West Point, N. Y., which latter place he entered in 1851, graduating in 1855. He was then assigned second lieutenant of the First United States Artillery, resigning in 1859. He then went to Indianapolis and began the practice of law. There he organized a company of zouaves. He then went to Florida and was commissioned in the regular army, Confederate States, and when the volunteer Confederate Army was raised he was made major of artillery, his first service being at Mobile Bay. He was then ordered to the Trans-Mississippi Department, and served through the early part of the war with Hardee's army, chief of artillery, and was senior officer of artillery in the battle of Shiloh. After this battle he was made chief of artillery in Beauregard's army. He was again ordered to the Trans-Mississippi Department with Gen. Hindman; was appointed brigadier-general, and commanded a division in the fight of Prairie Grove. Afterward he was ordered to the command of the harbor of Mobile; thence to the army at Vicksburg, where he commanded a brigade during the siege and at the surrender. After being exchanged he was again ordered to the defense of Mobile; thence to J. E. Johnston's army at Dalton, Ga.; and was chief of artillery through the campaign before Atlanta. He designed and executed an original system of fortifications at the Chattahoochee, which was very effectual in repelling all attacks, and which has been much admired by great artillery officers. Gen. Shoup was then made chief of Gen. Hood's staff, upon the appointment of the latter officer. After the war he was elected to the chair of physics in the University of Mississippi (Oxford, Miss.), and while there took orders in the Protestant Episcopal Church. He was elected to the chair of mathematics in the University of the South, at Sewanee, in 1870. In 1874 he took a parish in the diocese of Albany, N. Y., and was made canon in the All Saints Cathedral, Albany, N. Y. In 1877 he returned to the South, and was in charge of Christ Church, New Orleans, for a time. He was elected to the chair which he now fills in 1883. Dr. Shoup was married in 1871 to Miss Esther H. Elliott, daughter of the late Bishop Elliott of Georgia. He has a family of three children: Francis, Charlotte and Stephen. Dr. Shoup received the degree of D. D. from the University of the South in 1880.

JOHN SIMMONS, one of Winchester's prominent attorneys, was born April 28, 1846, in Franklin County, Tenn. His father, George Simmons, was a farmer of the county, and died in November, 1867. His mother was neé Mary Fancy. The paternal grandfather of John Simmons was William Simmons, who came to this county in the very early settlement of this part of the State. The maternal grandparents were French and Scotch-Irish; the paternal grandparents were English and German. The subject of this sketch received but a common school education. He remained on the farm till two years after the war, and then worked about at different vocations for a few years. In 1869 he began reading law at home, and in 1871 he was admitted to the bar, and has since been engaged in the practice of law. He was married, December 18, 1873, to Miss Anna Pennington, the result of this union being one son, Pennington. Mr. Simmons is a firm Democrat, and always has been, his ancestors having been old-line Whigs. His grandfather, Fancy, made the first donation to the Vanderbilt University in the sum of $1,000.

A. J. SKIDMORE, the trustee of Franklin County, Tenn., was born November 2, 1839, within one mile of where he now lives, being one of the family of children born to the marriage of William Skidmore and Sallie Keith. The father was a native of North Carolina; he immigrated to this county about 1813, and died in 1862, having been a farmer. The mother was born in Franklin County, Tenn., and she died in 1874. Mr. A. J. Skidmore was reared on a farm. At the age of nineteen he enlisted in Company I, Turney's First Tennessee, Confederate States Army, and was in the service about two years, and was discharged on account of disability. After the war he married and settled down to farming, where he has ever since resided, owning 135 acres of land three miles from Winchester. He also taught school about eight years after the war. He was elected in 1875 to the office of county assessor, which he held one term. In 1874 he was elected county trustee, and has filled his term of office with efficiency. He was married, in 1865, to Miss Sarah Jane Sells, the results of this union being five children, viz.: Mary J., Laura E., Bettie S., James F. and Hattie S. This wife died in 1874, and in 1878 he was married to Miss Nira Terry, of Jackson County, Ala. Five children have been born to this union, viz.: Maggie, Estella, Mattie and two unnamed. Mr. Skidmore, his wife and four children are members of the Methodist Episcopal Church South. He is a firm Democrat and always has been. He is a self-made, substantial citizen of the county.

DR. FLAVEL B. SLOAN, a prominent physician of Franklin County, was born in Polk County, Tenn., March 12, 1844. He was one of a family of eleven children born to James and Susan (Brown) Sloan. The father was born January 27, 1803, in Blount County, Tenn., and died October 15, 1880, in Polk County, Tenn., where he had followed farming all his life and having been an elder in the Presbyterian Church for fifty years· The parents of our subject were married November 15, 1827. The mother was born in Rockbridge County, Va., October 14, 1808, and died August 31, 1875, in Polk County, Tenn. Dr. Sloan was reared on a farm till the commencement of the war, when he joined the Fifth Tennessee Cavalry, in which he served six months and was discharged on account of bad health. In 1863 he again joined his command, and was afterward detailed private scout, first for Johnston and afterward for Hood. After the Tennessee campaign he again joined his company in South Carolina, and served in that until the surrender of Johnston's army. From 1865 to 1869 he attended the McNutt's Academy at Franklin, Tenn., where he also read medicine. He then attended the medical department of the University during the sessions of 1869–70 and 1870–71. He then began practicing in Franklin County where he has since followed his profession. He is a Democrat in politics and is a member of the Presbyterian Church.

GEN. E. KIRBY SMITH was born in St. Augustine, Fla., in 1824, being a son of Judge J. L. Smith, presiding judge of the United States Court in Florida. He was graduated from the West Point Military Academy, in the class of 1845. Almost immediately he was ordered to Corpus Christi, and before the age of twenty-one began his military career. He was before Vera Cruz, and at the first battles of Resaca de la Palma and Palo Alto. He was mentioned in the official report of John McIntosh, of the Fifth Infantry, for his brave conduct. He received two brevets in the campaign, one for the battle of Cerro Gordo, where he was one of the first to scale the heights, and one for gallant and meritorious conduct at Contreras. He was appointed instructor of mathematics at the military academy (West Point, N. Y.) for three years, and was selected to join the boundary commission, under Maj. Emory, in which service he received a high compliment in Maj. Emory's official report. On the organization of the cavalry he received the appointment of captain, high on the list, and was ordered to Texas, where he served ten years, eleven times successfully engaging the Indians, and was severely wounded in one engagement. On the secession of Florida he offered his services to the governor of that State. At this time he was lieutenant-colonel of cavalry. Returning from Texas he received, first an appointment as major of artillery in the Confederate service, and afterward that of lieutenant-colonel of cavalry. He was ordered to Lynchburg, Va., to muster in troops, and on Gen. Joseph E. Johnston taking command of Harper's Ferry, he accompanied him as chief-of-staff. After the evacuation of Harper's Ferry he received from President Davis the commission of brigadier-general. He was shot while gallantly leading a charge at Manassas, and was carried to the rear. Recovering from the wound he was assigned to the Department of Tennessee, Kentucky and the mountain region of North Carolina and Alabama. He led the advance into Kentucky, winning the victory at Richmond. He was then assigned to the command of the Trans-Mississippi Department, and defeated Banks, on Red River, and Steele, in Arkansas. He was the last general to surrender in the war. After the war he was president of the Atlantic & Pacific Telegraph Company, and built the lines from Cincinnati to New Orleans. He was appointed vice-chancellor of the University of Nashville, and reopened that institution after the war. In 1874 he came to Sewanee as professor of mathematics, and has since filled that chair. He was married, in 1861, to Miss Cassie Selden, of Virginia, the fruits of this union being eleven children, all now living.

JOHN M. STEWART was born in Franklin County July 25, 1847, being one of two sons, the progeny of Anthony and Rebecca (Holland) Stewart. The father was a native of Tennessee, and lived and died in Franklin County. The mother was born in Alabama, but was reared from childhood in Franklin County, where she died in about 1857. The subject of this sketch lived with his grandfather, in this county, from the age of ten to that of sixteen. In 1867 he had learned telegraphy, and then accepted the position of operator in the employ of the Nashville, Chattanooga & St. Louis Railroad until 1875, when he was appointed local agent at Cowan, where he has since resided and yet holds the same position. He was married, November 16, 1870, to Elizabeth Brazelton, the fruits of this union being six children, of whom four are living. Their names are Venna, Leala, Myra, Sterling, Orlin and an infant, the last two being deceased. The mother of these children died September 16, 1882, and October 6, 1884, Mr. Stewart was married to Mrs. Mattie Sherrill, nee Shook. To this union one son has been born, James S. Mr. Stewart has recently built himself a very fine residence—the best in Cowan. He is a man of public spirit and, has done much for the up-building of Cowan, especially for the schools, etc. Both himself and Mrs. Stewart are very highly respected. Mrs. Stewart is a member of the Cumberland Presbyterian Church.

JOHN W. SYLER, the surveyor of Franklin County, was born April 23, 1825, in this county, being a son of Jacob and Jane (Thompson) Syler, natives of Franklin County, Tenn., and North Carolina, respectively. The grandfather was John Syler, who came from Rockbridge, County, Va., in 1812, and settled in the west part of this county. Here he reared his family, all the Sylers of the county being descendants of his. Jacob Syler, like his father, was a farmer, a man of ordinary means. The mother came from her native State to this county when young and lived all her remaining life in Franklin County. John W. Syler, the subject of this sketch, was reared on a farm. He attended and graduated from the Davidson College, of North Carolina, and then entered the profession of teaching. For about ten years he was professor of mathematics, languages and science in the Robert Donald College, at Winchester, Tenn. He then taught the Carrick Academy, of Winchester, for many years, being engaged in the profession of teaching altogether about twenty years. He has also carried on farming all the time since he was a young man. He now owns about 10,000 acres of wild land. He has been superintendent of public instruction in this county for many years. In 1878 he was elected county surveyor of Franklin County, and now holds that office. From 1869 to 1872 he was engaged in merchandising. He was married, in 1853, to Miss E. V. Mann, the fruits of this union being ten children, eight of whom are now living, and six of whom are grown, viz.: Mollie L. (wife of Peter Weir, of Texas), J. F., Annie V. (wife of Fred Heep, of Texas), Bettie J. (wife of J. C. Arledge), John T., Emma, Walter S. and M. R. Mr. Syler is a Blue Lodge Mason. Politically he is a firm Democrat.

WILLIAM E. TAYLOR, clerk of the county court was born January 14, 1824, one and one-half miles south of Winchester, his parents being James and Milly (Mullins) Taylor, natives of Virginia and North Carolina respectively. The parents were married in Virginia, and removed to eastern Kentucky, from where they emigrated to Franklin County, Tenn., in 1810. The father died in 1866, having been a farmer and was born in 1781. The mother was born in 1784 and died in 1868. William E. was reared on a farm. When twenty-three years of age he was elected clerk of the county court, and held the office ten years and three months before the war. During the war he was engaged in farming, and continued in that pursuit until 1882 when he was re-elected to the clerkship of the county court. He was married July 25, 1855, to Malinda J. Turney, daughter of Hopkins L. Turney. He has a family of eight children, viz: James, Hop. T., Dick, Mary E., Milly, Ellen, Orpha, and Jennie. Mr. Taylor is a stanch Democrat, and a highly respected citizen of the county.

CHARLES H. WADHAMS was born in Edinburgh, Scotland, in 1828. When sixteen years of age he left home and went to London, where he became one of the Queen's Light Guards. Three days after the death of the Duke of Wellington he embarked for America, landing at New York. He then went to Lake George, and there became the chief steward of the noted hotel, William Henry, for six years. Leaving there he removed to Nashville, Tenn., and was steward in different leading hotels of that city. Then he had charge of Gen. Hood's bakery while his army was there, and then of Gen. Thomas' bakery after he had taken the city. After the war he went to Atlanta, Ga., and there worked in the American House, thence to Lookout Mountain for two months. He then removed to Franklin, Williamson Co., Tenn., remaining there five years in the bakery and confectionery business. He then came to Sewanee at the solicitation of the university dean in 1871, and engaged in his present business. He was married January 1, 1853, to Elizabeth Gibson, of Scotland. This union has been blessed in the birth of one child, Lizzie. Mr. and Mrs. Wadhams are members of the Presbyterian Church. Politically Mr. Wadhams is a Democrat. He is enterprising, and commands the respect of the people who know him.

JOHN W. WEBER, head-master of the grammar school in Sewanee, Tenn., was born in Columbia, Maury Co., Tenn., May 2, 1853. He is a son of Henri Weber and M. I. Weber. During the sessions of 1870 and 1872 he attended the Edgefield Male Academy, and entered the University of the South as a student September 12, 1872. He was elected fifth assistant in the grammar school in March, 1877, and fourth assistant in 1878, first assistant in 1879, and head-master in 1881, which position he now holds and is filling in a very satisfactory manner. He was married, March 18, 1879, to Maud J. Graves, daughter of Henry and Susan Graves, of Davidson County, Tenn.

M. N. WHITAKER, of the law firm of Estill & Whitaker, was born in Lincoln County, Tenn., January 29, 1860. His father was Newton Whitaker, a native of Lincoln County, Tenn., a farmer by occupation and a man of financial means. He, the father, died in August, 1879. The mother is yet living near Mulberry, Lincoln Co., Tenn., on the old homestead. Our subject was reared on a farm, and was educated mainly in the Mulberry Academy of his native county. He began reading law when nineteen years of age, and entered the practice of his profession when twenty-one. In January, 1883, he located in Winchester in his present partnership. He was married, October 15, 1885, to Miss Florence J. Griffin. Mr. and Mrs. Whitaker are both members of the Missionary Baptist Church. Mr. Whitaker is a firm Democrat in politics.

GREENOUGH WHITE. Ferdinand Eliot White was born in 1788, and was a merchant in the city of Boston. He was graduated from Trinity College, Hartford, Conn., in 1854. He was twice married, his second wife being Dorothy Gardner, who was born in 1799, and a niece of Madam Hancock. To them were born four daughters and three sons, our subject's father, John Gardner White, being born in 1833. Our subject's maternal grandfather, George Beach, was born in 1788, and for many years was president of the Phœnix Bank in the city of Hartford. For his second wife he married Maria, daughter of C. Nichols, of Hartford. She was born in 1799. One of her sisters married George

Beach, Jr., the eldest of Grandfather Beach's seven sons by his first marriage, and another sister became the wife of Isaac Toucy, Senator and Secretary of the Navy under James Buchanan. Our subject's mother was a Miss Beach. She was married to John Gardner White in June, 1862, and our subject, Greenough White, was born on September 17, 1863, it being the anniversary of the death of his uncle, William Greenough White, on the battle-field of Antietam. Greenough, our subject, was prepared for entrance to Harvard College at the private school of G. W. C. Noble, of Boston, and entered the university in the autumn of 1880, and in June, 1884, he received his degree as B. A. (*cum laude*, and with honorable mention in English). Through the following year he pursued courses in literature, ecclesiastical history and the history of art, and was graduated as Master of Arts in June, 1885. In the same month he was appointed assistant professor of modern languages in the University of the South.

B. LAWTON WIGGINS was born in Sand Ridge, Berkeley Co., S. C., September 11, 1861. His father was James Wiggins, Esq., planter. His mother was the daughter of Col. William Millard, for many years State senator in *ante bellum* days. In 1868 the family moved to Spartanburg, in the northern part of the State, for educational facilities. From Spartanburg they moved to Charleston, in 1873, where Mr. Wiggins attended the Holy Communion Church Institute. At the end of four years, having graduated there, he entered the University of the South, at Sewanee, Tenn., in 1877. In 1879 he became assistant to the professor of modern languages, and in August of the same year assistant to the professor of ancient languages, which position he retained until 1881, when he became first assistant in the Grammar School Department of the University. He received, in 1880, the degree of B. A., and in 1882 that of A. M., in which year he was elected professor of ancient languages and literature, which position he still retains. In the winters of 1883 and 1884 he attended the Greek Seminary of the John Hopkins University under that eminent scholar, Prof. B. L. Gildersleeve, and was made fellow by courtesy.

CLAIBORNE N. WILLIAMS is a native of White County Tenn., and one of Franklin County's enterprising farmers. He was born in 1830, and is of a family of thirteen children, born to Jesse and Malon (Sewell) Williams. Jesse Williams was born 1783, in North Carolina, and first married Caroline Maston, to whom five children were born, then she died, and he married the mother of our subject. They moved from White County, Tenn., to Mississippi, and from there to Franklin County, Ark., where they both died, 1855 and 1866, father and mother respectively. At the age of seventeen, our subject came from Mississippi, to Franklin County, Tenn., and procured for himself such educational advantages as the common schools of this county offered at that time. In 1854, he married Martha Hatchett, and followed farming until 1862, when he enlisted in Company K, Fourth Tennessee Cavalry, and remained with that command till the close of the war; then returned home and resumed farming at the place where he now resides, which he purchased in 1859. Mr. Williams devotes considerable attention to wheat raising and is very successful in that branch of agriculture. Mr. and Mrs. Williams are members of the Christian Church. To them have been born twelve children, nine of whom are still living, part being members of church with the father and mother, while part identify themselves with the Baptist Church. Politically Mr, Williams is a Democrat, and is in sympathy with the principles of prohibition.

DR. HARVEY P. WILLIAMS, one of Franklin County's most prominent physicans, who was born in Bedford County, Tenn., Feburary 14, 1850, being one of thirteen children born to the marriage of Aaron Williams and Patsie Brothers. The father was born in Buckingham County, Virginia, in 1801, and in about 1815, he immigrated to Rutherford County, Tenn., where he married about 1820. Dr. Williams remained with his parents until attaining the age of twenty-one, when he engaged in merchandising at Millersburg. He afterward traveled in Texas one year, and upon his return, began the reading of medicine under Dr. White, of Millersburg. After attending the medical college at Nashville, he began the practice of that profession, in Bedford County, in 1875. After one year he removed to Cowan, where he has very successfully continued to practice. His marriage ceremony was solemnized December 23, 1875, uniting him to Sallie E. Brothers, a native of Rutherford County. Dr. Williams is a member of the K. of H. the A. O. U. W. the I.O.O.F. and of the Christian Church. He has always been a Democrat in politics, and is an advocate of prohibition. Mrs. Williams is a member of the Cumberland Presbyterian Church.

GEORGE THORNTON WILMER, D. D., was born on the 8th of May, 1819, at Alexandria, then within the District of Columbia. His father, the Rev. William Holland Wilmer, D. D., was a native of Kent County, Md., where his ancestors were seated as early as 1693, at which time the American record of the family begins. He became rector of St. Paul's, Alexandria, was prominent in the successful effort to resuscitate the Episcopal Church in Virginia and in founding the Theological Seminary of the Diocese of Virginia, being one of its earliest professors. After leaving Alexandria he became rector of Bruton Parish, Williamsburg, Va., and president of the College of William and Mary. He died in 1827, in his forty-fifth year, and while holding both of these offices. The authorities of Williamsburg took charge of his burial; he was interred beneath the chancel of the parish church, and a memorial tablet, the contribution of Christians of all the denominations in the town, commemorates affectionate esteem of his character and services. The family of Dr. W. H. Wilmer removed to Fairfax County, Va. The pious care of his widow, a step-mother in name to many of the children, and a real mother to all the children of a large and dependent family, provided such means of education as a home school could supply, followed by such collegiate training, in the case of the sons, as they saw fit. George T. Wilmer, after a short stay at Bristol College, which he left without graduating, passed about two years in civil engineering; then two years in studying law, and in managing the small farming interests of the family; then three years at the Theological Seminary of Virginia, whence he was graduated in 1843; was ordained deacon by Bishop Meade. The larger part of his diaconate was passed at Wilmington, N. C., as assistant to Rev. R. H. Wilmer, rector of St. James', in that city, and subsequently bishop of the Diocese of Alabama. Rev. George T. Wilmer was admitted to priest's orders by Bishop Johns in 1844, and took charge of a parish in the counties of Botetourt and Roanoke, in the valley of Virginia; became rector of Bruton Parish, Williamsburg, in 1854; rector of a parish in Pittsylvania County in 1866; became rector of Christ Church, Mobile, Ala., and continued such rather more than two years; was for a short time in charge of Bishop Atkinson's Mission House, Asheville, N. C.; entered on his duties as professor of moral and intellectual philosophy and *belles-lettres* in the College of William and Mary, 1869; for about the last four years of his connection with the college, was also rector for the second time of Bruton Parish; in 1876 was elected professor of systematic divinity in the University of the South, and pending the organization of the theological department, assigned to duty as professor of metaphysics and English literature and other branches. From 1878 to 1885 he preformed the duties of professor of systematic divinity, professor of metaphysics, acting professor of political science and history, and lecturer on commercial law. Since the opening of the session of 1885–86, Dr. Wilmer has taught exclusively in the theological department. His degree of D. D. was conferred by the College of William and Mary in the year 1860.

JOSEPH D. WILSON, of the firm of Wilson & Francis, general merchants, was born in Pittsylvania County, Va., May 20, 1824. The father, Green B. Wilson, was a farmer by occupation, and in 1848 removed to Henry County. Tenn., where he died in 1866. The mother, *nee* Frances Q. Holderby, survived the father, and departed this life in 1874. Joseph D. was reared on a farm, and remained with his parents till after coming to Henry County, Tenn. He received but a limited early education. In Henry County he engaged in farming and in the tobacco business till 1885, when he removed to Winchester and engaged in his present trade in February of that year. He has been successful, and carries a stock of about $8,000. He chose as his helpmeet, Miss Annie E. Cox, the matrimonial ceremony being solemnized October 29, 1868. This union has been blessed in the birth of eight children, one of whom died in infancy. The others are Annie Q. Hunter L.

Ruth A., Asa B., Lydia M., Flora D., and Hoyland L. Mr. Wilson, his wife, and three children, are members of the Baptist Church. Politically, Mr. Wilson is a firm Democrat, and always has been. He is an enterprising and respected citizen of the county.

SAMUEL M. WOODWARD is a Tennesseean, born in Lincoln County, June 12, 1823. He remained at home until his marriage to Caroline Frame, August 3, 1845, also a native of Lincoln County. In 1854, he purchased his farm of 135 acres, where he has since lived, and has given his attention to agriculture and stock raising, and has been fairly prosperous in his business ventures. January 4, 1886, Mrs. Woodward died, having borne seven children, two of whom still survive: William B., born in 1846, and died in 1879; married Lizzie Lockhart in 1869, and was blessed by the birth of four children; James P., born in 1848, and died in 1864; John L., born in 1851, and died in 1858; Samuel W., born in 1853; Sarah A., born in 1855; Nicy M., born in 1858, and died the same year, and Susan E., born in 1861, and died in 1863. Mr. Woodward is a member of the Methodist Episcopal Church, and has always voted the Democratic ticket.

# GILES COUNTY.

CHARLES CLAYTON ABERNATHY, M. D., a successful practitioner, was born near Pulaski October 9, 1827. His early youth was passed on the farm and in attending the county schools. Later he attended the Wurtemberg Academy at Pulaski. He subsequently spent three years at Cumberland University at Lebanon. In 1848 he began the study of medicine under Dr. R. G. P. White, and in the spring of 1851 he graduated at the University of Pennsylvania. Located in Decatur County, West Tenn. In the same year he married Martha J. Stockard, of Maury County, and has two children by this union: Mary G. and Lizzie. After remaining five years in Decatur County, he moved to Pulaski, and here continued the practice until 1862, when he went on duty as a commissioned surgeon in the Army of Tennessee at the hospital at Chattanooga. In December, 1862, at his request, he was transferred to the Eighteenth Tennessee Infantry, Col. J. B. Palmer's regiment, Gen. John C. Brown's brigade, and served as the surgeon of this regiment until after the battle of Chickamauga, when he was transferred to the Third Tennessee Regiment, and continued to occupy that position until the close of the war. At the time of the surrender he was a prisoner of war at Fort Delaware, but was released July 19, 1865. In the fall of the same year he resumed the practice of medicine, and is still actively engaged in his profession. He is one of the leading physicians of this part of Tennessee. Mrs. Abernathy died in 1878, and the Doctor was married again, in 1880, to Mrs. Josephine C. McNairy, of Giles County. Mrs. McNairy was a Miss Wilkinson. Our subject is a Democrat, a Mason, and he and wife are members of the Methodist Episcopal Church South. He is a son of Charles C. and Susannah (Harris) Abernathy, and of Scotch-Irish descent. His father was born in Virginia in 1790, and his mother in Davidson County, Tenn., in 1800. The Abernathy family came to Tennessee in 1800, and settled in Davidson County, where the family resided until 1812. The grandfather died in 1835, and the father in 1876. The latter was clerk of the circuit court for twenty-four years. The mother of our subject died in 1845.

CHARLES ALFRED ABERNATHY, M. D., was born April 1, 1853, son of Alfred H. and Elizabeth T. (Butler) Abernathy, who were born in Giles County. The father for many years was one of the successful teachers of the county. Dr. Abernathy was educated in the common schools and Giles College, Pulaski. At the age of seventeen he quit farm work and began teaching, continuing for three years. During this time he was a disciple of Æsculapius, and subsequently attended lectures at the University of Louisville, graduating from the institution as an M. D. in 1875. He practiced one year in Pulaski, and then went to Prospect, Tenn., and formed a partnership with Dr. Theo. Westmoreland, but a year later moved to Lewisburg, Marshall County. In 1880 he returned to Pulaski, where he has since practiced his profession. In May, 1885, he formed a partnership with Dr. C. C. Abernathy, one of the oldest physicians of the county. The firm is styled Drs. C. C. & C. A. Abernathy. In February, 1884, Dr. Abernathy married Mrs. Ella (Ezell) Flournoy. The Doctor is a Democrat, a Knight of Pythias, and a member of the Methodist Episcopal Church South. Mrs. Abernathy is a Presbyterian.

LEWIS AMIS, of the firm of L. Amis & Bro., dealers in groceries and general merchandise, at Vale Mills, Giles Co., Tenn., was born December 5, 1836, in Pulaski, Tenn. He is a son of John and Martha A. Amis, both natives of North Carolina. John Amis was the son of John and Pollie Amis, natives of Granville County, N. C., and Martha Amis was the daughter of Thomas and Pollie (Robertson) Wilkinson, natives of North Carolina. The parents of our subject were married August 14, 1823, in Williamson County, and to them were born eight children, named Mary A., Nancy, Martha J., John W., James F., Field R., Lewis and Nancy E. J. Our subject was educated in the district schools, and his occupation has been merchandising and farming from early boyhood. In 1866 he was married to Rebecca E. Summerhill, daughter of Horace and Parmelia Summerhill, of Lauderdale County, Ala. To our subject and wife was born one son, John L. The Amis Bros. are Democrats in politics, and our subject is a member of the F. & A. M. and also the A. L. of H. The Amis family are members of the Methodist Episcopal Church South, and in high standing. They have been successful men in all their undertakings, and are regarded as prosperous and industrious business men. The older members of the family came here at an early date and have been known in this State for nearly a century. They are of Scotch-Irish descent.

HON. WILLIAM F. BALLENTINE, one of the county's most highly respected and influential citizens, was born August 24, 1832, in Pulaski, Tenn., and is the son of Andrew M. Ballentine, who was born in County Tyrone, Ireland, in 1791, immigrated to America in 1816, and in 1818 settled in Giles County, Tenn. In 1824 he married Mary T. Goff, daughter of John and Isabella Goff, natives of Virginia. In 1825 Andrew moved to Pulaski and engaged in the dry goods business. By this marriage he became the father of eight children, named John G., George W., Margaret J., William F., Andrew J., James H., Adilade and Virginia O. The father of these children died in 1863, and the mother is still living. Our subject was the fourth child born to his parents. He received a liberal business education at the Wurtemburg Academy, in Pulaski, and at the age of fifteen he withdrew from school and entered into active business as a dry goods merchant with his father and brother (George). In 1856 he purchased the tract of land where he now resides, and settled upon it in 1857. Here he followed agricultural pursuits until 1861, when he entered the army as captain in Col. Biffle's regiment of cavalry; afterward he was on detached service with the Second Kentucky Cavalry until the close of the war. Previous to the war, October 11, 1853, he married Sarah E. Leatherman, daughter of Charles and Eliza Leatherman, natives of Rutherford County, Tenn. Mrs. Ballentine was born April 5, 1835. In 1865 our subject moved back to Pulaski and engaged in mercantile pursuits, which he followed until 1868. He was one of the incorporators of the Pulaski Savings Bank in 1879, and was president of the same until 1880. At that time he moved back to his farm, where he now resides on 500 acres of valuable land, known as the Glenn Gower Stock Farm. He also has 800 acres of land in the Twentieth District, Giles County. In 1882 he was elected to the State Legislature from Giles County, and served one term. He is a Democrat, a member of the K. of H., and A. L. of H. and R. A. He and wife are members of the Methodist Episcopal Church South, at Mount Pisgah.

ANDREW J. BALLENTINE, farmer of Giles County, Tenn., was born in Pulaski, December 30, 1834, and is the fifth child born to the union of Andrew M. and Mary Ballentine. He received a liberal education in the Wurtemburg Academy and at the age of nineteen began clerking in his father's dry goods store, in Pulaski. He remained in this capacity a number of years and then began farming, which was interrupted by the breaking out of the war. He joined Gen. Logwood's Battalion of Cavalry, but was soon transferred to Gen. Gordon's staff. After the war he again began farming and has followed that and merchandising up to the present time. In 1869, he wedded Amanda Kennedy, daughter of John and Pattie Kennedy, natives of New York. Mr. and Mrs. Ballentine have four children: Orlean, Sallie W., Hick and Lady. Mr. Ballentine gives considerable attention to fine stock-raising, and owns some fine land south and north of Pulaski, both portions being well improved. Mr. Ballentine is a Democrat, and of Irish descent.

THOMAS W. BARBER'S birth occurred on the 23d day of May, 1843, in Giles County, Tenn. His parents, Isaac J. and Eliza A. (Gordon) Barber, were born in Virginia, in 1814 and 1815, respectively. They were Tennessee pioneers, and did much to clear and settle the State. The father died September 29, 1885, and the mother in October 1858. At the age of eighteen, our subject enlisted in the Confederate Army in Col. Wheeler's First Tennessee Cavalry, and served until the close of the war, participating in many of the most important and bloodiest engagements. January 20, 1867, he married Maggie A. Reid, born January 12, 1849, daughter of John P. C. Reed, of Giles County. Their children are named Henry R., Thomas Guy, Sammie C., T. Wesley, John I., Shellie M. and Lena M. Mr. Barber was raised under Whig influences, but since the war has not been identified with any party. He is a Mason, and owns a farm of 150 acres, cotton being the principal production. Mrs. Barber's parents were of Irish extraction. The father was a Tennesseean by birth, and was magistrate of Giles County for about thirty years and represented his county in the State Legislature one term. The mother's maiden name was Sarah A. Hazlewood.

JOHN L. BAUGH, an enterprising farmer, residing five miles south of Pulaski, in the Eighth District of Giles County, was a native of Williamson County, Tenn., born in 1841, and of German descent. His parents, Philip and Elizabeth Baugh, were natives of Tennessee, and were considered first-class citizens. Our subject secured a good education, and has been from early boyhood actively engaged in farming. In 1867 he was married to Mary D. Wilkins, and to them was born one child, a daughter, Annie. The mother of this child died in 1869, and in 1871 he wedded Docia Reed, who died in the fall of the same year. In 1874 he was again married to Lucy R. Grigsby, and this union resulted in the birth of two children. The family are consistent members of the Methodist Episcopal Church South. Mr. Baugh is a Democrat and a member of the F. & A. M. fraternity. In 1869 he moved to where he now resides, on 310 acres of excellent land, well improved. He is a rather succesful man in all his undertakings, and is regarded as a prosperous and industrious farmer.

JOHN A. BEASLEY, a practical and successful farmer, was born within one mile of his present residence October 14, 1822, being the fifth of eleven children of William M. and Elizabeth (Anthony) Beasley, who were natives of North Carolina, and were early settlers of Giles County, Tenn. Here they were married and raised their family. The father died in Madison County, Miss., in 1832, and the mother at the old homestead, in Giles County, in January, 1852. Our subject received a somewhat limited early education, and through life has followed farming. He served in the late war in the First Tennessee Cavalry, and served seventeen months. He was opposed to secession, and used his influence and votes to keep his State in the Union, but after secession became a fixed fact he followed the fortunes of his State. He was at Corinth, Iuka, and Thompson's Station, and at the battle of Iuka his horse was shot dead under him. He became exempt from service in 1863. October 24, 1844, he wedded Sarah C. Wells, born in Giles County July 28, 1828, daughter of Jesse Wells, an early settler of the county, born in Virginia in 1797, and to them were born eleven children: Jesse Fendle, William J. E., John E., Reble L., Dayton, Ann E., Sarah J., Eudora M. M., Ida J., Louella, and Daisy V. Mr. Beasley was formerly an old line Whig, but is now a Democrat. He is a Mason, and he and wife own 350 acres of land, and he is called one of the open-handed and honorable citizens of the county. He and his oldest daughter are members of the Cumberland Presbyterian Church, while his wife and the rest of the family belong to the Methodist Episcopal Church South.

HENRY L. BOOTH, trustee of Giles County and a native of that county, was born in 1844, near Bethel of said county. His father, Charles Thomas Booth and Mahala E. Jones, of Giles County, were married in 1843, and to their union were born six children: Henry L., Dewit M., Thomas M., Virginia A., Richard H. and Brown A. Booth. The father died in 1857. The mother is still living. The subject of this sketch received his early education in the common schools of Giles County. In 1862 he volunteered in the Thirty-second Tennessee Regiment, Confederate States Army, and served until the close of the war. He then attended school at the academy at College Grove, Williamson County, Tenn., leaving school in 1867. He then joined the Tennessee Annual Conference of the Methodist Episcopal Church South, serving the appointments of Rogersville, Moulton and Montevallo Station, Ala., and Savannah Circuit, Lawrenceburg and Carthage, Tenn. After which failing health compelled him to suspend active labors. He then alternated between the occupations of farming and teaching until he was elected trustee of Giles County August 7, 1884, which office he still holds. He was married October 6, 1873, to Ella Cullom, of Carthage, Tenn., daughter of Gen. William and Virginia A. Cullom, who were of Kentucky origin. To this union have been born three children: Henry Cullom, Virginia Ella and Leslie Ewell Booth. The subject of this sketch, in politics, is a Democrat, and a member of the Masonic fraternity.

JOSEPH W. BRADEN, circuit clerk, was born in Giles County February 14, 1846, son of Jacob G. and Harriet (Johnson) Braden, and is of Scotch-Irish origin. The parents of our subject died when he was a mere boy, and at an extremely early age he was compelled to fight life's battle for himself. He attended the country schools, and at the age of fifteen cast his lot with the Confederate States Army, in Company E, Eleventh Tennessee. He was captured twice, and both times made his escape. For one year after the war he attended school, his instructor being Edward Paschall, Jr. After this he clerked for some time in the store of Stacy, Morris & Co. In 1875 he was appointed deputy clerk and master under Maj. J. B. Stacy, and that continued for four years. He then farmed for for four years. In 1880 he married Miss Anna Bell Johnson, of this county. The fruits of this union were two children: Bessie and Rebecca S. Mr. Braden is a thorough Democrat, and in 1882 was elected circuit court clerk of Giles County. He has been one of the best officers the county has ever had, and is a highly respected citizen. Mrs. Braden is a member of the Presbyterian Church.

HENRY M. BRANNON, merchant, is a son of Robert and Elizabeth (Carson) Brannon, and was born in Franklin County, Tenn., October 21, 1842, and is of Scotch-Irish origin. Robert Brannon was born in Tennessee in 1795, and Elizabeth Brannon, his wife, was born in the same State in 1798. The former died in 1854, and the latter in 1849. Our subject received a fair education and came to Pulaski in 1859, where he remained until the breaking out of the war. In 1861 he enlisted in Company C, First Tennessee Regiment, Confederate States Army, and was in the leading battles fought in Virginia. He was captured at Petersburg, Va., in 1865, and was a prisoner two months in Fort Delaware. In 1867 he began merchandising in Pulaski, where he is still engaged in that business. In 1872 he wedded Mattie M. Bugg, daughter of Hon. R. M. Bugg, and to them were born six children: Annie L., Robert B., Pattie C., Thomas F., Lizzie M. and an infant not named. Mr. Brennon is one of the leading merchants of this portion of Tennessee. At the time of the organization of the Peoples National Bank he was elected one of the directors, and now holds that position. He is one of the prominent men of the city, and he and wife are exemplary members of the Methodist Episcopal Church South. He is a Democrat in politics, and a member of the Masonic fraternity.

CHARLES BUFORD, of the firm of Buford & Carter, in Pulaski, Tenn., dealers in hardware and agricultural implements, was born March 3, 1839, and is a son of Nicholas

C. and Elizabeth W. Buford, who were Tennesseeans by birth, and were married in 1838. To them were born the following family: Charles, Richard B., Elbridge G., Lewis C., William A., Irene, Lucretia, Thomas, Mark, Sallie, Lucy, Lena, May and Claud. Nicholas C. Buford died in 1869. Charles is the eldest of the family, and received a liberal education in Giles College, at Pulaski. In 1861 he enlisted in the Third Tennessee Regiment and served until 1864, when he was wounded at Resaca, Ga., and retired from active service. After his return he farmed, and in the fall of 1866 moved to Nashville and engaged in clerking and book-keeping until 1870, when he returned to Giles County, and until 1875 was a tiller of the soil in that and Shelby County. At the latter date he moved to Pulaski, and has since been engaged in his present business. In 1870 he and Rosa Carter were married. To them was born one child—Mabel. Mrs. Buford died in 1872, and in 1884 Ella Stokes became Mr. Buford's second wife. They have one daughter— Martha S. Our subject is a member of the Cumberland Presbyterian Church, and his wife of the Methodist Episcopal Church South. Mr. Buford is a Democrat and a member of the F. & A. M. fraternity.

FRANK G. BUFORD was born near where he now lives December 13, 1851, son of Hon. Thomas Buford, who was also born in Giles County, Tenn. He was the first president of what was formerly known as the Nashville & Decatur Railway, and was a member of the Tennessee General Assembly for a number of years. He was one of the most prominent men of Giles County at the time of his death, which occurred here in 1860. The Buford family is of English origin. The paternal grandfather of our subject was an extensive land-owner. Our subject is the fourth of seven children born to his parents. His mother, Mary Ann (Gordon) Buford, was a daughter of Thomas K. Gordon. Our subject was educated at the common schools and at the Washington and Lee University, in Virginia. He graduated from this institution in 1878, and after returning home engaged in teaching school for some years. Later he turned his attention to farming and stock-raising. Since 1876 he has been engaged in the breeding of trotting and pacing horses, but now gives his undivided attention to the breeding of pacing horses. He owns the famous pacer, "Tom Hal," sire of "Little Brown Jug," who has made the three fastest straight heats of any horse in America; time, 2:11¾, 2:11¾, and 2:12½. Among the famous sires that have been at Rockdale Farm are "Almont, Jr.," 2:29, sire of "Annie W.," 2:20; "Prince Pulaski," sire of "Mattie Hunter," 2:12¾; Gen. Hardee, sire of "Thunder," 2:22¾, and Buford's "Tom Hal." Mr. Buford is making a success in breeding pacing horses, and deserves the credit of being the first man in the United States to give his whole attention to and make a specialty of breeding pacers. In 1879 Mr. Buford married Lavina Childress, of this county, and by her has one child—Amanda. Mrs. Buford died in 1884. Our subject is a Democrat and one of the leading stockmen of Tennessee.

ADRIAN D. BULL, a retired merchant of Elkton, Tenn., is a native of the "Buckeye State," born in Greene County in 1815. His parents, John and Katherine Bull, were Virginians, who were married about 1793, and moved to Ohio in 1798. They became the parents of the following ten children: Benjamin F., William, Elizabeth, Arthur, Susan A., Katherine, Mary A., Adrian D., Richard R. and Caroline. The father and mother died in Ohio in 1825 and 1833, respectively. Adrian D. attended the common schools of the "Buckeye State," and in that State learned the saddler's trade. He came to Giles County, Tenn., in 1837, and located in Pulaski, where he worked at his trade. In 1838 he was married to Ursla Williams, daughter of John and Mildred Williams, and in 1843 moved to Elkton and worked at his trade until the outbreaking of the war. He then retired from active business until 1865, at which time he engaged in the dry goods business, continuing until 1881, when he sold his interest and retired from active life. He is essentially a self-made man, and is considered an estimable citizen. To him and wife were born the following children: Caroline, Julia A., John W., Ann L., Charles O., Evaline, Susan, and Mildred. They are members of the Methodist Episcopal Church South, and Mr. Bull belongs to the F. & A. M.

JAMES H. CAMPBELL, M. D., (deceased) was a leader in the society and every good work, and came of the pioneer family of John and Sarah Campbell. He was born in Maury County, Tenn., February 7, 1820, and spent his earliest days on a farm. His early education was liberal, and when young in years began the study of medicine, and graduated from the Kentucky School of Medicine, and as early as 1843 located at Campbellsville, Giles Co., Tenn., and began practicing his profession. He was twice married the first time in 1843, to Sarah M. Hunt, who died in 1863 leaving three children: John E., Mary E., and Anna M. Two years after his first wife's death the Doctor wedded Mary S. Alexander, born in Giles County, in 1842, and his widow and the following six children survive him: Alexander, Clarence, Colon, Sallie, Reece and Lillie. He was a Democrat and Mason, and a leading member of the Christian Church. He was an honest and respected citizen, and in his death the county lost one of its truest and best men. His death occurred in 1884. His widow yet resides on the homestead at Campbellsville. She is a member of the Cumberland Presbyterian Church, and is a daughter of D. A. and Saphronia Alexander, born in Tennessee in 1811 and 1817, and died in 1882 and 1851, respectively.

H. TAYLOR CAMPBELL, M. D., Lynnville, Tenn., is a native of Hickman County, Tenn., born February 9, 1848, son of Hiram H. and Susan (Sisco) Campbell, and is of Scotch-Irish origin. His father was born in Williamson County, Tenn., January 17, 1814, and his mother in Hickman County, Tenn., January 18, 1818. Our subject's grandfather was William Campbell of North Carolina. The family came to Tennessee about 1800, and here Hiram Campbell died October 18, 1851, and his wife July 15, 1857. Our subject is one of four children and spent his early days on his father's farm. He attended the common schools and Centreville Academy, and in 1870 began the study of medicine, attending lectures at the old Medical College, of Nashville, and the medical department of Vanderbilt University, from which he graduated in 1875. A year later he located at Pleasantville, in Hickman County, and there continued the practice of his profession until 1879, when he came to Giles County, and in 1881 to Lynnville. He is the leading physician of the town and has an extensive and lucrative practice. In 1877, he married Ardella C. Ross, of Giles County. They have three children: Willie R., Susan A. and Sophia M. Dr. Campbell is a Democrat, and he and wife are members of the Cumberland Presbyterian Church.

WILLIAM C. CARTER, a prominent farmer and stock-raiser, residing in Giles County, Tenn., son of Joshua and Mary Carter, whose natal State was North Carolina. They were married about 1827, and became the parents of five children: Jane, Joshua H., William C., John N. and Jacob D. The father died in 1878, and his wife in 1859. Our subject is the third of their children and was educated in the common schools of Giles County. He assisted at farm work in early life, and in 1867 settled on the farm where he now resides. He owns 400 acres of valuable and well improved land, and of late years has devoted his time to breeding and developing fine stock, in which he has been more than ordinarily successful. In 1867 the nuptials of his marriage with Sarah J. Simmons were celebrated, and to their union have been born two children: David P. and John W. Mr. and Mrs. Carter are members of the Presbyterian Church, and he is a supporter of Democratic principles. Mrs. Carter's parents are Merrill and Jane Simmons, of Giles County.

J. SAMUEL CHILDERS, wholesale and retail dealer in groceries, was born in Pulaski, Tenn., April 28, 1846, son of J. B. and Susan (Ezell) Childers, and is of Scotch-Irish and English descent. The parents were natives of Virginia and Tennessee, respectively. The former was born August 29, 1815, and the latter was born October, 1825, and died in Giles County in 1865. The Childers family immigrated to Tennessee in 1819, and settled in Giles County. They have for many years been one of the leading families of this county. Our subject, one of the prominent business men of this city, is the eldest of five living children. He was educated at Giles College in Pulaski, and in 1864 enlisted in Company K, First Tennessee Cavalry, and remained in the Confederate service until the close of the war. In 1865 he engaged in the merchandise business in Pulaski, and in 1868 he was joined in marriage to Miss Ada Pullen, of Giles County. This union was blessed by the birth of one child, Ben. From 1869 to 1874 Mr. Childers was in the dry goods business at Wales Station, this county, but in the latter year he returned to Pulaski, where he continued the dry goods business for two years, and then for four years was connected with a cotton factory. In 1874 he began the grocery business in this city, and has since continued that occupation. Mr. Childers is an enterprising man and a Democrat in politics. He is a Knight Templar, Pulaski Commandery, No. 12, and he and wife are members of the Methodist Episcopal Church South.

WILLIAM A. COFFMAN is the eldest of two children of Amers and Mary M. (Acock) Coffman, and was born in Logan County, Ky., March 23, 1832, and after attending the common schools began tilling the soil. He has been twice married, the first time in Giles County, Tenn., October 16, 1855, to Agnes E. Howard, daughter of Wesley Howard, and became the parents of these children: Rollin, who died November 10, 1882; Robert, died October 27, 1884; Benjamin F., James F., William, Julius C., Arthur, Mary J., Anna Lee and Sallie V. These children's mother was born in Giles County, Tenn., December 5, 1837, and died August 27, 1879. Our subject married for his second wife, Maggie R. Barbour. To them were born two daughters: Emma M. and Eva M. Her parents, John L. and Elizabeth E. (Guinn) Barbour; the mother's father, Wm. Guinn, being an eminent divine of the Methodist Episcopal Church, Tennessee. Mr. Coffman is an old-line Democrat and a member of the Methodist Episcopal Church South. He has a farm of 109 acres, on which he raises cotton and the cereals. His paternal grandfather, Adam Coffman, was a British soldier and served through the entire Revolutionary war. He was discharged at Montreal, Canada, but was afterward married in Maryland, and then came to Kentucky. Our subject's maternal grandfather was a soldier in the Revolutionary war in the Colonial Army, serving over seven years, and participating in the battles of Camden, Yorktown, Guilford Court House, Brandywine, and many others.

WILLIAM R. CRAIG, grain dealer, was born a few miles west of Pulaski, Tenn., November 21, 1852, son of W. J. and Virginia (Abernathy) Craig, and is of Scotch-Irish lineage. His father and mother were born in Tennessee and Virginia in 1820 and 1831, respectively. The Craig family came to Tennessee in 1815, and settled in Williamson County, and in 1840 came to Giles County, Tenn., and here the father died in 1884. William R. was the eldest of his six children. He was educated in Woodlawn Academy, and in 1870 came to Pulaski, and for three years was clerk in a grocery establishment. He then began business for himself, continuing until 1882, when he was burned out. In the fall of the same year he engaged in the grain business, and has continued the same up to the present time. He also deals in fruit, and annually ships large quantities of the same. In 1874 he and Sallie Ezell were united in marriage, and four children have blessed their union: W. Ezell, Robert P., Flournoy and Edward M. Mr. Craig is a Democrat and Mason, Knight Templar degree. They are members of the Episcopal Church, and he is one of the popular men of the county.

THOMAS E. DALY, of the firm of Moore & Daly, at Elkton, Giles Co., Tenn., was born March 16, 1859, son of Thomas B. and Martha A. Daly, whose natal States were Virginia and Tennessee, respectively. They were married in Giles County about 1844, and four daughters and three sons blessed their union: Mary V., Ella N., James W., Frederick R., Thomas E., Annie L. and Florence E. The father and mother died in 1873 and 1869, respectively. Thomas E. obtained his education principally at Oak Hill, Tenn., and in 1877 was engaged as clerk by A. D. Bull & Co., and remained with that firm until January, 1881, when he bought out Mr. Bull's interest in the business, and the firm is now known as Moore & Daly. January 2, 1881, Mr. Daly was married to Georgie Bull, daughter of Richard Bull, of Epton, and he and wife are members of the Methodist Episcopal Church South at that place. Our subject is a Democrat and of Irish descent, and belongs to an old and highly respected family.

WASHINGTON R. DICKERSON, farmer and stock-raiser, residing in the Thirteenth District of Giles County, Tenn., near Buford's Station, was born in Lynchburg, Va., October 21, 1811, and is a son of Terry and Nancy Dickerson, who were born in the "Old Dominion" and were married about 1805. Mary K., Allen A. and Washington R. are their children. The father died in 1818 and the mother in 1813. Our subject came to this State when a small lad, with some relatives, and settled in Maury County, where his education was very much neglected. He has farmed from boyhood, and in 1838 settled on a farm of his own. He owns 600 acres of as fine land as Giles County produces, besides 235 acres in the Fifteenth District and some valuable property in Pulaski, all of which he has made by his own good management and industry and the aid of his wife, who is in every sense of the word a helpmate. In 1843 he married Mary J. Stone, and eight children have blessed their union: Sarah K., Ophelia S., William A., Mary J., Betsy S., Rosa B. S., Washington R. and Jeffie. The family are Presbyterians, and our subject is a Democrat and of Irish lineage.

HON. Z. W. EWING, lawyer, a native of Marshall County, Tenn., is a son of L. A. and R. A. (Leeper) Ewing, and of old Scotch-Irish Presbyterian stock. His father was born near Athens, Ga., in 1809, and his mother in Bedford County, Tenn., in the same year. The father was a merchant and farmer and for many years was one of the leading magistrates of Marshall County. He died in 1853. The mother of our subject died in 1877, in Marshall County. Mr. Ewing was the seventh of eight children. During his youth his summers were spent on the farm at labor and in the winter season he attended the country schools. In 1859 he was a student at the Lewisburg Male Academy, and in 1860 went to Maryville College, in East Tennessee, where he remained until the breaking out of the war. He then joined Capt. R. H. McCrory's company, afterward Company H, Seventeenth Tennessee Infantry, Confederate States Army, and was promoted to lieutenant by commission, but served in the capacity of captain and major for two years. He was captured at Petersburg, Va., in 1864, and was confined under retaliation in the prisons of Fort Delaware, Fort Pulaski, Hilton Head and Sullivan's Island, upon the southern coast. He was released in 1865, and came home and resumed his studies. In 1866 he entered the University of Virginia, and there remained until the summer of 1868. In the fall of that year he taught school at Richmond, Tenn. In 1870 he went to Europe and spent a year in travel and the study of the German language. In 1871 he came to Pulaski and began the study of law in the office of Judge Thomas M. Jones. In the same year he wedded Harriet P. Jones, of Pulaski. They have one child—Marietta. December, 1871, he was licensed to practice law, and in May, 1877, he was appointed by Gov. Porter, as one of the three railway assessors for the State. In 1878 he was elected to the State Senate from the counties of Giles, Lawrence, Lewis and Wayne, and was chairman of and member of important committees. In 1879 he was appointed State visitor of the University of Tennessee, and delivered the annual address before that institution. September, 1879, he was appointed special attorney for the State and is now engaged in the practice of his profession. He has been a life-long Democrat, and has occupied many positions of public trust and has presided over one of the State conventions of his party. He is one of Giles County's most prominent men. Mrs. Ewing is a member of the Episcopal Church.

WILL S. EZELL, county court clerk, is a native of Pulaski, Tenn., and a son of P. H. and Mary A. (Shields) Ezell. The father was born in this county in 1816, and his mother was also born in this county in 1827. The Ezell family came to Giles County in 1808, and is one of the pioneer familes of this part of Tennessee. Our subject's birth occurred December 16, 1847. He was educated in Giles College, and in 1864 enlisted in Company K, First Tennessee. After the war he engaged as clerk in a store and for some time as book-keeper. He then engaged in the mercantile business for himself. In 1878 his father was elected county court clerk and our subject served as deputy county court clerk for four years. In 1875 he was united in marriage to Ada Faust, of this county, and the fruits of this union were four children: Otis M., Mary A., Edith and John F. In 1882 Mr. Ezell was elected county court clerk and has since held that office. He is a thorough practical business man and has made a good officer. He is a Democrat and a Knight Templar, Pulaski Commandery, No. 12. He came of an old and well respected family, and he and wife are members of the Methodist Episcopal Church South.

PINK M. EZELL, dealer in stoves, tinware and house-furnishing goods, is a native Pulaski, Tenn., born January 19, 1860, son of P. H. and Mary Ezell, old and prominent settlers of this county. Our subject is one of ten children, and is of Scotch-French descent. He was educated in the Pulaski schools, and when about sixteen years of age became salesman in the grocery store of W. R. Craig, and later clerked in a stove and tin store, and continued in this capacity until 1880, when he began business for himself, and has continued successfully in the stove and tinware business up to the present time. Mr. Ezell has made his own way in life, and is one of the prosperous young business men of Pulaski. In 1882 he united his fortunes with that of Mattie McCord, daughter of W. I. McCord, ex-editor of the Pulaski *Citizen*. Mr. and Mrs. Ezell have two daughters, named Mary and Margery. Mr. Ezell is a Democrat, and he and wife are church members.

ABRAM F. FINLEY is the son of Carroll and Nancy Finley, natives of Tennessee. They were married in 1835, and to them were born the following children: James L. D., Martha E., Newton M., Abram F., Josie, Charles C. and Mollie. The mother died in 1854. Our subject was born in Marshall County in 1845, and received a liberal education in the district schools of Marshall County. In early life he assisted his father in farming. At the youthful age of sixteen he joined the Confederate Thirty-second Tennessee Regiment of Volunteers (Col. Ed. C. Cook, commanding), and remained in service until the close of the war, and participated in most of the principal battles. He then returned home, and was engaged in farming until 1867, when he came to Pulaski and engaged in the liquor business. He has been very successful financially, as he started on a very small capital, but by industry he has made himself a wealthy man. He is noted for his liberality, and contributes to all charitable organizations. He is a Democrat in politics. The early members of the Finley family emigrated from North Carolina at an early date, settled in Marshall County, and were among the first settlers of Middle Tennessee.

CAPT. JOHN D. FLAUTT, cashier of the Giles National Bank, was born in Lincoln County, Tenn., October 2, 1835, son of James and Delilah O. (Dillon) Flautt, and is of German descent. James Flautt was born in Maryland, in 1800, and his wife in North Carolina, in 1804. He came to Tennessee in 1820 and to Giles County in 1838, and died in the latter place in 1883. Mrs. Flautt died in 1868. Our subject is the sixth of their seven children, and received the rearing and schooling of the average farmer's boy, besides attending Giles College, at Pulaski. From 1860 until May 14, 1861, he was a clerk in the dry goods store of D. C. Corbt & Co. At the latter date he enlisted in John C. Brown's Company, Third Tennessee, Confederate States Army, as private, and was commissioned regimental quartermaster in October, 1862, with the rank of captain, and thus continued until the close of the war. In December, 1865, he engaged in the hardware business in Pulaski, but in 1882 was elected assistant cashier of Giles National Bank, and January, 1883, was elected cashier. May 19, 1869, he wedded Salonia M. Rose, daughter of Col. S. E. Rose. They have five children: Marcella R., James S., Mary L., John H. and Meredith. Mr. Flautt is a Democrat, and cast his first presidential vote for Buchanan. He became a Mason in 1866, and he and Mrs. Flautt are members of the Presbyterian Church.

WILLIAM FOGG, deceased, was a farmer and a stock raiser of the Sixth District in Giles County. He was born in King George County, Va., in 1799, son of Frederick and Elizabeth Fogg, natives of Virginia. William received a good education and came to this State, settling in Giles County in the early part of this century. He was a tiller of the soil, and in 1832 he was joined for life to Frances Fogg, who died in 1852, in Giles County. In 1855 he took for his second wife Sarah L. Morris, the widow of Gen. Lafayette Morris, and the daughter of Levi and Mary A. Reed, natives of Tennessee. By this union our subject became the father of five children, viz.: Annie M., Frances E., William R., Frederick A. and Louisa M. Mr. Fogg came from a very highly respected family, and is of English descent. He owned 300 acres of good land, all well improved, and was in very comfortable circumstances. He died in 1868, mourned by a large circle of relatives and friends. He was a Democrat in politics.

THOMAS S. FOGG'S birth occurred in King and Queen's County, Va, June 20, 1820, the oldest and only surviving member of a family of five children born to James G. and Patsy (LaFaun) Fogg, and is of Scotch and French extraction. James Fogg was born in Virginia, in 1790, and came to Tennessee in 1823. He served in the war of 1812, and died in Giles County, Tenn., July 2, 1852. The mother was also a Virginian, born in 1795, and died in 1833, in Tennesee. Our subject's grandfather, James Fogg, served in the war for Independence and fought at Bunker Hill and Cowpens. Our subject has made farming his chief business through life, but in early life followed carpentering and traveled in all the Southern States. Mary M. Beasley became his wife December 24, 1846, and has borne him twelve children, nine now living: Thomas A., Walter S., Oscar G., Harry P., Edwin, Claude, Guy, Gertrude and Maie. Mrs. Fogg was born May 11, 1829. Mr. Fogg was an old-line Whig and since the death of that party has not affiliated with any political organization. He was made a Mason in 1847, and owns the "Pleasant View" farm of 500 acres, and is a liberal and benevolent giver, aiding all laudable enterprises. The most of the family are members of the Cumberland Presbyterian Church.

ANDREW L. GLAZE, M. D., a practicing physician located at Elkton, Giles County, was born February 25, 1837, in Limestone County, Ala., and is of Irish extraction. He received his early education in the schools of Alabama, and subsequently attended school at Elkton, Giles County. In 1858 he began the study of medicine with Dr. A. J. Held, of Elkton, and in 1859 entered the University of Nashville and attended one course of lectures. At the time of the breaking out of the war he was connected with the medical department of the Confederate Army where he remained until the close of the war. He then returned to Elkton, and was engaged in the practice of his profession. October 18, 1866, he was joined in marriage to Martha J. Stone, daughter of Thomas J. and Almira Stone, of Lincoln County. By this union our subject and wife became the parents of four children: Lilla, Madora, Mattie and Annie. In 1874, Dr. Glaze entered the University of Nashville, and graduated from that institution in 1875. He then returned to Elkton, and has been constantly engaged in his profession ever since. The Doctor is a Democrat and a member of the Methodist Episcopal Church. Mrs. Glaze died May 2, 1886.

GEORGE D. GRAY, M. D., of Buford Station, Tenn., was born in Mississippi, near Holly Springs, Marshall County, June 18, 1845. His father, Dr. George W. Gray, was born in Maryland in 1814, and came to Tennessee in 1828, thence to Mississippi, thence to Arkansas in 1854, where he resided and practiced medicine until his death in 1873. Our subject's mother's maiden name was Sallie Reynolds, who was born in Giles County, Tenn., and died in 1848. George D. received a liberal education at North Mount Pleasant, Miss., and began the study of medicine in the fall of 1865, attending lectures at the University of Louisiana, at New Orleans, and subsequently attended lectures at Washington University, at Baltimore, Md., graduating from that institution in 1868. He located in Arkansas, where he practiced his profession with success until 1883, when he came to Giles County, Tenn., and has successfully practiced his profession at Buford Station. In 1873, he married Sallie Sloan, of Arkansas, and by her is the father of five children: Dudley, George W., St. Clair N., Janie and Maud. Dr. Gray and wife are members of the Methodist Episcopal Church South.

BERRY C. HARDIMAN is a son of William J. Hardiman, and was born in Charlotte County, Va., June 5, 1839. The father came to Tennessee in the fall of 1856, by wagon, the journey lasting seven weeks. He was married to Mary A. Irvin, who was born in Virginia in 1816, and died in Giles County April 4, 1865. Our subject in youth received the advantages the common schools afforded. He served in the Fifty-third Regiment, Tennessee Infantry, three years, and was captured at the fall of Fort Donelson, but escaped by swimming the Cumberland River. He then joined Wheeler's Cavalry, and after being exchanged at Vicksburg returned to his former regiment. He was at Port Hudson, Chickamauga, Missionary Ridge, the almost continuous battle from Dalton to Atlanta, Franklin and Nashville, where he was wounded and disabled for further service until the close of the war. He was married, February 12,

1868, to Mattie M. Barnes, and seven children blessed their union, six of whom are living: William, Mary A., Ozellar, Mattie M., Revy L., and Ethel B. Mrs. Hardiman was born in Giles County, April 9, 1845, the thirteenth of fifteen children born to Jeremiah and Marilla (Gooch) Barnes. Mr. Hardiman was a Whig, but since the war has voted the Democratic ticket, and he and family are members of the Methodist Episcopal Church South. He owns 253 acres of good land, and is doing well financially. Uriah Hardiman, grandfather of our subject, served throughout the Revolutionary war.

HON. THOMAS B. HARWELL, a retired physician of Giles County, is the son of Gilham and Annie Harwell, natives of Virginia, who immigrated to Tennessee when quite small. They were married in 1820, and this union resulted in the birth of seven children: Sarah E., Thomas B., Samuel G., Annie W., Alfred F., Mary A. and William G. The father died in 1838, and the mother is still living. Our subject received his education in the Wurtenburg Academy, at Pulaski. In 1844 he commenced the study of medicine with I. J. Pepperson, of the above town, and in the fall of 1844 entered the Louisville Medical College, and attended one course of lectures. In 1850 he commenced the practice of medicine, and was engaged in this profession until 1867. He then abandoned his practice, and has since been devoting all his time to agricultural pursuits on the farm where he now resides. He has 600 acres of excellent land, all well improved, which is six miles south of Pulaski, near Harwell's Station. He has been a rather successful man in all his undertakings, and is regarded as a prosperous and industrious farmer. In 1875 he was elected to the Legislature from Giles County, and was re-elected to the same in 1879, representing Giles and Lincoln Counties. He is a Democrat in politics, a member of the F. & A. M. fraternity, and is also a member of the Methodist Episcopal Church South. He has also taken an active part in educational affairs of Tennessee, and is one of Giles County's leading citizens.

ROBERT A. HAZLEWOOD may be mentioned as one of the prominent and successful farmers of Giles County, Tenn. He was born in Campbell County, Va., January 15, 1822, and is the second of nine children of Little B. and Rachel (Walker) Hazlewood. His early education was obtained in the common schools. At the age of nineteen his inclination drew him westward, and he lived in Alabama two years, then came to Tennessee and followed farming and carpentering in Giles County. November 2, 1843, he married Amanda M. Hazlewood, daughter of Mitchell Hazlewood, and these children Mitchell F., Rachel W., Ann Eliza, Sarah J. (deceased), and Lucretia were born. Mrs. Hazlewood died December 17, 1851, and our subject married Serena S. Hazlewood, daughter of John Hazlewood. Henry, Thomas, William W. (deceased), John G. F., Allen W. and Felix S. are their children. Our subject's grandfathers, Hazlewood and Walker, were born in Virginia, and were Revolutionary soldiers, and his father was a soldier in the war of 1812. Robert A. served in the late war in the Fifty-third Tennessee Infantry, and was captured at Fort Donelson, and for seven months was a prisoner in Indianapolis. In March, 1862, he was discharged on account of age. Mr. Hazlewood is a Democrat from principle and education. He owns 160 acres of good land, and he and wife and four children are members of the Methodist Episcopal Church South.

ROBERT N. HERBERT, M. D., is a native of Williamson County, Tenn., his birth occurring near the village of Brentwood September 27, 1842, son of Robert N. and Elizabeth (Cummins) Herbert, and of English origin. His parents were born in Davidson County, Tenn., the father in 1811, and the mother in 1814. Of a family of nine children our subject is the fifth. He spent his boyhood days on a farm and in attending the common schools. At the breaking out of the late civil war he enlisted in Company B, Twentieth Tennessee Infantry, and served four years to a day, participating in some of the most hotly contested battles of the war. He began the study of medicine upon his return home, under Dr. B. W. Carmack, and graduated from the Nashville Medical College in 1867, and the same year located at Campbellsville, Giles Co., Tenn., where he has since been a successful practitioner of the healing art. December 7, 1867, he was married to Wessie Reams, who died September 2, 1874. November 14, 1876, Dr. Herbert married

Kittie Rogers, and four children have blessed their union: Robert C., Mary Wessie, Annie L. and Sallie E. Dr. Herbert is a Democrat, a Mason, and he and wife are members of the Methodist Episcopal Church South.

LEWIS S. HODGE, farmer, is a North Carolinian by birth, born February 21, 1817, and came to Tennessee with his parents, John and Sallie Hodge, at an early day. They located in Maury County, and became the parents of six children—three daughters and three sons: Gabriel L., Elizabeth, Lewis S., Mary, Samuel and Nancy. The father's death occurred in 1825, and the mother's in 1868. Lewis S. obtained such education as could be obtained in the common schools of Maury County at this early day. He has followed tilling of the soil from boyhood, and has resided on his present farm of 116 acres of valuable land since 1834. Willie J. Cavnor became his wife in 1835. She is a daughter of Thomas and Nancy Cavnor, of Giles County, and became the mother of ten children— seven sons and three daughters: John, James, Sallie, Samuel, William, Jackson, Harris, Nannie, Henry and Mary. Mr. and Mrs. Hodge are members of the Cumberland Presbyterian Church, and in his political views are subject is a Democrat.

WILLIAM J. HOWARD, is a son of John W. Howard, who was born in Butler County, Ky., in 1804, and came to Tennessee in 1825, and a few years later married Jane H. Butler, who was born in Giles County, Tenn., in 1809. The father was a farmer and died August 2, 1882. His wife died at the old homestead in 1875. William J. was the second of nine children, and was born in Giles County, Tenn., June 7, 1831. His preparatory education was obtained in the common schools, after which he took a course in Giles College, Pulaski, Tenn. He began farming for himself when about twenty-one years of age, and has followed that calling through life, and owns 518 acres of good land. March 3, 1859, Amanda M. Poor, of Logan County, Ky., became his wife, and of eight children born to them seven are living: George W., Drury R., Isaac B., Edward W., Berilla R., Amanda E. and Tennessee. Mrs. Howard was born June 12, 1837, and is the daughter of George A. and Berilla (Howard) Poor. Our subject served in the late war in the First Tennessee Cavalry, under Col. Wheeler, and was captured and taken to Jeffersonville, Ind., where he was paroled. Mr. Howard is conservative in his political views and belongs to the Masonic fraternity.

SAMUEL C. JOHNSTON, a native of Charlotte County, Va., was born in 1818, and came to Tennessee with his parents in 1833. They settled in Giles County six miles northwest of the county seat. His father, John Johnston, was born in Charlotte County, Va., in 1790, and followed the carpenter trade until after marriage, when he began farming. His wife, and the mother of our subject, Judith Cobb, was born in Virginia in 1785, and died July 19, 1847. The father is still living but is very feeble. Our subject was reared on the farm, and in 1840 wedded Dianna Smith, a native of Tennessee, born in 1824, and the daughter of Archibald and Frances (Wright) Smith. To Mr. and Mrs. Johnston was born one child, named Charles F.; he was born in 1841 and died January 28, 1866. Mrs. Johnston died in 1846, and in 1850 our subject immigrated to California, and spent fourteen months prospecting in the rich gold fields of the border State. He was a private in Thomas' Tennessee Regiment, Haynes' company, in the Mexican war. Mr. Johnston has always lived on the farm with his father; this tract contains 340 acres of good land. In 1854 he wedded Harriet E. Rolland, a native of Tennessee, born in 1834, and the daughter of John and Harriet (Carter) Rolland. To our subject and wife were born four children: Mary E., Mattie H., John R. and Margaret S. Mr. Johnson is a Democrat in politics, and a member of the Cumberland Presbyterian Church. Mrs. Johnston was also a member of the same church, and remained firm in the faith until her death, which occurred in 1885. The Johnston family are of Irish descent and have always made honorable and prosperous citizens.

MONROE M. JOHNSON, M. D., is a son of Matthew and Sina (Abernathy) Johnson, and was born January 3, 1828. His parents were born in North Carolina, and were there married in about 1818, and came to Tennessee the same year. Three daughters and four sons were born to this union: Franklin, John C., Harriet, James, Rebecca, Monroe M.

and Drusilla C. Matthew Johnson died in 1867, and his wife in 1860. Our subject received the advantages the common schools afforded, and supplemented that by a five years' course in the College Grove Academy, in Williamson County. In 1850 he began studying medicine under Dr. R. G. P. White, and in the fall of the same year entered Jefferson Medical College, at Philadelphia, Penn., from which institution he graduated three years later. He practiced in Old Lynnville until the breaking out of the civil war, when he enlisted and served in his professional capacity four years. He then purchased the farm of 252 acres where he now lives, and has practiced his profession and farmed ever since. Mary E. White became his wife in 1853. She is a daughter of Benton and Jane White, natives of Giles County, and became the mother of five children: Annie B., Alice B., Robert B., Walter T. and Helen W.; Anna and Helen only are living. Dr. Johnson is of Irish descent, and is a Democrat in politics and a member of the F. & A. M.

HON. THOMAS M. JONES, attorney at law, is a son of Wilson and Rebecca (McKissack) Jones, and of Welsh-Scotch descent. The father of Mr. Jones was a Virginian and immigrated to Giles County, Tenn., in 1817, and died here in 1818. His grandfather McKissick was a Revolutionary soldier. Our subject was born in Person County, N. C., December 16, 1816, and was the youngest of five children. He grew up on the farm and received a common school education. In 1831 he entered the University of Alabama, where he remained until the fall of 1833, after which he entered the University of Virginia and there remained until 1835. In the latter school he began the study of law, and after returning to Pulaski he began reading law in the office of Col. John H. Rivers & W. C. Flournoy, and remained here until 1836, when he raised a company for the Seminole war; was mustered out January, 1837, and the same year was admitted to practice law. In 1844 he was county elector on the Democratic ticket, and in 1845 he was elected to represent Lincoln and Giles Counties in the Legislature, and in 1847 was elected State senator for Giles and Maury Counties. He was elected a member of the Confederate Congress in 1861. Nine years later he was elected a member of the Constitutional Convention of Tennessee. For nearly fifty years he has been engaged in the law practice, and is now the oldest practitioner in Giles County bar. He has held the office of judge a number of times by appointment. He is one of the successful lawyers of this part of Tennessee. December 25, 1838, he wedded Marietta Perkins, of Williamson County, Tenn., and to this union were born nine children: Calvin (deceased), Charles P., Thomas W., Hume T., Harriet, Edward S., Lulie A., Lee W. and Nicholas T. Mr. Jones is a Democrat, a Mason, a Knight Templar, Commandery No. 12. Mrs. Jones died in 1871, and in 1883 Mr. Jones married Mrs. Ann Wood, of West Tennessee. He and wife are members of the Episcopal Church.

JAMES L. JONES (familiarly known as Lew Jones), county judge, was born in Giles County, Tenn., October 28, 1824, son of Edward Dandridge and Elizabeth H. (Rainey) Jones, natives of Virginia and North Carolina, respectively. The former was born in 1788 and the latter in 1790. The paternal grandfather of our subject was Abram Jones, a native of Virginia, who died in that State some time about 1792. About 1818 the father of our subject immigrated to Giles County, Tenn., and for nineteen years was county court clerk. He died in 1855. Our subject's mother died in Tennessee in 1854. James L. Jones was a country boy, and received his education in the common schools. In 1847 he enlisted in Company C, Third Regiment, Tennessee Foot Volunteers of the Mexican war. He was a lieutenant, and served until the close of the war. From 1848 to 1855 he was deputy county court clerk. Then for a number of years he was engaged in trading. In 1865 he was elected magistrate and also assistant assessor of internal revenue, which position he held until 1869. In 1873 he was elected county judge, which office he has held continuously since. His official record is one of the best ever made in Giles County. In 1860 he wedded Julia E. Blair, of Maury County, Tenn., and this union was blessed by the birth of nine children, six of whom survive: Edward B., Llewellyn, Mattie R., Elizabeth H., William R. and Mary. Mr. Jones was formerly a Whig, but is now a Democrat. He is a Mason, and he and wife are members of the Methodist Episcopal Church South.

JOHN W. JUDKINS is the son of Robert B. and Mary C. Judkins, natives, respectively, of South and North Carolina. They were married in this county in 1830, and to them were born nine children: Mary J., William S., John W., Martha A., Amanda C., Thomas D., Sarah M., Harriet V., and Enoch L. Our subject was born November 12, 1836, in Giles County, and received a liberal education in the common district schools of that county. In 1861 he wedded Tennessee C. Hopson, daughter of Renix and Rachel Hopson, natives of North Carolina, and this union resulted in the birth of one daughter, Tennessee C. Mrs. Judkins died in 1862, and in 1867 Mr. Judkins took for his second wife Mary F. Rains, daughter of William and Mary Rains, of Kentucky. By the last union our subject became the father of seven children: George A., Mary F., Martha O., Margaret E., Julia R., Lela J. and Robert R. In 1872 Mr. Judkins engaged in the grocery and general merchandise business in Pulaski, and still continues that business in connection with farming. He has a good farm of ninety-eight acres, all well improved, lying near the town of Pulaski. Mr. Judkins has been quite successful in all his undertakings, and is regarded as a prosperous and industrious farmer.

JASPER KELSEY, M. D., of Old Lynnville, Giles Co., Tenn., was born in Maury County in 1838, son of Thomas and Hester Kelsey, natives of the Palmetto State. They were married in Tennessee in 1828, and the following children were born to their union: Mary A., William T., Susan M., Robert A., George E., Newton and Jasper. Mrs. Kelsey died in 1848, and the father in 1872. Our subject's juvenile days were spent in attending school and assisting his parents on the farm. In 1860 he began his medical studies under Drs. Beard and Harwell, of Henryville, Tenn., but on the breaking out of the war he enlisted in the Twenty-third Regiment of Tennessee Volunteers, and served four years, participating in most of the principal battles of the war. After his return he resumed his medical studies, and in 1867 entered the University of Nashville, and was graduated as an M. D., from that institution in 1869. Since that time he has been actively engaged in the practice of his profession at old Lynnville, and is regarded as a reliable and successful physician. In 1868 he and Mary M. Compton were united in matrimony, and their union was blessed with the following family: Hettie E., Mary R., Annie T., Frederick W., Edna G., Alice V. and Verda Y. The family are members of the Methodist Episcopal Church South, and our subject is a Democrat and of Irish descent.

JOHN T. LOWRY was born where he now resides, September 1, 1841, the youngest of three children born to James B. and Elizabeth Lowry, born in South Carolina and Tennessee, respectively. They were married about 1835, and in 1840 located on the farm where our subject now lives. The father died in 1864, and the mother in 1869. John L. is of Scotch-Irish descent, and after attending the common schools in his youthful days, engaged in farming and tanning. He owns 350 acres of valuable land, well improved, and devotes considerable attention to the raising of fine stock. In 1867 he was married to Matura A. Gracy, daughter of Joseph B. and Elizabeth Gracy, and to them were born James B., David B., John S., Lizzie L., Eddie E. and Luther. Mr. and Mrs. Lowry are members of the Cumberland Presbyterian Church, and in politics he is a Democrat.

THOMAS MARTIN. Indissolubly connected with the history of Giles County is the life of Thomas Martin. The son of Rev. Abram Martin, he was born in Albemarle County, Va., on the 16th of December, 1799, and in 1818 moved to Pulaski, Tenn., to carve his own fortune in what was then the far West. Imbued with a deep religious fervor, which characterized his entire life, he early joined the Methodist Church, of which he was ever after an active and earnest member. In a comparatively short time, by economy, prudence, sobriety and an unusual facility for business, he had amassed a respectable fortune, which was entirely swept away by the treachery of his partner in business, who had been left in entire control of Mr. Martin's funds, while the latter was absent for a short time on a visit to his parents. Despite the blow, which would have utterly crushed the hopes and ambitions of most young men, he firmly refused to take the advice of friends and attorneys to avail himself of the plea of infancy, for he was not yet grown to man's estate, and assuming the entire obligations of his false partner, he started again in business with the declaration: "If God gives me life and strength, every dollar shall be paid." Against such energy and iron-will the fates themselves are powerless to prevail; the character and integrity shown in the beardless boy challenged the admiration of the entire business community; he was quickly offered a partnership by the principal merchant of Pulaski, and it was not long before the firm of Meredith & Martin became known throughout Middle Tennessee. About this time he married Miss Nancy Topp, and formed a co-partnership with his brother-in-law, Dr. Wm. Topp, a highly educated and accomplished physician, and one of those hardy pioneers, who, on the staff of Andrew Jackson, aided in achieving the laurels of "Old Hickory," and added not a little to the brilliant successes of the Seminole war. The new firm displayed the activity, which had accompanied all the enterprises with which Mr. Martin had been connected, and by utilizing the small streams which flow into the Elk River, secured a market for the cotton of Giles County in New Orleans, then, as now, the chief cotton mart of the world. Mr. Martin had now become the recognized financier of his section, and the subject of a railroad through the central portion of the State being agitated, his aid and counsel were eagerly solicited. He was not slow to perceive the advantages which railway communication with north Alabama would give to Giles County, and rode night and day to personally solicit the aid of every man, who could assist the enterprise. In a short time the idea became a fact; the Southern Central Railroad, which is now a part of the great Louisville & Nashville system, was built, and soon after Thomas Martin became its president. Though Mr. Martin took no active part in politics, he was a life-long Democrat, and thoroughly concurred with the doctrines of that party, and on the accession of James K. Polk to the Presidency he was tendered the secretaryship of the treasury, which office, however, he declined. Though he had always firmly refused a nomination for any political office, he consented to act as one of the commissioners to the Peace Conference, and did everything in his power to avert the dreadful calamities, which followed the civil war. Mr. Martin died in 1870, at the age of seventy years, leaving a large fortune, despite the losses which he had suffered by the war. He had several children; but Ophelia, who married Judge Henry M. Spofford, afterward United States Senator from Louisiana, was the only one living at the time of his death. His charities were numerous: he contributed largely to the building of the Methodist Church in Pulaski, and to the male academy, and endowed the large and handsome female seminary which bears his name. He never failed to aid the youth who was struggling with poverty, provided he was moral and industrious. In death, as throughout life, he was a zealous Christian, and died with the praises of the Redeemer on his lips: "Sweet Lamb of God, I'll see Thy bright face, joy! joy!" being nearly his last words on earth. "In business he was a giant," once remarked an admirer; he might have added that in all the grander attributes of human character, he was the ideal of splendid manhood.

JESSE MAYES, M. D., an old and prominent physician of Giles County, is the son of Jesse and Frances (Hill) Mayes, natives of Virginia. They were married in 1800, immigrated to this State and settled in Giles County in 1825. To this union were born ten children: Fletcher H., Thomas H., Mary, Susan, Elizabeth, Jesse, Fannie, Octavia, Samuel J. and Abigail. The father died in 1860, and the mother followed him in 1866. Our subject was born October 25, 1814, in Rockbridge County, Va., and attended the district schools. In 1834 he commenced the study of medicine with Dr. Edward R. Field, a prominent physician of Pulaski at that time. Our subject entered the Cincinnati Medical College in 1838, and after attending two courses of lectures he received an appointment from the government as assistant surgeon in the Indian emigration and held the position for the year 1840. At this time he returned to Giles County, and has since been constantly engaged in his profession and is regarded as one of the oldest and most reliable physicians of this county. In 1841 he married Mary E. Cook, daughter of Col. and Sallie Cook, of North Carolina, and to them were born three children: Julia F., Sarah F. and William H. (deceased). Dr. Mayes has 400 acres of land in partnership with his son-in-law, Jacob E. Morton, and is in very comfortable circumstances. In 1836 he was in the

Florida war, and served his time and received an honorable discharge at New Orleans. Dr. Mayes is a Democrat in politics, and all his family are members of the Methodist Episcopal Church South.

JOSEPH B. McCAUL, merchant, was born in Williamson County, Tenn., May 27, 1845, son of John A. and Elizabeth (Boon) McCaul, and is of Scotch-Irish lineage. John A. McCaul was born in Rutherford County, and died in Marshall County, Tenn., about 1858. The mother was born in the same county as her husband, and died about 1855. Joseph B. is the third of their ten children, and when about thirteen years of age began learning the saddler's trade, at which he worked until 1861, when he enlisted in the Twentieth Tennessee Infantry, but was discharged the same year on account of physical disability. He re-enlisted in the Eleventh Tennessee Cavalry in 1862, and served until the close of the war. From 1865 to 1867 he farmed and then engaged in the mercantile business at Bethesda, Tenn., remaining two years, and then came to Lynnville and began keeping a saddle and harness shop. At the end of eight years he engaged in the grocery business, and is the leading merchant in his line in the town. He also deals in grain. In 1868 he married Elizabeth V. Beatty, of Williamson County. He is a Democrat and Mason, and he and wife are members of the Presbyterian Church.

GEORGE W. McGUIRE, M. D., is the son of Cornelius W. and Sarah McGuire, natives of Virginia. They were married about 1825, in this State, and had born to their union thirteen children: Elizabeth, William H., Lucinda A., Harriet M., Calvin B., John P., James S., Robert R., Cornelius N., Mary P., George W., Narcissa E. and Docia A. The father died September 28, 1859, and the mother April 20, 1875. Our subject was born April 11, 1844, in Lincoln County, Tenn., and is of Scotch-Irish descent. He attended the county schools, and in 1866 began the study of medicine with a brother, Dr. C. B. McGuire, of Millville, Lincoln County. In the fall of that year he entered the University of Nashville, and graduated from that institution in 1869. After which he returned to Millville and commenced the practice of his profession with his brother. In 1874 he located at Dellrose, in Lincoln County, and practiced his profession with evident success. August 27, 1872, he married Ella O. Patterson, daughter of John C. and Elenor Patterson, of Giles County. To our subject and wife were born three children: James C., Cornelius N. and John P. The mother of these children died in 1881, and he then married Laura M. Legg, daughter of Andrew C. and Martha Legg, of Alabama. To the last union was born one child—Myrtle. In 1884 Dr. McGuire moved to Giles County, and purchased the land where he now resides. He is a very successful practitioner and is kept almost constantly busy visiting his numerous patients. He is Democratic in his political belief.

ANDREW J. McKIMMEN, a prominent stock-raiser, living one mile east of Pulaski, Tenn., was born in County Tyrone, Ireland, March 28, 1834, and is a son of Daniel and Jane McKimmen, who were natives of the "soil," and removed to the United States in 1843, settling on a farm in Giles County, Tenn., on which our subject now resides. They were the parents of the following children: Mary, Margaret, Emily, Andrew J., Isabella and Jane. The father died in 1878, and the mother in 1880. Our subject is their fourth child. He received a limited early education, and his time has been employed in breeding fine trotting horses, being the first man who introduced blooded trotting stock in Giles County (in 1856) and one of the first in the State. He is widely known and much respected by all. He and Georgie A. Everly were united in marriage in 1859. She is a daughter of Capt. George and Mary Everly, natives, respectively, of Virginia and Tennessee. Our subject is a Democrat, and is noted for his charity to the poor.

JAMES T. McKISSACK, farmer and stock-raiser, is a native of Person County, N. C., born in 1823, son of William and Janette McKissack, both natives of North Carolina. They were married in the early part of the present century, and to them were born five sons and three daughters: Susan P., James T., Gorham T., Don J., Alexander C., Lucy H., Jessie H. and William. Our subject was the second child born to this union. In 1833 he came with his parents to this State and settled in Maury County. He received a good practical education in the Jackson College, of Maury County, and in 1842 was engaged in the grocery and general merchandise business at Spring Hill, Maury County. In 1854, after moving around for some time, he settled in Pulaski, and was engaged in building the old court house and a number of other business blocks. Previous to this, in 1845, he married Sylvina C. Rowe, daughter of Louis and Lucy Rowe, and this union resulted in the birth of six children, named Lucy J., William L., Susan O., Edward F., Mary E. and Calvin C. The mother of these children died in 1880. In 1856 he purchased land near Vale Mills, in this county, and was engaged in farming and manufacturing until 1870, when he sold farm and business and moved to where he now resides, near Pulaski. He has 137 acres of valuable land, well improved. Mr. McKissack is of Scotch-Irish descent, and a Democrat in politics.

HENRY CLAY McLAURINE, whose birth occurred in Giles County, Tenn., January 8, 1840, is a son of William and Ann (Swan) McLaurine, and of Scotch-Irish descent. His parents were natives of Virginia, born in 1791 and 1797. The father was a tiller of the soil and died in this county in 1862. The mother died in 1866. Our subject is the youngest of eleven children, seven of whom are now living. He was reared on the farm and received his education in the district schools. During the years 1859–60 he clerked in a dry goods store at Molino, Lincoln County. In 1861 he enlisted in Company K, First Tennessee Cavalry, and for more than a year was a prisoner in Camp Morton. In 1866 he came to Prospect, in this county, and after clerking for one year engaged in the general merchandise business and there remained until 1882, when he removed to Pulaski. In 1873 he married Bettie M. Deaver, and in 1876 he ran for the office of sheriff and was deputy sheriff from 1872 to 1875. He ran for sheriff in 1876 against four Democrats and one Republican, and was defeated by the Republican by two votes. In 1882 he was elected county trustee and discharged the duties of this office in a highly satisfactory manner for two years. In 1885 he was commissioned postmaster at Pulaski, and confirmed January 12, 1886, by the United States Senate. He is a Democrat, a Mason, and he and wife are members of the Methodist Episcopal Church South. He is one of the county's best citizens, and a representative of one of the old families.

MARK McNAIRY, farmer, and a native of Giles County, Tenn., was born November 1, 1833, son of Frank and Mary McNairy, natives of Tennessee, who were married in Giles County about 1830, and were the parents of four children: Robert, Mark, John F. and William J. The father died in 1837 and the mother in 1853. The subject of this sketch received a fair education in the common schools, and subsequently attended the Giles College at Pulaski. In 1845 he moved to that town and was engaged in trading until 1865. In 1858 he led to the altar Lute Maxwell, daughter of William A. and Delila Maxwell, of Giles County, Tenn. By this marriage Mr. McNairy became the father of four children: Roy, Lycurgus, Minnie and Ellen. Mr. McNairy is a Democrat in politics and of Irish lineage. In 1865 he moved to the farm where he is now living, which consists of 240 acres. He has been successful at his occupation and is a prosperous, industrious farmer.

JAMES O. MITCHELL, of Lynnville, Tenn., is a native of Giles County, born December 19, 1833, son of Andrew and Eliza (Alexander) Mitchell, and is of Scotch-Irish descent. His parents were both born in North Carolina, the father in 1807, and the mother in 1809. His paternal grandfather was John Mitchell, also a North Carolinian. The Mitchell family came to Tennessee about 1809, and settled in East Tennessee. The father of our subject came to what is now Marshall County when a young man. He died in 1864, and the mother in 1865. James O. is the third of nine children, and grew to manhood on a farm, and was educated in the neighboring schools. In 1861 he enlisted in Company B, Third Tennessee Infantry, and participated in the battles of Raymond, Miss., Chickamauga, Missionary Ridge and the Georgia Campaign. Since the war he has been in business in this county. He was married, in 1856, to Frances Angus, who died in 1861. Mr. Mitchell's second wife was Sarah Kellam, whom he married in 1871, and who died four years later, leaving two children: Andrew and Nancy. Mr. Mitchell is a Democrat, and one of the substantial men of the county.

MARCUS M. MITCHELL is a native of Giles County, Tenn., born January 26, 1838, the second of three children and the son of Robert C. and Jane (Beasley) Mitchell, born in Virginia and Tennessee, respectively. The former came to Tennessee with his parents when a boy and there spent the rest of his life with the exception of a short period. He died in 1870, and the mother in 1863. Our subject resided with his Grandmother Beasley and obtained a practical business education in the common schools. By perseverance, honest dealing with his fellow-man, and economy, he is ranked among the wealthy farmers of the county, owning 322 acres of land. In the late war he served in the First Tennessee Cavalry, under Col. Wheeler, and participated in many hotly contested battles. He was finally released from service by his father taking his place, as the latter had no one depending on him, and our subject had a wife and one child. He was married, May 26, 1861, to Margaret H. Kimbrough, who bore him one child, a daughter—Almeda G.—born April 7, 1862 (wife of W. D. Abernathy). Mr. Mitchell is a Democrat, a man of generous and liberal disposition, and highly respected in the county where he resides.

ASA W. MOORE, of the firm of Moore & Daly, dealers in dry goods and general merchandise at Elkton, Tenn., is a son of David J. and Mary E. Moore, who were born in Virginia and North Carolina, respectively, and were married in 1828, in Alabama, and came to Tennessee the same year. Both parents died in 1857. Our subject is the seventh of their twelve children, and his early education was obtained in the common schools of Giles County. He attended the Pettusville High School, in Alabama, two and a half years, and at the breaking out of the war enlisted in the Ninth Alabama Regiment, and served until the close of the war, participating in many of the principal battles. After his return home he taught school until 1870, and at that time formed a partnership with A. D. Bull, and entered into his present business. Our subject has been successful as a business man and is considered one of the estimable citizens of the county. December 23, 1868, he was married to Eva Bull, and by her is the father of six children: David, Ethel, Joseph, Eva, Tom and Nellie. Mr. Moore belongs to the F. & A. M., and is a Democrat in politics, and belongs to the Methodist Episcopal Church South.

JACOB B. MORELL, farmer, was born in East Tennessee, in 1820, and is of German-Irish descent. His parents, Christian and Susan Morell, were natives of Virginia and Tennessee, respectively. They were married about 1812, and became the parents of six children: Elizabeth, John H., Jacob B., Samuel H., William and Christian. The father's demise occurred in 1827, and the mother's in 1859. Our subject received his education in the common schools of East Tennessee, and assisted his father in agricultural pursuits from early boyhood. He located in Giles County in 1842, and has been devoting considerable attention to milling. He is the proprietor of the Elk River Grist Mills, which are situated on Elk River, near Elkton. He has also 270 acres of good land, all improved. Mr. Morell has been a very successful man, financially, and all his property has been made by hard work and good management. January 16, 1844, he married Eleanor P. Phelps, and to this marriage were born an interesting family of eight children: Martha D., Allen P., Fredonia E., Emmett, Frances, Varina D., Pressley L. and Alice J. Mr. Morell is of Democratic principles, and is a man of sound judgment and good sense.

JOSHUA MORRIS is a son of Isaac Morris who was born in Delaware, June 29, 1766, and died July 16, 1856. He moved to North Carolina shortly after the Revolutionary war. Our subject's mother, Susanna Tacker, was born in Maryland in 1770, and died in 1840. Joshua Morris was born in North Carolina December 1, 1807 and is one of the old and leading citizens of Giles County. He was deprived the benefits of school, but gave himself a fair education, At the age of twenty he began life for himself, and a year later was married to Mary S. Tarkington, who bore him one child, named Isaac G. L., who died in 1853. Mary (Tarkington) Morris was born February 12, 1812, and died August 31, 1843. Our subject fought in the Florida Indian war and was faithful to his duties. He has held different county offices but is a farmer by occupation. By industry and perseverance he has accumulated considerable property, having at the present time 2,665 acres of land and all but 700 acres under fence, 500 acres of this land contain fine timber, such as oak, poplar and chestnut. He has twenty-seven tenants on his land, and has several tenement houses unoccupied. He has been a stock-raiser and was always successful; in fact, his every effort has been crowned with success. During the late war he was captain of a company for a short time. He is a Democrat in politics, and cast his first vote for Andrew Jackson. He has on his home farm, located on Big Creek, a cotton-gin and a grist-mill. He has living with him six great-grandchildren, which compose the entire family.

WILLIAM G. NANCE, dealer in confectionery, fancy groceries, cigars and tobacco, in Pulaski, Tenn., is a son of Sterling A. and Eliza Nance, natives, respectively, of South Carolina and Alabama. They were married in the latter State in 1830, and became the parents of six children: John D., Elizabeth, James F., Sterling A., William G. and Mary E. The father died in 1859 and the mother in 1872. William G. was born in Lauderdale County, Ala., in 1840. After acquiring his rudimentary education in the common schools, he, in 1855, entered La Grange College, at Florence, Ala., and attended one session. In 1857 and 1858 he attended the University of Murfreesboro, Tenn., where he finished his literary education. He then farmed in his native State until the breaking out of the war. In 1864 he enlisted in the Tenth Alabama Cavalry, and served until Lee's surrender. He then resumed farming, and in 1874 became clerk for J. Butler & Co., dealers in dry goods in Pulaski, Tenn. In 1878 he was compelled to suspend active business life, but in 1883 formed a partnership with his son, William J. Nance, in the liquor business, and continued the same until June, 1885, when he sold out and engaged in his present business. In November, 1860, he married Mollie Coffee, daughter of Joshua and Mary M. Coffee, of Alabama. They have five children: Willie J., Lula M., Adine P., Mamie and Sterling. Mrs. Nance died in 1874. Mr. Nance is a Democrat, and the family are church members.

WILLIAM C. NELSON, assistant cashier of the Giles County, Tenn., National Bank, was born in Limestone County, Ala., August 17, 1849, son of Isaac and Lizzie Nelson, and of English descent. The father was born in Giles County in 1822, and was a farmer and merchant by occupation. He died in 1854. The mother was born in South Carolina about 1824 and died in Giles County in 1854. Our subject's paternal grandfather was John Nelson, a native of Virginia, and an early immigrant to Tennessee. William C. was the third of four children and was raised on a farm. He received a practical education and, in 1871, began clerking in a dry goods store, where he remained until 1878, and then engaged in the clothing business, and continued that until 1881. At that time he opened a hardware store, and the same year became assistant cashier of Giles County National Bank. He sold his stock of hardware in 1885. In 1881 he married Georgie Adams, and is now the father of two children: Sue Adams and Lizzie. Mr. Nelson is a Democrat and a Mason, Knight Templar degree, and is at present eminent commander of Commandery No. 12. He is a Presbyterian and his wife belongs to the Episcopal Church.

ROBERT S. PARTRICK, owner and proprietor of the village of Bodenham, was born in Alabama in 1847. This village is composed of one water-mill, one cotton-gin, cabinet shop, blacksmith-shop and a general merchandising establishment. He immigrated from Alabama to this place about two years ago, and has been successfully engaged in business ever since. He was reared in Rogersville, Ala., and lived with his grandfather until fifteen years of age. He then enlisted in Company E, Seventh Alabama Cavalry, and remained in the service until the close of the war. He was a participant in some of the most hotly contested battles fought during that time. He returned to Alabama, and was engaged in different pursuits until coming to his present location. His father was a native of Kentucky, born in 1800, and came to Alabama when quite young. He married for his first wife a Miss Brooks, who bore him six children. She died about 1840. He then married Elvira Sham, she being the mother of our subject, and a native of Alabama, born in 1820. The last union resulted in the birth of four children. The mother died in 1854 and the father three years later. Our subject was united in marriage, in 1870, to Elizabeth Elledge, a native of Alabama, born in 1850, and to them were born three children: Infant (died unnamed), Ethel (who died in 1873), and Beatrice L. Our subject is a stanch Democrat, and cast his first vote for Horace Greeley. The Partrick family are of Irish descent, and emigrated from Ireland in the early part of the seventeenth century.

WILEY B. PEPPER, M. D., an old practitioner of medicine, and now a druggist of Lynnville, Tenn., is a native of Robertson County, Tenn., born near Springfield April 13, 1821, son of William C. and Sarah (Powell) Pepper, and is of English extraction. His father was a native of Virginia, and came to Tennessee with his parents in 1808. The family first settled where Nashville now stands, but later removed to Robertson County, and since then the Pepper family has figured prominently in the affairs of Robertson County, and there the parents of our subject deceased. Dr. Pepper's early life was spent on the farm. He received a liberal education at the Springfield schools, and began the study of medicine in 1844, graduating from the Memphis Medical College in 1849, and the following year located in Giles County, where he continued his profession two years. He then removed to Limestone County, Ala., where he remained until 1865, and just after the surrender of Lee at Appomattox he returned to his native county, and there lived five years, and in 1870 came to Lynnville, continuing the practice of his profession about six months, and then engaged in the drug business, which he has since continued. He was married, in 1853, to Miss Sarah E. Horwell, of Giles County. He was formerly an "old-line" Whig, but is now a Democrat, and was made a Mason in 1850. They are leading members of the Methodist Episcopal Church, and he is an honorable citizen.

RICHARD PEPPER, a successful farmer of Giles County, was born in Robertson County, Tenn., and is the son of William and Sarah Pepper. He received his education at Springfield, Tenn., and was a school-teacher for some time. October 14, 1867, he was united in marriage to Mattie E. Anthony, daughter of John B. and Sarah Anthony, of Giles County, and to our subject and wife was born one child—Tullia. Mrs. Pepper died April 16, 1873, and March 11, 1874, he married, for his second wife, Ella Westmoreland, daughter of Thomas A. and Elizabeth J. Westmoreland. . By this last union our subject became the father of three children: Annie, Kittie and Mildred. In 1876 Mr. Pepper located on the farm where he now resides, which consists of ninety-eight acres of fine land. He has been successful in most of his enterprises and is very comfortably situated. He is a Democrat in politics, and he and wife are worthy members of the Methodist Episcopal Church South.

REV. FRANCIS F. POLLARD was born in Virginia May, 1832, one of a large family of children born to the marriage of Uriah W. Pollard and Elizabeth Haley. Both born in Virginia, where the father died. The mother came to Tennessee with our subject in 1856, and died in Giles County November 28, 1861. Our subject's early education was obtained in the common schools. On the 31st of December, 1859, he and Ann E. Wells were united in marriage, and seven children were born to their union: William J., James B. (deceased), John C., Nancy A. E., Emeline, Mary F. and Sarah Helen. Mrs. Pollard was born on the farm where she now lives, August 5, 1831, daughter of Jesse Wells. Mr. Pollard served in the Ninth Alabama Cavalry, under Col. James C. Malone, but after six months' service was discharged for disability. He is a Democrat, and is, and has been, an active and efficient minister in the Baptist Church for twelve years. He owns a plantation of 407 acres, on which he raises cotton and the cereals.

JEFFERSON D. PULLEN, wholesale and retail grocer, is a son of John C. Pullen, who married Pauline Wheeler, and by her became the father of ten children. The father died in 1868 and the mother in 1877. Our subject is the ninth child, and in his juvenile days received a fair education. At the age of eighteen he began farming for himself and continued up to 1882, when he came to Pulaski, and engaged in his present business in partnership with J. S. Childress, and has succeeded beyond his expectations from a financial stand point. He was married in 1881 to Maggie Johnson, daughter of Samuel and Bettie Johnson, old and prominent settlers of Giles County. Mr. Pullen is a Democrat, and cast his first presidential vote for Hancock. He and wife are members of the Methodist Episcopal Church South.

RICHARD H. RAGSDALE, farmer and stock-dealer, was born in Logan County, Ky., January 1, 1847, son of Burrell Ragsdale, who was a native of Virginia, born in 1804, and an early settler of Kentucky. He was twice married; his first family of ten children was raised in Kentucky. His second wife, our subject's mother was Olive F. Foote, a native of Tennessee, and born in November, 1812. She died in Logan County, Ky., in the spring of 1874, followed by the father two years later. Richard H. served in the last year of the war, and December 25, 1867, was married, in Giles County, Tenn., to Anna L. Howard, born in 1849, and daughter of John W. Howard. Their children are James H., Jerry, Gray and Eunice. Mr. Ragsdale is a Democrat; and while he has not identified himself with any church, his wife belongs to the Methodist Episcopal Church South. He has 151 acres of fine land, and gives the most of his attention to raising stock.

ISAAC H. RAINEY, an enterprising citizen, was born in Giles County, Tenn., February 25, 1842; son of Horace D. and Eliza (Summerhill) Rainey, and of Scotch-English lineage. The father was born in North Carolina June 9, 1799, and the mother was born in the same State in December, 1799. The Rainey family came to Giles County about 1839. Our subject's father was a farmer by occupation, and his death occurred in this county in June, 1863; the mother died the year previous. Isaac H. Rainey is the eighth in a family of nine children. He assisted his father on the farm and attended the country schools. In 1861 he enlisted in Company K, First Tennessee Cavalry, and was a prisoner for five months. Since the war he has been engaged in the livery and farming business at Pulaski. In 1874 he was united in matrimony to Viola Wilkinson of Marshall County, and the fruits of this union were an interesting family of four children: Guy, Earl, Hugh and Paul. In 1877 he was elected marshal of Pulaski, and served in that capacity for six years. He has the only livery stable in Pulaski, and is doing a successful business. He is a Democrat, a member of the Masonic lodge, and he and wife are worthy members of the Methodist Episcopal Church.

RUFUS C. REYNOLDS, proprietor of the Belle Air Stock Farm, was born in Giles County, Tenn., son of Giles A. and Minerva (Childress) Reynolds, and of Scotch-English lineage. His parents were born in Virginia and Tennessee, respectively; the father in 1801, and the mother in 1811. They were married in 1829. The father came to Tennessee in 1825, and was by occupation a farmer. He died in 1867. The mother died in 1870. Our subject assisted his father on the farm and attended the schools in the county. He completed his education at the University of Mississippi, and subsequently engaged in breeding horses for the race course. In 1881 he purchased the famous "Almont, Jr." (Basticks), sire of "Annie W.," 2:20; "Judge Lindsay," 2:21¼, etc. In addition to the above, Mr. Reynolds owns fifteen extra well-bred brood mares. He purchased the old Reynolds homestead in 1870, known as Belle Air Stock Farm, settled by his father in 1875. Mr. Reynolds is one of the most successful stock-men of this section of Tennessee. He is a Democrat and a K. of P. His farm is located one mile east of Reynolds' Station on the Louisville & Nashville Railroad, and consists of 333 acres of well improved land.

GEORGE T. RIDDLE, cashier of the Peoples National Bank, was born in Pulaski, Tenn., May 23, 1844, and is the third of six children born to Thomas S. and Margaret (Speer) Riddle. He is of Scotch-Irish lineage. His father was born in Virginia in 1800 and his mother was a native of the Emerald Isle. The Riddle family came to Tennessee in early times, and here the father of our subject died in 1874. He was for many years engaged in active business in Pulaski and was county trustee for several terms, and was a leading citizen and a useful man. Our subject was educated at Giles College, this county, and at Bethany College, West Virginia, where he graduated in 1867. In 1862 he joined the Confederate Army and served in the ordnance department until the close of the war. Subsequent to his college and war life he began the study of law and was licensed to practice, but fearing his health he abandoned the idea of a professional life. In 1871 he was made book-keeper of the National Bank of Pulaski, and was made cashier of the same institution in 1873. He held this position until 1882, when the National Bank went into liquidation. He was then elected as director and cashier of the Peoples National Bank and now holds that position. He is one of the best financiers in Pulaski, and a most thorough business man. In 1872 he married Annie Lea.Skillern, of this county. He is a Democrat and a member of the K. of P., and he and wife are members of the Episcopal Church.

DR. JOSEPH COLEMAN ROBERTS was born on the Madison and Limestone County line, in Alabama, November 18, 1822, being of honorable parentage, not wealthy or distinguished, but highly respected for the sort of integrity and strength and purity of character and modesty in asserting their claims to high distinctions that constituted marked virtues among the agricultural classes in the earlier years of this country. He received an elementary education in the country schools of that day, and afterward attended the Frazier Academy, at Athens, Ala., and studied the classics, and at the age of about nineteen began teaching school, after which he entered the office of Dr. Frank Malone, at the Cross Roads, in Madison County, and in 1843–44 attended a course of medical lectures; after which he located in Limestone County and practiced his profession four years. He then went to New York City, and graduated at the University of New York in 1848. He returned home and located at Bethel, Giles Co., Tenn., where he has since resided. In 1849 he married Sarah I. Anthony, and to their union four children were born: J. C., Estella (who died in childhood), Walter A. and Sallie Bettie. The Doctor was laborious and persistent in his medical studies, and diligent and faithful in his professional engagements. At the beginning of the war the means he had accumulated had been invested mostly in slave property, and as a result of that conflict he was left comparatively penniless. He offered his services to the Confederacy, and served in the field and hospital as aid to Dr. Ford, acting in the capacity of assistant and director. When the army commanded by Beauregard and Bragg started on the Kentucky campaign, he was transferred to the Western Department, and was assistant to Dr. Wooten, now of Texas. After the war the Doctor located in Pulaski, Giles Co., Tenn., and by energy and frugality owns a neat and valuable brick residence on Main Street, and a farm of 600 acres of excellent land in the county. He has been constantly engaged in his profession for about forty-two years; has the reputation of being a studious, able and successful physician, and is engaged in active practice at the present time. His parents, George and Elizabeth (Kendrick) Roberts, were born in Georgia and were of English and Welsh ancestry. They moved to Alabama about 1800, and located where our subject was born. The father died in Lawrence County, Ala., and the mother in Mississippi. Their family consisted of seven sons and three daughters. Dr. Roberts is considered one of the county's best men. He is a Mason, a Democrat, and he and wife are members of the Methodist Episcopal Church South.

HON. SOLON E. ROSE, of Pulaski, is descended from an old and honored family of Scotland, whose history can be traced back for many generations. Col. William Rose, the father of the subject of this sketch, was a native of Virginia, born in 1779. He moved to Giles County, Tenn., in 1813, and was one of the early pioneers. He wedded Elizabeth W. Meredith, a lady of Welsh ancestry, who bore her husband a family of seven sons: Edward W., William M., Alfred H., Robert H., Fielding, David E. and Solon Eldridge. The father was one of the foremost men in the community in which he resided. He died in 1851, preceded by his wife in 1820. Solon E. Rose was born in this county August 18, 1818, was educated at Wurtenburg Academy in Pulaski, and was reared to years of maturity in his native county. At eighteen years he took part in the Florida war, participating in the battles of Withlacoocha, Panasophca and the Wahoo Swamp. In 1839 he began the study of law, and when in his twenty-second year was licensed to practice. After remaining for a time in Pulaski he removed to Lawrenceburg, and in 1843 was elected attorney-general, a position he retained six years, declining a re-election. From 1848 to 1859 he was president of the Lawrenceburg Bank, and was also connected with other enterprises. During the latter year he returned to Pulaski and formed a partnership with Judge J. A. Tinnon in the practice of the law, which continued until 1883, when Judge Tinnon was elevated to the bench. For the last fifteen years he has been president of the Giles National Bank of Pulaski. It would require a volume of no small dimensions to give in detail Mr. Rose's political career.   It will suffice to briefly state that he has been active in advancing the cause deemed best for his country's good; that he has occupied numerous positions of honor and trust, and that he has reflected honor and credit upon the same. He is a Democrat.   Mr. Rose selected for his helpmate through life Miss Marcella, daughter of M. H. and Ethalinda (Bumpass) Buchanan, and to their union four children were born: Solonia M., born November 16, 1844, now Mrs. John D. Flautt; William Haynie, born April 19, 1847, and now a resident of this county; Elizabeth E., born in 1849, and died in 1858; and Solon E. F., born December 19, 1850, now residing in Mississippi.   Mr. Rose began life without financial means, but by adhering to strict business rules in general, and the golden rule in particular, he has amassed a comfortable fortune and won the esteem of the best citizens of the State.

HON. JAMES C. SANDERS, a native of Tennessee, was born in 1816, and is the fourth of eight children born to William and Elizabeth (Bellantfant) Sanders.   The parents are natives of North Carolina, and immigrated to Tennessee about 1812, locating in Williamson County, where they remained a few years, after which they permanently settled in Giles County.   Here the mother died in 1872, and the father too passed from life about four years later.   Our subject passed his early life on the farm and in the district schools.   He lived with his father having entire control of the farm until about forty years of age.   He was bitterly opposed to secession and stood firm for the Union.   During the war he remained at home as quiet and peaceable as man could be under like circumstances.   In 1865 he married Catharine Parsons, a native of Tennessee, born about 1830, and the daughter of James W. and Massie (Gordon) Parsons.   Our subject began life a poor man, had but poor advantages for an education and yet he is a good neighbor and an energetic, industrious citizen.   In 1869 he was elected to the State Legislature to represent the counties of Marshall, Lincoln and Giles.   At the end of two years he returned home and confined himself to the farm until 1884, when he was again called upon to appear before the people as an independent candidate for representative, and was duly elected for the years 1885 and 1886.   Mr. Sanders resides in the Twelfth District, on an excellent farm of about 500 acres, which is fairly improved.

SAMUEL D. SCOTT is a native of Giles County, Tenn., born June 16, 1849, son of Thomas J. and Malinda W. (Holt) Scott, the former born in Illinois, in 1819, and was taken to Alabama at the age of two years.   He married and removed to Mississippi, and at the end of seven years moved to Tennessee, and then to Alabama, and in 1881 again to Tennessee.   The mother of our subject was born in Alabama, January 11, 1823. Our subject always had a predilection for farming, and has made that his occupation through life, and now owns 380 acres of fine land, on which he raises cotton principally, and also takes considerable interest in stock-raising.   November 12, 1868, he wedded Mary F. Whitfield, daughter of Alfred and Elizabeth (Simpson) Whitfield, one of the large landowners and prominent planters of Giles County.   To the union of our subject and wife were born the following children: James A. (deceased), Anna R., Minnie E. and Elizabeth W.   The mother was born June 24, 1850.   Mr. Scott is a supporter of Democratic principles, and he and Mrs. Scott are members of the Methodist Episcopal Church South.

JAMES SCRUGGS, farmer and stock-raiser of the Ninth District, was born in 1812, in Davidson County, Tenn., and is the fourth child born to the union of Thomas and Edna Scruggs, natives of Virginia.   They immigrated to this State in 1809, and to them were born nine children: Elizabeth, Nancy, James, Narcissa, Mary, Jane, William H., and Roxie A.   James, our subject, attended the common schools, where he received a liberal education.   When quite young he came to Giles County, and worked at the saddler's trade at Elkton until 1841, after which he began farming where he now resides.   He has 600 acres on Elkton Turnpike, and is in very comfortable circumstances.   All this he has made by hard work and good management, and is not in debt one dollar.   In 1834, he married Susan Nelson, daughter of John and Phœbe Nelson, natives, respectively, of Alabama and Tennessee.   This union of our subjects resulted in the birth of four children: William P., Mary E., James H. and Annie E.   Mr. Scruggs, in politics, is Democratic, and he and family are members of the Methodist Episcopal Church South, in high standing. In 1875, Mrs. Scruggs was paralyzed, and has never fully recovered from the stroke, but is much better. The Scruggs family is one of the fixtures of this county, and all are good citizens.

GEORGE E. SHORT, farmer and native of Giles County, Tenn., was born about three miles from Pulaski, Tenn., July 11, 1829. His parents, J. T. and Elizabeth (Abernathy) Short, were born in Brunswick Co., Va., in 1793 and 1803, respectively. They moved to Giles County, Tenn., in 1828, and settled about three miles southwest of Pulaski. The father was a planter, and followed that calling until his death, which took place in Giles County, in 1875. The mother died three years earlier. Of their ten children, our subject was the fifth. He was educated at the old field schools and at the schools of Pulaski. In the fall of 1862, he enlisted in the Third Tennessee Infantry, Capt. Ray's Company, Confederate States Army, and after nearly one year's service he was released on account of physical disability, and after peace was established he again resumed farming. He owns 480 acres of land, the greater part of which is in a fine state of cultivation. He resides in Pulaski. In 1858 he was married to Virginia M. Boisseau, who died February 23, 1881. In 1882, his marriage with Virginia C. Reynolds was consumated. They have one child: George Edward. Mr. Short is a Democrat, and he and wife are members of the Methodist Episcopal Church South, and are well respected citizens of the county.

PROF. WILLIAM J. SMITH, merchant, is a son of Lawrence and Mary J. (Overstreet) Smith, who were born in North Carolina and Tennessee in 1807 and 1818, respectively. The father immigrated to Tennessee about 1815, and settled in Maury County, and there died in 1879. William J., our subject, was born in Giles County, July 28, 1837, and after fitting himself for college at Pisgah, Tenn., completed his education in Lebanon University, at Lebanon, Tenn., and entered North Carolina University in 1862. In the late civil war he served in Company B, Forty-eighth Tennessee Infantry, and was captured at Port Hudson, but was soon paroled. After the battle of Missionary Ridge, he was in Gen. J. E. Johnston's army and later in Hood's army. He was captured at the second battle of Nashville and taken to Camp Douglas, and there held until the close of the war. For fifteen years subsequent to the war he taught school in Alabama, and was pronounced a competent and sucessful educator. Since 1881 he has resided in Lynnville, Tenn., and he and his brother, C. A. Smith, are associated in the merchandise business, the style of the firm being Smith Bros. Our subject is also engaged in farming; and in 1873 was married to S. E. Scruggs, at Portland, Ala. Prof. Smith is a Mason and is a member of the Presbyterian Church, and his wife of the Methodist Episcopal Church South.

NATHAN A. SMITH'S birth occurred in Giles County, Tenn., March 24, 1857, and he there received his education in the common schools. He has always followed the fortunes of a farmer's life, and in 1874 located on 143 acres of valuable and well improved land. In 1873 he was united in marriage to Loretta K. Shields, of Giles County, and five children are the result of their union: Susie, Jimmie, Owen B., John A. and one infant daughter. Mr. Smith is of Irish extraction, and in politics is a Democrat, and he and wife are members of the Presbyterian Church. His wife is a daughter of James and Eliza Shields, and he is a son of Nathan and Frances Smith, who were born in Virginia and Tennessee, respectively, and were married about the year 1835. Eleven children were born to them, named Elizabeth, Thomas G., David J., Susan A., Owen S., William C., Nathan A., Fannie, Sallie J., Charles V. and one infant, deceased. The father died in 1864, but the mother is still living.

HON. NOBLE SMITHSON was born December 7, 1841, near Nolensville, Williamson Co., Tenn., and resided in said county until 1853. He, with his parents, then removed to Lexington, Ala., and resided there until 1865, when he came to Pulaski, and has since continued to reside here. His father is the Rev. John G. Smithson, who was born in Virginia, in 1820, and who immigrated to Tennessee in 1830, and settled in Williamson County. He is a clergyman in the Methodist Episcopal Church South, and now resides near Pulaski. The paternal grandfather of our subject was Hezekiah Powell

Smithson, a Virginian, and a soldier in the war of 1812. At one time he was sheriff of Pittsylvania County, Va. The great-grandfather of our subject was Francis Smithson, also a Virginian, who died in Maury County, Tenn. The family came from North Cumberland County, Eng., to Virginia. The mother of our subject was Ann Vaughn Ladd, born in Williamson County, Tenn., in 1818, and was a daughter of Noble Ladd and Mary Burton Ladd. Her parents were natives, respectively, of Rockingham and Stokes Counties, N. C. She died near Pulaski, Tenn., July 20, 1886. Our subject's early life was spent on the farm. His father being in humble circumstances, he labored to aid him in the support of the family and received a good English education, and April 2, 1865, wedded Alice Patterson, of Giles County, and by this union has six children. He has been a member of the Independent Order of Odd Fellows and is now a Mason and Knight Templar. He is also a Knight of Honor and a member of the Ancient Order of United Workmen. He is a member of the Tennessee Historical Society and of the Bar Association of Tennessee. He is one of the leading lawyers of the State, and in politics is Independent. He is an advocate of woman suffrage, and district attorney-general for the Eleventh Circuit, composed of the counties of Williamson, Maury, Marshall, Giles, Lawrence, Lewis and Hickman, from November, 1867, to September, 1870. He was elected to the Thirty-eighth General Assembly as State Senator, from the Fifteenth Senatorial District, composed of the counties of Giles, Lawrence, Wayne and Lewis, November 6, 1872, for the next two years, 1873-74. He was chairman of the judiciary committee and also chairman of a special joint committee to investigate the affairs of the Bank of Tennessee. He was one of the thirteen senators who voted for the public school law of 1873, under which the present system of popular education has grown to be so efficient and beneficial to the State. He was a delegate to the National Greenback Convention at Indianapolis in 1876, which nominated Peter Cooper for the presidency. He has a large practice in the local courts and the supreme court of Tennessee, and is a distinguished lawyer and an eminent citizen.

REV. JOHN G. SMITHSON, a prominent farmer and stock-raiser, was born in 1820 in Pittsylvania County Va., and is the son of Hezekiah and Henrietta Smithson natives of Virginia. They were married about 1810 in Virginia, and to this union were born eight children: Hezekiah, Eliza, Henrietta, Paten, John G., Nathaniel, William and Henry C. The subject's father was a very prominent man in Virginia, and was sheriff of Pittsylvania County for many years. Our subject moved to Jefferson County, Tenn., in 1827 with his father, but afterward moved to Williamson County, Tenn., and received his education in the common schools of that county. In 1841 he was married to Ann V. Ladd, the daughter of Noble and Mary Ladd, natives of North Carolina. To Mr. and Mrs. Smithson were born fifteen children: Noble H., Mary H., Anne, Martha J., Rebecca J., Fountain D., John G., Paten C., Sarah E., Thornton L., William B., Isaac N., Alice D., Thomas F. and Henry C. In 1866 our subject purchased 350 acres where he is now residing. It consists of excellent land, three and a half miles west of Pulaski, all well improved and a part in cultivation. He has been a local Methodist Episcopal minister in this county since 1854. The Smithson family are all highly respected citizens, and the early members of the family were among the first settlers of Tennessee. Mr. Smithson owns a half-interest in the cotton and grist-mills known as the Vale Mills, which are very famous all over the country. He is also a stockholder in a turnpike, and a Republican in politics.

ISAAC NEWTON SMITHSON, of the firm of J. G. & N. Smithson, manufacturers of cotton goods, flour, meal, at the point known as Vale Mills in the Sixth District of Giles County, was born in 1858 in Alabama, and is a son of John G. and Ann V. Smithson, natives of Virginia, and Tennessee, respectively. Isaac received a liberal education in the Giles College, at Pulaski, and in early life assisted on the farm. He moved with his father to this State in 1866, and settled in Giles County. After completing his education at Giles College he was engaged as one of the teachers in that institution, and remained there one year. He then engaged in the book and stationery business until 1883, when he sold out his interest and moved to where he now resides at Vale Mills. The grades of flour manufactured by this firm are very fine, and their brand of flour known as "Excelsior" is extensively used in Middle Tennessee. September, 10, 1884, Mr. Smithson led to the altar Louise C. Harrison, daughter of Col. Thomas J. and L. E. Harrison of Indiana. Our subject is Independent in political belief, and he and wife are members of the Methodist Episcopal Church South. Mr. Smithson is a member of the K. of P., at Pulaski, and of English-Irish descent.

JOSEPH B STACY, clerk and master of the chancery court of Giles County, Tenn., was born in Franklin, Williamson Co., Tenn., October 4, 1827, son of Mahlon and Elizabeth G. Stacy, and of Scotch-Irish descent. His father was a native of North Carolina, born in 1797, and the mother of our subject was born in Williamson County, Tenn., in 1803. The Stacy family immigrated to Tennessee about 1803, settling in Davidson County; afterward removed to Williamson County, where they remained until 1828. Mahlon Stacy then removed to Giles County, where the mother of our subject died in 1876. The father died in 1880. Our subject is the second son of four children. He grew to manhood on the farm, received a practical education, came to Pulaski in 1845, and until 1851 was engaged as a clerk. He then engaged in merchandising, which he continued until 1859. In 1854 he married Miss Rebecca J. Johnson, daughter of Richard Johnson. The birth of four children blessed this union, two of whom are still living, to wit: Maria L. and Richard M. In 1862 Mr. Stacy joined the First Tennessee Cavalry, Confederate States Army, and was in the command of Col. James T. Wheeler. He took an active part in the battles of Corinth and Nashville. At the time of the surrender he was at Columbus, Miss. He returned to Pulaski in 1865, and the year following was engaged in general merchandising in this city. He continued this business until 1870, when he was appointed clerk and master of the chancery court, which position he has held continuously since, save a period of about six months. He is one of the best county officials the county has ever had. He is a true Democrat, and one of the leading stock-men of Giles County. He has given special attention to blooded horses and cattle since 1873, and has one of the best stock farms in Giles County. He is one of the most prominent men of this county, and he and wife are members of the Presbyterian Church.

JOHN T. STEELE, M. D., a prominent and successful practitioner, and a native of Giles County, was born October 1, 1826, and is the only child born to the union of Robert G. and Sarah Y. (Graves) Steele, natives, respectively, of North Carolina and Tennessee. The father was a tiller of the soil and a soldier in the war of 1812. Our subject received his education in the best county schools. In the year 1843 he began reading medicine with Dr. E. R. Field, of Pulaski, where he remained for two years. He then entered the old University of Pennslyvania, and graduated in the spring of 1848. He located in Pulaski, and entered into partnership with Dr. C. Perkins and practiced one year; after which he moved to Arkansas, locating at Augusta, and remained there three years. In 1853 he returned to Giles County, and since that time has been located in different parts of the county. In 1880 he located on the site where he now lives, which consists of a farm containing 215 acres of good land, with neat residences erected on it. He has also a saw and grist-mill erected on the farm, both in good running condition. December 1, 1853, he married Josephine C. Wilkes, a native of Maury County, born June 17, 1836. This union resulted in the birth of twelve children, seven of whom are living: Hume R., Robert W., Judith L., Hortense, Mattie R., John F. and Fannie C. Mr. Steele is a Democrat, and he and wife are members of the Methodist Episcopal Church South.

COLEMAN L. STEVENSON, a first-class farmer and stock-raiser, residing in the Ninth Civil District of Giles County, was born in that county December 26, 1832, and is the son of William P. and Malinda Stevenson, both natives of North Carolina. The father of our subject was born in North Carolina in 1810, and received his education in the schools of Giles County. He was a farmer by occupation, and by his marriage, in 1830, became the father of these children: Coleman L., Elam R., Joseph J., Presley W., William F., Sarah A. P., John H. and Wilber M. The father settled where he now resides in

1838, and has 300 acres of valuable land, all well improved.  He has four brothers who are ministers of the gospel, and his father was also a very prominent Methodist Episcopal minister.  Our subject's paternal grandparents were Rev. Elam and Lydia Stevenson, natives of North Carolina, who were married about 1805, and located in Giles County, Tenn., about 1813.  To them were born these children: Katherine, William P., James C., Abner A., Willis M., Minerva J., John B., Thomas C., Amanda, Elam A. and Gilbert. The grandfather died in 1875 and the grandmother in 1872.  Our subject, Coleman L. Stevenson, received a fair education, and has been engaged in farming from early youth. January 28, 1855, he was married to Louisa Jackson, daughter of Barrington and Nancy Jackson, natives of North Carolina, and to this union was born one child—William B. Mrs. Stevenson died February 1, 1856, and February 5, 1857, he was married to his sister-in-law, Dorcas Jackson.  The last union resulted in the birth of three sons: James M., Elam A. and Thomas M.  Besides his own children he took three orphan children to raise: Martha V., Nancy M. and Mary J.  They are the daughters of James and Mary Jackson (deceased).  In 1862 Mr. Stevenson enlisted in the Thirty-second Tennessee Regiment of Volunteers, and served until the close of the war.  He participated in most of the principal battles, and was a brave and gallant soldier.  Mr. Stevenson and family are consistent members of the Methodist Episcopal Church South.  He has a good farm of 265 acres where he now lives, and 400 acres in other parts of Giles County.  He is a Democrat in politics.

WILBUR M. STEPHENSON, farmer and stock-raiser of the Ninth District of Giles County, Tenn., was born on the 20th of January, 1841, and is a son of William P. and Malinda Stephenson.  In his youth he attended the common schools of Giles County, Tenn., and his early occupation was farming.  At the breaking out of the late civil war he enlisted in the Thirty-second Regiment of Tennessee Volunteers, and served until the fall of 1864, when he was compelled to abandon service owing to ill health. After recovering he resumed farming, and in 1884 settled upon his valuable and well-improved farm of 112 acres.  Besides this he owns a valuable tract of land lying along Elk River, and near the town of Elkton.  Our subject is a Democrat.  November 9, 1865, he led to the hymeneal altar, Martha J. Hampton, daughter of Matison and Melissa Hampton, of Lincoln County.  Mr. and Mrs. Stephenson are the parents of the following children: Matison P., John L., Maggie and Erskin.  Husband and wife are members of the Methodist Episcopal Church South.

GEORGE E. SUTTLE, a native of Giles County, and a successful farmer and stock-raiser, was born December 29, 1829, and is the son of Richard C. and Harriet A. Suttle, natives of Virginia, who were married in East Tennessee about 1826, and settled in Giles County in 1827.  They had an interesting family of ten children, named Mary E., George E., Saraphana, Lucius D., Willimina, Matherine, Leroy W., Delphina, William D. and an infant daughter that died in 1857.  The mother of these children is still living.  Our subject is of Scotch-Irish descent.  He received the rudiments of his education in the common schools, and then finished at the Murfreesboro University in 1853.  September 17, 1861, he was married to Theodosia O. Green, who was born April 11, 1842, and who is the daughter of Alfred B. and Sarah O. Green, natives of Tennessee.  By this union our subject became the father of seven children—two daughters and five sons: Lizzie L., William D., Harry H., Claud, two infants, boy and girl (twins), and James P.  Claud died July 16, 1874, and the twins died in 1877.  In 1869 he settled on the farm where he now lives, which consists of 443 acres of valuable land five miles east of Pulaski, on the old Elkton road.  He is regarded as a No. 1 farmer and an excellent citizen.  He also owns some valuable city property on East Hill in Pulaski.  Mr. Suttle is a Democrat, and he and children are members of the Methodist Episcopal Church South.  Mrs. Suttle is a member of the Presbyterian Church, at Pulaski.  The Suttle family is very old and highly respected.

EPPERSON TARPLEY, Esq., wagon and carriage manufacturer, was born in 1846 in Giles County, and is of Irish descent.  He attended the district schools, and afterward

GILES COUNTY. 873

finished his education in Giles Academy, in Pulaski. He then engaged in agricultural pursuits, and continued this occupation until 1867, when he entered into his present business. He has been rather successful at this, and is doing a good business. In 1862 his marriage with Malissa A. Kellum was solemnized. She is the daughter of Thomas J. and Nancy J. Kellum, of Giles County. The marriage of our subject resulted in the birth of six children: Lizzie V., Silas E., Elwood L., Alice B., Guy and Earl. The family are members of the Cumberland Presbyterian Church in high standing. In 1868 Mr. Tarpley was elected magistrate of the Eighth District of Giles County, and still holds that position. He is a Democrat in politics, and a member of the F. & A. M. fraternity. His parents are Silas S. and Susan V. Tarpley, natives of Tennessee.

CALLAWAY H. TIDWELL, ESQ., a prominent farmer and stock-raiser of the Sixth District of Giles County, is a son of Vincent and Phebe Tidwell and the grandson of Isaac and Elizabeth Tidwell, who immigrated to this State from South Carolina and settled in this county in the early part of the eighteenth century. Our subject's mother was the daughter of Silas Rackley of South Carolina, who came to Tennessee at an early date and settled in Lawrence County. The parents of our subject were married January 10, 1817, and their family consisted of eleven children: Callaway H., Jane E., Silas, Elizabeth, Charles W., Darling M., William G., Thomas B., James P., Melissa A. and Andrew J. Callaway passed his youthful days on the farm and secured a practical education in the country schools. In 1841 he was united in marriage to Leah Tucker, a native of Giles County, born February 17, 1825, and the daughter of Anderton and Stacy Tucker, natives of North Carolina, who immigrated to this State at an early day and made their home in this county. To Mr. and Mrs. Tidwell were born eleven children: Nancy J., Margaret A. Stacy E., William C., Martha C., Vincent M., Phebe M., Alice N., Mary W., Charles W., and Ozro H. Our subject settled where he is now living in 1874, and his farm consists of 500 acres of excellent land, all well improved and a part of the same in a high state of cultivation. He also owns 600 acres more, all well improved, in other parts of the county. He has been very successful financially, as he started in life with very little of this world's goods. He was elected magistrate in 1845, and has held the office in an able and capable manner. The family are members of the Methodist Episcopal Church South, at Trinity, and are all very highly respected citizens. Mr. Tidwell's political belief is Democratic.

JAMES J. UPSHAW, M. D., dealer in drugs and general merchandise, is a son of James and Elinor Upshaw, natives of Virginia and Tennessee, respectively. They were married about 1842, in Limestone County, Ala., and to them was born a family of three children: George L., William E. and James J. The father died November 6, 1858, and the mother in 1864. Our subject was born in 1858, in Giles County, received a fair education, and in 1876 began the study of medicine with Dr. James A. Bowers (deceased), of Elkton. He graduated from the University of Louisville in 1878, after which he came to Elkton, where he has remained ever since. He has had a good and lucrative practice, and was one of the county's best physicians. In 1883 he abandoned his practice, and has since devoted all his time to his present business. In 1878 he married Violet R. Patterson, daughter of John C. and Elinor Patterson, of Giles County. The result of our subject's marriage was the birth of two children: Louis B. and Minnie L. Dr. Upshaw is of English extraction, a Democrat, and he and wife are members of the Cumberland Presbyterian Church at Elkton.

REV. JOHN F. WALKER is a son of William B. and Ann (Scott) Walker. The father was born in Virginia in 1789, and after his marriage immigrated to Tennessee and located in Wayne County. On building his first house in 1816 the logs were cut from the forest, the house erected and the goods put in in one day. He was magistrate of his district twelve years, and died on the old homestead in April, 1873. The mother was born in 1794 and died in 1876. Our subject was born January 17, 1821, and received such early education as the primitive schools of his day afforded, and finished his education at Cumberland University, at Lebanon, Tenn. He taught school, and devoted his time until twenty-four years old to completing his education, when he was ordained a minister of the

Cumberland Presbyterian Church, and has been an active and efficient laborer in the cause forty-one years. He joined the Fifty-third Tennessee Infantry as chaplain, and was captured at Fort Donelson and kept a prisoner at Indianapolis, Ind., and later at Camp Chase, Ohio, where, through the influence of Gov. Tod, he was given the privilege of the city. He was confined at Johnson's Island for some time, when he, with a number of chaplains and surgeons, were released as non-combatants, and allowed to return home. March 21, 1855, he wedded E. A. Brown, and eight children were the results of this union: Herschel P., W. B., J. Luther, C. Herbert, Lura, Ida and Dezzie. Mrs. Walker was born January 17, 1831, daughter of Rev. B. Brown, who was an early pioneer of Tennessee and an efficient and popular divine. He died about 1875 and the mother in 1885. Mr. Walker is conservative in his political views. He owns a farm of 157 acres, and is a member of the Masonic fraternity.

DR. MARK S. WATERS, physician, and owner of the farm "Wood Lawn," was born August 30, 1833, the eldest of three children of David M. and Sarah F. (Toland) Waters, who were born in South Carolina and Alabama in 1813 and 1814, and died in 1860 and 1836, respectively. Our subject received the rudiments of his education in the common schools, and completed his literary education at Cumberland University. He began reading medicine with Dr. Elihu Edmundson, and attended two courses of lectures, and graduated from the old University of Nashville and later from the old University of New York, and now possesses an extensive practice. April 7, 1857, Maggie M. White, born April 20, 1835, became his wife. She is a daughter of James and Matilda M. (Gooch) White, who were born in Georgia and North Carolina in 1794 and 1800, respectively. The father died in 1877. He was a soldier in the war of 1812, and was pronounced one of nature's purest and best men. Our subject served in his professional capacity two years in the late war, but finally resigned his commission at Dalton, Ga. Dr. Waters is a conservative Democrat, well posted on the politics of the day. He and wife are parents of the following children: Thomas M., David S. (a promising young man and a medical graduate of the old University of Nashville), James W., Archibald C., Addison K., Guy S., Maggie L. and Fannie T. Dr. Waters is a Mason, and owns 280 acres of good land. He is a generous citizen and aids all enterprises for the public weal.

JOHN R. D. WILLIAMS, of the firm of Williams & Watson, lumber dealers, of Pulaski, Tenn., was born in Giles County in 1840, and is a son of William J. and Martha Williams, who were born in Tennessee and were married in 1839, and located in Giles County in 1840. Their family consisted of John R. D., Joseph, Mary, Lou and Melvin. The mother died in 1851. John R. D. was educated in the common schools, and in early life worked at the carpenter's trade. In 1861 he enlisted in the Ninth Tennessee Battalion of Cavalry, serving four years and participating in several of the principal battles. At the close of the war he was employed by the Government as bridge carpenter, but soon abandoned that occupation and engaged in building and contracting, following that business until 1877. He then entered into his present business in Pulaski, and has been very successful. In 1865 he was married to Maggie J. Walker, daughter of William M. Walker, of Maury County. The family are members of the Presbyterian Church, and Mr. Williams is a Democrat and a member of the F. & A. M.

DR. THOMAS L. WILLIAMS, a successful practitioner, was born in Giles County September 9, 1832, and is the son of George and Sarah (Graves) Williams, natives of Tennessee. They were married in Giles County in 1826, and moved to Mississippi in 1837, where they remained until 1839. To them were born three children: John, Thomas L. and George. The father died in 1852 and the mother in 1842. Our subject received his education in the common schools of Arkansas, and in early life was engaged in farming and blacksmithing. In 1856 he began his medical studies, which he continued until the breaking out of the war. He then enlisted in the Fortieth Arkansas Regiment of Volunteers, but owing to failing health he was soon discharged from the service. He then resumed his medical studies. In 1869 he graduated from the medical department of the University of Louisville, and returning to Elkton located there, where he has since remained. In 1859 he took for his wife Carrie Bull, daughter of Adrian D. and Ursula Bull, of Giles County. To our subject and wife was born one daughter—Katie. Dr. Williams is one of the county's best physicians, as his many patients yet living can testify. He has been very successful professionally as well as financially, and is a self-made man in every respect. He is a Democrat in politics, and he and wife are members of the Methodist Episcopal Church South. He is a member of the F. & A. M. and I. O. O. F.

SAMUEL S. WILLIAMSON was born within a mile of his present place of residence March 19, 1825. He has always been a tiller of the soil, and until attaining his majority resided with his parents. He was a soldier in the Mexican war, and fought at Vera Cruz, Matamoras, and was at one time confined to the hospital and pronounced incurable, but finally rallied, and is now enjoying the health usually allotted to man. He was married in Giles County, Tenn., March 9, 1854, to Jane P. Rainey, daughter of Horace D. Rainey, and to them were born three children: John E., Horace Glenn, and Lizzie C. (wife of J. B. Potts). Horace G. is a physician, who graduated from Vanderbilt University, Nashville, Tenn., and is practicing at Prospect. John E. died on the train eighty miles west of New Orleans December 22, 1883, while en route home from California, whither he had gone for his health. Mrs. Williamson was born in North Carolina October 7, 1825, and came to Tennessee in 1837. Our subject and wife are members of the Methodist Episcopal Church South, and he is a Democrat and belongs to the I. O. O. F. His parents, John and Susan (Sutherland) Williamson, were born in North Carolina and Virginia in 1784 and 1783 respectively. They were early settlers of Tennessee. The father died October 14, 1856, and the mother in 1859.

SAMUEL A. WILSON, a leading citizen of Giles County, was born in 1823, and is living on the farm of his birth. He was united in marriage in 1857 to Mary Herron, who was born in Mississippi in 1837, and the daughter of Thomas and Mary (Wynne) Herron, natives of Tennessee, born, respectively, in 1808 and in 1816, and died in 1844 and in 1879. To our subject and wife were born three children: Sallie W., Herron C. and Georgie W. Mr. Wilson remained on the farm with his father until 1843, when he went to Yazoo City, and engaged in merchandising in partnership with his brother for about five years. He then moved to Memphis, Tenn., and embarked in the dry goods business, which occupation he followed for four years. He then, in partnership with Norman & Carter, opened a cotton commission house, which also proved successful until the breaking out of the Rebellion. Mr. Wilson then went to Mississippi and opened a tannery, and was engaged in this business until the close of the war, after which he re-opened the cotton commission house, the firm being then known as Wilson, Carter & Co. In 1867 Mr. Wilson sold out and returned to Tennessee, locating on the farm of his birth, which consists of 400 acres of land in a high state of cultivation. Mr. Wilson is a Democrat in politics, and is a member of the Cumberland Presbyterian Church. His wife is also a member of the same church. His parents, James and Elizabeth (Weir) Wilson, were natives of Virginia, born, respectively, in 1783 and 1782. The father was a farmer by occupation, and participated in the war of 1812, and was also with Jackson in the Creek and Seminole Indian wars. He died in 1857, and his wife followed him the same year.

JOSEPH M. WRIGHT, a prominent man and successful dentist of Elkton, Tenn., was born in Lincoln County, Tenn., November 4, 1839, and is the fifth of a family of six children, and received his education in the common schools of his native county. His early days were spent in farming, and in 1867 he began the study of dentistry with G. A. Dewey, of Glasgow, Ky., and two years later began practicing. In 1870 he removed to Mississippi, and after a three years' residence in that State lived a short time in Giles County, Tenn., and then moved to Texas, where he resided until 1878. At that date he returned to Giles County, where he has since been actively engaged in the practice of his profession, and has met with good success financially and professionally. In 1874 he was married to Elmira N. Benson, daughter of Benjamin and Adaline Benson, and to them was born one child. Mrs. Wright died in 1881, and in 1884 Mr. Wright married Susan A. Graves. Both are church members, and our subject is a Democrat. His parents,

Jacob R. and Mary Wright, were Tennesseeans, and were married about 1830. Their children are Laminda, Minerva, Martha J., John D., Joseph M. and Jacob A. The father died in 1886, and the mother in 1844.

HUGH YOKLEY, farmer and stock-raiser, was born in Davidson County, N. C., in 1813, son of Andrew and Delia (Morris) Yokley, and is of Irish-Dutch origin. Both parents were born in the same State and county as our subject, and came to Tennessee and settled in Giles County in 1816, where they died. Hugh is the eldest of six living children, and attended the first schools of Giles County. He has lived the free, happy and independent life of a farmer, and settled on the farm where he now lives in 1841. He is an extensive land owner, and has been quite prosperous financially. In March, 1838, he wedded Martha Hannah, who was born September 29, 1817, daughter of James Hannah, a native of Ireland. They have six children: Sophronia, Martha A., Catherine, Henrietta, Eugenia and Hugh L. Mr. Yokley was formerly an old-line Whig, but is now a Democrat. He and wife are members of the Cumberland Presbyterian Church, and he belongs to the I. O. O. F. and G. T., and is considered one of the substantial and worthy citizens of the county.

---

# LINCOLN COUNTY.

J. S. ALEXANDER, proprietor of livery and feed stable, of Fayetteville, began business in 1876, and although his success was on a very small scale at first, he is at present the owner of eight vehicles and twelve horses, and is constantly increasing his stock. He was born in Lincoln County in 1838, son of Wiley M. and Nancy (Renegar) Alexander, born, respectively, in Tennessee and North Carolina in 1816. The father was an early settler of Lincoln County, and was a stock speculator and a man of exceptional business capacity. He was married in 1835, and died in 1881. He was tax collector and sheriff of the county several years. Of his eight children, four are living: W. S., J. S. (our subject), W. W. and Philomena (Mrs. A. J. Crisman). Our subject was educated in Mulberry, Tenn., and at the age of sixteen began clerking in a dry goods store, and two years later went to Shelbyville, where he was engaged in the grocery business for two years. In 1861 he enlisted in Company B, First Tennessee Regiment, and fought in the battle of Manasses, Gettysburg, Sharpsburg, Cedar Run, Seven Pines, Richmond, Chancellorsville, Harper's Ferry, Fredericksburg and Petersburg, where he was wounded and taken prisoner, and was taken to Washington, D. C., the day Lee surrendered. In 1865 he returned, after an absence of four years. December 22, 1868, he wedded Florinda H. Smith, daughter of Champion E. Smith. Mrs. Alexander was born in Lincoln County, Tenn., May 18, 1845, and is the mother of four children: George R., Claud, Frank and an infant son. He farmed four years after the war, and in 1873 came to Fayetteville, and established a retail liquor store, but ten years later engaged in his present occupation. He is a Democrat, and cast his first presidential vote for Stephen A. Douglas in 1860.

ANDERSON ALSUP, farmer, was born in Granger County, Tenn., July 16, 1809, and was educated in the schools near his home. In March, 1831, he married Sarah, daughter of John and Priscilla Davis. She was born in Lincoln County in 1815, and is the mother of four children: J. V., Amanda E. (Mrs. T. H. Kennedy), Mary A. (Mrs. R. P. Smith), and W. B. Mr. Alsup located on the old home-place after his marriage, and there has since resided, and at the present time owns about 400 acres of very fine land. He has been a successful business man, and has given his children good educational advantages. He has been magistrate of his district four years. He is a Democrat, and cast his first Presidential vote for Andrew Jackson. His wife belongs to the Baptist Church. Mr.

Alsup's parents were James and Abigail Alsup, born in Virginia and Pennsylvania, respectively, the former in 1769. He came to Tennessee at an early date, and died in Lincoln County in 1829. The mother departed this life in 1848.

WILLIAM H. ASHBY, farmer, is a son of Halifax and Eliza Jane (Hall) Ashby and was born in Lincoln County, May 28, 1830. He was one of a family of eleven children, ten of whom are living. The grandfather, also named Halifax, was born in England, immigrated to North Carolina, where he reared his family. Our subject's father was born in North Carolina, in March, 1807, and received his education in the schools in the vicinity. He was married in 1829, and followed agricultural pursuits, owning at the time of his death, which occurred in October, 1873, 250 acres of good productive land. The mother of our subject was born in North Carolina in May, 1808, and died in March, 1876. William, our subject, received his education in the common schools, and, November 2, 1852, was united in marriage to Mary Elizabeth Ramsey. This union resulted in the birth of nine children, seven of whom are living: Benjamin A., Sallie J. (wife of L. H. Wiley), James H., Felix B., Tinnie, Mary E. (wife of William Pylant) and Willie E. Mr. Ashby now owns 300 acres of valuable land and is in good circumstances. June 30, 1866, Mrs. Ashby died, and in August, 1868, Mr. Ashby wedded Ellen E. Wadley, a native of Tennessee, born March 9, 1840, and a daughter of J. B. and Matilda Wadley. To Mr. and Mrs. Ashby were born five children: John M., David W., Susan C., Eliza D., and Ida May. Mr. Ashby is a life-long Democrat and was formerly a member of the I. O. O. F. He and wife are leading members of the Cumberland Presbyterian Church.

TRAVIS D. ASHBY, farmer, and the son of Peter and Mary J. (George) Ashby, was born in Lincoln County, Tenn., in 1847. The father was born in Lincoln County, in 1821 and was a tiller of the soil. In 1844 he was married and became the father of three children: Elzina (wife of S. E. Keith, deceased), Sallie H. (wife of LaFayette Kimes), and Travis D., our subject. The father died in 1856. The mother of our subject was also born in Lincoln County about 1830, and is now living in the Fifth District, and is a devout member of the Methodist Episcopal Church South. Our subject remained with his mother till he was twenty-five years of age, and received his education in the district schools. December 25, 1872, he was united in marriage to Nancy J. Cunningham, daughter of Peter and Sarah Cunningham, and the fruits of this union were four children, three of whom are living: James N., Sallie E. and Luler T. About three years previous to his marriage he purchased 100 acres of land where he now resides, and through industry, frugality and close attention to business has added to his estate till he now owns 365 acres of good, productive land. He is a Democrat in politics, casting his first vote for Horatio Seymour. He is a Mason, and he and wife are among the most respected members of the Primitive Baptist Church.

J. W. BARNETT, groceryman and mayor of Fayetteville, Tenn., was born in Salem, Va., in 1846, son of John L. and Lucinda (Williams) Barnett. They were of Scotch-Irish and Welsh-English descent, born in Virginia, in 1814 and 1821, respectively. The father followed merchandising in Virginia for forty years, but is now living a retired life. He has been twice married (the mother died in 1854), his second wife being Mary A. Logan. Two of the three children by the first marriage are living. The second wife bore one child. Our subject attended Roanoke College, Virginia, and at the age of seventeen enlisted in the Salem Artillery of Hardway's battalion, took an active part in the battles of Spottsylvania, Cold Harbor, Richmond, Appomattox Court House and others, and served until the final surrender. In 1867 he began clerking in his father's store but removed to Pulaski, Tenn., in 1871 and continued clerking. In 1873 he came to Fayetteville and formed a partnership with F. W. Brown in a general merchandise store. In 1882 he established a staple and family grocery store, and has since been engaged in that business. In January, 1874, he married Julia C. Gordon, who was born in 1850, and has borne her husband four children: Clare Lou, Mary B., James W. and Julius L. Mrs. Barnett died in 1881, and the following year Mr. Barnett married Sadie E., sister of his first wife, born in 1845; and daughter of John T. Gordon. Mr. Barnett was chosen mayor of Fayetteville in 1885 and yet holds the office. He is a Democrat and a member of the K. of H. and A. O. U. W. He and wife belong to the Presbyterian Church.

A. F. BASS, merchant at McDowell's Mills, was born in Giles County February 7, 1854, and was one of three children of Farmington and Naomi Bass, born in Giles County, Tenn., in 1818 and 1817, and died in 1884 and 1876, respectively. They were married about 1840, and the father followed farming through life. Our subject received such education and rearing as is usually given a farmer's boy, and in 1881 he and Janey Bennett were united in marriage. Mrs. Bass was born in Giles County in 1860, and is a member of the Christian Church. After his marriage, Mr. Bass farmed for two years, and then began merchandising at Bunker's Hill, remaining one year. In 1885 he located at McDowell's Mills, where he keeps an excellent general merchandise store, and is doing a paying business. He takes an active part in all laudable enterprises and is doing much toward improving and building up the place. He gives his support to the Democratic party.

MRS. N. E. BENSON, of the Sixteenth District, was born in Lincoln County, April, 1828, and was one of two children born to W. and Cynthia Hayes. Her father was born in North Carolina in 1793, and died November 5, 1866. He was in the war of 1812, under Gen. Jackson, and was a farmer by occupation. The mother of our subject was born in Lincoln County, and departed this life December 19, 1865. The other child of our subject's parents was Commodore P., who was a farmer and resided in Lincoln County. He died December 25, 1867. Our subject received her education in the schools near home, and December 4, 1845, was united in marriage to Curran D. Benson, a native of Giles County, born September 10, 1820. By this union, Mrs. Benson became the mother of three children—one of whom is living: Thomas E., born November 14, 1846, and died August 22, 1876; E. F., born April 6, 1849, and died July 5, 1873; and Ella O., born June 15, 1857, and the wife of W. G. Harwell, a farmer of Giles County. They have five children: Robert E., William S., Fannie E., Sally M. and an infant. Mr. Benson (our subject's husband) owned over 100 acres of valuable land at the time of his death, which occurred August 20, 1868. The land was then divided among the children and wife. The wife now owns about 200 acres, located near Millville, and it is considered a fine farm.

DR. WILLIAM BONNER, dec'd., a native of Granville Co., N. C., was born October 7, 1798, and came to Tennessee with his father December, 1808. For two or three years the family lived in Williamson County, near Nolensville, and then came to Lincoln County, where William Bonner and his brother Moses continued to reside until their death. The whole of the southern portion of Middle Tennessee was then but sparsely settled, and William Bonner, seeing that physicians, even in urgent cases, could be had only by sending fifty or one hundred miles, young as he was, without prompting from others, determined to study medicine. In 1821 he went to Nashville and began the study of medicine under Drs. McNairy and Overton. He never ceased to speak of their kindness and of Mrs. McNairy as one of the noblest of women. In the winter of 1822-23 he attended a course of lectures at Lexington, Ky. In the spring of 1823 he began the practice of medicine in Lincoln County, and soon had a large and lucrative business, making money enough to pay his unpaid bills in Nashville and bear the expenses of a course of lectures in Philadelphia. He received his diploma in the spring of 1827. In extreme and desperate cases he informed his patients and resorted to desperate remedies, often with success. He took a tumor from the neck of a Mrs. Abernathy, when his brother and other learned and experienced physicians and surgeons declared she would die under the operation. She consented to the operation and afterward lived many years. Dr. Bonner returned to Lincoln County and continued the practice of medicine for thirty years. He married Lucy Rosseau Robertson on the 4th of July, 1827. He always seemed indifferent to notoriety, and operated more than twenty times for lithotomy and never lost a case. He collected over $100,000 from his practice and never sued for a medical bill. In connection with his practice he engaged in farming, and at the commencement of the late war he owned 8,000 acres of land and three or four hundred slaves. He was a man of wonderful energy and great physical and mental power. So strong, active and energetic was he for fifty years of his life, and so prosperous, that he never fully realized that any except those who were sick needed help. The result of the war and freedom to his slaves did not embitter him, but he constituted himself a guardian for every negro that lived with him. He died at Fayette September 20, 1879, at the age of eighty years, eleven months and thirteen days. He was a Democrat in politics, and never too tired to gain a vote for his candidate if he could, but in the sick room he eschewed politics and religion.

W. C. BRIGHT, M. D., is a son of John M. Bright, who was born in Fayetteville, Tenn., January 20, 1817. His father, James Bright, was a Virginian and an early pioneer of Tennessee. John M. was educated in Fayetteville and Hillsboro, N. C. In 1839 he graduated from the Nashville University. The subject of his graduating theme, "On the Classics," was a scholarly effort. He began studying law, and in 1841 graduated from the Transylvania University, at Lexington, Ky., with credit to himself and honor to the institution, delivering the valedictory address. He has since practiced in Fayetteville. In November, 1841, he wedded Judith C. Clark, daughter of Gov. Clark, of Kentucky. She died in 1855, and two years later he wedded Zerilda B. Buckner. Mr. Bright has always been a Democrat, and in 1844 stumped the State for Polk in his race for the Presidency. In 1847–48 he was a member of the State Legislature, and served on many important committees. In 1848, he made a canvass for Cass and Butler, and a leading journal wrote that it "would be hard to exaggerate the power and brilliancy of his speeches." The following are some of his speeches that have been published: "The Obligations of the American Youth," a speech against Know-nothingism, "Charity," "Life, Character and Public Services of the Hon. Felix Grundy," "Law, Lawyers, and Law-schools." During the late war he was inspector-general of Tennessee, with the rank of brigadier-general. In 1870 he was nominated and elected to the Forty-second Congress. Mr. Bright is very public spirited, and has done all in his power to further the interests of his State and county. His son, W. C. Bright, was born in Fayetteville in 1844, and was educated in Fayetteville and at Richland Academy, in Marshall County. His school-days were suddenly stopped by the breaking out of the war. May 4, 1861, he enlisted in Company C, Eighth Tennessee Regiment, and took an active part in the battles of Perryville, Murfreesboro, Peach Tree Creek, Chickamauga, and Decatur. At the last-named battle he was wounded in the left leg, which unfitted him for duty for about fifteen months. After his return home in 1865, he began the teacher's profession, but in the fall of the same year began studying medicine under Dr. Kennedy. From 1866 to 1868, he attended the medical department of the University of Nashville, and delivered the valedictory address in 1868. He immediately began practicing in his birthplace, where he has since resided with the exception of five years spent in Edgefield and Nashville. February 4, 1871, he wedded Annie Bramlett, daughter of Judge L. M. Bramlett. Mrs. Bright was born in 1849 in Giles County, Tenn. They have three children: Bramlett, Mary, and Judith. Dr. Bright is one of the leading physicians and surgeons of Lincoln County, and has a large and paying practice. He is a Democrat, and he and wife are members of the Presbyterian Church.

ANDREW J. CARLOSS is a son of Archelaus and Ruth (Pride) Carloss, is one of their thirteen children, and was born in North Carolina in 1815. The father was born in North Carolina in 1767, and was a son of Edward C. Carloss, who was born in Spain and immigrated to America when a young man. Archelaus' parents died when he was small, and he was apprenticed to learn the carpenter's trade, and while serving his apprenticeship assisted in building the first State capitol of North Carolina. He and wife died in North Carolina in 1845 and 1826, respectively. Andrew J. received a practical education, and at the age of nineteen came to Tennessee, where he has always made his home, with the exception of a short time spent in Alabama. July 30, 1839, he married Mary Ann Franklin, granddaughter of ex-Gov. Franklin, of North Carolina, who died at the age of fourteen years. Mr. Carloss owns 2,800 acres of land, and is a man of undoubted integrity. He has been a life-long Democrat. His wife was born in Alabama in August, 1821. Her parents, James and Frances Franklin, were born in North Carolina and Tennessee in 1794 and 1797, respectively.

HON. JO. G. CARRIGAN is an attorney at law, of Fayetteville, Tenn., and son of Hiram and Fannie (Randolph) Carrigan. The father came to the United States with his parents when a small lad, and lived, first in North Carolina, and then in Alabama, and finally, in 1854, came to Lincoln County, Tenn. He was a blacksmith by trade, but for the past ten years has lived retired from active business life. He and his wife became the parents of five children, four of whom are living: W. R. (who is a teacher and farmer), Susan (Mrs. G. W. Higgins), Josie (widow of A. W. Bonds), and Jo. G., our subject, who was born in Madison County, Ala., September 7, 1835, and received his education at New Hope Academy, Marshall County, Tenn., and Sulphur Springs Institute, Lincoln County, Tenn. He worked at the blacksmith's trade about six years and then entered the teachers' profession and taught one year. In 1856 he purchased a few law books and began his legal studies, being obliged to struggle along as best he could without the aid or instruction of other lawyers. He was admitted to the bar in 1858, and the same year became editor and proprietor of the *Messenger*, at Lewisburg, but at the end of one year began the publication of the *Union*, at Shelbyville, Tenn., which he continued until the breaking out of the war stopped further business. In May, 1861, he enlisted in Company G, Eighth Regiment Tennessee Infantry, Confederate States Army, and participated in the Cheat Mountain campaign (of which he has written a full account) and the battle of Perryville. In January, 1863, he was transferred to the quartermaster's department, but in December of that year was discharged, owing to the failure of his eyesight. In August, 1865, he was elected to the State Senate, and served on several important committees. His speeches on the elective franchise bill and the restoration of the people of Tennessee to the control of the State government attracted much attention. He moved to Fayetteville in 1867, where he enjoys the confidence of a large clientage and his brother attorneys. December 22, 1858, he was married to Fannie Higgins, who was born in Lincoln County in 1838 and has borne her husband two children: Emma (Mrs. A. M. McGlaughlin) and Beulah. Our subject is a fluent and ready speaker and an earnest advocate and safe counselor. He advocates the principles of the Democratic party, and is a member of the Christian Church. His wife belongs to the Cumberland Presbyterian Church.

JAMES H. CARY, farmer of the Twelfth District and a son of Robert and Sarah Blair) Cary, was born August 15, 1824, near his present residence. The father of our subject was born in Ireland in 1781, and was of Scotch-Irish descent. He was a weaver by occupation in his youth, and in later years devoted his attention to the cultivation of the soil. In 1798 he left his native country and came to the United States, landing at Charleston in February. He located in Chester District, S. C., where he was living at the time of his marriage, which occurred in 1807. In 1816 he immigrated to Lincoln County, and the following year settled on the Fayetteville and Pulaski road, six miles from Fayetteville, where he remained until his death, in 1869. He was one of the early settlers of Lincoln County, and was an industrious, hard-working man. He was the father of four children: Margaret, born in 1817; Isabella, born in 1819 (wife of James I. Tate), John, born in 1821 (and died March 31, 1886, leaving a widow and five children, who now reside on the old homestead), and James H., our subject, who lives half a mile from the old home place with his sister Margaret, and both are single. They have been industrious, persevering and economical, and as a result own 473 acres of excellent land, and have a good home. Mr. Cary is a Republican in politics, and cast his first vote for Lewis Cass in 1848. Margaret is a member of the Reformed Presbyterian Church, and has been for the past thirty-six years. In 1862 James enlisted in Company I, Starne's battalion, Forrest's command. He fought in the battle of Spring Hill, and at the end of five months returned home.

M. H. CAUGHRAN is a Tennesseean, born in Lincoln County in May, 1829. He is one of nine children, and the son of William and Elizabeth (Wiley) Caughran. The father was of Irish descent, born in South Carolina in 1786, and came to Tennessee in 1828.

He was a farmer, and died on the 14th of March, 1840. The mother was also born in South Carolina, in 1787, and died August 30, 1870. Our subject was educated in the common schools, and resided with his parents until twenty-two years of age. March 23, 1852, he was married to Julia, daughter of S. S. and Polly (Gibson) Buchanan. Mrs. Caughran was born in Lincoln County March 22, 1831. After his marriage Mr. Caughran looked after the interest of Mr. Buchanan's farm for ten years, and then purchased 100 acres of land near Petersburg, where he resided one year. He then sold this farm, and in 1865 purchased 185 acres of land near Fayetteville, where he resided ten years. He then purchased his present farm of 115 acres, and by his good business qualifications has accumulated quite an amount of property. He is a Democrat, and he and wife are members of the Presbyterian Church. In the late war he served in Company B, Twenty-eighth Tennessee Infantry for three months, then Gen. Bragg appointed him special messenger, taking care of Governmental supplies and distributing goods for the army. He remained in this capacity until nearly the close of the war.

H. T. CHILDS, farmer of the Eleventh District, was born in Lincoln County, of the same district, July 18, 1841, and was one of four children born to Thomas and Sally (Wilkins) Childs. The father was born in North Carolina March 9, 1796, and came to Lincoln County, this State, with his people, in 1818. He bought 200 acres of land in the Eleventh District, and yet more in other parts of Lincoln County. He died August 17, 1872. Our subject's mother was born in the Eleventh District in 1808, and departed this life October 19, 1883. Our subject was reared in the country, and received his education at the Sulphur Spring Institute. At the age of eighteen he enlisted in Company D, First Tennessee Infantry. He took an active part in the battles of Seven Pines, Cedar Run and Manassas, and was severely wounded in the last named battle. At the end of six months he was sufficiently recovered to return to active service again. In the battle of Chancellorsville he was again wounded, and did not return to duty for a year. He then joined Forrest's command, cavalry, and took part in numerous cavalry skirmishes. In 1868 he wedded Sally C., daughter of Allen and Martha Taylor, and a native of Lincoln County, born September 19, 1845. This union resulted in the birth of five children, four of whom are living: M. O., Mollie L., Annie N. and Thomas A. Mr. Childs owns 200 acres of valuable land, all well improved, and located near Fayetteville. In 1873 he was elected magistrate of his district, and this position he now holds. He is a strong advocate of good public schools, and a man who is scrupulously honest in all his dealings. He is a Democrat in politics, and a member of the Masonic fraternity.

DRS. R. E. & W. W. CHRISTIAN, physicians and surgeons of Fayetteville, Tenn., are the sons of Dr. D. W. and Americus (Faulkner) Christian. The father was of Scotch-Irish descent, and was born in Knox County, Tenn., in 1817. At the age of eighteen he began studying medicine under Dr. Cooper, and later graduated from the Louisville (Ky.) Medical College. He practiced in Kentucky and Texas, and during the late war resided in Louisville. In 1878 he established a drug store in Fayetteville, but died March 9, 1880, after living a useful and well-spent life. He was a true Christian, and left behind him an untarnished name. He was married May 16, 1844. His wife was born in Christian County, Ky., and since the death of her husband has resided with her two sons in Fayetteville. She is the second cousin of Gen. Robert E. Lee. Of her seven children five are living: R. E., Lillie M. (widow of Dr. B. C. Newman), Hattie Lee (Mrs. E. D. Stocking), Fannie Ella and W. W. R. E. Christian is a druggist, physician and surgeon of Fayetteville. He was born in Christian County, Ky., in 1846, and was educated in the common schools and at Louisville, Ky. In April, 1883, he entered upon his chosen profession, and in 1886 graduated from the medical department of the Vanderbilt University. December 20, 1882, he married Josephine Carneal, born in 1859, daughter of Walker Carneal. W. W. Christian was born in Lexington, Tex., in 1857. He attended school in Trenton, Paducah and Louisville, Ky., and Fayetteville, Tenn. In August, 1880, he purchased some medical books and began the study of medicine on his own responsibility. Two years later he entered Vanderbilt University, graduating as a physician and surgeon in February, 1883. After his father's death he and his brother, R. E., took control of the drug store which belonged to their father, but in July, 1884, the building caught fire and was consumed. They soon re-established, and keep a fine stock of drugs. These enterprising young men are building up a fine practice, and will rank among the leading physicians and surgeons of Tennessee. W. W. belongs to the K. & L. of H., and both brothers are members of the Methodist Episcopal Church South.

MRS. HARRIET CLARK was born in Washington County, Va., December, 1802. Her father, Zachariah Shugart, was born in Pennsylvania, and died in Virginia. The mother's maiden name was Elizabeth Offult; she was born in Montgomery County, Md., and died in 1819. In 1824 Harriet Shugart married William Clark, who was also a Virginian, born in 1792 and died in June, 1871. Of the six children born to them, four are living: Elizabeth B. (Mrs. William L. Thomas), James (deceased), William B., Rebecca M. (Mrs. Joseph Roe), Isabella J. (deceased) and C. S., a married son, with whom Mrs. Clark now lives on the old home-place. He is the youngest son, and has always looked after the interests of the farm. In 1872 he married Susan, daughter of Fenlie and Martha Smith. His wife was born in Lincoln County, in 1846, and she and her husband have three children: Martha, Willie and Lizzie. Our subject is said to be the oldest person residing in the district, but is yet quite hale and active. She belongs to the Presbyterian Church, and is a very estimable old lady.

HON. JOHN CLARK, farmer, was one of ten children born to James and Nancy Clark. The father was of Scotch origin, and a native of Blount County, E. Tenn. He was a farmer by occupation and lived to be over seventy-one years of age. The mother was born in the same county as her husband, and died at the age of forty-five. Our subject was also born in Blount County August 2, 1815, and got his education in the country schools. In 1838 he married Matilda Thompson, a native of Tennessee, born January, 1818. By this union he became the father of these children: James H., B. A., Nancy A., Martha J., J. P., Roena, Edward G., Will and Theodore. In 1859 Mrs. Clark died, and in the same year our subject married her sister, Priscilla Thompson. To the last union were born seven children: Margaret, Robert, Richard, Mollie, Charlie, Lina and Gertrude. In 1863 Mr. Clark was elected to represent two counties in the State Legislature, and in 1870, shortly after coming to Lincoln County, he was elected magistrate, and re-elected in 1874, but resigned before the term expired to accept the position of deputy sheriff. Mr. Clark owns 225 acres of desirable land, mostly well improved with good houses and out buildings. He is a Democrat in politics and a member of the Masonic fraternity.

W. B. CLARK, son of William and Harriet (Shugart) Clark, was born in Lincoln County, Tenn., in February, 1832. He received his education in the country schools, and, remained with his parents until he was twenty-two years of age. Febuary 22, 1872, he wedded Laura J. Mountcastle, a native of Mississippi, born in the year 1845, and to this union were born two children: William M. and Harriet E. Mr. Clark had 135 acres, which were given to him by his father, and upon this he located after marriage. In 1874 he sold out and went to Colorado, where he remained over five years, in that time, acquiring a homestead of 160 acres, besides purchasing the same number of acres. In 1880 he disposed of his property, returned to his birthplace, where he purchased 162 acres in the Twelfth District, and is at the present residing there. During the war he enlisted in the Confederate service, in Company G, First Regiment Tennessee Infantry, under Col. Turney; was in several skirmishes; but at the end of eighteen months was discharged on account of ill health. Mr. Clark is an enterprising, industrious farmer, and bears the reputation of being an honest man and a good citizen. He is a Democrat in politics, and he and Mrs. Clark are members of the Methodist Episcopal Church South. Mr. Clark's father was a Virginian, born in Washington County in 1792, and was an enterprising farmer, and, in connection with this occupation, worked at the blacksmith trade. About 1824 he came to Lincoln County, Tenn., and located in the Ninth District where he bought property and lived until his career ended in 1869. He was a soldier in the war of 1812, and for his services his widow draws a pension of $96 per year. He was twice married, his first wife being Barbara Tolbert. The mother of our subject was also born in Washington County, Va. She is still living, and since the death of her husband has made her home with her son, C. S. Clark.

LEWIS AND DR. J. C. COATS were born in Lincoln County, Tenn., in 1830 and 1853, respectively, sons of Thomas and Sarah Coates. The father was born in North Carolina about 1802, and came to Tennessee with his widowed mother when a boy. He was a farmer, and died November 2, 1874. The mother was born in South Carolina about the same time as her husband. Her death occurred June 9, 1870. Lewis Coats was married in 1851 to Mary Smith, who was born in Giles County, in 1830. Four children were born to them: J. C., Drucilla A. (Mrs. J. S. Parker), Mary L. (Mrs. J. P. Bruce), and Orlena T. Mr. Coats at one time owned 500 acres of land, but gave to his children until he now owns 260 acres. He was married when about twenty-one years of age, and as a Democrat cast his first presidential vote for Pierce. Dr. J. C. Coats was educated in the schools near his home, and when about twenty years of age entered the office of Dr. H. M. Beaty, in Blanche, and began the study of medicine, continuing two years. He then entered Washington University, at Baltimore, Md., and afterward took a course at Vanderbilt University, from which he graduated in 1878. He has since practiced in Blanche, and has treated all the diseases peculiar to that locality with commendable success. In 1880 he began keeping a general merchandise store, and has succeeded well from a financial stand-point. November 15, 1879, he wedded Alice E. Byers, born in 1862. They have three children: Mabel, Louis M. and an infant. The Doctor is a Democrat, and he and wife are members of the Methodist Episcopal Church South.

REV. A. B. COLEMAN, citizen of Lincoln County, and a native of the Keystone State, was born in November, 1830, in Indiana County. He is a son of James and Mary (Campbell) Coleman, both natives of Pennsylvania, and both of Scotch-Irish extraction. The father was born in Indiana County about 1795, and followed the occupation of farmer. He died in 1857. The mother was born in 1801, in Westmoreland County, and after the death of her husband, lived with her children. She died in 1884, in her eighty-second year. She was the mother of nine children five of whom are now living: John, Mary Jane (wife of Alexander Lyons), Margaret, Thomas W., and our subject, who remained with his parents till he was thirty years of age. His academic education was received at Elder's Ridge Academy, Pennsylvania, under the auspices of the Presbyterian Church, and at the age of eighteen he entered the teacher's profession, which occupation he continued for upward of ten years, but not without interruption, however, as he attended school some of the time. In 1857 he entered the Westminister College, Wilmington, Del., and commenced the study of the ministry proper. He graduated in June, 1859, and in 1861 he was licensed to preach. The following year he was ordained as minister, and sent to Minnesota to do missionary work, where he remained five years engaged in his religious duties. In 1867 he was sent South to organize and lay a foundation for their church work. He came to Lincoln County, Tenn., where he has since remained engaged in the good work. The same year of his arrival he dedicated the first United Presbyterian Church in the State of Tennessee. January 31, 1868, he married Hannah B. Taylor, a native of Lincoln County, born in 1840, and the daughter of Henry and Catherine M. Taylor. As a citizen Mr. Coleman is highly respected and bears the reputation of being a man of high character and one who leads a conscientious, straight-forward course through life, During the war he affiliated with the Union cause and was a strong supporter of the same. Mr. Coleman had the misfortune to lose his wife December 10, 1883.

WILLIAM COPELAND, distiller, and farmer of the Third District, and a native of Lincoln County, was born in 1829, and is one of ten children born to the union of John and Sarah (Massey) Copeland. The father was born in South Carolina in 1793, and was of Scotch-Irish descent. He was a minister of the P. B. Church; was also a soldier in the war of 1812, and was married in the same year. The latter part of his life was spent in farming in connection with his ministerial duties in Moore County, where he had a farm of 250 acres. He died in the year 1865. The mother was born in South Carolina in 1789, and died in 1857. Our subject received a good education, and when about seventeen began teaching, and taught several terms. At the age of twenty he took a trip to Arkansas, but returned home at the end of twelve months, and was elected constable. In 1852 he entered the mercantile establishment at Marble Hill in Franklin County, and clerked there for three years. November, 1854, he married Mary Ann George,-and by this union became the father of eleven children, eight of whom are living: Jefferson M., William C., Mollie H. (wife of John M. Franklin), Thomas N., Emily E. (wife of H. Snow), George M., Robert L. and Ida May. In 1857 Mr. Copeland sold his property, and entered the mercantile business at Smithland, where he remained three years. He then sold out and bought a farm of 300 acres, in the Fourth District, and for two years was revenue tax collector of Lincoln County. In 1867 he engaged in the distillery business, and this he still continues. In 1881 he purchased a distillery at Flintville, since which time he has been engaged in the business at that place. His machinery has a capacity of over three barrels per day. In 1885 he moved his family to the farm where they now reside. In politics he is a Democrat. He is also a member of the Masonic fraternity. Mrs. Copeland is a member of the Baptist Church.

JUDGE H. C. COWAN, farmer, was born in Franklin County, Tenn., November 15, 1809, son of Capt. James B. Cowan, who was of Irish descent, born in 1777, in Maryland. In 1797 he married Nancy Williams, who was born in Virginia in 1782. Their family consisted of six children. They came to Tennessee in 1806, locating in Franklin County, and there the father died in 1831. He was a captain in the war of 1812, and while living in East Tennessee two of his sisters were killed, while making maple sugar, by a band of Indians who came upon them suddenly. Retribution soon overtook them however, for a company of men was raised and seventeen Indians sent to the "happy hunting grounds" by the outraged settlers. The mother of our subject died in 1818. H. C. Cowan clerked for about five years in several places, and taught his first school in 1826, then went to Jackson County, Ala., and taught two short sessions. He then sold goods one year in Sparta, White Co., Tenn., when owing to some little disagreement he returned home and taught two five months' sessions, when he received apologies from his former employers and returned to them and sold goods a little over a year. He was then called home by the death of his father, and farmed and taught school, and in January, 1839, he became a resident of Lincoln County, and taught about fifteen sessions of school in and around Fayetteville, and in 1841 purchased 156 acres of land, where he settled and has since resided. At different times he has purchased 137, 45 and 75 acres. Two of his sons live on the latter farms. Mr. Cowan served as magistrate for forty-four years, and for fifteen years acted as chairman and one of the quorum of the county court, thus illustrating the respect in which he was held by the people. In 1869 he was elected judge of the county court, for eight years, but only served three years, owing to ill health. December 22, 1842, he married Agnes B. McDaniel, who was born March 29, 1814, and six children blessed their union, of which three are dead. Those living are, Andrew J., William Thomas and Louisa E. Judge Cowan began life poor in purse, but now owns 413 acres of fine land. He has a remarkably retentive memory, and is a man, who, by his exemplary life, commands the respect and esteem of all. He is a Democrat and a member of the Cumberland Presbyterian Church. His wife died November 24, 1881, and since that time his daughter has been his housekeeper.

W. S. CURTIS, a farmer, and a native of Madison County, Ala., was born November 14, 1823, son of Johnson D. and Isabella Curtis, natives of Georgia and North Carolina, respectively. The father was a farmer by occupation, and died in 1826. The mother was of Irish descent and died in 1824. Our subject was reared by his aunt, Mrs. McMurray, and received his education in the Giles County schools. In 1844 he married Margaret Bussell, a daughter of Robert and Nancy Bussell. Mrs. Curtis was born in 1822, and died August 19, 1858. By this union our subject became the father of five children: Robert J., a farmer of Giles County; T. D., a resident of Pulaski; W. A., a farmer of Giles County; James M., now in Lawrence County, Mo., and J. D., of Lincoln County, Tenn. After marriage, Mr. Curtis bought 150 acres of land in Giles County, where he located and remained six years. He then disposed of that property and bought 224 acres in the Sixteenth District of Lincoln County, where he is now living. He now owns 300 acres of very desirable land. October 23, 1859, he married A. Oliver, a native of Lincoln County, born January 13, 1834, and a daughter of E. P. and Sarah Oliver. This marriage of our subject resulted in the birth of eight children: Julia, wife of W. T. Woodward; C. L., E. S., C. M., F. J., A. L., J. H. and Alexander. Mr. Curtis has always been a hard working, industrious man, and has been quite successful in business, and has given his children the advantage of acquiring a good English education. He is a Democrat in politics and cast his first presidential vote for Taylor. He and wife are members of the New School Presbyterian Church.

JOHN M. DICKEY, farmer, was born in Franklin County in 1840, and received his education at New Market, Ala. When hostilities broke out between the North and South he enlisted in Company A, Forty-fourth Tennessee Infantry, Confederate States Army, and was in the principal battles of the war. He was captured and taken to Rock Island, Ill., where he was held till May 6, 1865, President Lincoln signing the petition for his release the day he was assassinated. Mr. Dickey then returned home and engaged in blacksmithing. November 18, 1861, he wedded Louisa McGehee, and became the father of five children: William M., Julia M., Lucy V., Edward W. and Fannie L. In 1870 Mr. Dickey purchased 300 acres of land, on which he is now residing. May 7, 1876, Mrs. Dickey died, and June 18, 1878, Mr. Dickey married Mrs. Laura V. Kyle, daughter of J. J. and Elizabeth Tucker, by whom he became the father of three children: Frederick C., John M. and Hughes D. In 1873 Mr. Dickey was elected magistrate to fill the unexpired term of Henderson Thompson, and has since filled the office in a satisfactory manner. He is a Democrat in politics and a Mason. Mrs. Dickey is among the most respected members of the Methodist Episcopal Church South. Our subject's parents were Ephraim M. and Louisa (Rich) Dickey. The father was born in Franklin County, in 1812, and was of Irish lineage. His education was considerably above the average, notwithstanding his meager advantages, and he was a blacksmith by occupation. He died in 1859. The mother of our subject died May 4, 1873.

HON. ISHAM P. DISMUKES (deceased), one of the leading members of the Fayetteville bar, was born in Lincoln County, Tenn., April 19, 1832, son of Marcus L. and Delia (Wadkins) Dismukes. He received a thorough literary education in the Fayetteville Academy, his preceptor being Prof. F. A. Dickinson. He began teaching school, and during his leisure moments was an earnest student of Blackstone. In 1855 he entered the law department of the Cumberland University at Lebanon, Tenn., and graduated in 1856. He returned to Lincoln County, and formed a law partnership with Hon. Edmund Cooper, of Shelbyville, and in 1860 Hon. J. G. Woods entered as partner, and after a short time Mr. Cooper withdrew, and W. B. Martin took his place. In 1861 Mr. Dismukes enlisted in Freeman's battery, and fought at Parker's Cross Roads, Chickamauga and Knoxville. He served until the close of the war, and was a brave and gallant soldier. December 17, 1867, he married Jennie Fulton, daughter of Hon. James and Mary (Morgan) Fulton. Mr. Dismukes' career from the very first was brilliant and successful. He was an able and wise counselor, and was unsurpassed in readiness of speech and brilliancy of thought. He had a large and paying clientage at the time of his death. He died of consumption, September 14, 1875, after living a life of great usefulness, and it may justly be said of him that his character was beyond reproach, and that he was an honorable and noble gentleman. He was candid in speech, honest in his motives, sincere in his manifestations of friendship, and incapable of a mean action. At his death the members of the Lincoln County bar passed a series of resolutions on his life and character. An eloquent tribute to his memory was delivered by his first law partner, Hon. Edmund Cooper. Since his death his widow has resided in Fayetteville, where she has a beautiful home.

ROBERT S. & DAVID G. DOUTHAT, boot and shoe manufacturers, of Fayetteville, Tenn., are the sons of John H. and Margaret (Burke) Douthat. The father is of

Scotch-Irish origin, and was born in 1816, in Fincastle, Va., and when a youth began learning the blacksmith's trade, which he mastered, and at which he worked for over fifteen years. He then began manufacturing wagons and plows, but for the past twenty-five years has been engaged in manufacturing boots and shoes. The mother is of German descent, and was born in Virginia in 1818. Eleven children blessed their union, ten of whom are living. Robert was born in 1844, and at the age of nine years began learning the shoe-maker's trade. In 1867 he left the paternal roof, and came to Fayetteville, where he continued working at his trade. October 27, 1867, he wedded Mary Ann Noblett, who was born in Tennessee, in 1844. In 1872 Robert and his brother, William B., established a boot and shoe shop in Fayetteville, continuing until 1884, when David G. was taken into partnership. In 1873 William was elected postmaster of the city, and his brothers, Robert and David, became sole proprietors. They are good workmen, and have been fairly successful in their business. They are stanch Republicans in politics, Robert casting his first presidential vote for U. S. Grant and David for R. B. Hayes. David was born in Virginia, in 1853, and, like his brother, learned the shoe-maker's trade, and left home when quite young, coming to Fayetteville. In August, 1875, he married Susan D. Bell, daughter of James H. Bell. Mrs. Douthat was born in 1855, and has borne four children: Robert H., John F., Margaret and David G.

CAPT. WILLIAM B. DOUTHAT, postmaster of Fayetteville, and a native of Christiansburg, Montgomery Co., Va., was born March 1, 1840, son of John H. and Margaret (Burke) Douthat. He received his education in Snowville, Pulaski Co., Va., and at the age of twelve was bound out for seven years to T. S. Bullard, of Snowville, to serve an apprenticeship at the shoe-maker's trade. He worked four years, abandoned his master, and commenced in life on his own responsibility. He went to Salem and worked for his brother, James H., ten months, after which he returned to his former home and set up a shop. During the late Rebellion he was a firm supporter of the Union. In 1863 he was about to be drawn into the Confederate side, when he, with upward of fifty others, started to join the Union forces, walking to Somerset, Ky., a distance of 150 miles, where they took the train for Nashville. He enlisted in Company C, Twelfth Tennessee Cavalry, U. S. A., and took an active part in the battles of Trune, Clifton, Lynchburg, Pulaski, Tenn., Florence, Sulphur Trestle and Richland Creek Bridge, Ala. In the action at Pulaski he was wounded twice, being shot in the right arm and hip. He was taken to the hospital at Nashville, where he remained two months. December, 1864, he rejoined his regiment and remained until October 7, 1865, when he was mustered out at Fort Leavenworth, Kas., and discharged at Nashville. He was appointed second lieutenant of Company A, Twelfth Regiment Cavalry, Tennessee Volunteers, United States Army. May 11, 1864, he was promoted to first lieutenant of the same company and regiment. April 16, 1865, he was assigned assistant adjutant-general on the staff of Brig.-Gen. G. Spaulding. He was assigned to duty as regimental commissary in June, 1865, and served until mustered out of service. He received a complimentary commission as captain October 20, 1865, for gallant and meritorious service. In 1866 Mr. Douthat went to Denver, Col., and remained there three years. In the spring of 1870 he came to Fayetteville, and the following year he and his brother, Robert S., formed a partnership in the manufacture of boots and shoes. In 1873 he accepted the position of postmaster at Fayetteville, and in 1885 disposed of his interest in the shoe shop, since which time he has given his attention to the office. In 1875 he married Emma Burgess, a native of Lebanon, Tenn., born July 7, 1848, and the daughter of Charles T. and Mary E. Burgess. This union resulted in the birth of one child—Carl B. Mr. Douthat has proved to be a most worthy and efficient postmaster. He has given universal satisfaction, and not one word of complaint has been offered for his removal under the new administration. He is a Republican in politics, and his wife is a member of the Christian Church.

J. H. C. DUFF was born in Lincoln County January 26, 1838, and remained with his parents until he reached his majority. He received a fair education in the common schools and afterward attended some time at Union Academy, Lincoln County, where he took a thorough course in surveying. At the breaking out of the war he enlisted in Company G, Eighth Tennessee Mulberry Riflemen, under Capt. William L. Moore, but was afterward transferred to Carne's Battery. He was in the battles of Perryville, Ky., and Chickamauga, and was captured at the latter place and sent to Camp Morton, Ind., where, February, 1864, he scaled the prison walls, under the cover of darkness, and without being seen, succeeded in making his escape. He was afterward captured again in Giles County, and made his escape once more. In 1866 he went to Bethel, Lincoln County, and married Jane C. Craig, but immediately returned to his father's, where he remained six years. This union resulted in the birth of nine children, eight of whom are living: Bessie C., Margaret E., Myrtle, Ruby, Henry N., Alfred F., Thomas D. and James B. F. In 1876 he was elected surveyor of Lincoln County for a term of two years. In 1885 he moved to the farm where he now resides. He in Independent in politics, is a Mason and an Odd Fellow, and he and wife are members of the Cumberland Presbyterian Church. His father, H. C. Duff, was born in South Carolina, August 28, 1808, and in 1845 immigrated to Lincoln County, where he purchased seventy-six acres in the Fifth District, and where he located and still resides. He has since increased his estate to 590 acres, but has given his son 200 acres. In 1837 he married Eliza D. Brown, who became the mother of our subject.

R. M. DUNLAP is a Tennesseean, born April 22, 1837. James E. Dunlap, his father, was of English-Irish origin, born in South Carolina, and came to Tennessee when a young man and married our subject's mother, Sarah E. James E. was a farmer by occupation, and died in 1859. The mother died in 1842. Our subject is one of their eight children. His education was obtained in the district schools and his boyhood days were spent on a farm. In 1859 he wedded Sarah E. Cole, who was born in Lincoln County in 1840, and departed this life in 1861. Two children were born to them: Sarah (Mrs. James Rhodes) and R. J., both living in Texas. In March, 1861, Mr. Dunlap enlisted in Company D, Forty-first Tennessee Infantry, and participated in the battles of Shiloh, Port Hudson, and numerous others. He was taken with the small-pox, and returned home in February, 1863. He has since been engaged in farming, and owns 230 acres of valuable land. In December, 1863, he married Sarah E., daughter of J. H. and Sarah Midley, of Fulton, Miss., born in 1835. They have nine children: Mary E. (deceased), Nancy E., James M., P. M., J. M., Patrick M., D. C., Shelton and Emma. Mr. Dunlap is quite skillful at almost any kind of work, and does his own blacksmithing and wagon work, and has been fairly successful in his agricultural pursuits. He is a Democrat.

JAMES M. DYER'S birth occurred in Lincoln County, Tenn., February 2, 1813. His early education was limited, but he has done much to eradicate this evil by reading, and is well posted on all the topics of the day. In 1834 he married Martha Newton, who was born in Shelbyville in 1813, and departed this life in 1874. Of their nine children three are living: Joseph H., Canthes V. and M. F. Our subject resided with his mother until about twenty years of age, and then sold dry goods throughout the western and middle portion of Tennessee for about three years. In 1849 he purchased 182 acres of land, and is now the owner of 282 acres of valuable land. In 1875 Mr. Dyer married Tennessee Larue. She was born in Marshall County in 1834. Notwithstanding many difficulties Mr. Dyer has encountered through life, he has now a good home and a comfortable competency. He is a Republican and was strongly opposed to secession. He held the position of magistrate twelve years, and he and wife are members of the Cumberland Presbyterian Church. He is a distant relative of the late Thomas A. Hendricks. His parents were James and Martha (Garland, cousin of Attorney-Gen. Garland) Dyer, born in Tennessee in 1779 and 1781, and died in 1817 and 1854 respectively. They were married in 1799. The father was a farmer, and a soldier in the war of 1812. Both our subject's grandfathers were soldiers in the Revolutionary war.

J. S. EDMISTON was born in Washington County, Va., in 1815, and was one of a large family of children of G. W. C. and Elizabeth (Steward) Edmiston, natives of Virginia, born in 1785 and 1791, and died in 1847 and 1839, respectively. They were married in the "Old Dominion," and immigrated to Tennessee in 1817, where they led the lives of farmers. J. S. Edmiston was educated in the schools near his home, and when about twenty-three years old purchased 140 acres of land near Swan Creek, where he remained four years, and then disposed of his property and bought out the heirs to the old home place, where he located and has since resided. He owns 450 acres of good land, well improved. He is a Democrat, and during the late war was strenuously opposed to secession. Previous to that conflict he was a Whig. He is also a Mason. His grandfather, William Edmiston, was a Virginian, and was a captain in the Revolutionary war. Two of his brothers were killed at the battle of King's Mountain. December 13, 1852, our subject married Margaret E., daughter of Russell T. and Eliza (Forsythe) Harreld, of Kentucky. Mrs. Edmiston was born January 16, 1833, and has borne seven children: William C., John H., Clara, Mary E., Catherine T., Robert R. and Thomas S. Our subject and wife are members of the Old Presbyterian Church, of Petersburg, Tenn.

JAMES P. EDWARDS, farmer of the Fifth District, and a son of James A. and Susan (Goodwin) Edwards, was born in Rutherford County August 4, 1839. The father was born in Rutherford County December 1, 1801, and is of Dutch-Welsh descent. He had the advantages of a district school education, and possessing an intellect above the average mind received an education accordingly. He is of noted ancestry, his great-grandfather once being Duke of Wales, and his mother a near relative of the elder Adams, also closely connected with the Buchanans, the early settlers of Nashville. He was married in 1825, and became the father of six children, four of whom are living. The mother of our subject was born in 1805 and died in 1867. The father died about 1875. Our subject received his education in the common schools, and later spent several years in the school at Tullahoma. During the war he enlisted under Capt. Meade, in Alabama, but did not enter the service on account of sickness. He was confined at home for several months, and upon his recovery entered the army as an enrolling officer, and continued in that capacity till the army retreated from Tennessee. He then went back with Gen. Forrest to take care of a sick brother, with whom he remained until his death near the close of the war. He was captured at Tullahoma and charged with bushwhacking, but acquitted himself nobly, and was released at the end eleven days. He then returned to Lincoln County, and commenced farming in cotton. December 1, 1870, he wedded Bettie Warren, and by this union became the father of ten children, nine of whom are living: Emma, Henry W., James A. and William Owen (twins), Edgar A., Bessie Polk, George W., Sue May and Anna Lynne. In 1882 Mr. Edwards purchased 60 acres, where he now resides. He is a Democrat in politics, and a member of the Masonic fraternity. He and wife are members of the Cumberland Presbyterian Church. Mrs. Edwards is a graduate of the Mary Sharp College at Winchester, Tenn.

HON. W. W. ERWIN, farmer, and a native of Tennessee, was born April 26, 1846. His parents, Robert and Jane E. (Woods) Erwin, were natives of Tennessee. The father was born in 1810, and the mother about the same year. She died September, 1885. The father is still living and is a saddler by trade. Our subject received his education at Moorsville Academy. December 23, 1869, he married Addie, daughter of Dr. John and Josephine Wood, and a native of Lincoln County, born March 30, 1853. By this union they became the parents of five children: Robert, Willie B., Edwin S., Ross and Leroy W. Mr. Erwin remained with his parents for some time, and received a good education in the schools of the county. He then engaged in teaching, and has followed this occupation for ten years. He has taught in Marshall, Giles and Lincoln Counties, and was principal of the Boonshill Academy for some time. In 1871 he moved on his present farm which consists of 150 acres of productive land. In 1884 he was elected to represent the people of Lincoln and Moore Counties in the Legislature of the State. Mr. Erwin is a Democrat, and he and wife are members of the Cumberland Presbyterian Church.

JOSEPH FARRAR, an old and influential resident of Lincoln County, Tenn., was born in North Carolina, June 11, 1811, and was the son of John W., and Elizabeth (Williams) Farrar. The father of our subject was born in Virginia in 1750, and moved to North

Carolina, and remained there until 1810. He was captain of a company in the Revolutionary war, under Gen. Greene, and served through its entire time. He was a cabinet-maker by occupation, and was with Daniel Boone, the first settler of Kentucky. He died in 1830. The mother of our subject was born in North Carolina, and died in Lincoln County, Tenn. Our subject received his education in the common schools, and December 22, 1831, he wedded Elizabeth, daughter of Robert and Polly Abernathy. Mrs. Farrar was born in Lincoln County, in 1814, and by this marriage became the mother of twelve children, four of whom are living: Nancy A. (wife of William West), James T., Pinkney E. and Miles J. After marriage our subject purchased one-half of the homestead, where he located and remained until 1853. In 1855 he bought 115 acres of land in the Thirteenth District, where he has since lived. He has since bought more land, and at one time owned 800 acres, but has divided it among his sons, reserving for himself about forty acres. Mr. Farrar is well known and highly esteemed far and near. He is an excellent citizen and a kind and obliging neighbor. He is a Democrat, and cast his first vote for Andrew Jackson. He and wife are worthy and consistent members of the Methodist Episcopal Church.

P. E. FARRAR, farmer, is a son of Joseph and Elizabeth Farrar. The father was born in one of the Carolinas in 1811, and came to Lincoln County with his parents when but a lad. After marriage he located in the Thirteenth District, where he still lives, and is a farmer by occupation. The mother of our subject was born in Lincoln County in 1814, and was married about 1831. She and her husband have been living together longer than any other couple in the district. Our subject was born in Lincoln County in October, 1850, and is one of twelve children born to his parents. He received his education in the district schools, and remained with his parents until he was twenty-five years of age. In 1875 he married N. J. Dickey, a native of Lincoln County, born in 1855, and the daughter of Alfred and Eliza Dickey. The fruits of this union were an interesting family of five children: Lizzie, Myrtle, Nannie L., Annie B. and Edna. After marriage our subject bought a farm in the Twelfth District, but remained there only three years, when he disposed of that place and bought 200 acres in the Thirteenth District, where he now resides. Mr. Farrar had two brothers who served in the late unpleasantness between the North and South. One brother, John, was killed after a service of about four years. Mr. Farrar and wife are members of the church and are among the county's best citizens.

WILLIAM B. FAULKNER, one of the principal citizens of the Twenty-fifth District, and a son of William and Ellen (Bolton) Faulkner, was born in Lincoln County in 1834, and is one of a family of seven children, four of whom are living. The father was born in Ireland in 1797, the grandfather in England and the grandmother in Scotland. The father of our subject received a fair education in the common schools, and was married twice, his first wife being Miss Patterson, by whom he had two children, one of whom died during the voyage to America. His wife died shortly after his arrival in this country, and in 1832 he wedded the mother of our subject. He was a farmer, a ditcher and blaster by occupation. His death occurred in 1870. The mother of our subject was also born in Ireland, in 1798, and died in 1843. Our subject received a fair education, and as his parents were poor he was compelled to work for a livelihood. He was employed for several years in a factory and afterward was engaged in trading and teaming in some of the Southern cities. During the war he enlisted in Company H, First Tennessee Regiment, and soon entered the Army of the Potomac, where he was quite a favorite of Stonewall Jackson's. At the end of a year he was discharged on account of ill health, but soon returned and engaged in some of the principal battles of the war. He was captured and held a prisoner until 1865. In January, 1866 he wedded Mrs. Charlotte Taylor, daughter of J. and M. Simmons. To Mr. and Mrs. Faulkner were born five children: Amanda E., Nancy J., Eliza B., Ellen F. and William A. Our subject located on ninety-four acres of land in the Twenty-fifth District, where he remained three years. He then purchased the same amount of acres in the same district, on which he located and still resides. Mrs. Faulkner died November 24, 1877, and in January, 1879, he married Mrs. Harriet A. Smith, daughter of David and Martha Sisk, by whom he had three children, two of whom are living: Mattie B. and Mary Pearl. Mr. Faulkner is a Democrat, a Mason and an Odd Fellow, and he and wife are members of the Methodist Episcopal Church South.

JOSEPH M. GREER is a son of Joseph and Mary (Harmon) Greer, and is one of eleven children and of Irish descent. The father was born in the "Keystone State " in 1754, and was an early pioneer of Tennessee, coming in 1790 and entering about 10,000 acres of land. They suffered all the hardships incident to pioneer life, but, unlike many of the early settlers, had the good will of the Indians. Mr. Greer was a farmer and merchant at Knoxville, Tenn., and was clerk of the first chancery court after the organization of the county. He died in 1835. Our subject was reared in Tennessee when there was no schools, consequently his education was acquired at home mainly through his own exertions. In 1847 he married Mary Edmiston, who departed this life September 19, 1858. They had one son—Joseph M.—who resides on the old home-place and looks after his father's farm. He was born September 13, 1858, and was educated at Petersburg and Fayetteville, and is now the owner of 535 acres of fine land, and is noted for his generosity and honesty. He votes with the Democratic party, and belongs to the Masonic fraternity.

PLEASANT HALBERT'S birth occurred in Williamson County, Tenn., in 1811. His parents, James and Elizabeth (Smith) Halbert, were born in North and South Carolina in 1771 and 1788, and died in 1833 and 1813, respectively. The father was a farmer, and in 1795 immigrated to Tennessee, but remained only four years, when he returned to his native State. September 9, 1801, he returned to Tennessee. He was married in 1810, and in 1813 came to Lincoln County, where he spent the remainder of his days. He was father of two children, only one now living—Pleasant Halbert—who made his home with his father as long as he lived. He was educated in the district schools, and October 8, 1833, married Nancy Crawford, who was born in 1810, and a daughter of John Crawford, who was an early pioneer of Lincoln County. Our subject and his wife became the parents of eight children, seven of whom are living: Martha (wife of Dr. J. E. Youell), Margaret E. (Mrs. Lemuel D. Sugg), James C., Mary J. (Mrs. Capt. J. H. George), Pleasant W. (a physician and surgeon), Naomi E. (Mrs. S. M. Clayton) and William H. (a physician and surgeon of Lebanon). Mrs. Halbert died August 5, 1850, and April 8, 1852, he wedded, Emily Buchanan, who was born July 23, 1814, and a daughter of John Buchanan. Of their three children two are living: Laura G. (Mrs. Pleasant Hobbs) and Isaac B. This wife died February 9, 1868, and July 1 of the same year Mr. Halbert married Martha V. Smith, daughter of David Smith. She was born in Alabama in 1826. Mr. Halbert owns 600 acres of land in the Eighth District, and is one of the old and highly respected citizens of the county. He has been a life-long Democrat, and has served as magistrate six years. He and Mrs. Halbert are members of the Cumberland Presbyterian Church.

JOHN HAMILTON, a native of Moore County, was born April 19, 1825, and is a son of William and Rachel Hamilton, natives, respectively, of South Carolina and East Tennessee. The father, when a young man, went to Tennessee, where he was married, and soon came to this part of the State. He was a farmer by occupation, and owned about 300 acres in what is now Moore County. He died in 1873. The subject of this sketch was reared on the farm, and secured a fair education in the district schools near Lynchburg. In 1847 he married Ann, daughter of Preston and Nellie Midkiff. Mrs. Hamilton was born in Moore County, in June, 1826, and by her marriage became the mother of four children: John, Nancy, James and Susan. Mr. Hamilton, after moving around for some time, bought 100 acres of land, where he located, and where he has since resided. He now owns 738 acres of valuable land. He has always been a hard-working, industrious man, and has been quite successful in his occupation. In 1857 he bought a mill, and has done considerable business, both in grinding grain and sawing lumber. He is a Democrat in politics, and Mrs. Hamilton is a member of the Lutheran Church.

WILLIAM HAMILTON, farmer, was born near his present residence in 1836, and is the son of David M. and Elizabeth (Morton) Hamilton. The father was a native of South Carolina, born in 1809, and was of Scotch-Irish lineage. He came to Tennessee in 1811 with his father, John Hamilton, who settled in the Twelfth District, bought property, and remained until his career ended, about 1813. While chopping a tree it suddenly split and flew back, striking Mr. Hamilton and killing him instantly. His wife returned to South Carolina in a short time to look after his unsettled business, going and returning on horseback through unbroken forests, bivouacking out of nights along the route. David M., our subject's father, lived in Lincoln County at the time of his marriage, which occurred in 1831. He lived in different parts of Lincoln County, but the last five years of his life were passed in the Fourteenth District. He owned 160 acres of land, and may properly be classed as one of the early settlers. He died in 1845, in the prime of life. The mother of our subject was born in Lincoln County, Tenn., in 1813, and was of Irish extraction. Her father, Alexander Morton, was a native of Ireland. He came to Lincoln County at a very early date, and was one of the first white men in the county. Since the death of her husband Mrs. Hamilton has lived with her children, and for the past eighteen years has lived with her son William. There were five children, four of whom are living. William was reared at home, and received a practical education in the public schools. October 22, 1857, he married Elizabeth E. Wyatt, daughter of Thomas Wyatt. Mrs. Hamilton was born in Lincoln County in 1835, and the result of her marriage was the birth of two children: David Knox and Mollie (wife of John Montgomery). After marriage Mr. Hamilton resided on the old home-place until 1868. In 1870 he had the misfortune to lose his wife, and January 8, 1878, he wedded Mrs. Anna (Telford) Massey, daughter of William Telford. The second Mrs. Hamilton was born in 1857, in Marion County, Ill., and this marriage resulted in the birth of one child, Cora Agnes. In 1872 Mr. Hamilton purchased 100 acres of land in the Twelfth District, where he has since resided. He is one of the farmers of Lincoln County who is possessed with modern ideas of cultivating the soil. He is a Republican in politics, and he and wife are members of the United Presbyterian Church.

THOMAS HAMPTON is one of a large family of children born to the marriage of Preston and Sarah Hampton, who were born in North Carolina and Tennessee in 1777 and 1788, and died in 1859 and 1830, respectively. They were farmers. Thomas was born in Lincoln County, October 29, 1815. He resided at home until twenty-six years of age, and three years later was united in marriage to Martha J. Smith, who was born in 1826 and died in July, 1883. Seven children were born to them, four of whom are living: William, E. T., Mary A. (Mrs. W. F. Hamilton), and Sarah (Mrs. Robert Cleghorn). Mr. Hampton traveled in the West two years before his marriage and for two years after his marriage, farmed his father-in-law's farm, then purchased 175 acres which he afterward increased very much, but gave to his children until he now owns 121 acres. In 1885 Mr. Hampton married his second wife, Mrs. Elizabeth (Yant) Pampen. She was born in Lincoln County, September 25, 1835. Our subject suffered heavy losses by the late war, but in the main has been more than ordinarily successful. He and wife belong to the Baptist Church.

DAVID L. HARRIS, son of John and Susan (Lee) Harris, was born in Lincoln County, Tenn., in 1830, and is one of two children, our subject only living. The father was Scotch-Irish by birth, born in Virginia about 1804. He came to Tennessee at an early day, where he married and afterward resided a few years, but ended his days in Kentucky, in 1843. He was twice married, his second wife being Jane Abernathy, by whom he had three children. After his parents' death our subject resided with his uncle, Joel M. Harris, with whom he remained until twenty-one years old. He learned the tanner's trade of his uncle, and afterward became one of the firm and remained such until the business was abandoned about 1879. He owns a farm of 800 acres, upon which he located in 1860. In 1857 he married Julia Conaway, by whom he had seven children: William N., Alice B., Sarah L., Joel L., John M., David D., and Samuel S. Mrs. Harris died March 24, 1870, and the August following Mr. Harris married Sarah Bray, and Thomas, Susan T., Fannie, Maud and Ira are the children born to this union. Iron and coal have recently been discovered in almost inexhaustible quantities on Mr. Harris' farm, and when developed may prove of great value to the county. Our subject is a wealthy land owner, and was formerly a Whig, but since the war has affiliated with the Republican party. He belongs to the F. & A. M. and I. O. O. F.

O. R. HATCHER, M. D., was born on the 30th of August, 1846, one of five children of Octavus and Caledonia (Pillow) Hatcher, who were born in Virginia and Tennessee, in 1818 and 1826, respectively. The father was brought to Tennessee when about eight years of age, became a merchant, and died in 1856. Our subject, O. R., was educated at College Grove, under Profs. Wynn and Carey, and then entered the medical department of the Nashville University and attended six months, and then went to New York, to Bellevue Medical College, where he graduated as an M. D. in 1872. In February, 1873 he and Mary Woodard were married. She was born in 1849 and has borne three children: John U., Nellie I., and William L. Dr. Hatcher practiced medicine in Fayetteville about five months, and then moved to Hazelgreen, Ala., but two years later returned to Lincoln County, where he has since resided and practiced his profession with much success. He and his brother, A. H., have a farm of 282 acres under the latter's supervision. The Doctor is a Democrat and a Mason, and he and Mrs. Hatcher are members of the Methodist Episcopal Church South.

SAMUEL HAYNIE, farmer, was born in Bedford County, in 1833, and remained at home until he was twenty-five years of age. He received a fair education in the neighboring schools, and December 20, 1856, led to the altar Anna Moore, a native of Lincoln County, Tenn., born June, 1832, and the daughter of Andrew and Rachel Moore. The union of our subject and wife resulted in the birth of ten children, seven of whom are living: Samuel J., Robert H., Mary J., Hugh L., Thomas J. J., Anna L. and Emma L. Mr. Haynie resides on the old home-place, which now consists of 302 acres under a good state of cultivation. In 1863 he enlisted in Company D, Eighth Tennessee, and took an active part in the battle of Murfreesboro. He was in the retreat toward the south, and soon after returned home and resumed farming. Mr. Haynie taught school several terms before marriage and also several after marriage. He is a life-long Democrat in politics. Our subject's parents, James and Elizabeth (Bailey) Haynie, were married about 1830. The father was born May 18, 1810, and was of Scotch-Irish descent. He was a farmer by occupation, but, being a natural genius, could manufacture or repair nearly all kinds of machinery. He died in 1878. The mother of our subject was born in North Carolina and died in 1882.

HENRY HENDERSON, trustee of Lincoln County, was born in the Twenty-first District of that county in 1825, and is the son of David and Elizabeth (Lee) Henderson. The father was a Virginian and was of Scotch extraction. In 1806 he came to Lincoln County, and was among the pioneer settlers of the same. He was in the war of 1812, was wounded in the right arm, which rendered him a cripple for life. About 1814 he was married, and afterward located in the Twenty-first District, where he died in 1857. He was a tiller of the soil and at the time of his death owned upward of 1,100 acres of land. The mother of our subject was born in North Carolina in 1800 and died November, 1871. They had ten children, only four of whom are living: James, Sandy, Henry and Daniel W. Our subject was reared at home and received his education in the public schools. In 1855 he was elected surveyor of Lincoln County, and served in that capacity until 1876, with the exception of a short interval during the Rebellion. In 1858 he married Mrs. Sarah (Blake) Crawford, daughter of William Crawford. Mrs. Henderson was born in Lincoln County, Tenn., in 1827, and by a previous marriage became the mother of four children: Delia F. (wife of Pleasant Snoddy), James E., W. B. and Annie (wife of G. D. Wicks). By her last union was born one child, Victoria May (wife of Thomas Phillips). In 1861 Mr. Henderson bought 285 acres in the Nineteenth District, where he has since resided. In 1876 he was elected county trustee, and at the expiration of his term was re-elected, and so has continued for five successive terms. He is a Democrat in politics and a member of the Masonic fraternity, being a Royal Arch Mason. He is a member of the Methodist Episcopal Church South, and his wife is a member of the Cumberland

Presbyterian Church. He was major of the Second Battalion, Seventy-second Regiment of the Fourth Division of Tennessee Militia for three or four years, being commissioned by the governor of Tennessee, and was first lieutenant of a company in said battalion for a number of years.

AUSTIN HEWITT, of Boonshill, Tenn., was born in 1840 near Norwich, Conn., son of Elkanah and Lucy Hewitt, born in Virginia and Connecticut, respectively. The father was born in 1808, and was a brick-mason by trade. He was a resident of Connecticut many years, and there died. The mother's death occurred in 1849. Austin remained with his parents until about sixteen years of age, and then went to Macon, Ga., and was overseer of a brick manufactory. After a short residence in South Carolina he went to Arkansas and while there enlisted in Company D, First Arkansas Infantry, and took an active part in the battles of Manasses, Shiloh, Perryville, Murfreesboro, Chickamauga, Missionary Ridge and was with Thomas at the time of the surrender. He served three years and rendered his country valuable service. July 3, 1864, he married Martha E. Reed, born in Lincoln County in 1844, and began farming. In 1871 he purchased 172 acres of land, which he has increased to 540 acres. He takes much interest in stock-raising, and besides his home farm has valuable property in Pulaski, Giles County. He is conservative in politics and cast his first presidential vote for S. J. Tilden. Mr. Hewitt wishes to retire from active business life and to dispose of his farm, which is well adapted to grazing stock and raising all kinds of grain.

H. C. HIGGINS is a son of Owen W. Higgins, who was of Scotch descent, born in Kentucky in 1802. He came to Lincoln County, Tenn., in 1806 with his father, and eventually became the owner of 200 acres of land, about five miles from Fayetteville. He was married about 1824 to Fannie H. Stone, and by her was the father of eleven children, eight of whom are living: Nancy (widow of Daniel Tucker), Sallie (Mrs. Daniel B. Shull), Mary (Mrs. Isaac Holman), George W., a lawyer in Fayetteville; Martha D. (Mrs. James Cato), Fannie E. (Mrs. J. E. Carrigan), Virginia (widow of Prof. Peter Hunbaugh) and our subject, H. C. Their father died in 1865, and their mother, who was born in 1806, in Virginia, died in 1871. The subject of our sketch was born near his present place of residence in 1846, and was educated in the neighboring schools and at Fayetteville, and made his home with his mother as long as he remained unmarried. December 22, 1868, he wedded Fannie Stone, daughter of L. L. Stone. Mrs. Higgins was born in Lincoln County, and has two children: Berry Owen and Julia. Mr. Higgins and wife own 488 acres of land, and have a beautiful and comfortable home. Mr. Higgins is a man of good business qualities, and in politics is very conservative, casting his first presidential vote for Seymour and Blair. He is a member of the I. O. O. F., and he and wife are members of the Cumberland Presbyterian Church.

J. B. HILL, jeweler of Fayetteville, Tenn., was born in Lincoln County, Tenn., in 1832, son of Ebenezer and Mary T. (Bryan) Hill. The father was born in Mason, N. H., October 14, 1791, and died at the residence [of his son, in Manchester, May 16, 1875. At the age of fourteen he went to Amherst and worked in a printing office. He then went to Troy, N. Y., and while there enlisted in the war of 1812, and served until the close. He went to Huntsville, Ala., in 1819, and the following year came to Fayetteville, where he has continued to reside with the exception of two years. In March, 1823, he began the publication of a weekly paper called the *Village Messenger*, which he continued to issue until July 18, 1828. In 1825, with his brother J. B. Hill, he issued the first number of *Hill's Almanac*, which grew into popularity until 1862, when the war prevented its continuance. It was considered an almost indispensable article in every household and office. In 1833 and 1834 he published the *Independent Yeoman*, a hebdomadal journal, edited by himself. He published several works, and established and conducted a circulating library. He possessed more than ordinary mental ability, and was a terse and fluent writer, and his editorials were noted for their shrewd common sense and logic. He was married in 1824, and about four years previous to his own death his wife died. Our immediate subject, J. B. Hill, was educated in the schools of Fayetteville. He began learning the jeweler's trade at the age of twenty-two, and finally wedded Maggie Bearden, who has borne him five children: Charles B., Mary, Eben, Maggie B. and Emily H. Maggie is but six years of age, but is a fine performer on the violin, playing by ear almost any tune she ever heard with almost perfect time and expression. Mr. Hill served in the late war in Company C, Forty-first Regiment, Tennessee Infantry, and was afterward appointed quartermaster-sergeant. Mr. Hill and wife are members of the Cumberland Presbyterian Church, and he is the leading jeweler of Fayetteville and a much respected citizen.

DAVID F. HOBBS, a prominent citizen and farmer, is one of eleven children born to Nathaniel and Sarah Hobbs. The father was of English descent, and was born in North Carolina in 1789. He was married in 1812, and came to Lincoln County in 1832, locating in the Sixteenth District. He was a cabinet-maker by occupation, and died in 1861. The mother of our subject was also of English origin, was born in the same State as her husband and about the same year. She died in 1875. Our subject was born in North Carolina July 25, 1820, and received his education in the schools near home. In 1841 he married Sarah Shipp, a native of Lincoln County, born 1823, and the daughter of Louis and Mary (Cole) Shipp. To our subject and wife was born one boy, Pleasant, now a merchant in the Thirteenth District. After marriage Mr. Hobbs engaged with Dr. Bonner, and remained with him nineteen years, overseeing and looking after the interest of the plantation. In 1865 he purchased 155 acres of land in the Thirteenth District, where he located, and has since remained. He has since bought more land, and now he and his son own about 800 acres. He is a Democrat in politics, and cast his first presidential vote for James K. Polk. Pleasant Hobbs, son of our subject, was born April 4, 1844, and received his education in Lincoln County. In 1870 he wedded Laura Halbert, a native of Lincoln County, born in 1854, and by this union became the father of five children: Tula H., Sarah E., David F., Jr., B. and B. M. Pleasant Hobbs, since he has grown to manhood, has been a partner with his father on the farm. December, 1880, he began the mercantile business in the Thirteenth District, where he still continues. September, 1885, J. D. Sugg entered into partnership with them, and the firm is now known as Hobbs & Sugg. They are doing a good business in the sale of dry goods and groceries, and carry about $4,000 worth of stock. Pleasant is a Democrat in politics, and a member of the Masonic fraternity. He and wife are also members of the Methodist Episcopal Church.

COL. J. H. HOLMAN attorney, at law at Fayetteville, Tenn., is a son of James W. Holman, who was born in Lincoln County, Tenn., in 1812. He was a farmer and Primitive Baptist minister. In 1830 he married Jean Flack, who was born in Lincoln County in 1812, and in 1881 came to Fayetteville, and has since resided with his children. He owns 800 acres of land, and has been a minister of the gospel since 1845. His father, Rev. Hardy Holman, was a Virginian, and moved to Kentucky previous to 1800. He was among the very early pioneers of Lincoln County, and surveyed the town plot of Fayetteville. Our subject is one of eight children, four now living; Dr. Thomas P., a resident of Lincoln County; Sue M. (Mrs. Dr. W. A. Millhouse), Jennie P. (Mrs. John G. Tolley), and J. H., our subject, who was born in Lincoln County in 1836, and received an academic education in the schools of his county. In 1856 he entered Union University, at Murfreesboro, but in the spring of 1857 was appointed lieutenant in the regular army by President Pierce, and held the position until the breaking out of the war between the North and the South, when he was appointed lieutenant-colonel of the First Regiment Tennessee Volunteers. In 1863 he was promoted to the rank of colonel, which position he held until the close of the war. He was at Cumberland Gap, Perryville, Lawrenceburg, and in many skirmishes, and was wounded on three different occasions, but not seriously. He was paroled May 24, 1865, at Houston, Tex. He was taken prisoner at Winchester, Tenn., in 1863, and retained at Camp Chase, Ohio, and Johnson's Island for thirteen months. After returning home he began the study of law, and in 1867 was admitted to the Lincoln County bar and began practicing with his brother, D. W. Holman. November 23, 1865, he and Lizzie C. Kimbrough were united in marriage. Mrs. Holman was born in 1840, and was a daughter of Rev. Bradley Kimbrough, a Baptist minister. In 1870 Mr. Holman was elected attorney-general of the Sixth Judicial Circuit, holding the office until 1877, and has since devoted his attention to his profession. In 1878 he was appointed commissioner to the Paris Exposition by Gov. Porter, and during his absence traveled in various portions of Europe. He belongs to the Masonic fraternity, Union Chapter.

THOMAS P. HOLMAN, M. D., an influential farmer of Lincoln County, Tenn., is a son of James W. and Jean (Flack) Holman, and was born March 3, 1834. At the age of sixteen he began teaching school, and followed that occupation at irregular intervals for upward of six sessions. He entered Union University, Murfreesboro, Tenn., and graduated at the age of twenty-four years. He then became a follower of Æsculapius, and continued his studies to the time of the late civil war. In 1862 he joined Company C, Eleventh Tennessee Cavalry, and participated in the battles of Murfreesboro, Massy Creek, Chickamauga, Chattanooga, Dalton, Resaca, and numerous other engagements of less note. He was captured at Fayetteville in 1864, and taken to Camp Chase, Ohio, but was exchanged at the end of six weeks, and immediately rejoined his command. He returned home in 1865 and taught school one session, and then kept a hotel in Shelbyville for about one year and a half. In 1867 he entered the medical department at Washington University at Baltimore, Md., and graduated as an M. D. in 1869. He was appointed resident physician of Bay View Asylum at Baltimore, but the following year returned to Tennessee and began his practice at Mulberry. January 5, 1875, he wedded Silena Moore, daughter of Capt. Lewis Moore, who was killed at Jonesboro in 1864. Mrs. Holman was born in 1850, and has borne her husband the following children: Burke, Wayne, Leon, Fannie Lynne, Ross, and Moore. Dr. Holman owns 300 acres of land near Fayetteville, to which he gives the most of his time and attention. He met with good success in his practice, but owing to his enfeebled constitution was compelled to abandon it. In politics he is a Prohibitionist in principle and practice. He belongs to the Freemasons, and his wife is a member of the Christian Church.

B. F. HOUSTON, oculist and aurist of Petersburg, was born in Marshall County, Tenn., September 11, 1852. B. F. Houston, father of our subject, was born in Tennessee in 1807, and was a farmer by occupation. He died February 1, 1862. He was married to N. B. Usery, who was born in 1813 in Giles County, and died in November, 1878. Our subject was educated at the Mooreville Institute under Prof. Burney. September 11, 1872, M. A. Elliott, who was born in Franklin County December 9, 1850, became his wife. They kept a boarding house at Louisville two years, and then returned to the old home and he began taking charge of his mother's farm. In 1874 he began the study of medicine, but on account of weak eyes was obliged to abandon the study for some time. In 1879 he moved to Petersburg, and after a time went to Florence, Ala., and took special instruction on the eye and ear under the well known doctor, A. M. Parkhill, and now has an extensive practice in Lincoln, Marshall and the adjoining counties, also a number of counties in Alabama adjoining the State. He has acquired a reputation, especially in the treatment of the eye. He and wife are members of the Christian Church.

CAPT. WILLIAM W. JAMES, farmer of the Fifth District, was born in 1828, in Lincoln County, Tenn., and was one of eleven children born to Thomas and Martha (Duke) James. The father was born in Norfolk, Va., in 1790, and was of English lineage. His education was fair, and when about twenty years of age, he, in company with an elder brother, immigrated to Lincoln County, but soon went to Alabama, and engaged in the war of 1812, under Gen. Coffee. They were in the battle of New Orleans, and at the close of the war immigrated to Lincoln County and located near Mulberry, where he purchased a farm. In 1825 he was married, and at the time of his death, which occurred in 1866, he owned several good farms. The mother died about 1874. Our subject received his education in the neighboring schools, and the age of nineteen entered as clerk in a mercantile establishment at Fayetteville. In 1849, he, in company with about thirty-five others, started to cross the plains for the *El Dorado*. He engaged in mining while there, and at the end of two years returned home and engaged in the mercantile business at Mulberry Village, where he continued until 1861. In 1859 he wedded Susan V. Freeman, and to them were born eight children, five of whom are living: Thomas D., Sarah A,, William W., Alice P., and John M. In 1861 Mr. James was made captain of Company A., Forty-first Tennessee Infantry, and was taken prisoner at Fort Donelson. He was exchanged at Vicksburg, and soon after was discharged on account of poor health. In 1869 he purchased 300 acres of land at Mulberry, where he now resides. In politics he is a life-long Democrat, casting his first vote for Franklin Pierce. He is a member of the Masonic fraternity, and of the I. O. O. F., and he and Mrs. James are among the most substantial members of the Missionary Baptist Church.

GEORGE A. JARVIS, postmaster and merchant, of Petersburg, Tenn., was born on the 13th of June, 1840, at Richmond, Va., son of Gus and Rebecca (Smith) Jarvis. He was educated and reared in his native town, and May 20, 1869, married Lula Green, who was born in Lincoln County, Tenn., August 12, 1847, and two children are the result of their union: George A. and Minnie E. In 1857 Mr. Jarvis became salesman for Joseph Akin, of Maury County, and remained with him until the breaking out of the war, after which he acted as traveling salesman for Louisville houses for seven years, and in 1872 came to Petersburg. Since 1874 he has been in the mercantile business, and has also had the postoffice at Petersburg. Mr. Jarvis is a Democrat, and belongs to the I. O. O. F. and K. of H. fraternities. April 27, 1861, he entered the Confederate Army, serving in Company B, Second Tennessee Infantry, commanded by William B. Bate, the present governor of Tennessee. He served as lieutenant. He afterward became a member of another company, and served in the quartermaster's department. He participated in many battles, and May 1, 1863, was captured and taken to Johnson's Island, where he remained a prisoner twenty-two months. He returned home in May, 1865.

T. A. JEAN, farmer and mechanic, is a native of Lincoln County, Tenn., born in 1836, and is one of eleven children of John and Ann (Shaw) Jean. The father was of Irish lineage, born in North Carolina in 1797, a merchant and farmer by occupation. He came to Tennessee in 1815, and two years later married. He died in 1883, at the advanced age of eighty-six years. He was twice married, his second wife being Patsey Taylor. The mother was born in 1801, in North Carolina, and died in 1845. At the age of ten years our subject became the architect of his own fortunes, and for about eight years was a farm laborer, and for his first year's labor received $3 per month for his services. January 27, 1856, he married Martha E. Rutledge, who was born in 1829, in Lincoln County. The following are their children: William McHenry, John Alex, Elizabeth A., Thomas M., Mary C., Martha L. and George W. In 1882 Mr. Jean purchased 141 acres of land near Fayetteville, on which he located and has since resided. He is very skillful with the use of tools, and does his own blacksmithing and repairing in general. He is a Democrat in politics, and his first presidential vote was cast for Breckinridge, in 1860. He served in the late war in Forrest's escort, and was in many severe skirmishes. His principal duty was scouting, and during his entire service he was neither wounded nor captured. He returned home in 1865, after an absence of three years. He and Mrs. Jean are members of the Methodist Episcopal Church South.

DR. GEORGE W. JONES, physician and surgeon of Mulberry, and a son of C. G. and Nancy (Moore) Jones, was born in Maury County in 1835. The father was born near Lynchburg, Va., in 1803, and was of English lineage. At the age of twenty-six, he, in company with an elder brother, immigrated to Maury County, Tenn., making the entire journey on foot. In 1831 he was married and became the father of nine children, of whom our subject is one. He died January 2, 1874. The mother was born in North Carolina in 1805, and is now living on the old farm in Maury County. Our subject remained at home until he was twenty-one years of age, and received his early education at Rock Springs. In 1865 he entered the medical department of the University of Nashville, where he graduated in 1858. He immediately located in Mulberry and began practicing his profession. In 1858 he wedded Lizzie Whitaker (daughter of Newton and Fannie Whitaker) and to this union were born eight children, five of whom are living: Charley N., Clarence G., Lelia W., George M. and Jennie M. In 1859 he removed to Mississippi, where he remained till 1861, after which he returned to Mulberry, and has since resided there. During the war he was elected sergeant of Company C, Fifth Kentucky, and was soon afterward made lieutenant of his regiment, but was discharged after the battle of Murfreesboro, on account of disability. Since that time he has continued the practice of his profession, in which he has made a complete success. He is a member of the I. O. O. F., and K. of H. He and wife are members of the Missionary Baptist Church.

W. L. KILPATRIC, merchant of Fayetteville, and farmer, living two miles south of that village was born in south Alabama, October 20, 1857, son of I. T. and M. V. Kilpatric. The father was born in South Carolina in 1818, and was of Irish lineage. He moved to Georgia when a youth, and was married there, and moved to Alabama; thence to Lincoln County, Tenn., in 1883 where he located and now resides. The mother was born in Georgia in 1827 and died in January, 1884. Our subject received his education in the various schools of Alabama. In 1879 he married Mary Wilson, a native of Lincoln County, born May 1, 1865, and the daughter of Matthew T. and Jane C. Wilson. By this union our subject became the father of one child—Alva W. After marriage our subject located on the farm, where they have since resided. He now owns over 500 acres of excellent land, well improved. In 1882 he and his brother, T. B., engaged in the mercantile business at Fayetteville. In 1886 he purchased his brother's interest, and took another partner, T. I. McCowan, and now do business under the name of Kilpatric & Co. They have been very successful in the sale of dry goods, clothing, etc. Mr. Kilpatric is a Democrat in politics, and cast his first presidential vote for Grover Cleveland. J. E. Kilpatric, brother of W. L., was in the late war, enlisting in 1864 when but seventeen years of age, and remaining until the surrender. Our subject and wife are members of the Presbyterian Church.

WILLIAM J. LANDESS, farmer and tanner of the Sixth District, was born October 9, 1852, in Lincoln County, Tenn. The father of our subject, John Landess, was born in Kentucky, November 11, 1799, and was of Dutch extraction. He acquired a good business education and was a tanner by occupation. He located in the Sixth District, where he soon established a lucrative business. April 5, 1831, he married Mary H. Stone, and became the father of eleven children, ten of whom are living, our subject being one of them. The father died September 11, 1876, and the mother is still living on the old homeplace. Our subject received his education principally at the Oak Hill School, taking quite a thorough course in the languages. November 28, 1878, he led to the altar May Boone, a native of Lincoln County, born February 8, 1856, and the daughter of Capt. Nathan and Orpha Boone. This union resulted in the birth of three children, two of whom are living: John B. and Alberta K. Mr. Landess is now residing on the old homeplace where he was born. He is the owner of 300 acres of good land, well cultivated, and succeeded his father in the tannery business, in which he has been quite successful. He is a Democrat in politics, casting his first vote for S. J. Tilden. He and wife are members of the Primitive Baptist Church. Mrs. Landess was educated at the Female Institute at Winchester.

R. W. LONG is a son of Joseph Long, who was born in North Carolina, and came to Tennessee and married Matilda Flack. The mother was born in 1804 and died in 1873. Our subject received a common school education, and after his marriage, in 1857, to Tabitha Bledsoe, he tilled the home farm for his mother, who was a widow. His wife was born near Petersburg, November 10, 1836, and seven children blessed her union with Mr. Long: Alva M. (Mrs. J. C. Moore), Nora I. (Mrs. C. A. Talley), Thomas A., Fannie E. (Mrs. O. B. Taylor), James B., Helen B. and Affa C. In 1872 our subject and family moved onto their present farm of 200 acres, comprising seven acres of all kinds of fruit trees. Mr. Long has given his children good educational advantages, and is conservative in politics, voting rather for the man than the party. He served in the late war in Company F., Forty-first Tennessee Infantry, and took an active part in the battles of Fort Donelson, Franklin, Nashville and several minor engagements. He was captured at the fall of Fort Donelson, and imprisoned seven months at LaFayette and Indianapolis, Ind. He was the wagonmaster in the quartermaster's department two years. He returned home in the fall of 1864. He and wife are members of the Methodist Episcopal Church South.

J. W. LLOYD, senior partner of the firm of Lloyd & Blake, proprietors and publishers of the Fayetteville *Express*, was born October 3, 1843, in Huntsville, Ala., son of W. B. and Martha P. (Tatum) Lloyd, born in Virginia in 1818 and 1817, and died in 1873 and 1851, respectively. They were married in 1838, and soon after moved to Huntsville, Ala. Our subject's mother died when he was quite young, and at the age of thirteen he became an apprentice at the printer's trade, working on the Huntsville *Advocate* four years. He then commenced life for himself as a journeyman, and the following thirteen years worked in most of the large cities in the South, assisting on the leading daily and weekly papers. In April, 1873, he came to Fayetteville and assisted in the establishing the Fayetteville *Express*, the proprietor and publisher being J. B. Smith. In 1876 Mr. Lloyd and F. O. McCord purchased the press, but in 1880 Mr. J. W. Goodwin purchased Mr. McCord's interest, and for two years the firm was known as Lloyd & Goodwin. From 1882 to August, 1883, the firm was Lloyd & Carrigan, and in January, 1884, Mr. Blake took a one-half interest. The *Express* is a newsy paper and is devoted to the interests of the people. Mr. Lloyd has been in the newspaper business nearly thirty years and knows the needs and wishes of his patrons. He is a Democrat in his political views, and cast his first presidential vote for S. J. Tilden in 1876. February 23, 1881, he married Kate Jones, daughter of Capt. Joel J. Jones, who was killed in the battle of Perryville, Ky. Mrs. Lloyd was born in Lincoln County, Tenn., in 1853, and has one son—Sumner.

J. J. MADDOX, farmer of Lincoln County, is a son of John and Elizabeth Maddox, who were born in 1811 and 1812, respectively. They came from the Carolinas, and were among the early settlers of Tennessee, and were farmers. The father died in 1880 and the mother in 1872. Our subject received a liberal education, and December 18; 1873, led Martha A. Sherrell to the hymeneal altar. She was born in Lincoln County July 3, 1855, and is the mother of six children: R. S., J. S., B. M., A. A., M. S., and L. J. In May, 1861, Mr. Maddox joined the company known as the "Camargo Guards," and was in the battle of Murfreesboro and many minor engagements. He returned home in 1863, and three years later purchased the farm on which he now lives, consisting of 368 acres of land. Mr. Maddox is well respected by his fellow-man, and takes an active interest in all institutions which promote the advancement of the county. He is a Democrat and Mason, and he and wife are members of the Methodist Episcopal Church.

W. L. McCANN was born in Jackson, Ala., in 1827. His father was of Irish descent, born in the "Palmetto State" in 1800, and moved to near Alabama in 1825, and after a two years' residence came to Tennessee, where he died in 1867. The mother was born in South Carolina in 1804, and died in May, 1882. W. L. McCann was educated in the Eighteenth District of Lincoln County, and in 1851 married Miss M. J. Rawls, daughter of L. H. and Sarah Rawls. She was born in Lincoln County, Tenn., November 3, 1832. Mr· McCann purchased his present farm in 1872, which consists of 386 acres of excellent farming land, well improved with good buildings and a fine orchard. He has been very successful, as he began business for himself since the war with little or no means, and now owns an excellent tract of land. He is a Democrat, and during the late war was strongly opposed to the principles of secession. He belongs to the Masonic fraternity.

COL. C. A. McDANIEL is a son of Fielden and Lucy (Barker) McDaniel, and was born in Lincoln County, Tenn., in 1823. The father was of Scotch-Irish descent, born in Virginia, in 1781, but a resident of North Carolina at the time of his marriage, which occurred about 1803. In 1808 he came to Middle Tennessee, and was a resident of Lincoln County, Tenn., after 1810 or 1811. He died in 1840, being one of the early residents and pioneers of the county and suffering many privations incident to pioneer life. The mother was born in North Carolina, in 1783, and died in 1839. Our subject is one of their nine children, and resided with his parents until their respective deaths, then he and his brother Charles bought the old homestead and began tilling the soil. When the news came that gold had been discovered in California, he, with a number of friends, started for the "Golden Gate," going overland, the trip taking nine months. There he remained seven years engaged in mining. He returned home in November, 1856, and in December,

1857, was married to Margaret Buchanan, daughter of Andrew Buchanan. Mrs. McDaniel was born in Lincoln County in November, 1831. They have four children: Mary Lou (Mrs. J. B. Whitaker), Andrew C., and Fielden and Felix (twins). In 1848 Mr. McDaniel had purchased 100 acres of land, on which he settled after marriage, and where he has since made his home. He now owns 374 acres of good and well improved land. In 1847, at the age of twenty-three, he was elected to the State Legislature, being the first native representative of Lincoln County. In 1854 he represented Calaveras County, Cal., in the State Legislature, and has been a life-long Democrat. He served in the Mexican war and was slightly wounded at the battle of Monterey. He took an important part in the late war, and assisted in organizing the Forty-fourth Regiment, Tennessee Infantry, and he was chosen colonel of the same. He was wounded in the right arm at Shiloh, but served until the close of the war with the exception of nine months. He returned home in May, 1865. He and wife are members of the Methodist Episcopal Church South.

M. L. McDOWELL, miller of the village known as McDowell's Mill, Tenn., was born in Murfreesboro, Tenn., May 14, 1843, son of James and Harriet McDowell, born in 1818, in Tennessee and North Carolina, respectively. The father is a carpenter, and he and wife are yet living. His grandfather was born at Staten Island, N. Y., and he and his wife and family, with the exception of three sons, were murdered by the Indians. Our subject was educated in the Murfreesboro Academy, and in 1861 he enlisted in Company A, Second Tennessee Infantry, commanded by W. B. Bate, the present governor of Tennessee, and participated in the battles of Bull Run, Shiloh, Richmond, Chickamauga and Murfreesboro. He was wounded at Richmond, Ky., and was unfitted for further service, but remained with his company in preference to a hospital. He returned home in 1864, and in 1865 wedded Mary A. Cawthon, daughter of M. B. and and M. J. Cawthon, of Alabama, and seven children were born to them: George L., E. R., H. E., M. L., S. J., M. B. and Myrtle L. Mr. McDowell farmed in Alabama a number of years, but met with reverses, and moved to Tennessee and began working at the carpenter's trade at Lynchburg, and erected very nearly all the fine houses in the place. While there he was mayor, magistrate and notary public. In 1880 he moved to Giles County, and was in the milling business two years in that county, then came to McDowell and erected his present mill. There was no village at the time of his location, but the place has now about 100 inhabitants, two dry goods and grocery stores, a postoffice, blacksmiths and carpenters shops and nine dwelling houses, and a fine schoolhouse is in process of being erected; all of which has been brought about by the energy of Mr. McDowell. He belongs to the Masonic and I. O. O. F. fraternities, and in politics is a Democrat.

C. C. McKINNEY, attorney at law and magistrate of District No. 8 of Lincoln County, Tenn., was born where he now resides, in 1828. His father, Dr. Charles McKinney, was of Scotch-Irish extraction, and was born in Wayne County, Ky., in 1788, and educated at Center College, Danville, Ky., where he also read medicine. He married Mary Russell in 1810, and came to Lincoln County, Tenn., in 1812, being one of the pioneer settlers and physicians of the county. His visits to the sick were made by following the old Indian trails and foot-paths, and he was known far and near as a man possessed of remarkable intelligence and honesty. He was surgeon in the war of 1812, and died in 1864 full of years. The mother was of direct Scotch descent, born in 1790. She died in 1863. They were the parents of fourteen children, only three of whom are now living. Our subject's paternal and maternal grandparents were born in Ireland and Scotland, respectively, and both were early emigrants to America. C. C. McKinney received an academical education, and in 1850 became a disciple of Blackstone, Hon. James Fulton being his preceptor. He was admitted to the bar in 1851, and has since practiced his profession, and regarded as a successful, earnest advocate and safe counselor. He was in partnership in the practice of law two years with W. B. Martin, and thirteen years with F. P. Fulton. In August, 1885, Mr. McKinney was elected magistrate of his district, and yet holds that position. He has always resided in Fayetteville, and has displayed qualities of head and heart which have enabled him to surmount many difficulties. He is a

Democrat, but previous to the war was a Whig. He is also a Mason. In June, 1856, he married Ellen Dennis, born in Alabama, in July, 1837. They have two children: James D., who is the pharmacist in W. A. Gill's drug store, in Fayetteville, and Charles F., who is salesman in the dry goods store of J. A. Lumpkin. Mr. and Mrs. McKinney are members of the Cumberland Presbyterian Church.

R. D. McMILLEN is a son of Joseph McMillen, who was of Irish origin, born near Knoxville, Tenn., in 1784. He was a tailor by trade, and died in 1859. Our subject's mother was of Scotch descent, born in Kentucky in 1787 and died in 1863. Our subject was born in Fayetteville August 17, 1822, and, being the youngest of twelve children, was left to look after the old home place and care for his parents. He owns 267 acres of valuable land near Petersburg, and has been a successful business man. In 1858 he married M. J. Millard, daughter of Willam and Mary Millard. She was born in Lincoln County in 1833, and died in 1878, having borne seven children, six of whom are living: Margaret F. (deceased), Effie (Mrs. C. Rosborough), William J., Sarah, Thomas, Minnie and Lucinda. They have received good educational advantages, and have made the most of their opportunities. Mr. McMillen is a conservatiye Democrat, but was formerly a supporter of the Whig party, and is a man well versed on all the questions of the day. He belongs to the Masonic fraternity.

MRS. CHARLOTTE MERRELL, a native of Lincoln County, Tenn., born June 1, 1813, is one of the two children born to James and Elizabeth (Daugherty) Grant. Our subject's father was born in Virginia, and, after living there some time, immigrated to North Carolina. He was a farmer by occupation, came to Tennessee in 1812, and died in the Sixteenth District April 3, 1841. The mother of our subject was born in North Carolina about 1761, and departed this life January 26, 1836. Charlotte received her education in the schools near home, and October 14, 1838, she married William Merrell, a native of North Carolina, born January 26, 1815. By this union were born nine children, five of whom are living: Robert and Thomas are living in Lincoln County; Susan is the wife of William Soloman, and she with her husband and three children, Charley, Dewit T. and Dorinda are living with our subject on the old home place; Charley is living in Colorado, Texas. Mr. Merrell died October 31, 1880, and left a fine farm of 200 acres lying on the western portion of the Sixteenth District of Lincoln County and a portion in Giles County.

J. S. MERRELL'S birth occurred in Giles County, Tenn., in March, 1839. His father was born in North Carolina, in 1798, and came to Tennessee when a lad, and afterward became a farmer. He died in December, 1866. His wife was born in Tennessee, and died in 1852. Our subject's early education and raising was like the average boy of his period. To his marriage with Josie Reed in December, 1860, were born the following family: Martha (deceased wife of A. J. Smith), Cynthia (Mrs. P. A. Hall), Susan, Cora G., Hugh F., Mollie B. and James E. Since 1866 Mr. Merrell has farmed in the Seventeenth District of Lincoln County, where he owns 145 acres of fertile land, well improved. In connection with overseeing his farm he carries on blacksmithing, and is a skillful wood-workman. He takes much interest in educational affairs, and has given his children good educations. He is a Democrat and a Mason, and he and wife are members of the Missionary Baptist Church. In 1861 he enlisted in Company F, Forty-fourth Tennessee Infantry, and was in the battles of Murfreesboro, Chickamauga, Siege of Knoxville, besides many smaller engagements. He was a brave and faithful soldier, and returned home in December, 1863.

JAMES A. D. MIDDLETON, lumberman and prominent citizen, and a son of Alexander D. and Jane Smith (Brodie) Middleton, was born July 24, 1842, in New York City. The father of our subject was born in Scotland about 1815, and was a descendant of Scotch ancestors. He was a marble-cutter by occupation, learning this trade in New York City. The mother of our subject was also born in New York City about 1817. After the death of the father, which occurred July 26, 1849, the family went to Virginia, and soon after to ———— County, Mo., where they remained two years. They then removed to St. Louis in 1851, where they remained till after the death of the mother, which occurred in 1865. Our subject remained at home until nineteen years of age, and received his education principally in the free schools of St. Louis, Mo. On the 31st of July, 1868, he wedded Mrs. Cordelia J. Hague, daughter of G. W. Alexander, of Lincoln County. They have two interesting children: C. Jennie and Walter P. J. Previous to his marriage he went into the army with Lieut.-Col. Mortimer Okean as a hostler, and there he remained until 1865, when he landed at Tullahoma. After staying there two years he received an appointment in the internal revenue service, where he remained until April 30, 1884, with the exception of about two years, 1868 and 1870, when he was postmaster at Mulberry. May 1, 1884, Mr. Middleton commenced his present occupation. He is a Republican in politics, and a Prohibitionist, aud cast his first vote for Abraham Lincoln. He is an Odd Fellow, Knight of Honor, a Good Templar and a member of the Methodist Episcopal Church South, as are also the two children. Mrs. Middleton is a member of the Cumberland Presbyterian Church.

DR. W. L. MOORES, a physician of the Thirteenth District, was born in Lincoln County, Tenn., in 1842, and was one of two children born to William H. and Elizabeth (Sugg) Moores. The father was of Welsh origin and was born in Lincoln County, Tenn., about 1820. He was a tiller of the soil, and died in 1845. The mother of our subject was of English origin, born in Robertson County, Tenn. in 1801, and died in 1874. Our subject received a good literary education in the counties of Lincoln and Giles. In 1862, he enlisted in Freeman's battery, and took part in the battle of Parker's Cross-roads, and other minor engagements. He was captured while sick at home, July, 1863, and taken to Camp Chase, where he remained seven months, after which he was conveyed to Fort Delaware and remained there a year. In June, 1865, he began the study of medicine and at the end of a year and a half entered the Cincinnati College of Medicine and Surgery, where it required three years to complete the course, but owing to his rapid progress was allowed by the faculty to take all his examinations at the end of the second year, and received his diploma in 1867. In the same year he married Sarah J., daughter of Mill and Lucretia (Fox) McCollum, her mother being a cousin of Gen. B. F. Butler. Mrs. Moores was born in Giles County, July 5, 1844, and by her marriage became the mother of six children: Cyrus L., James A., Ira, Edna, Matt W†, and William C. Dr. Moores has always been an active, energetic man, and has a large and increasing practice. He has met with commendable success and is continually laboring for the good of the people. He is postmaster at Cyruston, and this office has been in the hands of the family for fifty years. He is a Mason, a K. of H., and a member of the Methodist Episcopal Church and is secretary of the same. Mrs. Moores is a member of the Presbyterian Church. Dr. Moores has a small farm where he resides, and has a fine young orchard. He is making a specialty of the study of horticulture, and he also has on his place a fish-pond and is a pisciculturist to some extent.

J. K. MOORES, farmer, was born in the Thirteenth District, where he now resides, and is one of nine children born to his parents, Daniel and Elizabeth Moores. The father was born in New Jersey in 1789, and came to Lincoln County with his parents when but nineteen years of age. He followed agricultural pursuits and was married in 1816. He was a soldier in the war of 1812, and died in 1849. The mother of our subject was born in the southern part of Pennsylvania in 1796, and died in October, 1876. Our subject was reared at home, received his early education in the country schools and afterward completed at Viny Grove Academy. In 1856 he wedded Louisa Smith, a native of Lincoln County, born in 1839, and a daughter of the well known Constant and Margaret Smith. By this union our subject became the father of four sons: John, now living in Obion County, Tenn.; Knox and Cyrus, in Texas; and Ross, who still remains with his father. Mr. Moores taught school for some time, and after marriage located on the old homeplace, where he has since resided. In 1868 his wife died, and in 1872 he wedded Mrs. D. J. Wilson, who was born in Lincoln County in 1837, and who is the daughter of Maj. and Elizabeth Ruth. The result of our subject's marriage was the birth of two children: Astor and Bessie. He is a Democrat in politics, a Mason, and he and wife are members of the Cumberland Presbyterian Church. In 1870 he was elected to the office of magistrate, which position he held for six years in a satisfactory manner. Mr. Moores now owns 250 acres of good land, all well cultivated and improved.

WILLIAM T. MOYERS, carpenter, is a son of Samuel H. and Sarah (Phelps) Moyers, and was born in Fayetteville, Tenn., in September, 1827, and at the early age of twelve years left home and became the architect of his own fortune, working at the tinner's and copper-smith's trade for three years. At the age of sixteen he began working at the carpenter's trade, and has followed that calling through life. In October, 1853, he was united in marriage to Martha G. Rowe, who was born in Lincoln County in 1837, and daughter of William Rowe. Mr. and Mrs. Moyers became the parents of fourteen children, nine of whom are living: Edna (Mrs. Ephraim Pitts), Thomas, Robert, Hardy, Fannie, Nama, Curtis, Jesse and Jacob. Mr. Moyer is a Democrat in politics, and cast his first presidential vote for Lewis Cass. He is the oldest native inhabitant of Fayetteville, and is a member of the F. & A. M., I. O. O. F. and K. of H. fraternities. His father was of German descent, born in Virginia in 1791, a shoe-maker by trade. The grandfather, Peter Moyer, was a native German, and came to America previous to the Revolutionary war, and to Tennessee in the early part of the present century. He assisted in leveling the canebrakes where Fayetteville now stands, and took up his abode in the village. He lived to be one hundred and one years of age, and was a man of powerful physique. When eighty-four years old he felled a large oak tree, and split 100 rails in order to reach home by 1 o'clock to see a game fight. He served through the entire Revolutionary war. Samuel Moyer was an 1812 soldier, and was married about 1820. He kept a boot and shoe store in Fayetteville a number of years, and in 1843 moved to the country, where he resided until his death, December 24, 1869. The mother was born in Tennessee in 1810, and died in October, 1871. Nine of their thirteen children are now living.

HON. DAVID J. NOBLITT, physician and surgeon, and a son of Abraham and Sarah Ann (Razar) Noblitt, was born in Bedford County, March 16, 1836. He worked at home until he was eighteen years of age, paying $50 a year for the remainder of his time. He received his early education at the free schools, and when he first left home entered the Charity School, taking an English and Latin course there for two years. He taught two years, and in 1857 entered the medical department of the University of Nashville, where he graduated in 1860. In 1861 he enlisted in Company F, Forty-fourth Tennessee, and was appointed assistant surgeon of the regiment, in which capacity he remained till after the battle of Murfreesboro, when his health failed, and he was compelled to resign his position. November 22, 1860, he wedded Sylvania C. Boone, daughter of Samuel and Cynthia Boone, and this union resulted in the birth of two children: Leona N. and Boone E. In 1866 our subject purchased 190 acres of land at Booneville, where he located and still resides, and where he continues to practice his profession, and is now one of the leading physicians of this county. He owns 185 acres of land under a good state of cultivation and good improvements. In 1872 he was elected to represent Lincoln and Giles Counties in the lower house of the State Legislature, and re-elected in 1874. He is a Democrat and a Mason. Mrs. Noblitt is a member of the Primitive Baptist Church. Our subject's father was born in North Carolina July 4, 1812, and was of Anglo-Polish descent. He was of noted ancestry, his great-grandfather being connected with the English Navy in the days of William Penn, and came with him to the new world to aid and assist him in his colonization. Abraham, our subject's father, was a farmer, and died in 1845. The mother of our subject is still living, and is making her home with our subject. Her father was a cousin to Patrick Henry, of Revolutionary times.

B. S. PAPLANUS, a merchant of Petersburg, Tenn., was born in Hungary, Europe, and being left an orphan at an early age, he resolved to make the New World his home, and accordingly came to the United States in 1871, landing in New York, but only resided in the metropolis a short time, when he went to Ohio, and peddled in that State about one year, and then came to Tennessee in June, 1872, where he pursued the same vocation until the fall of 1878. In September of the same year he began merchandising in

Decatur, Ala., but remained in that place but a short time, when he returned to Tennessee and located in Petersburg, where he engaged in business, He started with a small stock and limited patronage, but has increased his business year by year, and by fair dealing, industry and courtesy he has gained the esteem of the people, and has built up a trade second to none in the county. He goes to headquarters to buy his goods, and is an energetic business man and shrewd financier, and a valuable addition to the county. He also deals in corn, wheat and country produce, and in 1885 purchased more dried fruit than was ever purchased by any merchant in the county, shipping at one time six car-loads.

JOEL PARKS was born near his present residence in 1837, son of William and Mary (Thurston) Parks. The father was born in North Carolina in 1786, and was a farmer by occupation. He came to Lincoln County, Tenn., when a young man and purchased 300 acres of land near Fayetteville, where he resided until 1850, when he removed one-half mile northwest of Fayettville, where he resided until his death in 1863. He was a successful farmer owning over 600 acres of land. The mother was born in North Carolina, and died in 1840. Of their eleven children, four are living: Elizabeth (widow of Hugh Thomison), Martha (Mrs. John Roach), Catherine (widow of Joseph Cashion), and Joel, our subject, who was educated in the schools of his native county. He made his parents' house his home until the breaking out of the war, when he enlisted in Company K, Eighth Regiment Tennessee Infantry, and fought at Perryville, Murfreesboro, Resaca, Marietta, Jonesboro, Franklin, Nashville, and other engagements of minor note. He was wounded at Murfreesboro by a shell, and was released from active duty about one month. He returned home in December, 1864, and lived on the old home-place with his sister, Mrs. Cashion until 1876, when the estate was settled. In October, 1878, Mary, daughter of Frank Renegar, became his wife. She was born in Lincoln County in 1850, and has borne her husband one daughter—Sarah Elizabeth. In the spring of 1877, he erected a house on his portion of the old homestead, where he moved and has since resided. He is a Democrat in politics, and cast his first presidential vote for S. J. Tilden, in 1876. He belongs to the Masonic fraternity.

ELISHA T. PARKS, farmer, and a native of Lincoln County, was born August 1, 1839, son of Benjamin T. Parks, a native of Lincoln County, born in 1815, and a farmer by occupation. In 1838 he married Martha Thomison, and located where the village of Kelso now stands. After remaining here till 1850, he moved to what is now known as the Twenty-first District, and remained there till 1856, when he purchased 520 acres in the Fifth District, where he located and remained till his death, which occurred in February, 1857. The mother was born in Lincoln county, in 1816, and died in 1880. Our subject received his education in the school of the vicinity, and after the father's death, assisted his mother on the farm. At the breaking out of the war he enlisted in what was first Company H, afterward Company K, Eighth Tennessee, of Mulberry Riflemen. He was wounded at the battle of Murfreesboro, and returned home in December, 1862, where he remained till July, 1863. He then joined the army in Georgia, and served through the Georgia campaign. He was captured at Petersburg, and taken to Nashville and finally to Columbus, Ohio, where he was held for about five months. November, 1865, he married Mary Ann Alexander (daughter of Col. L. S. and Mary Alexander), and this union resulted in the birth of four children: Benjamin N., S. O., Ernest and Cora A. Directly after marriage Mr. Parks located on the old home-place where he still continues to reside. He has 100 acres of excellent land, all well cultivated, and is living in one of the oldest houses in the vicinity. It was built eighty years ago. In 1882 he was elected magistrate and filled the office to the entire satisfaction of the public. In politics he is a life-long Democrat, and he is also a Mason. Mrs. Parks is a member of the Primitive Baptist Church.

W. E. PATRICK, a worthy and well-to-do farmer of the 21st District, was born near his present residence in 1832, and was the eldest of six children of John and Mary Patrick, who were born in Lincoln County, where they always lived with the exception of about nine years spent in Alabama. Our subject attended the schools near his home and assisted his parents on the farm. In 1855, he was married to Margaret George, who was born in Lincoln County in 1832. Seven children were born to their union, named James B., A. J., G. F., T. L., P. F., H. C. and Fannie B. In 1876 he purchased a farm of 160 acres of good and well cultivated land in the Twenty-First District, where he has since resided. He has been fairly successful in his business enterprises and gives his aid to all worthy enterprises. Mr. Patrick is a Democrat in his political views, and he and wife are members of the Methodist Episcopal Church South.

MRS. E. R. PATTERSON, is a daughter of James and Rebecca Cheatham, and is one of the two surviving members of their family of four children. She was born in Lincoln County, Tenn., in 1819, and her parents were born in Virginia, and came to Tennessee at a very early date. The subject of our sketch was reared at home, and in 1844 was married to D. S. Patterson, who was born in Sumner County about 1821, and came to Lincoln County, when a boy. He owned about 800 acres of land at the time of his death, which occurred April 4, 1862. Their family consisted of eight children: Maria S. (Mrs. Dr. H. L. Patterson), James S. (deceased), Elizabeth (deceased), Dr. William A. (deceased), Davidson H., who conducts the home-place, Cornelia R. (Mrs. W. B. Stevenson), Belle V. (Mrs. W. S. Patterson), and Emma J. (Mrs. J. E. Reeves). They were all given good educations and two of them were graduates of colleges. Davidson H. and his brother are well-to-do in worldly goods. His early education was obtained in the common schools, which he completed at Bethany College.

JAMES H. PATTERSON is one of eight children, and was born in Tennessee July 9, 1832, son of William and Rachel (Clendening) Patterson, and of Irish descent. William was born in North Carolina and came to Tennessee, where he married Miss Clendening, who was born in 1790 and died August 8, 1877. James H.'s early education was obtained in the schools near home and at Briar Patch Spring schools. He owns 485 acres of land near Blanche, and in 1880 sold 300 acres. [Besides this he owns 500 acres in different tracts. Mr. Patterson is a man noted for his charity, and is esteemed and respected by all. Of his father's eight children only three are living: J. C., who is a farmer in Giles County; and our subject and his sister Violet, who keeps house for him. November 7, 1861, he enlisted in Capt. Rhodes' company—Company G, Forty-fourth Tennessee Infantry—and was made first lieutenant, and was promoted to the rank of captain. He was discharged in 1862, on account of ill health, and returned home. J. H. Patterson (deceased), an uncle of our subject, will be remembered by many of the old residents of Sumner County, as he was widely known. Dr. John Patterson, his son, is one of the leading physicians of Murfreesboro.

W. S. PATTERSON is a son of L. M. and L. P. Patterson, who were born in 1834. The father served in the late war in Company G, Forty-fourth Tennessee Infantry, as lieutenant, and was killed at the bloody battle of Shiloh. The mother is residing with her children. The rudiments of our subject's education was obtained in the common schools near his early home. He afterward completed his education at Blanche Academy, which was under the management of J. A. Holland. W. S. was born June 21, 1859, and in 1881 was united in marriage to Belle V., daughter of D. S. and E. R. Patterson. She was born in Lincoln County, in 1859, and has borne her husband two children: Alma V. and L. E. Mr. Patterson has resided on the old home place since his marriage, and owns 305 acres of valuable land; he is an industrious farmer, and fully deserves his good fortune. He gives his support to the Democratic party.

LEWIS PEACH, marble and stone cutter, of Fayetteville, was born in 1836 in Davidson County, Tenn., and is the son of William and Susan Peach. The father was born in 1809 in Williamson County, Tenn., and was a marble-cutter by trade. His father, Jonathan Peach, was a native of South Carolina, born in 1783. He was one of the pioneers of Williamson County, assisting in forming one of the first settlements. William lived in his native county at the time of his marriage, and soon afterward moved to Davidson County. About 1842 he moved to Nashville, where he resided and worked at his trade. He assisted in cutting the stone for the State capitol, and since the conflict has been living a retired life with his son Lewis. The mother was born in 1813 in Williamson

County, Tenn., and died in 1865. They had nine children, five of whom are living. Our subject received his education in Nashville, and at the youthful age of thirteen began learning the marble and stone-cutter's trade, under the direction of his father. This he has since continued with the exception of four years during the Rebellion. In 1862 he enlisted in Company C, Eighth Regiment of Tennessee Infantry, and took part in some of the principal battles. Owing to the weakness of his eyesight he was placed on detached duty. In December, 1864, he returned home and re-opened business at Petersburg, Tenn. In 1873 he came to Fayetteville, where he has since resided. July, 1871, he wedded Susie J. Sheffield, a native of Bedford County, born in 1844, and the daughter of James W. Sheffield. Mr. Peach has devoted his entire time and attention to the marble and stone-cutting business, and has proved to be a skilled workman and artist. He turns out fine specimens of art, his work giving almost universal satisfaction. He has the only tombstone and marble business in Lincoln County. Mr. Peach is very conservative in politics, voting for principles and not for party. He is a Mason, and his wife is a member of the Primitive Baptist Church.

R. PETTEY, proprietor of the leading hotel in Fayetteville, was born January 8, 1829, in north Alabama, son of Dr. John W. and Annie (Harris) Pettey. The father was a North Carolinian, born in Wilkes County, February 28, 1791, and a physician in his neighborhood of considerable note. He was also a farmer, and about 1825 he left North Carolina and immigrated to Madison Co., Ala., where he purchased 160 acres. Previous to his death, which occurred September 23, 1876, he was the possessor of 360 acres. The mother was born January 18, 1798, in North Carolina, and reared to maturity a family of thirteen children, seven of whom are now living. She died June 13, 1869. Our subject received a limited education in the country schools, and remained with his parents until he was about twenty-one years of age. In the fall of 1849 he left the parental roof and immigrated to Lincoln County, where he lived with his brother W. W. as a clerk. In 1855 he came to Fayetteville, where he has since resided, and in 1858 he and his brother W. W. established a dry-goods store on their own responsibility, the firm being known as W. W. & R. Pettey. They continued in business until the civil war, when our subject enlisted in the Confederate service in Company G, First Tennessee Regiment, under Col. P. Turney. He was wounded at the battle of Seven Pines, the ball passing through his right lung and through the entire body. He did not recover sufficiently to re-enter the field. In 1867 he resumed his clerkship, working in various kinds of merchandise establishments. October 29, 1869, he wedded Margaret C. Norris, a native of Alabama, born November 26, 1841, and the daughter of Dr. George D. and Martha W. (Ragsdale) Norris. The result of our subject's marriage was the birth of four children: Gertrude, Annie C., Burton, and Mabel. In 1873 Mr. Pettey and his brother W. W. established a book or stationery store, and in the following year W. W. became proprietor of a hotel. In 1876 our subject sold his interest in the store and brought his brother's interest in the hotel, and from that time to the present has been engaged in that business. Mr. Pettey is a courteous and obliging gentleman, and is quite popular among the traveling public as a first-class hotel proprietor. Mrs. Pettey as a land lady is pleasant and entertaining. In politics Mr. Pettey is a stanch Democrat. He and wife are members of the Cumberland Presbyterian Church.

SQUIRE PICKLE, of Lincoln County, Tenn., was born in Bedford County January 27, 1815. His parents, Henry and Rachel (Nealy) Pickle, were born and married in North Carolina. They came to Bedford County, Tenn., soon after, and there spent the remainder of their lives. Our subject attended the neighboring schools during the fall and winter, and after attaining his majority became the architect of his own fortunes. After his marriage to Martha Harris, which occurred in 1840, he purchased 120 acres of land in Bedford County, but four years later disposed of this land and came to Lincoln County, where he now owns 188 acres of good land. Mrs. Pickle died in 1860, having borne one daughter, now deceased. In 1861 Mr. Pickle married Mrs. Harriet Scott. Our subject and his wife are well-to-do in worldly goods, as well as in the respect and esteem of their neighbors and friends. He is a Democrat, and is ever ready to support worthy enterprises.   On his farm is a well seventy feet deep, which was bored in 1883, the water having excellent mineral ingredients and possessing superior medicinal qualities.   It was analyzed with the following results: Saline sulphur, chloride of sodium, sulphate of sodium, carbonate of sodium, chloride of magnesium, sulphate of magnesium, carbonate of magnesium, sulphate of calcium, carbonate of calcium, also traces of phosphates, iodine and bromine.

JOHN PIGG is one of nine children and the son of Edmund and Rebecca Pigg, who were born in Virginia and North Carolina in 1804 and 1808, and died in 1884 and 1875, respectively.   Our subject was born June 9, 1847, and spent his early days on his father's farm.   In 1876 he was married to Ida Dyer, who was born in Lincoln County in 1857, and is a daughter of J. W. and Narcissa Dyer.   Mr. and Mrs. Pigg have three children: James E., Rebecca and Ida M.   Mr. Pigg resided with his parents until twenty-eight years of age, but after his twenty-first birthday began doing for himself.   He was in partnership with his father and brother, Claybone, in the farming interests eight years, and then worked on the home-farm four years longer.   He now owns a farm of 450 acres, on which he resides, besides 200 acres in another tract; and, in connection with his brother, Joseph, owns 1,000 acres in Lawrence County.   He is an energetic and honest business man and as such has the respect of all.   He raises, buys and ships a large amount of stock, and in politics he is a Democrat.   He is a member of the Masonic fraternity.

ISAAC S. PORTER, a son of Benjamin and Elizabeth (Casey) Porter, was born in Lincoln County, Tenn., in 1817.   He was reared principally by his mother, as his father died when he was about ten years of age.   He attended the neighboring schools, and in 1838 married Emeline, daughter of George W. and Ann Dennis, by whom he had twelve children, ten of whom are living: George W. D., Benjamin F. P. (deceased), David S., Isaac H. M., Robert M., Lawrence L. T., Elizabeth C., Eliza C., Helen L., Jane F. and Julia F.   Mr. Porter owns 235 acres of valuable and well improved land.   His two sons George and Benjamin were in the late war and participated in many of its principal battles, the latter being killed at Resaca, Ga., May 15, 1864.   Mrs. Porter was born in Tennessee in 1816, and her father and mother in North Carolina in 1791, and 1789, respectively.   Mr. Porter was a Whig, but since the war has been a Democrat.   His father was born in Boston, Mass., in 1763, and in 1804 married the mother, who was born in Virginia in 1778, and they together came to Tennessee in 1809.   The father died in Lincoln County in 1828.   The mother died in Texas in 1857.

J. C. REED, an enterprising citizen of the Fourteenth District, was born in Williamson County, Tenn., in 1820, son of J. C. and Agnes Reed.   The father was born in North Carolina about 1785, and immigrated to Williamson County, Tenn., with his parents when but thirteen years of age.   He was a tiller of the soil, and died in 1848.   He was one of the minute men in the Seminole war under Gen. Jackson.   The mother of our subject was born in Pennsylvania about 1790, and was of Irish origin.   She died in 1828.   Our subject was reared on the farm and attended school until he was large enough to assist on the farm.   In 1847 he wedded Louisa, daughter of Jesse and Eliza Fee.   Mrs. Reed was born in Lincoln County in 1833, and by her union with Mr. Reed became the mother of eight children: Eliza A., John M., Sarah E., J. L., S. W., M. A., Martha and H. C.   After marriage our subject lived on the home place for thirteen years, after which he began for himself with but little means.   He is now a well-to-do farmer, owning about 750 acres of fair land.   He is a Democrat, and his first presidential vote was for James K. Polk.   Mrs. Reed is a member of the Methodist Episcopal Church.   Her father, Jesse Fee, was born in North Carolina in 1805.   He was a farmer by occupation, and died very suddenly May 22, 1867, from what was thought to be heart disease.

R. C. RIVES, saddler, of Petersburg, was born in Marshall County March 12, 1838. His father, Green Rives, was of English descent, born in Virginia in 1773, and came to Tennessee in 1830.   He was a schoolmate and personal friend of Winfield Scott, and was married three times.   Our subject is the son of his wife Susan (Woodard) Rives, who was born in Virginia in 1810.   She died in 1850, as did her husband.   Our subject was reared on a farm, and March 12, 1862, married Rebecca J. Gillian, who was born in Alabama April 2, 1839. To them were born twelve children, these five now living: Anna, Mary C., Sarah, Lutha G. and Bertie. After his father's death our subject resided with his brother twelve months, and then learned the saddler's trade. After some time he and his brother B. W. became partners in business, continuing until the war, when he enlisted in Company C, Eighth Tennessee Infantry, but after a short time was discharged on account of ill health. After the war he again opened a shop at Petersburg, where he has since resided, with the exception of four years, when he had a shop at Belfast, and spent one year at Lewisburg. Since December, 1885, he and O. S. Christopher have been partners in business, and keep the largest stock in the county. Mr. Rives is conservative in politics, but of late years has voted the Democratic ticket. He belongs to the Masonic fraternity, and he and wife are members of the Presbyterian Church.

JOHN ROACH, an old and well respected citizen of Lincoln County, and a native of Warren County, Tenn., was born December 28, 1823. His father, James Roach, was a native of Ireland, born in 1788, and followed agricultural pursuits for a livelihood, in connection with all kinds of mechanical work. When about nineteen years of age he left Ireland and came to the United States, landing at Savannah, Ga., where he lived at the time of his marriage, which occurred about 1805. In 1828 he came to Lincoln County, where he died in 1831. He was one of the early settlers of Warren County. The mother of our subject, Elizabeth (Ivy) Roach, was born near Savannah, Ga., in 1789. Her father was of English and her mother of Scotch extraction. She was the mother of fifteen children, ten of whom lived to be grown, and five are living now, viz.: Ellen, Susan J., Martha, William D. and John. Our subject was reared without a father's care or guidance or a mother's tender love and training. After the death of his parents there were five children left, all of whom were bound out. John was bound out till he was twenty-one years of age, and was to receive for his services a horse, saddle and bridle, valued at $125; a suit of clothes, worth $35; and twelve months' schooling. He was married a short time before his time was out, and received his horse and saddle. His wife was Martha D. Parks, daughter of William Parks, his guardian. Mrs. Roach was born in Lincoln County June 13, 1825, and by her marriage became the mother of six children: Benjamin T., William A., Clayborn M., Mary E. (wife of Madison Luna), Othena (wife of William A. E. Pitts), and Martha E. (wife of William R. Cashion). Between the years 1845 and 1856 he became the possessor of 280 acres of land in the Eleventh District, where he remained until July, 1866, when he disposed of his real estate and, October 4, bought 280 acres in the Seventh District, where he now resides. October, 1861, he enlisted in Company C, Thirty-second Regiment Tennessee Infantry, and was elected first lieutenant. He fought in the battle of Fort Donelson, in which action he received a wound in the throat and arm, and was disabled from duty for the remainder of the year. After recovering from the wound he was taken with the fevers, and was never able to return to duty. He has been a life-long Democrat, and his first vote was cast for James K. Polk. In 1852 he was elected magistrate of his district, and for nine years filled that office. He is a Mason, and he and wife are members of the Primitive Baptist Church.

IVISON T. RODES, station agent at Fayetteville, Tenn., for the Fayetteville Branch of the Nashville, Chattanooga & St. Louis Railroad, and the Fayetteville Branch of the Duck River Valley Railroad, is the son of Thomas J. and Mildred Martin (Dickerson) Rodes, born in Virginia in 1807 and 1811, respectively. They came to Tennessee in 1837, and the father died in Coffee County in 1864. After his death Mrs. Rodes married Ira Kinnaughan, and in 1885 she, too, passed away. Our subject was born January 19, 1838, and received an academical education in Coffee and Warren Counties. He resided with his parents until twenty-five years of age. October 16, 1860, he and Emma Miller were united in marriage. Mrs. Rodes is a daughter of Peter Miller, and was born in October, 1838. The following are the names of their children: Thomas M., James E., both railroad contractors; Mary M.; William C., telegraph operator at Fayetteville; Arthur S., who assists his father; Ivison T., Jr., and Henry Ernest. Mr. Rodes' early life was spent in farming, and in the fall of 1863 he enlisted in Company H, Eleventh Tennessee Cavalry, and in 1864 was appointed lieutenant of Company A, Twenty-eighth Regiment, and served until the close of the war. He was at Murfreesboro and in numerous minor engagements, returning home in May, 1865, and soon after began his career on the railroad as conductor, express agent and mail agent on the McMinnville Branch for three years. In October, 1873, he came to Fayetteville, and for two years was conductor on the branch from Decherd to Fayetteville, and was then given his present position. During his long career on and in the service of the road he has ever proved upright, straightforward and courteous. He is a Democrat, a Mason, a member of the K. of H., a Good Templar, and himself and family are members of the Methodist Episcopal Church South. Mr. Rodes lost his wife in 1880, and March 24, 1882, he wedded Florida Lasater, of Manchester, Tenn.

W. M. ROSBOROUGH'S father was born on the Atlantic Ocean in 1777, while his parents were on their way to the United States from Belfast, Ireland. They located in South Carolina, and there our subject's father and mother were married. The father died in 1845, and the mother in 1877. W. M. Rosborough was born in Lincoln County, Tenn., June 13, 1827, and after his father's death, he took care of his mother until her death. His father was a large land owner, and at his mother's death he inherited her dower, and now owns 230 acres of good land. He was married to Harriet Thomas in 1876. She was born in Lincoln County in 1831. Our subject is an excellent neighbor and citizen, and is a conservative Democrat in politics, and, although he served in the Confederate Army, was opposed to the principles of secession. He served in Company C, Eighth Tennessee Infantry. He was wounded four times at Murfreesboro and was compelled to abandon service two years. He then rejoined, and was at Kenesaw Mountain, Peach Tree Creek. Jonesboro. Franklin, Nashville and others. He returned home in 1865. Mr. Rosborough is an Odd Fellow, and he and wife are members of the Presbyterian Church.

J. H. RUSSELL, proprietor of a hotel at Petersburg, is a native of Marshall County, born March 18, 1842, one of ten children of John M. and Ella J. (Radford) Russell. The father was a Georgian by birth, born in 1805, a farmer and extensive tobacco grower. He located in Marshall County, Tenn., in 1835, and there remained until his death in 1862. The mother was born in the same neighborhood as her husband, in 1807, and died in 1866. Our subject attended New Hope Academy and resided under the paternal roof until 1861, when he entered the army, joining Company A, Eighth Tennessee Infantry, and took part in the battles of Murfreesboro, Shiloh, Winchester, Huntsville, and several smaller engagements. He served three years, was wounded seven times, but lost little or no time from active field duties. He returned home in January, 1864, and began farming, and remained in this business about four years. February 11, 1864, he married Mary J. Waters, who was born in Marshall County, in 1845, and bore her husband five children: George H., Fannie E., W. T., Susan B., and Myrtle. About 1868 Mr. Russell removed to Petersburg, and has since kept hotel. He keeps a first-class house and is obliging and hospitable in the treatment of his guests. He is a Democrat and a member of the Masonic fraternity.

ISAAC RUTLEDGE, farmer of the Fifth District, is a native of North Carolina, born in 1819, and a son of Isaac and Ruth (Steelman) Rutledge. The father was a native of North Carolina, and of French descent. He was a farmer by occupation, and died about 1836. Mrs. Rutledge was also born, reared and married in North Carolina, and died in Lincoln County, Tenn., in 1828. Our subject was reared by his father, his mother having died when he was small, and had the advantage of a district school education. In 1842 he married Martha J. Wagoner, and this union resulted in the birth of six children, four of whom are living: Margaret A., wife of James C. Shofner; Daniel H., of Texas; Ruth R., wife of R. B. Logan, and Nanny J., wife of Andrew Edwards, of Rutherford County, Tenn. Mrs. Rutledge died in the latter part of the year 1857, and in 1858 our subject wedded Rebecca A. Buchanan, and by her became the father of eight children, six of whom are living: Orville C.; Lola L., wife of G. G. Osborne, of Bedford

County; Fannie L., wife of Elder T. C. Herndon, one of Kentucky's best divines and instructors; John L., Rosa Lou and Garland M. In 1861 he enlisted in the Confederate Army, Fifth Kentucky Regiment, and was in most of the principal battles. During the battle of Baton Rouge he was shot through the body, and lay on the battle-field twenty-four hours before he received aid. He was then taken prisoner, but not thinking he could recover he was turned over to his friends, and has never entirely recovered from the effects of his wound. He is of Democratic principles, and he and wife are members of the Primitive Baptist Church. In January, 1886, he sold his farm of 305 acres to his son, Orville C., who is now living at home, and who is a promising young man. He received the best educational advantages the Fifth District can afford, and is a Democrat in politics, casting his first vote for Grover Cleveland. He is a member of the Primitive Baptist Church.

D. M. SANDERS is a native of Lincoln County, Tenn., born in 1846, and his early days were spent in attending the district schools and assisting his parents on the farm. After attaining man's estate he was married to Mrs. Martha J. Watson in December. 1865. She was born in Lincoln County in 1842, daughter of James and Betsy Bowles, and their union was blessed with the birth of two children: John B. and Arena. In 1882 Mr. Sanders purchased 316 acres of valuable land, on which are good buildings and a fine orchard. His farm, which he has accumulated by hard labor and good management, is located on Coldwater Creek near Fayetteville. Mr. Sanders is a Democrat, and during the late war served in Capt. George's company—Company G, Twentieth Tennessee Cavalry, a short time during 1864. His parents, M. and Eveline Sanders, were born in Alabama and Tennessee in 1820 and 1824, respectively. They were married in Tennessee, whither the father had moved in his youth. The father was a farmer, and died March 26, 1880. His wife resides with her son Mack.

E. M. SCOTT is a son of John L. Scott, who was born in Lincoln County, Tenn., in 1824, and whose people came from North Carolina at a very early date and located where Nashville now stands. Our subject's grandfather was a Revolutionary soldier, and died in Tennessee when over ninety years of age. Our subject's father died in 1854. The mother was born in Lincoln County in 1822, and is now the wife of Squire Pickle, and resides in the Eleventh District. At the age of sixteen our subject joined the army, serving in Company C, Eighth Tennessee Infantry nine months, and then joined Company K, Fourth Tennessee Cavalry, and participated in many bloody engagements. He was captured near Knoxville, but made his escape the same day. He returned home May 18, 1865. In 1866 he married M. T. Chitwood, daughter of William Chitwood. She was born in Lincoln County in 1849, and six children were born to their union: Ophelia, John L., Clemmie, Willie, Thomas R. and Ella. Mr. Scott has always been a farmer, and is the owner of 181 acres of valuable and well improved land. He and wife are members of the Primitive Baptist Church, and he is a Democrat in politics.

D. C. SHERRELL, citizen and merchant of Dellrose, and a native of Lincoln County, Tenn., is a son of Dr. Joseph L. and Martha Sherrell. The father was born in Lincoln County October 2, 1824, and is now a retired physician, residing in the Sixteenth District. The mother was also born in Lincoln County, Tenn., and died in 1862. Our subject received an excellent education, and January 1, 1880, was united in marriage to Mary E. McCoy, who was born in Giles County, January 1, 1862, and whose parents were M. E. and Elinor McCoy, of Bradshaw, Giles County. To our subject and wife was born one child: Horace E. Previous to his marriage D. C. Sherrell entered the employ of Hill, Miller & Co., merchants of Pulaski, Giles County, as salesman, and afterward entered into partnership with W. H. Stone, and began merchandising at Dellrose, where he has since continued. From 1873 to 1876 he was alone in the business, but in 1881 W. E. McCoy bought an interest in the business, and the firm is known as D. C. Sherrell & Co. He and his brother, B. A., are also in the drug business, and are doing a good business for a country town. Mr. Sherrell has also a harness shop at the same place. Mr. Sherrell is a man much respected by all his acquaintances, and is an excellent citizen and an obliging neighbor. He is a Democrat, and he and wife are members of the Methodist Episcopal Church South. Dellrose can boast of a telephone. The line runs from Pulaski to their village, and the only one at the present time in Lincoln County.

JAMES C. SHOFNER, farmer, and a son of Jephtha H. and Nancy (Logan) Shofner, was born June 5, 1845, and is one of a family of eleven children, seven of whom are living. The father of our subject was born in Lincoln County in 1811 and was of Dutch extraction. He was a farmer and died March 11, 1886. The mother of our subject was born in Lincoln County, Tenn., in 1816 and is now living on the old homestead. Our subject received his education in the Mulberry and Greenwood school, and during the late war he enlisted in Gen. Forrest's escort under Capt. Boone, when he was but sixteen years old, and was in many of the principal battles. He was captured while at home and paroled. In 1865 he wedded Mary A. Rutledge (daughter of Isaac and Jane Rutledge) and the fruits of this union were nine children, seven of whom are living: Lena L., Mattie J., Walter N., Pearl, Mary, Alice R. and Reuben T. Soon after marriage Mr. Shofner purchased 150 acres of land of his father near Booneville, where he still resides. In 1883 he connected himself with R. A. Musgrove in the mercantile business at Booneville, and is succeeding in an admirable manner. He is a Democrat in politics, and he and Mrs. Shofner are worthy members of the Baptist Church.

REV. ARCHIBALD S. SLOAN, of the Twentieth District, and son of James and Jane (Thompson) Sloan, was born in Newbury, S. C., December 8, 1821. He was one of a family of eight children, only three of whom are living, viz.: Rev. H. T., pastor of Cedar Springs and Long Cane, S. C., which position he has filled for thirty-eight years; Mrs. Jane Chalmers, of Newbury, S. C.; and our subject. The father of our subject was born in South Carolina in 1796, and was of Irish extraction. He was a farmer by occupation, and was married in 1819. At the time of his death, which occurred in 1869, he was the owner of about 800 acres of good land. Mrs. Sloan was a native of South Carolina, born in 1803, and died in 1872. Our subject received the rudiments of his education in the schools of the neighborhood, but subsequently entered Erskine College, South Carolina, where he took a regular course, graduating in 1844. In 1846 he was licensed to enter the ministerial profession under the Associate Reformed Presbyterian Church and soon after emigrated to Lincoln Connty, and after moving around for some time began his ministerial career at Prosperity, where he remained as pastor for twenty-seven years. March 14, 1848, he wedded Elizabeth J. Stewart, a native of Lincoln County, born September 20, 1829, and to this union were born seven children, six of whom are living, viz.: Nora J. (wife of H. T. Sloan), Mary F. (wife of John Lindsey), James T., Olivia C. (wife of E. H. Parkinson), Thomas W. and Ebbie C. Mr. Sloan has a fine farm in a good state of cultivation. While yet preaching at Prosperity his charge increased till he was compelled to abandon his practice at that place, since which time he has been pastor at Bethel and New Hope; virtually he has preached the gospel to the same people for forty years, being among the earliest Christian workers. In 1886 his son, Thomas W., graduated at Erskine College, South Carolina, the same place from where his father graduated forty-two years previous.

J. H. SMITH, farmer, was born in Maury County, Tenn., in 1834, and received his early education at the schools near his home. He afterward attended New Hope Academy, Marshall County, Tenn., and Erskine College, at Due West, S. C. Here he graduated August 8, 1860. In September, 1863, he united his fortunes with those of Nancy M. Downing, a native of Marshall County, born October 23, 1834, and a daughter of John and Eliza Downing. This marriage resulted in our subject becoming the father of four children, three of whom are living: John F., Anna E. B., Eliza M. (deceased), and Elmer R. After graduating, Mr. Smith entered the teacher's profession, and taught until hostilities broke out between the North and South. At the close of the war he resumed teaching and his wife also engaged in that occupation, which they continued for eleven years. In 1871 Mr. Smith purchased eighty-nine acres of land in the Thirteenth District, where he located, and where he has since resided. He now owns 187 acres of land in a good state of cultivation. Mr. Smith has given his children good educational advantages, and has given his support to all laudable public enterprises, and especially to educational and religious institutions. In 1876 he was elected to the office of magistrate and held this position for six years. He is independent in political belief and was much opposed to the principles of secession. He is a Mason, a K. of H., and he and wife are members of the Methodist Episcopal Church. Mrs. Smith attended school for some time at Columbia Tenn., and afterward assisted in teaching at Waco College, at Waco, Texas. Here she carried on her studies and graduated from that institution in May, 1860. Mr. Smith is a son of Franklin and Elizabeth Smith. The father was of French-Welsh descent, and was born in 1802. He died November 2, 1863. The mother was a native of South Carolina, born in 1807, and died in July, 1859.

W. R. SMITH, a prominent citizen of the Eighth District, and also a farmer and butcher, of Fayetteville, was born in Lincoln County July 20, 1838. He was one of three children born to John N. and Nancy B. Smith. The father was born in Georgia in 1816, and was of German lineage. He died August 19, 1859. The mother was born in North Carolina in 1806, and now resides with her son, W. R. Our subject received the rudiments of his education in the schools near home, and subsequently completed his education at the Sulphur Springs Institute. In 1859 he married Martha E. Koonce, a native of Lincoln County, born March 1, 1843, and the daughter of Needham and Burdotta Koonce. Mr. Koonce was a well known and much respected citizen of Lincoln County. He was a brick-mason and contractor, and helped lay the foundation of the State penitentiary, at Nashville, being a young man at the time. To Mr. and Mrs. Smith were born eight children: Mary E. (wife of John Monday), Lizzie B. (wife of O. P. Gray), Anna (wife of Charles McCloin), Robert A.; Willie R., Burrell, Roscoe and Nannie B. In 1866 he purchased eighty acres of land in the Eighth District of Lincoln County, where he soon located and has since resided. He now owns 275 acres in the Eighth District and 280 in the Twenty-first District. Besides conducting the farm, he and his cousin, J. H. Smith, have a meat market in Fayetteville, and also have the stock-yard at that place. Mr. Smith has on his place a fish-pond, and has for a number of years past been engaged in raising fish, mostly of the carp species. Mr. Smith has been extensively engaged in handling cattle, and for some time past has been making a study of their diseases. Mr. Smith has given his children the advantage of a good English education, and gives his support to all laudable public enterprises, especially educational institutions. He is conservative in politics, and is considered one of the county's best citizens. Mrs. Smith is a member of the the Methodist Episcopal Church.

REV. A. P. SMITH, a farmer and minister, residing near Petersburg, was born at New Philadelphia, Ohio, December 27, 1855, son of John T. and Mary A. (Brown) Smith. The father was born in Virginia, October 26, 1827, and moved to Ohio with his father, who had been a large slave-holder in Virginia. Not believing in slavery, however, he sold his negroes and moved to Ohio, where he followed merchandising, and died in 1872. A. P.'s mother was born at New Philadelphia. Her maternal grandparents were Stephens by name, and belonged to the nobility of England. On their voyage to America their daughter formed the acquaintance of a gentleman by the name of Brown, and married him, although her parents were strongly opposed to the union. A. P. Smith's mother was the result of this union. She died in 1874. Our subject graduated from the New Philadelphia High School in 1875, and completed his education in the Vanderbilt University at Nashville. December 22, 1882, he married Carrie, daughter of D. R. and Jane (Greer) Smith. The father was born in Virginia in 1814, moved to Lincoln County, Tenn., in 1838, and was married when about twenty-seven years of age. He was a merchant and farmer, and died July 4, 1865. The mother was born in 1825, and died June 1, 1873. Their five children still retain an interest in the home farm. J. B. resides in St. Louis, Mo., and J. G., Virginia, Carrie and B. B. reside at or near the old home. In 1878 A. P. Smith entered the Tennessee Conference as a Methodist Episcopal minister, and in 1880 entered the editorial profession, and edited the *Upper Cumberland*, a Democratic paper, but four years later disposed of it, and engaged in agriculture. He is a local minister, and delivers many lectures in favor of temperance. His brother, John, lives in Janesville, Iowa, and his sister, Ola (Mrs. W. H. Morgan), is clerk of the State Senate, and Alice is the wife of Clark Cook, of Lebanon.

RICHARD SMITH, merchant and farmer of the Twenty-fifth District, was born in Lincoln County, in 1827, and is one of nine children born to Richard and Elizabeth (Arwood) Smith. The father was born in North Carolina about 1779, received a very meager education, and was obliged to make his way in life without the benefit of that blessing. When twenty-one years of age he was married, and followed the occupation of a farmer till his career ended in 1852. The mother was born in North Carolina about 1784, and died in 1850. Our subject remained with his parents until he was twenty years of age, and received his education in the common schools. February 25, 1847, he was united in marriage to Eliza Faulkner, a daughter of William and Ellen Faulkner. Soon after his marriage our subject began farming as a tenant, and this continued for two years. He then entered the mercantile business at what is now Smithland, and is still engaged in that occupation. In 1862 he enlisted in Company A, Forty-fourth Tennessee, and entered the Army of the Cumberland as a drummer, where he remained about seven months, after which he returned home, and resumed his business. Although having very little of this world's goods to start with, he is now in very comfortable circumstances, and is the owner of about 550 acres of good land. He is a Democrat in politics, and a member of the Masonic fraternity, also of the I. O. O. F. He and Mrs. Smith are members of the Methodist Episcopal Church South.

J. FRANKLIN SMITH may be mentioned as a prosperous farmer of Lincoln County, Tenn. He was born in 1835, and is one of ten children of Lemuel and De Bolious Smith, born in 1790 and 1808, and died in 1855 and 1863, respectively. At the age of seventeen Franklin entered a newspaper office at Athens, and worked on the *Herald* about eight years. In 1863 he entered the army, joining Wharton's brigade and Malone's battalion, but remained only a short time, when he returned home. Since the war he has followed tilling the soil, and owns 371 acres of very desirable land, well improved. In December, 1879, he began merchandising near home, keeping a general line of goods, and has a large patronage and is doing well. He is a Democrat, and, although he was in the war a short time, he was opposed to secession. He belongs to the I. O. O. F.

W. J. STEGALL, saw-mill contractor and farmer, of Fayetteville, Tenn., was born in Rutherford County, in 1823, son of Jesse and Elizabeth (Webb) Stegall, born in Mecklenburgh County, Va., in 1794 and 1801, respectively. The father, in 1818, determined to seek his fortune in the far West, and accordingly located in Rutherford County, Tenn., where he bought property, and lived until 1832, and the following ten years resided in Bedford County. From 1842 to 1860 he was a resident of Marshall County. In 1866 he went to Waco, Tex., where he died in 1867. The mother died in 1842. Mr. Stegall was twice married, and the father of sixteen children, ten by his first wife and six by his second. Our subject secured a limited education in the old-fashioned log schoolhouse of early days. February 2, 1847, he wedded Rebecca McCleary, who died in 1848. In 1850 Melvina (Temple) Wilhoit became his second wife. She was born in 1832, in Shelbyville, Tenn., and has borne three children, two of whom are living: Ewing B. and William W., the former a carpenter of Fayetteville, and the latter a resident of Florida. Mr. Stegall has been a resident of Fayetteville since 1856, with the exception of four years during the war. He joined Col. Hatton's regiment in 1861, and later was given a position in the quartermaster's department. February 2, 1865, he wedded Mrs. Florence M. (Batie) Foster, who was born in Georgia in 1848. For a time Mr. Stegall worked, and had an interest in a carriage-shop, but soon disposed of his interest and engaged in contracting and building and speculating in stock. He owns 220 acres of land, one business house and twenty-two houses and lots in Fayetteville. He is a Democrat, and a member of the Masonic fraternity. He and wife are members of the Methodist Episcopal Church South.

W. B. STEVENSON was born January 1, 1856, of Irish descent, son of C. L. and

Louisa Stevenson, who were born in Giles County, Tenn., in 1832 and 1834, respectively. The father has been twice married, our subject being the only issue of his first marriage. The mother died February 1, 1856. W. B. Stevenson completed his education at Bethany High School, and has since been a successful agriculturist. In 1875 he married Nelia, daughter of David S. and Elizabeth Patterson. Mrs. Stevenson was born in June, 1856, and has borne three children: Jerrena R., Zana M. (deceased) and Annie Hencil. Mr. Stevenson owns a large and well cultivated farm, and is a man of good business qualifications. He raises considerable stock, his farm being adapted to grazing as well as raising cereals, and he takes much interest in establishing and supporting educational and religious institutions. He is a Democrat, and he and wife are members of the Methodist Episcopal Church South. For the last four years he has been experimenting in growing hedge fences, and has been very successful, and now has hedge on his place, three years old, which is sufficiently large to confine stock.

DR. WILLIAM STEWART, physician and surgeon, residing near Molino, Tenn., was born in Newberry, S. C., February 9, 1809. His parents, John and Elizabeth (Drennan) Stewart, were born in the Emerald Isle. They came to the United States, and the father participated in the Revolutionary war, serving the entire time. He was a farmer and died in 1826. In 1827 the mother came to Tennessee with her children, and here she died in 1844. They were the parents of seventeen children. Our subject was educated in his native State, and came to Tennessee when nineteen years of age. He began studying medicine at the age of twenty-three, and October 12, 1831, married Nancy McClain, who was born in Davidson County, Tenn., in 1811. Of their ten children nine are living: John P., James L., J. Milton, Robert A., Henry M., Elizabeth A. (Mrs. A. J. Davis), Joseph B., Mary J. (widow of J. W. Dandridge), and Oliver Sidney. Our subject farmed for some time in Bedford County after his marriage, and then began practicing medicine, soon acquiring a lucrative business. In 1848 he settled in Lincoln County on the old home place. In 1860, not being satisfied with his medical knowledge, he went to Macon, Ga., and took a course of lectures in the Reform Medical College, and graduated in the same year. August 29, 1869, Dr. Stewart lost his wife, and September 27 of the following year he married Fannie Sheddan, who was born in Blount County in 1836. Dr. Stewart has been exceptionally fortunate in the practice of his profession, and is considered a skillful physician and surgeon. He owns 205 acres of land, and in politics still holds to the old Whig principles. In 1865 he represented Lincoln County in the State Senate. Dr. Stewart is a strong advocate for temperance and has done much to eradicate the evil of intemperance in communities where he has resided. Not one of his large family of children has ever used liquor in any form, and the same may be said of them in regard to tobacco, tea and coffee. The Doctor and his wife have been members of the United Presbyterian Church for many years.

J. D. STONE, a prominent citizen of the Seventh District, was born in Lincoln County, Tenn., December 25, 1839, one of six children born to the marriage of L. L. Stone and E. P. Drake, who were born in Bedford County, Va., and Madison County, Ala., respectively. The father's birth occurred in 1801. He came to Tennessee, with his parents, when about sixteen years of age. He was a farmer and owned upward of 1,000 acres of land. He died in 1880. The mother departed this life in 1872. Our subject received his rudimentary education in the common schools of Lincoln County, and afterward attended Nashville University. In 1861 he wedded S. A., daughter of D. B., and Julia Shull, and their union resulted in the birth of five children: Julia (Mrs. J. A. Gowell), Eva, B. B., E. E. and Rose. Our subject has always resided on the old homestead. After the death of his father he fell heir to a portion of the family estate, and he now owns 615 acres of very desirable land, well improved. He has given his children good educational advantages, and has done much to aid educational and religious institutions. He is conservative in politics, and his wife is a member of the Cumberland Presbyterian Church. In 1861 he enlisted in Company B, Forty-fourth Tennessee Infantry, and was at Shiloh, Chickamauga, Perryville, Murfreesboro and many minor engagements. He

was wounded at Shiloh and gave up active duties for about three months.  He was captured at Murfreesboro, and held a prisoner at Camp Douglas, Chicago, for about four
months.  He returned home in May, 1865.

DR. B. S. STONE, a physician of Dellrose, was born in Giles County, Tenn., June 15,
1849, and was a son of Thomas J. Stone, and a grandson of Thomas C. Stone, and a great-
grandson of Joshua Stone.  Thomas J., the father of our subject, was born August 7,
1806, and went to Giles County, with his parents, in 1812, locating at Pulaski.  He was
married in 1839, and was a farmer by occupation.  His death occurred April 17, 1874.
The Doctor's mother was born in Giles County in 1816, and died in 1849.  Our subject received a good literary education at Bethany and Elkton, Giles County.  He then entered
the office of Dr. A. L. Glaze, a very prominent citizen and a brother-in-law of Mr. Stone,
where he remained about twenty months.  He then entered the medical department of the
Vanderbilt University, where he graduated in 1875.  Previous to this, December 24, 1874,
he married Annie Sherrell, a native of Lincoln County, born December, 1856, and by this
union they became the parents of four children: Emmet R., Mary V., Joseph S. and Andrew A.  After graduating Dr. Stone located in the Sixteenth District. and began the
practice of medicine,  In 1881, for the purpose of getting a more central location to his
practice and a pleasant place, he removed to Dellrose, and has recently built a fine residence on an excellent farm of 300 acres.  He has a large practice, and is entirely devoted
to his professional duties.  He has had flattering success in all treatments of patients, and
is a man well;known and much esteemed throughout the county.  He is independent in
political belief, and he and wife are members of the Methodist Episcopal Church.

GEORGE STUART, farmer, whose birth occurred in North Carolina in March, 1814,
is a son of Thomas and Sarah Stuart.  The father of our subject was a descendant of
Irish ancestors, and was born in North Carolina.  He immigrated to West Virginia, and remained there until his death.  The mother was also born in North Carolina, and died in
Moore County, Tenn.  Our subject was reared on the farm, and received a rather limited
education in the schools of those early days.  He came to Tennessee, with his widowed
mother, when about seventeen years of age, and in 1831 married Harriet Woodard, a native of North Carolina, born in 1816, and the daughter of William and Sarah Woodard.
To Mr. and Mrs. Stuart were born these children: Sarah (wife of Thomas Lockey), Eliza
(wife of William Tucker), Thomas, Green, Mary (widow of D. M. Summers), Robert,
Martha (wife of Joseph Clark). and Docia (wife of Dr. Walter McMullen, of Texas).  Soon
after marriage our subject moved to Millville, and was engaged in the milling business
for seven years.  In 1849 he bought 100 acres in the Thirteenth District, where he located
and where he has since resided.  He has since bought more land, and now owns 300 acres
of good land.  Mr. Stuart has reared a large family, and helped them to a good start in
life.  He began for himself with no means, but by energy and good business qualifications
has amassed a considerable amount of property.  Mr. Stuart is a Democrat in politics,
and during the late civil war had two sons in the army.  Thomas entered in the first
company that was organized, and served four years.  He was captured, and taken to Fort
Delaware, but made a daring escape by swimming the bay.  Mr. Stuart and wife are
members of the Methodist Episcopal Church, and are noted for being good citizens and
kind neighbors.

HON. L. D. SUGG, an old and respected farmer, was born in Robertson County,
Tenn., March 3, 1826, and is a son of Cullen E. and Sidney (Conrad) Sugg.  The father
was born in Robertson County, Tenn., in 1798.  He was of Scotch descent and was married about 1822, and was a blacksmith and farmer by occupation.  He came to Lincoln
County about 1826.  The mother was born in Springfield Tenn., in May, 1802, and died
in February, 1886.  His people first went to Davidson County at a very early date
and built block-houses to protect themselves from the Indians.  The father died in 1849.
Our subject in youth received the rudiments of his education in the schools near
home, and afterward completed his education in the Viny Grove Institution, under Parson
Bryson and Prof. John A. Steward.  In 1856 he married Margaret Holbert, daughter of

Pleasant and Nancy Holbert. Mrs. Sugg was born in Lincoln County July 9, 1836, and her marriage resulted in the birth of seven children: Douglas, Ethel (wife of E. Wilson, Naoma, Eula (wife of Edgar Thurston, of Alabama), Sidney, Nancy and William. Mr. Sugg now owns 600 acres of good land, all well improved. He is a man well known through out the county, and is much esteemed for his many good qualities. In 1878 he was chosen to represent the people in the House of Representatives, and that position he filled to the satisfaction of his constituents and in a creditable manner to himself. He is a Democrat and a member of the Masonic fraternity.

H. H. SUGG, citizen and farmer, was born on the farm where he now lives in the Thirteenth District February, 20, 1831, and is a son of Cullen and Sidney (Conrad) Sugg. Our subject received the rudiments of his education in the schools near his home, and finished at Fayetteville, and Forest Hill, Giles County. In November, 1855, he wedded Sallie Bruce, a native of Lincoln County. She died the same year they were married, and May, 1858, our subject took for his second wife Mrs. Elvira, daughter of Cornelius and Mrs. Allen. The result of this union was an interesting family of two children: Edward and Kate E. (wife of J. K. Whitaker). After his marriage he located on the old home-place, and remained there until 1859, when he bought 320 acres near by, and moved to that: At the end of ten years, he exchanged with his brother T. J. for the old home place, and now owns 340 acres of valuable land. In 1865, he wedded Miss L. Yowell, a native of Petersburg, Tenn., born in 1837, and to this union were born four children: Henry, Sabra, Susie and William. Mr. Sugg has been quite successful in business, and has given his children good educational advantages. He is a Democrat in politics, and he and wife are members of the Christian Church. In 1862 he enlisted in Capt. Freeman's Company of Artillery, and was in the battle of Chickamauga and a great many artillery engagements. He was captured in 1863, but was soon afterward exchanged.

W. C. SUGG is one of seven children born to the marriage of Cullen E. and Sidney Sugg, and was reared at home, receiving his education in the schools near his home and Viney Grove Academy. In 1858 he married Mary S., daughter of Dr. John and Josephine Wood. She was born in Lincoln County in September, 1841, and bore her husband eight children: J. D. (merchant), Jennie (wife of S. A. Bingsley), Mary A. (Mrs. J. C. Whitaker), W. C., Jr., Vic, Ida W., Lemuel H. and Thomas F. Our subject and his brother, L. D., farmed together about ten years when he purchased 500 acres of land, on which he located and which he has increased to 820 acres. His farm is well improved with good barns and fine orchards. Mr. Sugg has trafficked a great deal in both land and stock, and is a shrewd financier. Besides his home farm he owns 400 acres elsewhere. Most of his children have had the advantage of a collegiate education and he is a man of broad views and keen intellect. He is a bitter antagonist to all monopolies and everything that tends to oppress the laboring man. He is conservative, voting always as his conscience dictates.

NEWTON C. SULLIVAN, farmer and magistrate of the Twelfth District, was born in Lincoln County, Tenn., in 1823, and is the son of Cornelius and Mary A. (Gunter) Sullivan. The father was a native of Cheatham County, N. C., born in 1793, and followed agricultural pursuits as a livelihood. He was married in 1812, and in 1818 came to Lincoln County, Tenn., locating in the Fifth District, but afterward moved to the Twelfth District, where he remained until his career ended in 1846. He was of Irish extraction. The mother was born in 1794, in Cheatham County, N. C., and since the death of her husband she has lived on the old place, but is now living with her children. She is yet living, and is ninety-two year sold. About four years ago she fell and injured her hip, which renders her helpless in regard to walking, but her mind is perfectly clear and active. She is the oldest lady in the county. Our subject was one of eleven children, seven of whom are living. He was reared at home, and received a fair education in the schools of the county. At the age of nineteen he left home, and commenced working as a day-laborer on the farm. In 1844 he went to Mississippi and became an overseer on a plantation, where he remained for six years. He then returned to his birthplace, and in March,

1851, he married Margaret Mauldin, daughter of Harris Mauldin. Mrs. Sullivan was born in Marshall County in 1836, and by her union to Mr. Sullivan became the mother of eleven children: Harris H., Mary E. (wife of James A. Brisco), George W. J., Susan D., Newton C., Julia F. (wife of James Barns), Alva H., Sarah M., Octavia A., Cornelius B. and Willie B. Our subject enlisted in the Confederate service in 1861, in Company E, Forty-first Regiment, Tennessee Infantry, under Col. Bob Farqueharson, and fought in the battles of Murfreesboro, Chickamauga, Knoxville and numerous severe skirmishes. After the fight at Fort Donelson the Forty-fourth Regiment, followed Gen. Sidney Johnston to Corinth, Miss., and joined under Col. John S. Fulton, where he remained until the latter part of the year 1863. In 1865 our subject located on 290 acres in the Twelfth District where he has since resided. He now owns 415 acres. In politics he has been a life-long Democrat, casting his first vote for Lewis Cass. He is a Mason, and Mrs. Sullivan is a member of the Methodist Episcopal Church South. In 1874 Mr. Sullivan was elected magistrate to fill a vacancy, and for the past ten years has adjusted his constituents difficulties, with impartial fairness, and there has never been an appeal taken from his decisions. The Sullivan family are noted for longevity. Susan, our subject's great aunt, lived to be one hundred and seven years old. Nancy, her sister was ninety, and Jerry, their brother, was also ninety.

CAPT. W. A. SUMMERS was born in Limestone County, Ala., February 20, 1838, and received his rudimentary education in the common schools, and afterward attended Oak Hill Institute, and graduated in 1870. While a student he conducted some of the classes in the college. June 9, 1870, he married Annie, daughter of J. L. and C. L. Walker. Mrs. Summers was born in Giles County, Tenn., September 14, 1848, and was educated at Bethany Institute and Oak Hill College, and was a teacher for some time. She has borne three children: Tully A., Willie H. and Laura K. Mr. Summers taught school eight years after his marriage, and was very successful in that calling. In 1878 he was compelled to give up teaching, owing to ill health. He began farming, and now owns 300 acres of very desirable land. He is a Democrat in politics, and in 1861 enlisted in Company E, Thirty second Tennessee Infantry, and upon the reorganization of the army he was promoted to the rank of captain. He participated in the battles of Fort Donelson, Chickamauga and Missionary Ridge, and received a severe wound. After his recovery he was at Resaca, Kennesaw Mountain and many other engagements. and was a brave soldier, rendering valuable service to the Confederacy. He was a prisoner for some seven months, and returned home in June, 1865.

JAMES H. TAYLOR, farmer and prominent citizen of the Twenty-fifth District, and a son of Young and Sarah C. (Poston) Taylor, was born in Lincoln County April 11, 1822, and is one of a family of nine children, only two of whom are living. The father of our subject was born in 1789, and had no advantages for acquiring an education. He was married when about twenty-two, and was employed for many years as an overseer of slaves. About 1818 he immigrated to Lincoln County, and farmed as a tenant for several years. He then purchased 240 acres in the Fourth District, where he remained until his wife's death in 1866. His death occurred about 1874. Our subject received a practical education in the neighboring schools, and February 15, 1844, was married to Martha Simmons, by whom he had six children, four of whom are living: Jarred S., Sarah (wife of Thomas B. George), Franklin P. and William. After marriage our subject farmed for several years as a tenant, but imitating the example of his father, and inheriting his strong will and determined character, was so far successful in his labors as to soon be able to procure a home of his own. In 1849 he purchased one-half interest in 400 acres of land at Smithland, on which he located and continues to reside. He has since increased his original tract to over 1,000 acres, but has donated considerable to his children, and now has about 550 acres of fine land. Mrs. Taylor died April 17, 1881, and November 11, 1884, Mr. Taylor married Mrs. Rettie Reagor, who was born in Lincoln County May 22, 1846. Our subject is a Democrat in politics, and cast his first vote for James K. Polk. Mrs. Taylor is a member of the Christian Church.

JARRED S. TAYLOR, farmer, and a son of James H. and Martha (Simmons) Taylor, was born in Lincoln County in 1847, and is one of a family of six children, four of whom are living. He received a liberal education in the common schools, and taught during the years 1869 and 1870. He afterward engaged in farming, and in March, 1871, united his fortunes with those of Mollie McLaughlin, daughter of William H. and Margaret K. McLaughlin. The result of our subject's marriage was the birth of eight children: Bernice, Beulah, William H., James M., Guy F., Andrew E., Maggie E. and Horace. Mr. Taylor began farming at first as a tenant, but in 1874 purchased land in Smith land and began clerking in a mercantile establishment at that place. In 1883 he, in company with his brother, entered the mercantile business on their own responsibility in the same place. In 1884 he disconnected himself with the firm, and removed to where he now resides, one mile north of the village, on a farm of 140 acres. Mrs. Taylor was born in Lincoln County in 1842, and she, as well as her husband, are members of the Christian Church. Mr. Taylor is a Democrat, and cast his first vote for Horatio Seymour. He is also a member of the Masonic fraternity.

YOUNG A. TAYLOR is a son of Edmund and Jane (Poston) Taylor, and was born in Lincoln County, Tenn., in 1826. His early schooling did not exceed four months. When the war broke out between the North and South he enlisted in Company A, Forty-fourth Tennessee Infantry, and was in the battles of Murfreesboro, Chickamauga, and Petersburg. He was wounded at Horse Shoe Bend, and was obliged to give up further service. He resumed farming on his farm of 126 acres, which he had purchased before the war, and which he has since increased to 308 acres. When twenty-three years old he was married to Elizabeth Styles, who died in 1859, leaving four children: Mary A., Sarah, Francis, and James. In March, 1861, Mr. Taylor wedded Martha McClure, by whom he had ten children, nine now living: Temple C., Young A., William F., Zylphia E., John H., Ida B., Cora F., Ardella, and Andy W. Our subject's parents were born in Virginia and North Carolina, respectively, and were married in the latter State. The father was a farmer, and died a few years previous to the war. The mother died in 1874.

TEMPLE C. TAYLOR, farmer, and a son of Edmond and Jane D. (Poston) Taylor, was born in Lincoln County February 4, 1825, and is one of ten children, six of whom are living. The father was born in Virginia and married in North Carolina. He was a farmer by occupation and owned 204 acres of land. His career ended a few years previous to the civil war. Mrs. Taylor died about 1874. Our subject was reared at home and received no education worth speaking about, having attended school only about six weeks in his life. During the war he enlisted in Company A, Forty-fourth Tennessee Infantry, under Capt. Styles, and was engaged in many of the principal battles. He then returned home after four years of honorable service. He had purchased a small farm previous to the war, and after his return sold it and purchased 265 acres where he is now living. October 9, 1878, he married Mrs. Clemmenza L. McClellen, daughter of Martin and Nancy N. Wisener. Mr. Taylor is a Democrat, and he and wife are members of the Cumberland Presbyterian Church. Previous to entering the army our subject made a pair of shoes which he wore during the entire service. Mrs. Wisener was born July 26, 1812, and is now living with her daughter, Mrs. Taylor. Mr. Wisener was born March 18, 1786, and died when Mrs. Taylor was quite small.

THOMAS TAYLOR, son of James and grandson of Edmund Taylor, was born in Lincoln County, Tenn., in 1824. His father and grandfather were Virginians. The former married Jensie Shelton in Virginia, and became the father of eleven children, four now living. He has always made farming his occupation, and at an early day came to Tennessee and settled among the canebrakes, where he afterward became the owner of 400 acres of land. He died in 1844, after a well-spent life. The mother died in 1852. Thomas received very meager educational advantages. November 15, 1853, he married Mary, daughter of Hillery H. and Dovey Hill, and nine children are the results of their union: James H., Young A., Elizabeth J., John F., Robert J., Jennie L. and Susan F. Mr. Taylor farmed his father's place until both parents' deaths, and in 1861 purchased sixty-nine acres of land, which, by the aid of his wife and his own energy and economy, he has increased to 800 acres. During the late war he served gallantly in Company B, Forty-fourth Tennessee Regiment, C. S. A. He has been a life long Democrat.

EDWARD TAYLOR, farmer, was born October, 1821, in Lincoln County, and is one of a family of seven children born to William and Priscilla (Alexander) Taylor. The father was born in Virginia in 1790 and received his education in the neighboring schools. He was a mechanic and farmer by occupation and immigrated to Tennessee, with his parents, when but a small boy. He was married about 1819, and in 1842 purchased 150 acres where Edward now resides. He died in 1858, and Mrs. Taylor several years previous. Our subject received a fair education, and after reaching his majority began farming his father's place. December, 1849, he was married to Eliza Forester, by whom he had one child: N. Alexander, who is now at home. He is a young man of exemplary habits, industrious and honest. After marriage our subject continued to farm for his father for several years, and at last purchased his father's fine tract, which now consists of 160 acres. December, 1883, Mr. Taylor had the misfortune to lose his wife. Mr. Taylor is a Democrat in politics and is strenuously opposed to monopolies and is an ardent friend to all laboring men.

JOHN A. TAYLOR, merchant and farmer, and a son of John A. and Elizabeth (Stubblefield) Taylor, was born in Lincoln County in 1849. The father was also a native of Lincoln County, born about 1810. He was married about 1828, and became the father of eleven children seven of whom are living. He was a tiller of the soil, and at the time of his death which occurred April, 1850, owned about 225 acres of good land. The mother was born in Lincoln County about the same time as her husband, and died March, 1873. Our subject was reared by a mother's tender care, his father having died when he was but an infant. He received his education in the district schools, and December 8, 1870, was married to Mary E. Reynolds, daughter of John and Malinda Reynolds, by whom he had seven children, four of whom are living, viz.: Ella, Alda O., John A. and C. Wilson. At the time of his marriage our subject was engaged in the grocery business at Kelso, where he continues to reside. In 1872 he purchased a stock of general merchandise, and is now carrying a stock to the value of about $800. He now owns real estate in the village, besides a valuable farm of 150 acres in the Twenty-third District. Mr. Taylor is at present depot agent at Kelso. He is a member of the I. O. O. F. and of the K. of H., and he and Mrs. Taylor are members of the Cumberland Presbyterian Church. Mrs. Taylor was born in Franklin County, in 1846, and her parents were also natives of the same county.

SAMUEL H. TAYLOR is a son of Henry and Catherine M. (Sloan) Taylor, and was born in the district where he now resides, in 1834. His grandfather, Henry Taylor, Sr., was a South Carolinian, and in 1806, located in Lincoln County, Tenn., and was one of the first white men to assist in forming a white settlement within its borders. His son, Henry Taylor, settled on the old homestead after his marriage, and there passed the remainder of his days. He died in 1855. The mother was born in South Carolina, in 1807, and since her husband's death has made her home with her children. Samuel H. is her third child. He was educated in the neighboring schools, and attended one session at Viny Grove Academy. October 10, 1854, he married Miss L. Ormand, daughter of James and Mary (Ray) Ormand. Mrs. Taylor was born in Franklin County, Ala., in 1831, and became the mother of nine children, five of whom are living: Mary Emma C. (Mrs. Samuel H. McDill), Ormand B., Lorena A., Albert P. and Oscar S. Mr. Taylor lived twelve years on the old homestead after his marriage, and in 1867, purchased eighty acres of land in the Twelfth District, where he has since made his home. In 1884 he purchased a portable saw-mill which he operates in connection with his farming. It has a capacity of 6,000 feet per day. Attached to this is a mill for grinding corn, both for rough feed and table use. Mr. Taylor is a Republican, but cast his first Presidential vote for James Buchanan. In 1864 he was elected magistrate, and in 1868 was chosen tax collector of Lincoln County. He has been an elder in the United Presbyterian Church for the past twenty-six years. His wife died August 30, 1885, and since then his daughter Lorena has been keeping house for him.

H. D. A. THOMAS first saw the light of day in Lincoln County, Tenn., January 7, 1824, being one of twelve children. William Thomas was of English birth, born in Kentucky, about 1789 and was a resident of Lincoln County, Tenn., at the time of his death, October 1, 1872. He was a teacher by profession, and served in the war of 1812, and was married, about 1814, to Rebecca Lyon, who was born in North Carolina in 1794, and died in 1868. The subject of this memoir was reared at home and educated in the common schools, and after attaining his majority began carving out his own fortune, but continued to reside with his parents until thirty-four years of age. After his marriage to Lyntha Millard, in 1858, he purchased his present farm of 250 acres. His wife was born September 3, 1829, daughter of William and Mary (Wade) Millard, and has borne the following children: Mary J. (Mrs. Thomas Bryant), Rebecca ( Mrs. R. L. Moore), Elizabeth, Cora E. and Marcus. Our subject has given his children good educational advantages, and is considered one of the honorable and public-spirited men of the county. He is a Democrat, and was opposed to secession during the late war, although he assisted in the Confederate Army. He is a Mason and K. of H., and he and wife are members of the Presbyterian Church. They have in their possession a Bible that was printed in 1655, that is supposed to have been printed in England and descended through her father and grandfather to Mrs. Thomas.

E. T. THOMAS was born in Lincoln County March 1, 1819, son of William and Rebecca (Lyon) Thomas. (See sketch of H. D. A. Thomas for parents' biography.) He attended the country schools near his home in youth, and for two years after his marriage resided on the old home place. In 1843 he married Jane Moore, daughter of John and Esther (Harkins) Moore. She was born in 1823 and died in 1883, having borne eleven children, seven of whom are living: Esther (Mrs. H. C. McKinzie), Albert, Rebecca (Mrs. J. S. Smiley), William, Josie (Mrs. P. H. Smith), Nannie (Mrs. J. T. Holland), Mary (Mrs. James Poindexter). Mr. Thomas has given considerable land to his children, but still owns 270 acres, all of which he made by his own indomitable energy. He is conservative in politics, and cast his first presidential vote for W. H. Harrison. He is a Mason. For his second wife he took Mrs. Elizabeth Beasley, widow of Daniel Beasley, who died in the army in 1862. She reared and educated three children: Clemmey (Mrs. Cyrus Cathey), Sallie (wife of Prof. Douglas Allen) and John F. (a Methodist Episcopal minister). Mrs. Thomas is the daughter of Rev. Felix and Ann McGaw.

JAMES M. THORNTON is a Virginian, and son of Reuben Thornton of the same State, born in 1797, and married to Mary Tiffen in 1818, by whom he had nine children. They came to Tennessee in 1833, and here the father farmed, and died in 1863. The mother died in 1864. James M. was born in 1822, and received a limited education in the district schools, but by desultory reading and study now has a good English and business education. At the age of twenty-one he became overseer for James Vance, with whom he remained three years. In the meantime, in 1844, he married Lucinda, daughter of William and Mary Vance. She was born in Alabama in 1825, and bore her husband eight children, seven of whom are living: William A., Mary E., John M., P. L., R. D., R. B., J. B., T. H. (deceased) and Laura J. Our subject was overseer for Mat Vance a number of years, and then came to Lincoln County, and for six years did business for Henry Kelso, and then entered the employ of Dr. B. Bonner, and looked after the interests of his plantation. After renting land two years he, in 1866, purchased 287 acres of land, which cost between $10,000 and $11,000. He afterward purchased 450 acres of land at a cost of $16,000. He gave this land to his four sons. Mr. Thornton began married life very poor in purse, but by industry and good business qualifications has a fine home and a comfortable competency. He is a Democrat, and cast his first presidential vote for James K. Polk. He belongs to the Masons and has reached the degree of Chapter in that Order. He and wife are members of the Methodist Episcopal Church South, and he and his sons are strong advocates of temperance.

JACOB VANCE is a native of the "Palmetto State," born in 1814, son of James and Nancy (Hill) Vance, of North Carolina, born in 1786 and died in 1848 and 1857, respectively. Of their six children four are living: Malinda (Mrs. Robert Crutcher, of Texas), Sarah (Mrs. Samuel Jones, of California), Maria (widow of Asbury McWilliams, of Giles County) and our subject, Jacob, who was reared and educated in Giles County and resided with his parents until twenty-two years of age. September 24, 1839, he wedded Mary Ann Eddings, daughter of Abraham Eddings. Mrs. Vance was born in October, 1821, in Alabama. To them was born one child—W. P. (deceased). In 1849 Mr. Vance purchased 400 acres of] land in Giles County, but sold out in the fall of 1850, and the following year came to Lincoln County and purchased 478 acres near Fayetteville, where he is now residing. His farm is highly improved and furnished with good buildings and fences. Mr. Vance is esteemed as an honest and industrious citizen, and in his political views has been a life-long Democrat, casting his first presidential vote for Hugh L. White, in 1836. He is a member of the Cumberland Presbyterian Church. His son, W. P. Vance, died at the age of twenty-five years, when all earth's brightness was promised him. He was respected and loved for his many virtues by all who knew him, and idolized by his parents and relatives. His remains were followed to the tomb by the I. O. O. F. and the members of the Agricultural Association.

JOHN WARDEN was born in North Carolina in 1826, son of Robert and Elizabeth (Pilcher) Warden. His early education was very limited, he never having received more than six months' schooling during his life. At the age of six years he was brought to Tennessee by his parents, and made his home with them until he was twenty-one years old. October 27, 1847, he married Rachel Ashby. She was born in Lincoln County December 1, 1825, daughter of Alex Ashby. They have three children: Vina Jane (Mrs. George Millstead), John Wilson and Travis Alex. Mr. Warden resided in the Sixth District of Lincoln County until May, 1864, when he purchased 100 acres in the Seventh District, and there has since resided. He lost his wife May 9, 1854, and the following year he married Martha A. Duncan, daughter of Judge Duncan. They have six children: Martha Ellen, Mary Elenora, William James, Hardin Daniel, Judge and James Ebenezer Goodloe. Their mother died June 30, 1880, and March 20 of the next year he married Mary C. Ashby, a sister of his first wife. In 1861 Mr. Warden joined Company A, Forty-first Regiment Tennessee Infantry, and was in the battles of Fort Donelson, Raymond, Vicksburg, Jackson and Chickamauga. He was captured at Fort Donelson, and taken to Camp Morton, Ind., where he was retained seven months. He returned home in December, 1863. He is conservative in politics, and he and wife are members of the Primitive Baptist Church. His father was born in North Carolina in 1790, and was married in 1830. After living two years in Illinois he came to Lincoln County, Tenn. He died in 1862. The mother was born in North Carolina in 1799, and died in 1861. Of their eleven children eight are living: Hardin, Emeline (widow of John H. Steelman), John, Daniel, Jane (Mrs. James Isom), Darinda (Mrs. G. W. McAfee), James M. and Franklin H.

THOMAS J. WHITAKER, citizen and farmer of the Thirteenth District, was born in Lincoln County April 23, 1823, and is one of a family of seven children born to Benjamin and Mahaldah Whitaker, and the grandson of John Whitaker, who built the first gristmill in Lincoln County. He was the first chairman of the county court, and will be remembered by many of the oldest citizens now living in the county. The father of our subject was born in Kentucky, and came to Lincoln County with his parents at a very early day. He was a farmer by occupation, and died in the Eighth District September 12, 1869, being over eighty years of age. The mother is supposed to be a native of Georgia, and died about 1840. Our subject received a good, practical education in the common schools near home, and in 1847 was married to Elizabeth R. Moores, a native of Lincoln County, Tenn., born November 19, 1821, and died November 30, 1880. By this union six children were born, four of whom are living: W. N., M. E., Susan. Dora and In 1847 our subject bought 167 acres of land in the Thirteenth District, where he has since resided. The place is pleasantly located, well improved, and is near Fayetteville Elkton road, twelve miles west of Fayetteville.

ALEXANDER J. WHITAKER, son of Joseph and Ann (Jeffries) Whitaker, was born in Lincoln County in 1833. The father was born in Kentucky in 1788, and'was of English extraction. He was married twice, the first time to Martha Hughes, by whom he had six children, only two of whom are living. Mrs. Whitaker died in 1830, and in 1832 Mr. Whitaker married his second wife, by whom he had two children: Julia F., wife of T. D. Hill, and the subject of this sketch. The father died in 1874 and the mother in 1863. Alexander was reared at home, and received his early education in the district schools, but later attended the academy at Mulberry for about seven years, where he took quite a thorough course. January 10, 1855, he wedded Sarah J. McMillen, daughter of Dock and Madeline McMillen, and by this union became the father of eight children, five of whom are living: Joe D., Charley B., Edna, Fannie E. and Henry. Soon after marriage our subject located on his father's farm, and in 1867 purchased 150 acres of land, on which he is now residing. In 1865 Mr. Whitaker was elected magistrate, and has held the same office ever since. At the breaking out of the war Mr. Whitaker enlisted in the Fifth Kentucky Infantry, and took an active part in the battles of Shiloh and Chickamauga. He is independent in polititical belief, a Mason, K. of H., and both he and wife are members of the Missionary Baptist Church.

HON. W. W. WILSON is the son of William and Susan Wilson, natives of Kentucky and North Carolina, respectively. The father was born in February, 1799, and came to Lincoln County with his parents when but six years of age. He followed agricultural pursuits as a livelihood, and was quite successful at this. He died in March, 1856. The mother was born in 1797, and departed this life in 1845. Our subject was born in Lincoln County, April 28, 1827, and received his education in the school near his country home, and at Viny Grove, under Prof. Erwin. In 1848 he married Miss A. Whiting, a daughter of Robert and Mrs. Whiting. She was born in Robertson County in 1829. Mr. Wilson began teaching, and has followed that occupation for about ten years. In 1851 he bought ten acres of land in the Thirteenth District, where he located, and has since lived. He now owns 250 acres in a very desirable place, and is doing a good business. About 1858 he was elected magistrate, and again in 1864. He has held the office considerable of the time since, up to 1880, when he refused to accept the position any longer. In 1872 he was chosen by the people to represent them in the State Legislature. He is a man well known throughout the county, and his being elected to offices of trust at different times shows that the public appreciates his services. He is a Democrat, and a member of the Masonic fraternity. Mrs. Wilson is a member of the Cumberland Presbyterian Church.

J. B. WILSON, the proprietor of a furniture and undertaking establishment in Fayetteville, Lincoln County, Tenn., was born in that place February 3, 1834. He is the eldest child of a family of five children—three sons and two daughters—born to Union A. and Mary (Shanks) Wilson, and was educated in Fayetteville. At the age of sixteen he began learning the cabinet-maker's trade in his father's shop, and continued working for him until 1854, when his father, his brother, C. S. Wilson, and himself entered into a co-partnership of undertaking and dealing in furniture, in which they continued until 1859. He was married to Miss M. A. Whitaker October 6, 1856, and eight children were born to this union—six daughters and two sons—of whom only four are living: Martha A., Mary M., James B. and Myrtle C. At the breaking out of hostilities between the North and South our subject enlisted in Company C, Forty-first Tennessee Regiment Confederate States Army, in December, 1862. For his second wife he took Mrs. Lucy A. (McDaniel) Fullerton May 10, 1882, who was born April 28, 1850. She was first married to Robert G. Fullerton December 1, 1868, by which marriage there were three daughters born, only two now living: Willa A. and Lucy G. J. B. Wilson is a practical business man and has an extensive trade. He has been the leading furniture dealer and undertaker in Fayetteville for the last twenty years. He has been a life-long Democrat, is an elder in the Presbyterian Church, and is also a member of the I. O. O. F.

C. S. WILSON. In 1858 C. S. Wilson established a sale and feed stable in Fayetteville, Tenn., and soon after, on a very humble scale, engaged in the livery stable business.

He steadily prospered in his undertakings, and in March, 1885, owned twenty-six vehicles and twenty horses. On the 4th of that month the building caught fire, and the building, thirteen buggies and fifteen horses were consumed. Mr. Wilson immediately began erecting a much larger building, 82x125 feet, with a capacity of feeding sixty-eight horses. He is doing an extensive business, meeting with the success his efforts deserve. He was born in 1835 in Fayetteville, and is a son of Union A. and Mary (Shanks) Wilson. When about fourteen years of age he began learning the cabinet-maker's trade, continuing eight years. In 1869 he became proprietor of the Shanks House, and managed that hotel for four years. In 1878 he purchased 200 acres of land, which he has managed in connection with his stable. In November, 1861, he and M. E. Lauderdale were married. She was born in 1840, and is the mother of four children: Charles, Beulah, Augusta and Fannie. Mr. Wilson has been a business man of Fayetteville for the past twenty-five years, and is in every respect an honest and worthy citizen. He is a Democrat, and belongs to the K. of P. His father was born in Tennessee in 1813, and was a cabinet-maker by trade. In 1832 he married, and after his first wife's death he wedded Rebecca Price, who yet survives him. He was the father of thirteen children, and died in 1875.

J. W. WOODARD, a native of Lincoln County, was born March 9, 1843, son of M. C. and Lucinda Woodard. The father was of Irish descent, and was born in Lincoln County in 1810. He was a blacksmith and farmer by occupation, and died in September, 1860. The mother of our subject was also born in Lincoln County about 1818, and now resides at the old home-place in the Thirteenth District with her son, W. S. Our subject received his education in the schools near home, and remained with his parents until the breaking out of the late war. In 1861 he enlisted in Company F, Forty-fourth Tennessee Infantry, and took part in the battles of Shiloh, Chickamauga, Murfreesboro, Petersburg, and was captured at this place and taken to Fort Delaware, where he remained about four months. He returned home in July, 1865, after over four years' service, and was in many of the hottest battles of the war without receiving a single wound. In 1866 he married M. E. Hampton, a native of Lincoln County, born in 1845, and the daughter of Samuel and Annie Hampton. To our subject and wife were born six children: Samuel M., James G., John H. F., Lillian, Robert M. and Martha L. After remaining on the old home-place about four years our subject purchased about 100 acres of land in the Thirteenth District, where he located and remained about thirteen years. In 1883 he bought 135 acres in the Sixteenth District, where he located. He still retains the farm in the Thirteenth District and owns 485 acres of valuable land. He also owns a mill and is doing a good business in grinding grain and sawing lumber. Besides this, he looks after the interest of the farm. He is a Democrat, a Mason, and he and wife are members of the Methodist Episcopal Church.

M. W. WOODARD, attorney at law, of Fayetteville, Tenn., was born in Lincoln County, in 1846, the third son of Robert S. and Mary (McKinney) Woodard, born in Tennessee and North Carolina, in 1821 and 1825, respectively. The father was a teacher and farmer in early life, and was married in 1842. In 1847 he was elected tax-collector of Lincoln County, serving one term. In 1856 he was elected clerk of the circuit court, and held the position until the late war. In 1864 he was re-elected and held the office until 1868. Soon after the organization of the Lincoln County Savings Bank he was chosen assistant cashier, but at the organization of the First National Bank he was chosen its cashier, which position he held until his death in 1877. During the many years he was in public life he was the administrator of many large estates. His father, Reuben Woodard, was born in 1792, in North Carolina, and was a pioneer settler of Tennessee. He was a brick-mason, and lived to be eighty-six years of age. Our subject's mother, since her husband's death, has resided on the old homestead with two of her children. Their family consisted of eleven children: James L., Galen D., M. W., Annie B. (Mrs. Thomas Dryden), Mary E. (Mrs. Dr. O. R. Hatcher), A. B., Robert P., J. Reuben, W. K., Addie (Mrs. Eugene Higgins) and one deceased sister (Mrs. Sallie Francis). Our subject was educated in Milton College, Fayetteville, and in 1868 began studying law, and in 1871 was admitted to the bar and began immediately to practice. In 1873 he was appointed judge of the county court, and filled the position for eighteen months. In 1883 he and Hon. R. L. Bright formed a law partnership, and the firm is known as Bright & Woodard. They constitute one of the leading law firms of Lincoln County, and our subject is one of the leading and useful members of society. October 25, 1871, he married Ida L. Hatcher, who was born in Maury County, Tenn., in 1854. The following are the names of their children: Irene, Octa L., Bessie, Robert S., Bernard H., Fannie, John and Ida. Mr. and Mrs. Woodard are members of the Presbyterian Church, and he is a Democrat and belongs to the Masonic fraternity and I. O. O. F.

ELDER J. G. WOODS was born in Franklin County, Tenn., in 1823, and is a son of William and Mary (Harris) Woods. Wm. Woods was born in Virginia in 1776, and Mary Harris, his wife, was born in Kentucky in 1782. They died in Franklin County, Tenn., in 1838 and 1840, respectively. Wm. Woods was of Scotch-Irish descent, and a tiller of the soil, and for upward of thirty years was a Primitive Baptist minister. He was one of the earliest settlers and largest land owners of Franklin County. Of his large family of children, only three are living: Mourning S., Mary A. (widow of John Miller), and J. G., who is the youngest. J. G. Woods was educated in the pioneer log schoolhouse of primitive days. After his parents' death he resided on the home farm about three years, and on November 30, 1843, he was married to Susan J. Boyce, daughter of Joseph and Martha J. Boyce, who was a daughter of Paul Dismukes. Susan J. was born in Madison County, Ala., in 1825. J. G. and Susan J. Woods had six children, to wit: James H., Archibald M., William E., Joseph G., Mary A. and Mattie E. Archibald M. died in infancy, and Mary A. died after she was grown. Since 1844 Mr. Woods has been a resident of Fayetteville. He and James H. Cobb were engaged in the tanning, saddlery and harness business for a number of years, and they were also engaged in buying and shipping produce South. In 1850 they erected the first livery and feed stable in the town, and two years later they closed their partnership business, after which our subject served as constable and justice of the peace for several years, during which time he studied law and was admitted as a practicing attorney in 1858. He continued to practice law until 1875. In 1857 or 1858, upon the re-organization of the Winchester & Alabama Railroad, he was elected one of its directors, and continued a director until the road was sold by the State. He was also president and receiver of the road for some time. At the organization of the First National Bank of Fayetteville he was elected one of the directors, and in November, 1874, was elected president of the same, but resigned in January, 1885, owing to ill health. He was licensed to preach by the Primitive Baptist Church in the fall of 1873, and ordained in 1874, and has been actively engaged in the ministry from that time until the present, except when prevented by bad health. His wife Susan J. died in 1865, and the following year he married Lou S. Webb, who is a daughter of Hartwell and Nancy Webb, and was born in 1825. He has been a member of the Masonic fraternity since 1851.

JAMES H. WRIGHT is one of twelve children of Jacob and Nancy Wright, and was born in Lincoln County, Tenn., in 1812. His father was of English descent, born and married in Virginia. He came to Tennessee and followed the life of a farmer, and died when about ninety-six years of age. The mother was born in Ireland, and came to the United States with her parents. James H. obtained the rudiments of his education in the schools near his home, and in 1839 married Nancy, daughter of John and Elizabeth Trantam. They have thirteen children: Elizabeth (Mrs. John Alsup), Josie (Mrs. John Myers), Fannie (Mrs. Ruf. Smith), Ethlinda (Mrs. Robert Maury), W. L., A. W., S. H., J. H., R. L., D. N., J. H. and Cordelia, and one son, Marshall, who was killed at the battle of Chattanooga. Mr. Wright has always farmed, and by the sweat of his brow has become the owner of 300 acres of valuable and well improved land. He has been successful. He has reared a large family of children and given them good educational advantages, and has a comfortable competency. Mr. Wright is a Democrat, and he and Mrs. Wright are members of the Christian Church.

WILLIAM R. WYATT, farmer and miller of Fayetteville, Tenn., was born in Lincoln County, in 1844. His father William Wyatt was of English-Irish descent; born in 1802 in South Carolina. He came to Tennessee in 1804, and to Lincoln County in 1807 or 1808, and was a teacher and farmer by occupation, being very successful in both occupations. He married Sallie Breckenridge in 1834, and died in 1880. His wife was born in South Carolina in 1804, and died in 1884. The Wyatt family came to Tennessee when the country was almost a wilderness. The bottom lands were covered with cane, and the country was infested with Indians and many wild animals. They did their share in helping to settle and clear the lands of Lincoln County. Of the seven children born to William and Sallie Wyatt, three are living: Margaret Jane, Mollie E. and William R., who received such education as could be obtained in the old fashion schoolhouses of his boyhood days. July 4, 1864, he and Sallie McCown were united in marriage. She was born in South Carolina in 1845, a daughter of Joseph I. and Mary (Bryson) McCown. Mr. and Mrs. Wyatt have six children: Eva, Delia, Lizzie, Jennie, Joseph and Flora. Mr. Wyatt resided with his parents four years, and in 1868 purchased 200 acres of land about five miles from Fayetteville, where he settled and resided until January 1, 1886, when he moved to town to educate his children. By energy and industry Mr. Wyatt is the owner of 400 acres of land. He is a Republican in politics, and his first presidential vote was cast for U. S. Grant in 1868. He and wife are members of the United Presbyterian Church. In 1884 he purchased a saw-mill which he operates in connection with his farm.

JOHN YOUNG, lumberman and builder, was born in New Hampshire March 24, 1842, and is one of nine children born to Benjamin and Melinda (Everett) Young. Our subject remained at home until he was eighteen years of age, and received his early education in the district schools of New Hampshire. After immigrating to Illinois he attended a graded school, where he received a good practical education, and after this he was engaged in farming and threshing for several years. He was in the army, and served several years in the quartermaster's department. In 1867 he came to Lincoln County, and settled at Flintville, where he purchased some property. In 1870 he wedded Sarah M. Bradford, and the fruits of this union were five children, four of whom are living: Sarah, George, John and James. In 1879 Mr. Young purchased a milling property, and has since been engaged in sawing lumber and grinding grain. Although commencing life with but little of this world's goods, Mr. Young now owns, exclusive of town and mill property, about 200 acres of land near Flintville. The father of our subject was born in New Hampshire about 1810, and was of English origin. He received a good business education, and engaged in agricultural pursuits. In 1856 he moved to Illinois, and is living there at the present time. The mother of our subject was also born in New Hampshire, about 1810, and is still living.

## MOORE COUNTY.

The firm of BILLINGSLEY & BAILEY was formed November 4, 1885, by S. A. Billingsley & T. G. Bailey. The senior member of firm is a native of Bledsoe County, Tenn., born October 31, 1856, and was reared in his native county. His father was a farmer. Our subject engaged in merchandising for two years at Spencer, Tenn., before coming here. February, 1884, he went to Mulberry and there engaged in teaching, being principal of the schools at that place until June 4, 1886, when he resigned. December 16, 1885, he married Jennie Sugg, of Cyruston, Lincoln Co., Tenn. The father of Mr. Billingsley was a minister, and his grandfather was a member of the first Tennessee Legislature. The father of our subject died in 1878, and his mother is still living. Mr. Bailey, junior member of the firm, was born in the present limits of Moore County, and is a son of Thomas R. and Nancy M. (Edwards) Bailey, natives of North Carolina and Alabama resectively. The father was a farmer, and died April 4, 1884; the mother still survives. Mr. Bailey engaged as clerk in a store in Lynchburg, for two years, and then formed a partnership with T. H. Parks & Co., continuing with that firm until December, 1882. He held an interest in R. B. Parks & Co.'s store until March 10, 1884, when he retired and attended school five months. In November, 1885, he joined the present firm, which is doing a general merchandising trade with a stock of $2,500. Both are Democrats, and are young and enterprising business men.

J. L. BRYANT & CO. This firm is now composed of H. B. Morgan and J. W. Motlow. It was first established in 1872, by J. L. Bryant (now deceased) and H. B. Morgan. J. L. Bryant had himself been in business in Lynchburg since 1866. He was born September 25, 1824, in Lincoln County, and was reared in West Tennessee, and when a young man returned to Moore County, and on August 24, 1845, married Finetta B. Leftwich, and engaged in merchandising at Charity, in this county, continuing in mercantile pursuits until his death. In 1865 he was at Shelbyville, and removed from there to Lynchburg. He was also an extensive farmer and stock trader. He was drowned April 5, 1883, at Shelbyville. He was a very popular man, and was identified with the social and public interests, and was one of the most successful business men of Moore County. There now survives him a family of two daughters and his widow. H. B. Morgan was born October 14, 1842, in Lincoln County, Tenn., being a son of W. A. and Mary (Davidson) Morgan, both now living near Montgomery, Ala. Young Morgan remained on the farm until 1861, when he enlisted with the "boys in gray" and served till the battle of Franklin, in 1864, in which he lost an arm. He returned home in June, 1865, and farmed for one year. He then became deputy sheriff of Lincoln County, holding that office four years, and was then elected sheriff for four years. In 1872 he entered the above named firm, and has been very successful. He was married in 1868 to Mrs. Mary J. Reece, nee Bryant, daughter of J. L. Bryant. To this union one daughter has been born—Jessie B. Mrs. Morgan was the mother of one daughter by her former marriage—Johnnie Reece. Mr. Morgan is a public spirited citizen of the county, and is highly respected. J. W. Motlow was born in Lynchburg, November 17, 1851, being a son of John T. and Finetta B. (Broadway) Motlow, who reside near Lynchburg. He was reared on a farm, and at the age of twenty-one began farming for himself, which he continued until 1882, when he entered the firm of J. L. Bryant & Co. He was married, January 1, 1880, to Miss Willie Alice Bryant, daughter of J. L. Bryant, the result of this union being one daughter—Aetna. Mr. Motlow is a Democrat in politics, and is an enterprising citizen of Lynchburg.

S. E. H. DANCE, M. D., the leading physician of Lynchburg, Tenn., was born March 30, 1834, son of Stephen M. and Sarah (Smith) Dance, born in Virginia and North Carolina, and died in 1853 and 1862, respectively. They came to Lincoln County about 1826. The father was a farmer of ordinary means and a local minister of the Methodist Episcopal Church. Our subject spent his boyhood days on a farm and at the time of his father's death was attending Emory and Henry College, Virginia. He returned home and began the study of medicine and attended one course of lectures, in 1854–55 in the University of Tenn. He graduated from the Louisville (Ky.) Medical College in 1856 and began practicing his profession in Lynchburg. During the war he was assistant surgeon of Turney's First Tennessee, and in 1862 was promoted to surgeon of the Eighth Tennessee, continuing until near the close of the conflict, when he was made medical director for the reserves of Tennessee. After his return from the battle field he resumed his profession in Lynchburg, in which he has met with good success. September 16, 1856, he married Miami A. Berry, and eight children blessed their union—Edward M., William H., Charles H., Frank P., Fannie, Robert R., Harry H. and Clifford C. In 1883 Dr. Dance and his son, William H., opened a drug store in Lynchburg. He is one of the stockholders of the cotton-mills, and also owns an interest in the grist-mills of Dance & Waggoner, at Lynchburg.

JACK DANIEL, proprietor of the distillery at Lynchburg, Tenn., was born in Moore County, in 1848. His father, Gallaway Daniel, came from North Carolina to Moore

County when eight years of age, and in later years followed tilling the soil as an occupation. Our subject has always been a farmer, and in 1876 erected his distillery, which he began operating two years later, under the firm name of Daniel & Call, continuing thus five years. It has a capacity of fifty bushels per day and turns out some of the finest brands of " Lincoln County" whisky.  Mr. Daniel is the owner of a large and productive farm, which he manages in connection with his distillery, and on which he raises large numbers of live-stock.

BENJAMIN M. EDENS, one of Moore County's pioneer citizens, was born in Madison County, Ala., July 13, 1822, and is one of five surviving members of a family of nine children born to Samuel and Nancy (Franks) Edens. The father was a native of South Carolina, and came to Limestone County, Ala., where he married the mother of our subject. They came to Lynchburg, this county, in 1825, located, and engaged in farming. The father's death occured about 1866, and the mother followed him about 1870. Our subject remained with his parents until his majority, after which he began farming for himself. September, 1849, he led to the hymeneal altar Pauline Blythe, a native of Moore County. This union resulted in the birth of nine children, seven of whom are living. Immediately after marriage they settled on the farm where they now reside. At that time it was an unbroken wilderness, but by hard labor and perseverance, and after enduring many privations customary with the pioneer settlers, he now owns a fine tract of over 200 acres of mostly cultivated land. Mr. Edens cast his first vote in 1844, and has always voted for the nominees of the Democratic party. He and family are members of the Methodist Episcopal Church.

REV. JAMES S. ERVIN, merchant, and a native of what was then Lincoln, but is now Moore County, Tenn., was born April 4, 1832, and is a son of James S. and Jemimah (Merrill) Ervin. The parents were natives of North Carolina, and immigrated to this county in 1816 and 1818, respectively. The father was an industrious farmer, and died November 7, 1881; the mother followed November 9 of the same year. Our subject remained with his parents until eighteen years of age, when he married Catherine Womack, November 7, 1849, a native of Bedford County. The fruits of this union were sixteen children, twelve of whom are still living. The mother of these children died April 5, 1880, and September of the same year Mr. Ervin was united in marriage to Rebecca Dillingham, a native of this county. In 1855 our subject moved to Bedford County and followed agricultural pursuits till 1866, when he came to this county and located on the farm where he has since resided. He has a fine tract of 150 acres at County Line, and also has another farm in the county of 130 acres. In 1869 he engaged in merchandising in County Line, and has continued that business ever since. In 1857 he was ordained minister in the Baptist Church, of which he and his family are worthy members. Politically he has always been identified with the Democratic party, and is a strong advocate of temperance.

ALEXANDER FORESTER, farmer, was born in Moore County (then Lincoln County) in 1820, and is one of eleven surviving members of a family of fourteen children born to Isaac and Matilda (Hodges) Forester. The father was born in South Carolina in 1790, and came to Moore County previous to the war of 1812, in which he participated under Gen. Coffee, and afterward under Gen. Jackson. At the close of the Indian war he returned to Moore (Lincoln) County, and soon after was married. The parents are both still living, having now enjoyed the companionship of each other about seventy years. The youngest child is now forty-three years old, and the oldest is our subject. The parents have had eighty-nine granchildren, sixty-nine of whom are still living. They have over sixty great-grandchildren, all still living but three or four. They also have two great-great-grandchildren, both living. Our subject at the age of twenty-three left his home, and in 1843 was united in marriage to Minerva Eaton, a native of Moore (Lincoln) County. Eight children blessed this union, seven of whom are still living, and five are married and have children. In 1862 Mr. Forester enlisted in the Confederate Army, in a Kentucky regiment of infantry, but afterward, just before the battle of Murfreesboro, was transferred to Newman's battalion. In 1863 he was discharged, owing to advanced age, after having participated in the battles of Shiloh and Baton Rouge. March 20, 1863, he returned home, and has since followed farming on the place where he now resides, a good farm of 270 acres. The whole Forester family are stanch Democrats, although none have ever aspired to office.

HON. W. W. GORDON was born in Winchester, Tenn., May 20, 1848. His father, Dr. Amzi B. Gordon, was a native of the county of Bedford, moving to Franklin County in about the year 1841, where he began the practice of medicine, soon building up a large and lucrative practice. He was a zealous member of the Baptist Church and one of the founders of the celebrated Mary Sharp College, at Winchester. He died in 1855. His mother is a daughter of John March, a highly respected farmer of the county, and a sister of Hon. Hayden March, who represented Franklin County several times in the Legislature. Mr. Gordon received only the rudiments of an English education at Carrick Academy, in his native town, the suspension of the schools during the five years of war depriving him, as it did thousands of the youth of the South, of the means of obtaining an education. He entered a printing office during the war, partly for the educational advantages thus offered, but principally for the meager salary thereby obtained for the support of his widowed mother and sister. He moved to Nashville soon after the war, working in the various departments of the newspaper offices of that city. He spent several years in visiting the principal cities of the Union. In 1870 he was married to Miss Mary E. Fletcher, daughter of G. G. and Ann Fletcher, of Shelbyville, Tenn. He has but one child, Russell W., born in 1871. In 1874 he moved to Lynchburg, Moore County, and in April of that year established the *Sentinel*, continuing its publication for five years. During that period he was four times elected mayor, and was chosen twice by the county court as superintendent of public instruction. Attracted by the excellent schools of his native town, he returned to Winchester in 1883, to educate his son. In 1884 he was elected representative of Franklin County in the Forty-fourth General Assembly of the State. He is an enthusiastic advocate of popular education, a Democrat in politics, and a member of the Methodist Episcopal Church South.

JOHN E. GORE, farmer, of Moore County, was born in April, 1826, in Bedford County, Tenn., and is a son of Amos and Mary A. (Cowser) Gore. The parents were both natives of South Carolina, and came to Bedford County in the early settlement of the county. Our subject left the parental roof at the age of eighteen, and in 1844 went to Mississippi, where he remained three years engaged in farming and boating. He then came home and bought a small farm in this county (then Franklin County). In September, 1849, he was united in marriage to Jane Cunningham, a native of this county, and in 1866 bought the farm where he now resides, a tract of 200 acres, splendidly watered by several springs, one of which issues from a cave near his residence. affording splendid water facilities, which is not used except for drinking purposes. To our subject and wife were born eight children, five of whom are still living: Elizabeth, William L., Rebecca (Mrs. Duckworth), Robert E. and Joshua. Politically Mr. Gore has always been identified with the Democratic party, but has never aspired to office. He and family are members of the Baptist Church.

DR. A. H. PARKES, whose birth occurred on the farm where he now resides, in Moore County, October 11, 1836, is one of seven surviving children, born to the union of Martin L. and Susan (Smith) Parkes. The father was a native of North Carolina, born in 1793, and came to this county about 1818. He was an officer in the war of 1812, and was magistrate in Lincoln County for several years. He was a tiller of the soil, and died December, 12, 1845. The mother was born August, 8, 1803, in Virginia, and came to this county in 1818, where she was married the same year. She died August, 11, 1881. At the age of seventeen, our subject began the study of medicine with a brother in Lynchburg, where he remained three years, after which he attended a course of lectures in the medical department of the University of Nashville. He then practiced for one year, and in the fall of 1858, entered Jefferson Medical College at Philadelphia where he graduated the following March. April. 1861, he joined Turney's First Tennessee Infantry, and in the fall of the same year was elected lieutenant. May, 1862, he returned home, and since that time has been actively engaged in the practice of his profession in connection with farming. November 26, 1867, he married Mary E. Killer, daughter of J. A. Killer, a lieutenant in the Mexican war. Three children were the result of our subject's marriage, all of whom are living, viz.: Laura M., Susan B., and Albert H.

M. N. PARKES is one of the ten children born to the union of Martin L. and Susan B. (Smith) Parkes. The father was born in North Carolina in 1793, and immigrated to what is now Moore County, Tenn., in 1818, where he lived the balance of his life. The country then was dense forests and canebrakes. He was a blacksmith and a farmer, and was a man of simple means. He was a member of the Primitive Baptist Church, and was a soldier in the war of 1812, being a lieutenent and also a recruiting officer. He died in 1845. The mother was born in 1803, and removed here when quite young. Our subject was born January 19, 1839 near Lynchburg; was reared on a farm, and learned the tanner's trade when a boy, which occupation he followed for thirteen years. He then engaged in the cotton factory at Lynchburg, and after that was burned down, he engaged in milling till 1876, when he engaged in the retail liquor dealing, with John L. McWhirter, under the firm name of McWhirter & Parkes, till 1878. He then bought Whirter out, and engaged with D. S. Evans, as Parkes & Evans, the present firm. Mr. Parkes has been quite successful in his business, considering the reverses he has met with. In 1866 he married Mary F. Womack, which union resulted in the birth of six children, four of whom are now living: Mary A. (wife of William H. Dance), John B., Charles M. and Lerna. Mr. Parkes is a Democrat and one of the enterprising men of the county. Mrs. Parkes is a member of the Christian Church.

RUFUS B. PARKS, clerk and master of the Chancery Court of Moore County, Tenn., is one of four children born to Allen W. and Fannie (Miller) Parks, natives of North Carolina, born in 1797 and 1802, respectively. They took up their abode permanently in Tennessee in 1826. The father was a farmer, merchant, and in latter days kept hotel, and was magistrate a number of years. He died November 18, 1884, and the mother January 6, 1877. Rufus B. was born May 5, 1827, near Lynchburg, and received a good practical education. For about four or five years after attaining the age of nineteen he clerked in merchandise stores and then engaged in the business for himself, continuing until the breaking out of the war, when he enlisted in Company E, Fifth Kentucky Infantry, and was afterward transferred to the Ninth Kentucky Infantry, in which he was lieutenant. On account of poor health he resigned and came home, but soon joined the Twenty-third Tennessee Battalion and served until the close of the conflict. After his return he farmed alone until 1883, when he engaged in merchandising also, which he followed until 1885. He owns 120 acres of land. In 1849 he was married to Emily J. Roundtree, who died November 30, 1884, having borne him four children: Rufus A., Alice A. (Mrs. Loderick Robertson), Edwin L. and May. Mr. Parks has been a member of the Christian Church, in which he is deacon, for forty years. Politically he is a Democrat, and has been magistrate about six years. He was elected to his present position in 1883, and is an efficient and trustworthy officer.

HON. R. A. PARKS, editor of the Lynchburg *Falcon* and attorney at law, was born October 21, 1849, in Lynchburg. His father is Rufus B. Parks, whose sketch appears next above. His early life was spent with his parents and in school. He engaged in teaching school and studying law when a young man. In June, 1872, he obtained license to practice law, and has ever since continued to do so, in the firm of Holman & Parks, from 1872 to 1884, and since then in the firm of Holman, Holman & Parks. He was united in marriage, November 14 1872, to Miss Susan A. Holt, of Moore County. This union has been blessed in the birth of six children, four of whom are now living: Roy H., Pearl, Harry R. and Margaret. Mr. Parks is a Democrat in politics and takes an active interest in political affairs. He has held the office of recorder of Lynchburg, and is now filling his second term of office as mayor of the town. He represented Lincoln and Moore Counties in the lower house of the Legislature from 1882 to 1884. He is a member of the I. O. O. F., having joined that fraternity in December, 1884. Since February, 1884, he has been editor and proprietor of the Lynchburg *Falcon*, and has made it a good paper.

THOMAS H. PARKS, of the firm of Parks, Taylor & Co., of Lynchburg, Tenn., is a son of Ambrose Lee and Eleanor E. (Watts) Parks. The father was born in North Carolina. After his marriage he moved to Missouri, where he resided until 1846, and then came to Lynchburg, Tenn., where he was engaged in the wheelwright and wagon-making business. Both parents died in 1850. Thomas H. was born in Missouri October 19, 1840, being but nine years old when his parents died. He made his home with an uncle in Alexander County, N. C., until seventeen years old. In 1858 he came to Lynchburg, Tenn., and engaged in the carpenter's trade, relying upon his own exertions for support. He joined the Confederate Army, Turney's First Tennessee, Company E, and served until the close of the war, with the exception of nearly two years spent in prison. He began dealing in live-stock after the war, and about 1870 began selling goods in Lynchburg, but on a very limited scale. He has increased his business from time, to time and is now doing well financially and is one of the leading business men of Lynchburg. He was married in 1869 to E. A. M. Taylor, daughter of Squire J. H. Taylor, and their union has been blessed with six children: Minnie M., John L., Willie K., Emma P., Thomas H. and Nellie H. Mr. Parks is a Democrat, and owns about 200 acres of land. He and wife and eldest daughter are members of the Christian Church.

E. Y. SALMON, M. D., was born in the "Palmetto State," on the 26th of June, 1830. His father, William H. Salmon, was a physician and immigrated to Alabama in 1833, and afterward removed to Texas in 1863, where he died. He was identified with public interests in Alabama, and held the office of clerk, for twenty-four years. The mother died in Texas at an advanced age. Our subject was reared in Alabama, and resided with his parents until nineteen years of age. He volunteered to serve in the Mexican war in 1846, but peace was declared before he reached the Army. He went to California in 1849, and mined for eighteen months, and then engaged in trading. In 1854 he returned to Alabama, then went to Texas, where he studied medicine two years, and then entered the medical department of the University of Tennesse, and graduated in 1857. He practiced in Lynchburg until 1861, when he organized the first company that was organized in the State, which took the name of the Lynchburg Rangers, Company E. He served in Turney's First Tennesee, as sergeant and captain. After his return, he practiced at Lynchburg until 1872, when he was made clerk and master of the chancery court of Moore County, two terms. In 1882, he removed to Nashville, where he was engaged in the manufacture of veterinary medicines, which he has continued ever since. His summer home is in Lynchburg, where he is one of the most popular citizens. He and Margaret Taylor were married in 1858, and of the six children born to them, one is dead: Bettie F. (wife of Dr. J. C. Franklin, of Nashville), Eliza B., William T., Nannie B., and H. Carrie are those living. Dr. Salmon and family are members of the Christian Church, and he is a firm Democrat in politics.

JOHN N. SULLIVAN, farmer, was born November 2, 1838, in Moore County, and is one of ten children born to Dempsey and Naoma (Neece) Sullivan. The parents were both born in this county in 1811 and 1812, respectively, the father being of Scotch-Irish descent. He was a farmer, although he also engaged in the mercantile business for a few years in Lincoln County, and dealt largely in stock from 1845 to 1855. The mother died September, 1884. The father is still living, a hale, hearty man of seventy-five. John N. remained with his parents until the war, when he enlisted in the Eighth Tennessee Infantry, with which he remained till severely wounded at the battle of Murfreesboro. In March, 1875, he was united in marriage to Elizabeth Logan, also a native of this county, and the fruits of this union were an interesting family of nine children, one of whom died in infancy. Shortly after marriage, Mr. Sullivan engaged in the tannery business in Bedford County, where he continued for fourteen years, afterward purchasing the farm where he is now residing, which consists of 400 acres of good land. On this farm is quite an eminence, from which is afforded an excellent view of the surrounding country. Mr. Sullivan and family, are members of the Christian Church. He is identified with the Democrats, and is an advocate of the principles of prohibition.

JOHN H. TAYLOR was born in Oglethorpe County, Ga., February 26, 1801, and is the only living member of a family of seven children of Woody B. and Nancy (Seay) Taylor; who were born and married in the "Palmetto State," and moved to Georgia, and in 1809 to Tennessee. At that time the country was covered with canebrake, and Lynchburg contained only two log cabins. Woody B. Taylor died in 1840, and the mother in 1846. John H. resided with his parents until July 18, 1826, when he wedded Elizabeth Ford, who was born in South Carolina and has since lived in the vicinity of Lynchburg. To this venerable couple ten children were born, seven of whom are living. Politically Mr Taylor is a stanch Democrat, and he and wife are members of the Baptist Church. W. B. Taylor is the second of John H. Taylor's children. He was born near his present residence March 15, 1829, and resided with his parents on the farm until his marriage, March 2, 1869, to Susan T. Keller, a daughter of Dr. J. A. Keller, a native of the county. He moved to Illinois in 1842, and there enlisted in the Mexican war as first lieutenant, and died from the effects of the service in 1847. The family then came to Lynchburg, where the mother, whose maiden name was Lauriette Walker, now lives. Mrs. Taylor was born September 23, 1840, and is a member of the Christian Church. Mr. Taylor served in the late war in Company E, Turney's First Tennessee, and October 1, 1864, lost an arm at Petersburg, Va. He resided in Alabama a short time, but soon returned to Moore County, Tenn., where he owns 180 acres of very fine land.

JAMES C. TIPPS, a popular citizen of Moore County, and one of six surviving members of a family of twelve children born to Michael and Leah (Seivalley) Tipps, was born August 6, 1839, on the farm he now owns, near Marble Hill, Moore County. The father of James C. was a native of North Carolina, born 1809, and came to Moore County (Franklin) when four years of age. He was a tiller of the soil and magistrate for several years. He died in 1883. The mother, a native of Moore (Lincoln) County, was born January 24, 1810, and is still living. At the age of nineteen our subject left home, and September 2, 1858, was married to Mary Stoball, native of Coffee County, Tenn. Eleven children were the results of this union, all of whom are living. At the time of his marriage he began farming for himself and continued this occupation till the commencement of the late war, when he enlisted in the Forty-first Tennessee Infantry, with which he remained till the close of the war. He then returned home, and in partnership with John Seivalley was engaged in merchandising from 1875 to 1880. He was constable for four years, beginning 1866, and deputy sheriff for two years. He was appointed postmaster of his village in 1875, and still holds that position. Mr. Tipps has in his possession a deed written by Gen. Jackson, conveying land to our subject's grandfather. Mr. Tipps and family are members of the Lutheran Church.

J. H. TRIPP, M. D., of Marble Hill, was born March 18, 1843, in Lincoln County, Tenn., and is one of a family of seven children born to Henry and Nancy (Gattis) Tripp, both natives of North Carolina. They were married in Lincoln County, Tenn., and the father followed agricultural pursuits until his death in 1846 or 1847. The mother is still living in Lincoln County. Our subject remained and assisted his mother on the farm until the breaking out of the late war, when he enlisted in the Forty-fourth Tennessee Infantry, and remained with this until the surrender at Appomatox Court House. He then returned home and engaged in farming for several years, and also secured a limited education by attending common schools for about fifteen months. He attended the Washington Medical College at Baltimore, Md., session of 1870-71, and then practiced at Marble Hill till 1876, after which he attended Medical College at Louisville, Ky. Here he graduated and resumed his practice at Marble Hill till the session of 1884-85 of the medical department of the University of Tennessee, at which place he also graduated, and has since continued the practice of his profession at his home in this county. August 22, 1876, he married Sally A. Bean, to which union one child was born, Myrtle. The Doctor and wife are members of the Methodist Episcopal Church.

INDEX

Prepared By

Colleen M. Elliott and Lois M. Ott
Fort Worth, Tx.